GOA-KANARA PORTUGUESE RELATIONS
1498-1763

Xavier Centre of Historical Research (XCHR) Studies Series

No.1 : João de Barros: Portuguese Humanist and Historian of Asia/ *C.R. Boxer*

No. 2 : Coastal Western India: Studies from the Portuguese Records/ *M.N. Pearson*

No. 3 : The Black Legend of Portuguese India: Diogo do Couto, His Contemporaries and the Soldado Prático-A Contribution to the Study of Political Corruption in the Empires of Early Modren Europe/ *George Davison Winius*

No. 4 : Health and Hygience in Colonial Goa (1510-1961)/ *Fátima da Silvà Gracias*

No. 5 : Trade and Finance in Portuguese India: A Study of the Portuguese Country-Trade, 1770-1840/ *Celsa Pinto*

No. 6 : Goa and the Revolt of 1787/ *Charles J. Borges* (Ed.)

No. 7 : Goa and Portugal: Their Cultural Links/ *Charles J. Borges* and *Helmut Feldmann* (Eds.)

No. 8 : Goa-Kanara Portuguese Relations 1498-1763/ *B.S. Shastry* and *Charles J. Borges* (Eds.)

No. 9 : Goa's Foremost Nationalist: José Inácio Candido de Loyola: The Man and His Writings/ *Charles J. Borges* (Ed.)

No. 10 : Goa and Portugal: History and Development/ *Charles J. Borges, Óscar G. Pereira* and *Hannes Stubbe* (Eds.)

No. 11 : Conversions and Citizenry: Goa under Portugal 1510-1610/ *Délio de Mendonca*

About the Author

Prof. B.S. Shastry was born on 17 August 1938 and passed away prematurely in Goa on 8 June 1991. He worked for his doctorate under the well-known historian and archivist P.S.S. Pissurlencar. He started his career in Goa as a lecturer in history at the Chowgule College (Margao, Goa) and later came to head the departments of history at the Centre of Post-Graduate Instruction and Research (Panaji) and the Goa University (Bambolim), respectively.

Gifted with a pleasing personality, Prof. Shastry was research guide to a number of students and was often invited to take part in international and national conferences on topics of Indo-Protuguese history. He wrote and edited a number of books including *The Kings of Keladi and the Portuguese* (in Kannada), Dharwar, 1972; *Studies in Indo-Protuguese History*, Bangalore, 1981; *Goan Society through the Ages*, New Delhi, 1987; *Bibliography of Dr. Pissurlencar Collection*, Bambolim, 1989; and *Socio-Economic Aspects of Portuguese Colonialism in Goa (19th-20th centuries)*, Belgaum, 1990.

About the Editor

Charles J. Borges. S.J. is Director, Xavier Centre of Historical Research, Alto Porvorim, Goa. He has been a Jesuit since 1967 and after his training in philosophy and theology, did his M.A. and Ph.D. in history from the Bombay University. He is author of *The Economics of the Goa Jesuits 1542-1759* and had edited or co-edited a number of books including *Goa and the Revolt of 1787, Goa and Portugal: Their cultural links*, and *Jesuits in India: In historical perspective*. He has many published articles to his credit and has also lectured in India and abroad.

XCHR Studies Series No. 8

GOA-KANARA PORTUGUESE RELATIONS 1498-1763

B.S. Shastry

Edited by

Charles J. Borges
Director
Xavier Centre of Historical Research
Alto Porvorim, Goa

CONCEPT PUBLISHING COMPANY PVT. LTD.
NEW DELHI-110059

ISBN: 978-81-7022-848-6

Edition 2026

Published and Printed by

Concept
Since 1974

Concept Publishing Company Pvt. Ltd.
A/15-16, Commercial Block, Mohan Garden,
New Delhi-110059 (India)
T: 91-11-41101460
E: publishing@conceptpub.com, *W*: www.conceptpub.com

CONTENTS

Author's Preface

Being interested in research in modern Indian history, particularly South Indian history, I was looking out for a suitable topic. Dr. P. S. S. Pissurlencar, whom I consulted, suggested that I might study the Portuguese activities in Kanara. The suggestion was of sufficient interest and attraction, and I gratefully accepted it.

Dr. Pissurlencar became not only my guide, but also a source of inspiration for me. I have endeavoured, to the best of my ability, to make use of his profound knowledge of source-materials. Unfortunately, his health was delicate for long and he expired on July 19, 1969. However, it was my good fortune that he guided this thesis, to its virtual completion, before he ceased to be and I could submit the synopsis with his approval on March 27, 1969.

It was absolutely necessary for me to learn Portuguese, for I was aware that a study of the Portuguese activities in Kanara would not be worth the name if it were not based upon Portuguese documents. I began to learn the language as soon as the topic for research was decided upon. During the course of about four years, I have acquired a fair working knowledge of the language. It has, therefore, been possible for me to base my thesis on Portuguese sources, published as well as unpublished.

Most of the published sources, which I have made use of, are found in the Centre of Historical Research, Panaji. This Centre was established by the University of Bombay entirely with the help of a donation made by Dr. Pissurlencar of his personal collection of books, manuscripts, micro-films and photostat copies, comprising more than 4,000 items all put together. As long as the collection was in the personal possession of Dr. Pissurlencar, before he gave it away about three years ago, he used to lend certain books to his research students, including me, to take them home for study; but later on, when he no longer had the collection in his possession, this facility was stopped. This became a matter of great inconvenience to me as I was a student residing nearly thirty miles away in Margao, where I was a lecturer at the Chowgule College. Virtually no study was possible during the working days and it was impracticable to travel daily to Panaji. Besides, for a year or so, in 1965-66, when the collection was in the process of being transferred from the hands of Dr. Pissurlencar into those of the University, practically no book could be secured from the collection even to consult in Panaji, for the books, etc. were simply bundled up and kept in one place or another before being housed in the Menezes Bragança Hall building where they are preserved at present. All these necessitated a period of nearly four years to complete my thesis. It would have been longer still, but for Principal D. B. Wagh of Chowgule College, who, with his sympathetic and encouraging attitude towards my efforts at research, enabled me to spend in Panaji one working day every week by freeing me from the College work on such days. Thus, during these free days, as well as on holidays and in the vacations I could stay in Panaji to study at the Centre and at the Historical Archives.

I gratefully record here my deep indebtedness to Prof. G. V. Kantak, who is looking after the Centre, for the fullest cooperation possible that he extended to me. It is virtually impossible for me to repay his thousand and one acts of kindness towards me.

I am thankful also to Dr. V. T. Gune, Director of the Historical Archives, Panaji, to his assistant, Mr. Gajanan Ghantkar, and to other members of the staff of the Archives for giving me facilities to consult the unpublished documents preserved there.

Margao
September 22, 1969

B.S. SHASTRY

Editor's Preface

The Xavier Centre of Historical Research, Goa, has great pleasure in including in its Studies Series, the present work *Goa-Kanara Portuguese Relations 1498-1763* written by the late Prof. B.S. Shastry. Though parts of it have been published in different places, it is being published in its entirety now to make known the work of the well-known Indo-Portuguese scholar who carved a niche for himself in studies dealing with Portuguese presence along the west coast of India.

Since Prof. Shastry submitted his thesis for the doctoral degree in 1969, much new information has been presented on the same theme, yet the present work has retained his findings in their original form.

It is our hope that *Goa-Kanara Portuguese Relations 1498-1763* will serve to show the dedicated work of the late historian who made Goa his home and its history his life-long study.

May his memory live on.

I wish to thank his wife, Usha Shastry of the Goa University and their children, for helping in part publication costs and also for their constancy in keeping alive the historical legacy of Prof. Shastry. I also wish to thank in a special way Ms. Ernesta Bhobe for competently typing the entire manuscript for publication.

4 November 1999

Dr. Charles J. Borges
Director, XCHR

List of Abbreviations

APO-BP: Arquivo Portugues Oriental by A. B. de Bragança Pereira.

APO-CR: Arquivo Portuguez Oriental by J. H. da Cunha Rivara.

Assentos: Assentos do Conselho do Estado by P. S. S. Pissurlencar.

Cartas: Cartas de Afonso de Albuquerque published by the Royal Academy of Sciences, Lisbon.

CEO: Conquista Espiritual do Oriente by Paulo da Trindade.

Commentários: Commentários do grande Afonso de Albuquerque.

D-AB: Década 13 da História da India by António Bocarro.

D-DC: Da Asia by Diogo de Couto.

D-JB: Asia by João de Barros.

Documentação: Documentação para a História das Missões do Padroado Portugues do Oriente: India by António da Silva Rego.

DRI: Documentos Remettidos da India ou Livros das Monções published by the Royal Academy of Sciences, Lisbon.

EF: The English Factories in India by William Foster (1618-1669) and by Charles Fawcett (1670-1677)

História: História de Descobrimentos e Conquista da India pelos Portugueses by Fernão Lopes de Castanheda.

JBBRAS: Journal of the Bombay Branch of the Royal Asiatic Society

KV: Keladinripa Vijaya by Linganna.

LCC: Livro da Correspondencia de Canará

LCF: Livro das Cidades e Fortalezas que a Coroa de Portugal tem nas partes do India, etc. ed. Francisco Paulo Mendes da Luz.

Lendas: Lendas da India by Gaspar Correa.

LPCF: Livro das plantas de todas as fortalezas, cidades e povoações do Estado da India Oriental by António Bocarro. In APO-BP.

LRI: Livro de Regimentos e Instruções

LRV: Livro de Reis Vizinhos.

Monções: Livro das Monções do Reino.

Orçamento: Orçamento do Estado da India (1574) by Diogo Velho.

Regimentos: Regimentos das Fortalezas da India by P.S.S. Pissurlencar.

Subsidios: Subsidios para a história da India Portuguesa by R. J. de Lima Felner.

VSCV : Vijayanagara Seicentenary Commemoration Volume.

1

INTRODUCTION: THE PORTUGUESE ARRIVAL IN INDIA

May 17, 1498 is an epoch-making date in East-West relations.[1] On that day Vasco da Gama, the Portuguese nobleman and navigator, reached Calicut on the Malabar Coast. He had set sail from Portugal on July 8, 1497 with four ships and 170 men. Doubling the Cape of Good Hope, he reached Melinde on the eastern coast of Africa on April 14, 1498. He developed friendly relations with the king of Melinde and procured the services of a Muslim pilot who knew the sea-route from Africa to India. This pilot, Ahmad Ibn Májid, was a native of Gujarat and was an expert sea-farer of the western coast of India.[2] With his guidance, da Gama easily reached Malabar.

I do not wish to go into the various motivating forces which impelled the Portuguese and the different causes and circumstances which enabled them to become the first European nation to discover the sea route to India via the Cape of Good Hope.[3] It is enough to state that the main motivating factors which brought them to India were religion and commerce. It is said that when da Gama sent one of his sailors to Calicut, he was asked by two Muslim Tunisian merchants who spoke Castilian: "What the devil brings you here? In search of what have you come from such a long distance?" Pat came the reply from the sailor: "We come in search of Christians and spices".[4]

Da Gama in fact supposed that the Malabaris were Christians and their temples were chapels. The Portuguese believed that the Indians had been converted to Christianity by St. Thomas. No wonder, therefore, that da Gama and his companions offered prayers before "the image of Mary" in a temple in Calicut.[5] This mistake was discovered soon afterwards and the Portuguese realised that the Hindus were far from being Christians. However, the King of Portugal then desired that the Hindu rulers and their subjects be converted to Christianity.[6]

The advantages of the spice trade with the East was, no doubt, the more important motivating force which brought the Portuguese to India. During the centuries that followed the fall of Jerusalem in 1187, the Muslims monopolised the eastern trade controlling the Egyptian and Syrian ports through which goods from the East had to pass on to Europe. Spices, particularly pepper, were in universal demand in Europe, but the price was steep and made exorbitant by the Muslim rulers of Cairo and Persia who imposed high taxes on the articles on their way to Europe.[7] The Portuguese of the 15th century were aware that any European nation which would discover the sea route to the East, and to India, and would use that route for bringing spices direct to Europe, would become economically prosperous. The Muslims of North Africa and Persia would then be outflanked and their monopoly over the Eastern trade would be paralysed. This aim of the Portuguese was fulfilled with amazing speed within a decade or two after the arrival of Vasco da Gama in India.

Da Gama was well received at Calicut by the Zamorin who was a Hindu. The Muslim traders of Calicut tried to prevent any trade relations between the Zamorin and da Gama. Their intrigues resulted in some misunderstanding between the Zamorin and the Portuguese. Nevertheless, da Gama could load his ships with spices and other articles. He then sailed northwards along the coast till Anjediv, off the Karwar coast in North Kanara, from where he set sail for Africa on his way back to Portugal. He reached home on August 29, 1499. Of the four ships, one was lost on the return voyage and out of the 170 men who had left Portugal in 1497 only 55 returned. The voyage was, however, a great success. Da Gama could show his countrymen the various spices and precious stones that were available in India and tell them of the articles which the Indians demanded.[8]

The King of Portugal then evolved a definite policy with regard to the East. He concluded that the advantage of the eastern trade would be better secured by force than by peace, and that he should send priests to christianize the East. Accordingly, on March 9, 1500 a large fleet of 13 ships and 1,200 men, under the command of Pedro Alvares Cabral, set sail from Lisbon for India. In addition to the men-of-war there were eight Franciscans, eight priests and a vicar.[9] Cabral, after experiencing misfortunes, reached Calicut on September 13, with only six vessels. He succeeded, after an interview with the Zamorin, in setting up a factory at Calicut but misunderstandings soon arose and he left Calicut with only three laden ships. However, he could procure goods at Cochin for his remaining ships. On January 9, 1501 he sailed from the Indian shores, leaving behind at Cochin about 30 Portuguese. When he reached Portugal on the last day of July of the same year he had only five ships out of the original thirteen. However, they were so richly laden that a great deal of profit was realised after selling the cargo of the merchandise of the East.[10]

In the meantime, in March 1501, a third fleet of four vessels, under the command of João da Nova, had left for India. The King of Portugal had apparently decided by then to send such a fleet to India every year. The fleet of 1501 avoided Calicut which was then hostile to the Portuguese and went to Cochin where it was soon laden with merchandise which was kept ready by the Portuguese left behind by Cabral. The fleet was back at home safely on September 11, 1502.

In February 1502, da Gama was sent again to India with a larger fleet of 20 ships. His brother, Estevão, commanding 5 ships, sailed from Portugal in April of the same year. The two met at Anjediv. Da Gama has two significant instructions from his sovereign: one was to block, as much as possible, the Muslim trade between India on the one hand, and the Persian Gulf and the Red Sea on the other; the second instruction was that he should endeavour to divert the eastern trade entirely to Portugal. Thus, the monopoly of the eastern trade was to be transferred from the hands of the Muslims into those of the Portuguese. Accordingly, Muslim trading vessels were attacked on the Indian Ocean. On reaching the Malabar Coast he demanded of the Zamorin that the latter should expel from his kingdom all the Muslim traders. The Zamorin naturally refused to comply and da Gama caused wanton and cruel destruction to the Zamorin's ports, vessels and subjects. He then proceeded to Cochin where he succeeded in establishing a factory. Leaving Vicente Sodre with 6 vessels and a caravel to guard the coast, da Gama left for Portugal reaching there on September 1, 1503.[11]

In 1503 and 1504 too, the King of Portugal sent fleets to India. However, in 1505 the policy of sending out to India an annual fleet was given up. Instead, it was decided to appoint a Viceroy who was to stay in his post in India for a term of three years. The first Viceroy to be appointed was Francisco de Almeida who set sail from Lisbon on March 25, 1505 with a fleet of 22 ships and 1,500 men. He had instructions to build fortresses at Kilwa, Anjediv, Cannanore and Cochin, and thus to establish Portuguese supremacy in the Indian Ocean. In February 1509, Almeida inflicted off Diu a crushing defeat to the fleet of the Sultan of Egypt which had come to the Gujarat coast at the request of the king of Cambay.

Almeida was succeeded by the great soldier-statesman, Afonso de Albuquerque on November 5, 1509. With him began a new era in the history of the rise of the Portuguese power in India. He conceived the idea of establishing a territorial empire in India and succeeded in implementing it to a considerable extent. He captured and occupied Goa in 1510 and made it the headquarters of the Portuguese power in the East; in 1511, he conquered Malacca which gave the Portuguese control over the trade between India and China; and in 1515 he established Portuguese sovereignty over Hormuz, thus acquiring command over the entrance of the Persian Gulf. It was Albuquerque, therefore, who firmly laid the foundation of Portuguese supremacy in the East and effectively curbed the Muslim monopoly of trade with India and the East Indies. Though a territorial empire worth the name was never built by the Portuguese in India, their naval supremacy in the Indian Ocean and their control over the Eastern trade continued to remain unquestioned until the turn of the 16th century when the Dutch and the English entered the eastern waters as competitors.

This present study deals with Kanara. The territorial boundaries of a region do not remain permanent; they change for one reason or another. Kanara is divided into two districts: North and South Kanara both included in the state of Mysore. Kanara as a whole has a coast washed by the waves of the Arabian Sea and extending from the village of Majali, about 5 miles to the north of the Kalinadi, to the village of Talpadi, about 8 miles to the south of the river Netravati. The district of Belgaum and the territory of Goa are to the north of Kanara. The district of Dharwar lies to the northeast and the districts of Shimoga and Kadur border on the east. Coorg is to the southeast. Kerala lies to the south.

At the time of the arrival of the Portuguese, Kanara had different boundaries. Duarte Barbosa writes: "Proceeding from this city (of Goa) along the coast, on the way to Malabar, there is a river which they call *Lingua* (the Kalinadi), which is the demarcation of the kingdom of the *Daquem* (Deccan) with that of Narsinga (the Vijayanagara empire), and at the mouth of the river, on a hill, there is a fortress which they call *Cintacora* (Chitakul or the present Sadashivagad), which the Sabaia (Yusuf Adil Khan of Bijapur) possesses here for the defence of his land, in which he has continually many foot soldiers and cavalrymen, and here ends the kingdom of the *Daquem* on the northern side, which extends along the coast up to Chaul..."[12] Further, "Passing this *Cintacora*, the immediate land beyond (the river) is of the great kingdom of Narsinga which is so vast that it has five very big provinces, and each one, its own language. The first is along the coast up to Malabar, which they call *Tolinate* (Tulunadu)..."[13] And again after referring to Mirjan, Honavar, Baindur, Barkur, Basrur and Mangalore, the ports along the coast downwards, he writes with regard to Kumbala: "This place of *Cumbola* had a lord who commands and governs it, appointed by the king of Narsinga, and stands face-to-face with the kingdom of Cannanore, and here ends the kingdom of Narsinga on the coast of the province of *Tolinate*."[14]

The province of *Tolinate*, no doubt, is the province of Kanara, one of the five big provinces in the Vijayanagara empire. Thus, according to Barbosa the territories of Kanara began from the southern bank of the Kalinadi. In the south, Kanara included, as the above narration of Barbosa implies, Manjeshwara and Kumbala, which are now found incorporated in the territories of Kerala. He mentions that Kumbala was subject to the emperor of Vijayanagara and the territories of the province of Kanara terminated there.

João de Barros takes the southern boundary of Kanara a little more downwards. He writes: "... from *Aliga* (the Kalinadi) to another river named *Cangerecorá* (Chandragiri), which is five leagues to the north of the *Monte de Eli* (Mount Deli), a notable Cape on this coast, it will be 46 leagues. On this coast lie these localities: *Ancolá* (Ankola), *Egorapá* (?), *Mergeu* (Mirjan), the city of *Onor* (Honavar), capital of the kingdom, *Baticalá* (Bhatkal), *Bendor* (Baindur), *Bracelor* (Basrur), *Bacanor* (Barkur), *Carnate* (Karnad), Mangalore, *Mangueirão* (Manjeshwara), *Cumbatá* (Kumbala), *Cangerecorá*, by which runs a river of this name which is the extremity and demarcation...; all these localities belong to the province of Canara, subject to the king of *Bisnagá* (Vijayanagara) ..."[15] Thus for Barros, Kanara extended from the Kalinadi in Karwar to the river Chandragiri in Kasaragod.

Regarding the northern boundary of Kanara, Afonso de Albuquerque, in one of his letters to the King of Portugal writes: "... the other land of *Cintaquola* up to Goa is in your obedience..."[16] *Cintaquola* is the Portuguese corruption of Chitukul, modern Sadashivagad on the northern bank of the Kalinadi. This land was traditionally included in the kingdom of Goa, as stated in a treaty between the Portuguese and the emperor of Vijayanagara, Sadashiva Raya.[17] Thus, the Kalinadi was certainly the northern boundary of Kanara.

On the basis of the above authorities[18] one may conclude that at the time of the Portuguese arrival in India, Kanara comprised the area between the Kalinadi and the river Chandragiri, and between the Western Ghats and the Arabian Sea.

The period for the present work is from 1498 to 1763. The Portuguese came into contact with Kanara in 1498. Vasco da

Gama sailed northwards from Malabar along the coast till his arrival in mid-September at a group of islands off Kundapur, two leagues from the mainland. He developed friendly relations with the locals there who brought him fish and other provisions in return for the shirts and other articles he gave them. Before sailing he placed on one of the islands, with the permission of the local people, a Portuguese banner with the cross and the coat-of-arms of the King of Portugal,[19] probably as a mark of conquest and possession. Today these islands are known as Pigeon Islands, situated about 20 miles south of Bhatkal.[20]

From the Pigeon Islands the Portuguese fleet proceeded to Anjediv, a group of five islands, about five miles southwest of Karwar, and two miles from the mainland. The Portuguese stayed there from September 24 to October 5, cleaning and repairing their ships, filling fresh water, and procuring provisions. Da Gama came to know from some natives who brought him pumpkins and cucumbers that there was plenty of cinnamon available there, but no other variety of spices. He took with him, as a sample, two large branches, full of leaves of a cinnamon tree from a thicket where there were many such trees.[21]

The locals seemed to have become friendly with the Portuguese. On one occasion 12 of them in two small boats went to them and offered them a large bundle of sugarcane. They requested da Gama to allow them to go on board the Portuguese ships in order to have a look. He suspected something and was irritated with the request. Just then some more locals arrived in two boats. Seeing that da Gama was not well disposed towards them the first group of twelve asked the latter not to land. And then they all sailed away. [22]

Thus the Kanarese and the Portuguese came to know each other to some extent right from the beginning of the latter's arrival in India. That contact continued in various spheres–political, commercial and religious–until the end of the Portuguese hold over Goa on December 19, 1961.

1763, however, marks an important stage in Portuguese-Kanarese relations. In that year Hyder Ali Khan, *de facto* ruler of Mysore, brought to an end the line of the Keladi rulers which had dominated Kanara for about 200 years. The dynasty of the Keladi chiefs was established in 1499 when Chauda Gauda was appointed the Nayaka of Keladi by Vira Narsimha, emperor of Vijayanagara. The event virtually coincided with the coming of the Portuguese to India. It is true that until the middle of the 16th century, there was no direct relations between the Portuguese and the Keladi rulers: but in 1554 or a little earlier, Sadashiva Nayaka, one of the successors of Chauda Gauda, was appointed Governor of Chandragutti, Barkur and Mangalore.[23] The Keladi Nayakas thus entered the Kanara region and came into direct contact with the Portuguese. Since then as shown elsewhere, there were active relations between the two powers, sometimes friendly and at other times hostile, until the last ruler of the dynasty, namely, Rani Virammaji, was overthrown in 1763 by Hyder Ali who initiated a new chapter in the history of Kanara. A period of a little over two centuries and a half from 1498 to 1763, therefore, may be considered as a distinct period of the Portuguese-Kanarese relations. I have laid emphasis on the political aspects of the Portuguese-Kanarese relations.

REFERENCES

1. K. M. Panikkar considers this as the beginning of the "Vasco da Gama epoch" in East-West relations, for the Western dominance over Asia began with the coming of Vasco da Gama to India and lasted for about 450 years until the British withdrew from India in 1947. His work *Asia and Western Dominance* has the sub-title *A survey of the Vasco da Gama epoch of Asian History, 1498-1945.*
2. C. R. Boxer in his work: *Four Centuries of Portuguese Expansion, 1415-1825: A Succinct Survey*, quotes with near approval (p. l) a 16th century Spanish historian, Francisco López de Gómara, who says that the discovery of the sea route from Europe to India by Vasco da Gama was "the greatest event since the creation of the world, apart from the Incarnation and Death of Him who created it". *D-JB*, I, pp. 151-2.
3. Several books and papers have been produced in this respect. Oliveira Boleó, in his work: *Descobrimentos Marítimos e Explorações Terrestres*, (pp. 36-42, 54), enumerates the following causes: (i) Portugal had an excellent coast; (ii) during the 14th century she consolidated her territorial boundaries in

Europe and in 1415 she began her career of overseas expansion with the capture of Ceuta in North-West Africa; (iii) to fight against the Muslims, be they in Africa or in distant lands, and to spread Christianity among the pagans, became her national policy; (iv) she took advantage of the nautical studies of the day in Europe; (v) the fear of the '*Mar Tenebroso*' (Sea of Darkness) beyond the Cape of Bojador was removed with the voyage of Gil Eanes in 1434; (vi) it was believed that there was a Christian king, Prester John, at the flank of the Muslim empire who constantly fought against Islam; one of the purposes of the voyages of discovery therefore was to find out his kingdom and unite with him against the Muslims; (vii) economically, Portugal was deficient in many products; the desire and necessity to improve her economy impelled her to further voyages of discovery after the conquest of Ceuta; (viii) ethnically, a large portion of the population of Portugal consisted of the descendants of the ancient sea-faring peoples like the Greeks, the Celts and the Visigoths; (ix) The Portuguese secured (in 1428) a copy of the *Book of Marco Polo*, which gave them some valuable knowledge regarding the East, including India and China; and (x) Prince Henry the Navigator (1394-1460), by far, was the most eminent human agent who organised and directed the voyages of discovery, taking full advantage of the above factors and circumstances. He was motivated by (a) an intellectual curiosity of knowing the geography of the world; (b) a spirit of proselytization and crusade–to convert and fight against the infidels; and (c) a desire to develop overseas commerce and to colonise. His career as an explorer, conqueror and crusader began in 1415 when he captured Ceuta. By the time he died in 1460 his sailors had gone as far as the Mountain of Lion (Leão) on the West Coast of Africa; his policy was continued by his successors without a break.

4. Alvaro Velho, *Roteiro da Primeira Viagem de Vasco da Gama*, p. 40.
5. *D-JB*, I, pp. 157-8.
6. António da Silva Rẹgo, *Portuguese Colonisation: A Study of Royal Ordinances (Regimentos)*, p. 26.
7. R. S. Whiteway, *The Rise of the Portuguese Power in India*, pp. 7-8.
8. *Cambridge History of India*, V, p. 4.
9. *D-JB*, I, pp. 181-2.
10. *Cambridge History of India, V*, p. 5.
11. *Ibid.*, p. 6.
12. Duarte Barbosa, *Livro de*, tr. A. R. Machado, pp. 93-4.
13. *Ibid.*, p. 94.
14. *Ibid.*, p. 100.
15. *D-JB*, I, p. 357.
16. *Cartas*, I, p. 28. The letter dated December 22, 1510.
17. Simão Botelho, "O Tombo do Estado da India", in *Subsidios*, p. 256.
18. Tomé Pires (*Suma Oriental*, tr. Armando Cortesão, pp. 60-1, 65-66) differs from these authorities regarding the boundaries of Kanara. According to him Kanara extended from Anjediv to Mangalore. Mirjan, Honavar, Bhatkal, Basrur, Brahmawar, Barkur, Udipi and Mangalore were its ports. Though

Manjeshwara belonged to the emperor of Vijayanagara, it was not a Kanarese port. Kumbala, of course, was far below and it was, therefore in Malabar. It may be pointed out that though Tomé Pires was in India, his stay here was for about a year and nine months (*Ibid.*, pp. xxiv-xxvi, xxix). Duarte Barbosa, on the other hand, was in India from about 1500 to 1516 or 1517 (Longworth Dames, *The Book of Duarte Barbosa*, p. xxxiii). He knew Malayalam very well (*Ibid.*, p. xxxvi). His statements regarding the Kanarese boundaries, therefore, must be considered as more authentic. João de Barros too can be considered as having acquired greater knowledge of the Kanarese boundaries, though he never came to India. For as an official, long connected with the India House at Lisbon, he was familiar with Indian affairs and as an official historian, he studied documents relating to India.

Later Portuguese writers also support Barbosa and Barros. Simão Botelho (*op. cit.*, pp. 246-8), writing in 1554, included all the ports from Sadashivagad to Kumbala in Kanara. He was the superintendent of the Treasury and was in India between 1532 and 1554, visiting various ports, factories and fortresses. Even in the 17th century, the 'district of Canara' was described as extending between Goa and Cannanore, as can be seen in a royal ordinance dated March 19, 1612 (*DIR*, II, p. 228).

19. *História*, I, p. 60; Alvaro Velho, *op. cit.*, p. 70.
20. *Gazetteer of the Bombay Presidency*, XV, pt. II, *Kanara*, p. 101.
21. Alvaro Velho, *op. cit.*, p. 71.
22. *Ibid.*, p. 74.
23. N. Lakshminarayana Rao, "The Nayakas of Keladi", *VSCV*, p. 258.

2

THE PORTUGUESE ARRIVAL AT KANARA

The Vijayanagara Empire

Any discussion on the political and commercial situation in Kanara at the arrival of the Portuguese in India must be prefaced with the statement that this whole coastal region was subject to the sovereignty of the Vijayanagara emperors. In 1336, Deva Raya, the Bairasu Odeyar of Barkur, whose authority extended at least from Karkal in South Kanara to Kumta in North Kanara, made over his kingdom to Harihara I, the first emperor of Vijayanagar.[1] The rest of Kanara also came under Harihara's control. The whole region of Kanara remained under the Vijayanagara emperors until the latter half of the 16th century.[2] Many Portuguese writers confirm that the province of Kanara from the Kalinadi to the river Chandragiri was a part of the great Vijayanagara empire when the Portuguese came to India.

There were, however, a number of local chiefs in Kanara who governed small areas at the time of the arrival of the Portuguese. The Vijayanagara emperors allowed full independence to these chiefs within their respective jurisdictions, provided they maintained their quota of horses, foot soldiers and elephants in readiness for immediate use and paid their annual tributes.[3] That is why we find these chiefs entering into treaties with the Portuguese, independent of the Vijayanagara emperors, and the Portuguese treating them as if they were independent kings, even though they knew very well that the chiefs were feudatories of the emperors. It may be true that the Portuguese, for their own glorification, treated the chiefs as kings,[4] but the virtual independence the latter enjoyed under the Vijayanagara emperors may be considered as an additional factor for the Portuguese attitude towards them.

Gersoppa, Barkur, Mangalore, Ullala and Kumbala were the feudatory principalities of Kanara at the time of the arrival of the Portuguese. It is interesting to see the positions of the chiefs of these principalities and their respective territorial jurisdictions at the turn of the 15th century and the beginning of the 16th and the commercial importance of the ports and towns.

Gersoppa

The principality of Gersoppa was created by the Vijayanagara emperors. A Jain family was recognised as the ruling house of this principality. The house was related by marriage to the Bairasu Odeyars of Barkur.[5] The principality of Gersoppa extended, according to one Portuguese source, "from Honavar and Mirjan to Anjediv".[6] In fact it extended from the south bank of the Kalinadi to Gersoppa itself on the south bank of the river Sharavati, for another source mentions the Kalinadi as the river "where the kingdom of Honavar separated from that of Goa".[7] `The kingdom of Honavar' meant the kingdom of Gersoppa, as the Portuguese often used the former expression to denote the kingdom of Gersoppa.[8] Anjediv, Mirjan and Honavar were its principal ports and Gersoppa, about 16 miles inland was its capital.

Who was the ruler of Gersoppa at the arrival of the Portuguese? This is difficult to answer. Probably it was Berforé, who may be identified with Basavaraja of Gersoppa [9] and who sent an ambassador to Goa in March 1510, at the instance of his suzerain, Krishna Deva Raya, and who offered to assist the Portuguese against the Adil Shah of Bijapur.[10] Afonso de Albuquerque gives us some clues regarding the reign-period of Basavaraja. He wrote to the King of Portugal: "..*Merião* (Malhar Rao) was the nephew of the King of *Onor* (Honavar) who gives you *Mirjeu* (Mirjem)", and his uncle owing to some discontent, banished him from his kingdom and at his death bestowed the kingdom to a younger brother of his (Malhar Rao's); and there was always a fight between both the brothers; and *Merião* always endeavoured to oust his younger brother as he (Malhar Rao) was the true heir: this brother, while he ruled, I found him to be a very bad man, friend of the Muslims, of little truthfulness and hardly paying the dues of *Mirjeu* ... and would to God that the king of *Onor*, his brother, died ... and he (Malhar Rao) succeeded to the kingdom".[11]

The letter is dated April 1, 1512. At the time of writing this letter, Malhar Rao was the chief of Honavar, that is, Gersoppa, as can be seen from the letter itself. He succeeded his younger brother, who had just died then. The younger brother's name however, is not indicated, but he had succeeded the king who had given Mirjan to the Portuguese. The Portuguese secured Mirjan, probably in the first half of 1506, after a war between them and the king of Gersoppa in October of the previous year.[12] Thus, Malhar Rao's uncle was ruling in 1505 and 1506. He seems to have been on the throne in 1509 also. For in an order of Albuquerque to the treasurer of Cochin, dated December 1 of that year we come to know that a present was given to the son of "Tyno, king of Onor".[13] Probably Malhar Rao's uncle was this 'Tyno'.

Basavaraja may be identified with 'Tyno' for the rulers of Gersoppa seem to have had the title '*Wodearu Pritani*'[14] and 'Tyno' may be considered as referring to the ending of the word '*Pritani*'. Basavaraja cannot be identified with the younger brother of Malhar Rao, for Albuquerque found the younger brother unfriendly towards the Portuguese, whereas Basavaraja offered to help them against the Bijapuris. Thus, one may conclude that Basavaraja Odeyar Pritani ('Tyno' or 'Berforé' for the Portuguese) was the king of Gersoppa at least from 1505 to 1510. He was succeeded by his younger nephew, who in turn was followed by the latter's elder brother, Malhar Rao in the beginning of 1512.

From the above quoted letter of Albuquerque, dated April 1, 1512 another deduction may be made. Malhar Rao is mentioned as the nephew of the king of Gersoppa, who gave Mirjan to the Portuguese, and that he was the real heir to the kingdom. This indicates that Malhar Rao belonged to a ruling family in which the

'*Aliyakattu*' prevailed in respect of inheritance, namely, the sister's son and not one's own son was the heir. If 'Tyno' is identified with Malhar Rao's uncle, then the latter had a son, yet the son did not succeed his father to the throne, even when Malhar Rao was exiled. Instead, Malhar Rao's younger brother became the ruler. It is true that 'nephew' stands for one's brother's son also. However, Barros clearly states that Malhar Rao was the nephew of the king of Honavar, and the heir of the same kingdom of Honavar, following the custom of the people of India (in which) the nephews, the sons of sisters were the heirs and not one's own sons."[15]

The Gersoppa chiefs were frequently at war with Goa. The latter kingdom had been annexed by Harihara II in 1366, but it was lost to the Bahamanis in 1472 during the reign of Virupaksha II. The latter's successor Virupaksha III, endeavoured to retake it but in vain. Goa, in fact, remained in Muslim hands up to 1510 when it was conquered by the Portuguese. In the meantime, every emperor of Vijayanagara had an eye on the territories of Goa, and it is likely that the chiefs of Gersoppa had instructions to create trouble for the Muslims of Goa. Barros confirms this, though the reason given by him is different. It may not be out of place here to give a long quotation from his work in which he vividly describes the political and commercial relations among Honavar, Vijayanagara, the Deccan and Goa. He writes: "This port (of Honavar) and that of Bhatkal, which is seven leagues ahead, with others of this coast, belonged to the king of Vijayanagara, and the king of Honavar (was) his vassal. These ports were for a little less than 40 years, the most celebrated along the whole coast, not only because the land was fertile by itself and abundant in provisions, where there was great shipment to all places, but also (because) it was the entrance and exit of all the merchandise for the kingdom of Vijayanagara, from which the king had great revenue, mainly from the horses of Arabia and Persia, which came here as the ports of the greatest profit, on account of the great value they had in Vijayanagara, as these horses were the principal force with which he defended himself against the Muslims of the kingdom of the Deccan with whom he was at war continually, and who had encircled him on the northern side and had taken many of his territories."

"And owing to this fertility of the land and the trade of these ports, there was a great number of native Muslims there, whom they call *naiteás* (Navayats), who used to purchase the horses and sell them to the Deccan Muslims, on account of which the king of Vijayanagara received great damage, as they waged war against him with the horses and more (damage) at the hands of the purchasers of the horses which he needed on account of the doubled price".

"Finally, as a people harmful to his state, he ordered the king of Honavar, his vassal, that he should kill as many of these Muslims as he could, so that the others would flee from his land out of fear. And in the Muslim year of 917, which is the year 1479 in the era of Christ our Redeemer, there was a slaughter of these Muslims in all the territories of Honavar and Bhatkal, in the manner of a conspiracy, in which more than 10,000 died; and the others who were formed into a group, the people of the land giving them an occasion for their exit, went to live in the island of Tissuari, wherein the city of Goa is founded ..."

"On account of the outrage which was done unto these Muslims, they began, in hatred of the Hindus of Honavar, to people Goa and attract merchandise there, mainly the horses, so that they (the horses) could pass on to the kingdom of the Deccan, a work they accomplished shortly, as these things were shipped by the Muslims, who desired to favour their parties against the Hindus, on account of which the ports of Honavar and Bhatkal began to feel the damage. And in order to oblige the ships loaded with horses as well as other merchandise, which used to sail into these two ports always, to go to them and not to that of Goa, he (the emperor of Vijayanagara) sent to the king of Honavar four Hindu captains, who, with a fleet of ships, would compel all the ships to sail into his port and would rob and cause all the damage they could to those (ships) which defended themselves".

"Of which fleet ... Timmayya ... was the Captain-major, ... who did all the damage which he could to the Muslims by the coast, ... And before he came to this post, the king of Honavar had other captains, by reason of which there was always a war between the king of Honavar and the governors of Goa, and on account of this the fortress of *Cintacora* (Sadashivagad) came to be provided as the frontier of enemies".

"The Muslims prevailed so much against the king of Honavar, especially after the *Sabaia* (Yusuf Adil Khan) became the lord of Goa, that the king of Honavar, having the habitation of the city at the mouth of the river, shifted it inside (along) the river ... "[16]

From the above quotation it is clear that there were frequent wars between Gersoppa and Goa after the massacre of 1479. Ten years prior to the massacre, Goa had fallen to the Bahamanis. Thus, when the emperor sent four captains to the assistance of the king of Gersoppa he not only intended to hinder the commerce of Goa, but also to keep the Muslim master of Goa engaged so that it would be a good distraction for him, as he would be compelled to keep a portion of his army in Goa to defend it. Gersoppa, however, does not seem to have gained much against Goa.

The Gersoppa chiefs seem to have had differences with the rulers of Bhatkal or the Barkur chiefs also. In 1508, when Francisco de Almeida was in Malabar, Timmayya requested his help, apparently on behalf of the king of Gersoppa, against Bhatkal. However, when Almeida reached the Bhatkal river he found that the two chiefs had stopped fighting in obedience to their suzerain, Krishna Deva Raya, who had come to the temple of Gokarna to weigh himself in gold.[17]

From Varthema and Duarte Barbosa we get a good deal of information regarding the commercial importance of Honavar. The former says that the 'king of Honavar' had seven or eight ships which were on continuous voyage. There was much rice in Honavar. The people there lived longer than the Italians for its climate was very good.[18]

Barbosa records that much trade was carried on in Honavar by the Malabaris who took a considerable amount of black rice from there in exchange for coconuts and coconut-oil, palm-jaggery and palm-wine. Every year an infinite number of *zambucos*, big and small, came to Honavar from Malabar for this trade of rice, which was the staple article of food among the Malabaris.[19]

In addition to Honavar, there were other ports and towns under the Gersoppa chiefs. With regard to Mirjan, Barbosa says that it was situated on the bank of a great river of the same name (the modern Tadri river). A big quantity of very coarse black rice was grown there. This rice was purchased by the Malabaris who came there in small *zambucos*. The rice was exchanged for coconuts, coconut-oil and jaggery which the people of Mirjan liked very much.[20]

Anjediv, by far, attracted the Portuguese right from the beginning. Vasco da Gama had spent 12 days there in September-October 1498 on his return voyage. He found there a 'church' built of stone; but it was damaged by the Muslims and therefore it was covered with straw. The locals worshipped three black stones there which were in the centre of the 'church'. There was a beach in front of the 'church' and there were two tanks on the island.[21]

Varthema says that both Hindus and Muslims lived in Anjediv. The climate there was not good, nor was the soil very fertile. Between the island and the mainland there was a very good port and in the island excellent potable water.[22]

The Anjediv group of islands seem to have been very much utilised as a place of rest by the Muslim and Hindu sea-farers during the course of their navigation along the coast and between India and the ports of East Africa and the Middle East. The Portuguese also made similar use of the islands, which, however, do not seem to have been well populated on account of their poor climate and infertile soil. The Gersoppa chiefs, in whose principality they were included, apparently neglected their development for these reasons. The islands were virtually nobody's land until the Portuguese decided to make them their own in 1505 by building a fortress.[23]

Barkur

In South Kanara, or Tulunadu proper, Barkur and Mangalore were the two important governorships under the Vijayanagara emperors. The Portuguese called Barkur *Bacanor*. The town of Barkur was on the north bank of the Sitanadi. Basrur or Bracelor of the Portuguese writers was included in the territorial jurisdiction of Barkur, for Barbosa mentions them together,[24] and, besides, they were not very far from each other. Basrur was located on the south bank of the river Haladi.

Inscriptions belonging to different governors of Barkur from 1490 to 1510 have been discovered at Chaulikeri, Handali, Koteshwar, Kalassa, Giliyara, Manigarakeri, Basrur and Bandar. There were at least three chiefs at Barkur, in succession from 1498 to 1510, Sadharanadeva Odeya (1498, 1499), Basavarasa Odeya (1502, 1507, 1508) and Mallappa Nayaka (1510).[25] Kedali Basavappa Arasu Odeyar, mentioned in an inscription of 1506 found by Buchanan in Baindur,[26] may be identified with Basavarasa Odeya. Thus, Baindur came under the principality of Barkur. Tomé Pires included Bhatkal also within the kingdom of Barkur.[27] Thus the region from Bhatkal to Basrur belonged to the Barkur chiefs.

Commercially, Bhatkal was the most important port in Kanara.[28] It was located about 25 miles south of Honavar. It was a river-port located about a mile from the shore. Many Muslim merchants resided in Bhatkal and there was a lot of traffic there. A great quantity of rice and sugar, especially white sugar, was produced and nuts and figs were available. However, there was neither wheat, nor barley, nor vegetables in Bhatkal.[29]

According to Barbosa, there was a great commerce of many articles of trade in Bhatkal. There were Muslims and Hindus among whom were prominent merchants. Every year, many ships from Hormuz came to the port of Bhatkal to take white rice and powdered sugar, which was available there in great abundance. They packed the powdered sugar in small bags. A lot of iron was also shipped. These three articles, namely, rice, powdered sugar and iron were the main merchandise of this place. There was also some pepper which was brought to that port by the Malabaris. There were many good *miramulanos* which were sold to the Muslims of Arabia and Persia.[30]

The ships from Hormuz brought to Bhatkal many horses and pearls which were sold there for the Vijayanagara empire. However, after the Portuguese occupation of Goa, the Hormuz ships took these articles to Goa. Some ships from Mecca also came to Bhatkal for spices. The *zambucos* from Malabar came there to take iron and sugar in exchange for much palm-sugar, coconuts, coconut oil, palm-wine, pepper and some drugs. The Portuguese after occupying Goa did not allow the ships from Mecca and Malabar to trade with the ports of Kanara but some of the ships ventured to go there for trade in spite of the Portuguese orders and regulations.[31]

There was much demand in Bhatkal for copper, which was carried inland for making coins, boilers and other utensils which the people of the land used. Quicksilver, vermilion, coral, aluminium ore, and ivory were sold there.[32]

On account of the great commercial importance of Bhatkal special administrators seem to have been appointed at the port. Tomé Pires says that Damj Shetty (probably Dama Shetty) was 'governor' of the Hindus and Cojatar, namely Khwaja Atter, was the Muslim there.[33] Barbosa mentions the very same Dama Shetty (Damachat) and another Reimas, probably Ramdas. The former was very rich with plenty of money and beautiful precious stones and the latter was the nephew of the Vijayanagara emperor.[34] The *Commentários* also speaks of two administrators of Bhatkal, namely Naodaquiçar, probably Nandakishore, and Condanechatim, probably Gundanna Shetty, who proposed to negotiate a treaty of peace with Albuquerque.[35]

At Baindur a great quantity of very good rice was gathered. Rice was cultivated there in valleys and marshy plains. There were two crops a year. All the rice that was exported from Bhatkal came from Baindur.[36]

To the ports of Barkur and Basrur came ships for rice from abroad as well as from Malabar. Much rice was exported to Hormuz, Aden and Xaer and more to Cannanore and Calicut. Though the Barkur country was small it was well-populated.[37]

The town of Basrur had a republican form of government. The people elected the oldest among themselves as the 'senators'. The merchants of Basrur were so rich that the people spoke of their wealth in terms of *bharas* of gold, each *bhara* weighing four quintals or 235.008 kilograms. Considerable quantities of rice, ginger and pepper were produced in Basrur. Much cloth of fine quality was also made there.[38]

Mangalore

Mangalore, like Barkur, was a separate administrative unit under the Vijayanagara emperors. However, a common governor over the two regions was many a time appointed. Thus, Annappa Odeyar was the governor of Mangalore and Barkur in 1418.[39] So also, in 1554 or a little earlier, Sadashiva Nayaka of Keladi was appointed governor of Chandragutti, Barkur and Mangalore by Ramaraja.[40]

Varthema, who might have been in Mangalore some time between 1504 and 1508, says that "fifty or seventy ships are loaded with rice" in the port of Mangalore.[41] Duarte Barbosa says that it was populated by Muslims and Hindus. Many ships came to the port of Mangalore to take loads of black rice, which was sold at Malabar. Ships laden with the Mangalore rice went to Aden also. Some pepper was grown there. The Mangalore river was amenable and beautiful. There were groves of coconut palms, sumptuous edifices, many rich and grand houses of Hindu worship, and also many mosques.[42]

Ullala

Ullala, the Olala of the Portuguese writers, does not seem to have attracted them until after the second decade of the 16th century. At the time of the arrival of the Portuguese in India, chiefs belonging to the Chautar family ruled over Ullala and its neighbourhood to the south of the river Netravati. Like all the chiefs from the river Kalinadi to the river Chandragiri, the Chautars also were the feudatories of the Vijayanagara emperors.

Kumbala

Duarte Barbosa found Kumbala to be under a lord who was subject to the emperor of Vijayanagara. It was on the frontier of the province of Kanara. The territorial jurisdiction of Kumbala seems to have extended as far as the north bank of the river Chandragiri in Kasaragod to the south of which commenced the territories of the king of Cannanore.

Very poor black rice was collected at Kumbala and the Malabaris came there to purchase and load it in their *zambucos*. They sold it to the poor class of people in Malabar and the islands of Maldives. This rice was very cheap and the merchants gained more in dealing in it than in white rice. Coir, which was used in making cable and ropes and which was a safe article of trade everywhere was given in exchange for the rice.[43]

Causes of the Portuguese success against native chiefs

The first and the foremost cause of the Portuguese success in India was their possession of an excellent navy. During the 15th century they developed scientifically the art of building ocean-going ships which were equipped with cannons. These cannon-carrying ships were a novelty on the shores of India when the Portuguese arrived here.[44] Outside Europe, only the Ottoman empire had a navy equipped with artillery but when the Portuguese reached India, the Turks had no navy in the Indian Ocean to challenge them. By the time the Ottomans thought of attacking the Portuguese in this quarter, the latter had strongly established themselves.[45] Though the Vijayanagara emperors had a navy it was not strong enough to compete with that of the Portuguese. In India gunnery was not developed then. This being the case, the native chiefs of Kanara cannot be blamed if they could not resist the Portuguese. The Gersoppa chief, no doubt, had a fleet under the command of Timmayya, but the ships were not equipped with guns and they do not seem to have been fit for fighting in deep waters.

Further, even though the Portuguese bombarded cities and ports, and caused damage to ships of merchandise on the Kanara coast, the Vijayanagara emperors had no desire to incur the hostility of the Portuguese by coming to the aid of the local chiefs and fighting the former. For both the Vijayanagara emperors and the Portuguese had in Muslims a common enemy to fight. Vijayanagara frequently fought with the Muslim rulers of the Deccan. Friendship with the Portuguese could be of great help to her in procuring military equipment from abroad, particularly the horses from Hormuz, which otherwise went to her enemy through the port of Goa, in spite of

Timmayya's efforts to prevent it. That is why Krishna Deva Raya offered his friendship to the Portuguese when Goa was taken by them.

The Kanarese trade, like the trade of all the East with the West, was under the monopolistic control of the Muslims. Therefore, Vijayanagara had every reason to rejoice if her enemy was deprived of this monopoly by the Portuguese. The native chiefs might have complained to their suzerain concerning the Portuguese high-handedness against them but he apparently preferred to take no notice of the complaint, so that the Portuguese could, being free from the necessity of facing the Vijayanagara forces, devote their energy to curb the Muslims.

REFERENCES

1. J. Sturrock, *The South Canara District Manual*, pp. 63, 64.
2. Occasionally, during the course of these two centuries, the Bairasu Odeyars revolted against their suzerains, but they were usually suppressed. Thus, they endeavoured to regain their independence during the reign of Harihara II (1377-1404), but in vain. Again in the reign of Virupaksha II (1465-85), Immadi Bairarasa Odeyar revolted but when the imperial forces marched against him and encamped at Mangalore he took to flight. (Hayavadana C. Rao, *Mysore Gazetteer*, vol. II, pt. III, pp. 1510-1, 1770-1).
3. R. Sewell, *A Forgotten Empire*, p. 131.
4. *Ibid.*, p. 119.
5. *Gazetteer of the Bombay Presidency*, vol. XV, pt. II, *Kanara*, p. 283.
6. Tomé Pires, *Suma Oriental*, tr. Armando Cortesão, pp. 60-1.
7. *Commentários*, II, p. 116.
8. The Portuguese sources show that Honavar and Gersoppa were not two different principalities, but were one and the same. The Portuguese used the expression: "the king of Honavar" or "the king of Gersoppa" to denote one and the same ruler. Afonso de Albuquerque who had close contacts with Kanara says at one place that Mirjan was given to the Portuguese by "the king of Honavar" (*Cartas*, I, p. 47) but in another place he states that the very Mirjan was given by "the king of Gersoppa" (*Ibid.*, I, p. 172). Tomé Pires (*op. cit.*, pp. 60-61) states that the region from Anjediv to Honavar belonged to the king of Gersoppa. Gaspar Correa writes (*Lendas*, tomo I, pt. I, p. 289) that Honavar belonged to the king of Gersoppa and (*Ibid.*, pt. II, p. 565), that Malhar Rao was the king of Honavar. If Honavar belonged to the king of Gersoppa Malhar Rao, king of Honavar was the king of Gersoppa. Thus the expressions "king of Honavar" and "the kingdom of Honavar" in Portuguese sources mean the king of Gersoppa and the kingdom of Gersoppa respectively.

9. *Gazetteer of the Bombay Presidency, op. cit.*, p. 109.
10. *Commentários*, II, pp. 183-184.
11. *Cartas*, I, p. 47.
12. *Infra*, pp. 30-36.
13. *Cartas*, IV, p. 209.
14. *Gazetteer of the Bombay Presidency, op. cit.*, p. 283.
15. *D-JB*, II, p. 237.
16. *Ibid.*, I, pp. 347-8.
17. *História*, II, pp. 424-5.
18. L. de Varthema, *Itinerário*, tr. Vicenzo Spinelli, p. 134.
19. Duarte Barbosa, *Livro de*, tr. A. R. Machado, p. 95.
20. *Ibid.*, pp. 94-5.
21. Alvaro Velho, *Roteiro da Primeira Viagem de Vasco da Gama*, p. 73.
22. L. de Varthema, *op. cit.*, pp. 133-4.
23. *Infra*, pp. 85-6.
24. Duarte Barbosa, *op. cit.*, p. 98.
25. K. A. N. Sastri, and N. Venkataramanayya, *Further Sources of Vijayanagara History*, p. 149. The figures inside the brackets show the years in which the inscriptions belonging to the respective chiefs have been found.
26. J. Sturrock, *op. cit.*, p. 67.
27. Tomé Pires, *op. cit.*, p. 61.
28. *Ibid.*, p. 62.
29. L. de Varthema, *op. cit.*, p. 133.
30. Duarte Barbosa, *op. cit.*, p. 96.
31. *Ibid.*
32. *Ibid.*, p. 97.
33. Tomé Pires, *op. cit.*, p. 62.
34. Barbosa, *op. cit.*, pp. 96-7.
35. *Commentários*, II, pp. 291-2.
36. Barbosa, *op. cit.*, p. 98.
37. *Ibid.*, pp. 98-9.
38. *D-DC*, VIII, p. 279. Also X, pt. I, pp. 380-1.
39. G. M. Moraes, *Mangalore*, p. 4.
40. *Supra*, p. 8.
41. L. de Varthema, *op. cit.*, p. 133.
42. Barbosa, *op. cit.*, p. 99.
43. *Ibid.*, pp. 99-100.
44. K.M. Panikkar, *Asia and Western Dominance*, p. 29.
45. *Ibid.*

3

GERSOPPA'S HAND IN THE PORTUGUESE CAPTURE OF GOA

The kingdom of Gersoppa played an important role in the Portuguese capture of Goa, which became the permanent headquarters of the Portuguese empire in the East. To be sure, the early contacts between this kingdom and the Portuguese were not a happy event. In 1502 Vasco da Gama arrived with his fleet at the Honavar river chasing the fleet of Timmayya, whom he wrongly believed to be a Muslim pirate. Estevão da Gama, Vasco da Gama's brother, was sent into the river with men, who, on entering the river, came across some palisades from where the natives shot at the Portuguese from small guns and bows. Estevão, however, affected a landing and the enemy took to flight. This place, probably a part of the city of Honavar, was burnt after which the Portuguese safely returned to their fleet. Having thus accomplished the wanton and unnecessary burning of the ships and of the city, the Portuguese fleet proceeded towards Bhatkal.[1]

Better relations, however, developed between the Portuguese and the kingdom of Gersoppa during the vice-royalty of Dom Francisco de Almeida (1505-09), though not without a clash. The Viceroy constructed a fortress at Anjediv in accordance with the instruction of King Manuel of Portugal. This clearly showed the intention of the Portuguese to establish themselves in India and to control the Indian trade and commerce on the western coast. The exploits of the Viceroy against the Muslims in East Africa were already known to the kings of India. No wonder, therefore, that the king of Gersoppa desired friendship with the Portuguese rather than hostilities. In the beginning of October 1505 he sent an ambassador to the Viceroy at Anjediv with a present of provisions. According to Correa, Timmayya himself was the ambassador.[2]

The Viceroy readily agreed to be at peace with the Gersoppa chief and in order to show the greatness of Portugal, he put forth the spoils which he had brought from Mombasa. There were valuable and costly items among them and the ambassador was awe-struck on seeing them.[3]

Barros gives a different version of this peace negotiation between the Portuguese and the king of Gersoppa. The Viceroy sent a message to him by way of informing him of the Portuguese arrival at Anjediv. He expressed his happiness in having him as a neighbour with whom he desired to have friendly relations, as commanded by his own sovereign, the King of Portugal. He also informed the chief of Gersoppa that he had certain matters to discuss with him. He requested the chief to let him know how they could meet each other for a discussion.[4]

No reply came from the Gersoppa chief to this message, nor to others which the Viceroy sent later. However one of the captains of the chief informed the Viceroy that his lord was in the hinterland, busy in the negotiation of a war and therefore not in a position to respond personally to the messages of the Viceroy. Almeida thought that this excuse and delay were deliberate on the part of the Gersoppa chief as he desired to gain time to prepare himself for a showdown with the Portuguese. Yet he received the messengers of the captain with politeness and hospitality, sending him a present and his compliments. On the following day two ambassadors from the chief himself came to the Viceroy. They pretended to be innocent of what had happened between him and the captain. They told him that on hearing of the arrival of the Portuguese fleet at Anjediv and of the construction of the fortress on the island, their chief, who was busy with a war far away from the coast, sent them to him with a view to developing friendly relations with the King of Portugal. The chief offered the Viceroy, through these ambassadors, all that was needed with respect to provisions and other things for providing the fortress. After replying to these general offers, the Viceroy asked them why no response had been made to his own message. The ambassadors said that their chief was not aware of these. Regarding the role of the captain, the ambassadors told him that their chief would be hurt for not having been informed of the message, but that it was legitimate for captains to act cautiously in such matters as long as they would let their chief know of the matter and would soon come back with his answer. The Viceroy pretended to be happy with this, believing that the truth would be known from the reply that the ambassadors would bring from their chief. He sent them away with his compliments, and presents in return for what they had brought with them.[5] The ambassadors apparently did not come back. In spite of the Viceroy's suspicion, however, the Gersoppa chief seems to have desired friendship with the Portuguese then.

A few days later an incident occurred which led to a clash between the Portuguese and the chief. As Correa says, a ship belonging to the Muslims and coming from Hormuz loaded with horses, was seen by the Portuguese from Anjediv. The Viceroy ordered a caravel to chase the ship. It, however, had to be towed by boats into the sea as there was no favourable wind at the bay where it was anchored. This caused a little delay. Nevertheless, on seeing the caravel, the Muslims entered the Honavar river, but the crew, out of fear for the Portuguese, erred at the bar and the ship went aground. The Portuguese caravel did not enter the river, for the crew did not know the bar. Dom Lourenço, son of the Viceroy, who commanded the caravel, put out four boats and with his men approached the ship. The Muslims fled to the land. The Portuguese then began to remove the horses from the ship into their own boats. While they were doing so, there suddenly arose a tempest with a strong wind which forced them to give up the work and hasten back to Anjediv. The next day when the sea was calm, the Portuguese went to the ship again to fetch the horses, but the horses were already taken possession of by the king of Gersoppa. The Viceroy sent a letter requesting him to give up the horses, but the king refused to do so saying that the horses belonged to him since they were found lost within his jurisdiction. The Viceroy then considered the peace between the Portuguese and the Gersoppa chief as breached.[6]

According to Barros the ship carrying the horses was a large *zambuco* which approached Anjediv in order to take shelter there from a strong wind which had been blowing for two days. The crew soon realised that the island was occupied by the Portuguese with a large fleet.[7] The *zambuco* therefore changed its course and sailed towards Honavar. Dom Lourenço de Brito, and two of the Portuguese captains, were sent with their men to chase it. On approaching the *zambuco* the Portuguese found in it only twelve horses. When the storm broke out they entrusted these horses to the care of some local Muslims who could not, however, return them to the Portuguese, for the Gersoppa chief took them away. On the latter's refusal to surrender the horses, there followed a war between the two parties.[8] Thus, for the sake of a few horses the professed friends fought with each other.

Almeida embarked from Anjediv on Thursday, October 16, 1505 and reached the mouth of the Honavar river the same night in moonlight. On Friday morning he sent Fernão Soares in a boat to find out whether the ships could enter the river. Soares, after an inspection, returned and reported that ships, other than the caravels and small vessels, could not enter the river and that many big ships equal in size to those of the Portuguese were aground in the river. He also found out from the people that the enemy could amass 4,000 soldiers at short notice. Besides, some Muslims told him that they desired peace with the Portuguese, that they would urge the king to pay for the horses, and that their ships lying at the port should not be burnt in the meantime. The Viceroy waited the whole day to see if the Muslims would get the king to pay for the horses, but in vain. He then decided to attack the city. 600 men were ordered to embark in boats and other small vessels. They reached the city in the moonlight and before it was dawn, the Viceroy soon realised that it was not desirable to attack until the morning since his men did not know the land well and the moonlight was not enough to guide them. The attack, was, therefore postponed. The inhabitants of the city, in the meantime, took shelter in a nearby hill along with their women, children and goods, for fear that the Portuguese would fall upon the city any time. They desired very much that the king pay for the horses, but he did not want to, since he was 'greedy',[9] as if the Portuguese demanded the horses or compensation out of generosity!

The next morning, October 18, two Muslims again went to the Viceroy and told him, on behalf of the merchants of Honavar, that they desired peace and that they would entreat the king once again to pay the Portuguese for the nine horses. This time his reply was that he would burn the ships lying at the port even if the horses were paid for, for he was sure that among the ships there were some belonging to the Calicut ruler, who was an enemy of the Portuguese on the Malabar coast. The envoys denied the presence of the Calicut ships and went away never to return.[10]

While these dilatory negotiations were going on, the Gersoppa chief did nothing but sent his troops to fight the Viceroy whom he considered young and inexperienced. The Viceroy sent his son, Dom Lourenço, with some soldiers to effect a landing and to burn the ships. The enemy took to flight. On seeing the fire the Gersoppa chief sent additional troops. In all there were 4,000 men most of whom were bowmen and others were shield men with lances. The Gersoppa soldiers drew up in formation at the end of the city. The Viceroy too sent reinforcements to his son, and he himself began to move to see that the fire was not extinguished by the enemy. The bowmen, well-protected by the shield men, rained arrows on the Portuguese, led by Dom Lourenço, one of whom was killed. The Portuguese, however, managed to put the defenders to flight, killing 13 of them. The Viceroy, who was observing all this from his boat, ordered his son to come back, fearing that he might chase the enemy too far and put himself in danger. Dom Lourenço began to retreat accordingly but seeing this the enemy thought that the Portuguese were doing so out of fear and attacked them on the river bank. The enemy fled, however, when the Portuguese began to bombard from their ships. In the meantime, the Viceroy himself received a wound on his toe of the left foot from an arrow shot from the enemy. The wound was not a serious one and was soon cured. The Portuguese burnt 14 of the enemy ships and a great part of the city, and killed 22 of the enemy troops and wounded many more. On their side, one Portuguese soldier was killed. The Viceroy was the only one wounded.[11]

Barros, however, writes that the Viceroy did not have the intention of destroying the city, because it belonged to a vassal of the emperor of Vijayanagara with whom the Portuguese wanted to be on friendly terms. What the Viceroy wanted done, therefore, was to burn the ships belonging to Timmayya and others.[12]

Losing all hope of withstanding the Portuguese attack, the Gersoppa chief decided to seek peace. He sent two envoys to the Viceroy with the message that he repented for what he had done, that he realised his error in breaking the friendship with the Portuguese, that he would pay for the horses on account of which the battle was fought, and that he would become a vassal of the King of Portugal to whom he would pay tribute. The envoys themselves were to be hostages and they were to be beheaded if the chief did not send the promised money the following day. The Viceroy replied grandiloquently that he did not mind so much the taking of horses by the chief but his violence of truth, which ought to be guarded always, especially by the kings! He conceded peace because he did not want war! However, he did not have time then to settle terms of peace since he had much to do in Cochin where he ought to have been by that time. On reaching Cochin he would send his son with whom the chief could come to terms and pay for the horses. In the meantime he would give the chief a Portuguese flag so that no harm would be done to him by any of the Portuguese fleet. On these terms the Viceroy sailed for Cochin the same day, October 18.[13]

According to Barros, Timmayya played an important role in the negotiations for peace. The Viceroy was being treated for his wound in a ship in the afternoon of the day of the attack when Timmayya sought permission to see him. The request was granted. The Viceroy was impressed by Timmayya's personality. He had a noble and intelligent bearing. His dignified and honourable behaviour convinced him that he could give him credence as the trusted envoy of the Gersoppa chief. Timmayya begged to be excused for not coming earlier, the cause for the delay being the various affairs entrusted to him by his chief. He told the Viceroy that he had paid for this delay, because some of the ships burnt by the Portuguese belonged to him personally, that he had come to him to declare himself a vassal of the king of Portugal, which was not a new desire but one which he had right from the first day on which the Portuguese had arrived in India; that the Gersoppa chief also proposed to become a vassal of the Portuguese king; that the chief could not come personally to the Viceroy as he was indisposed; and that the offer of the vassalage, both of Timmayya and of his chief be accepted as they would always be loyal to the King of Portugal. Payment for the horses was promised. Compensation for damage, if any, was also offered to the Portuguese, though the soldiers of Honavar had done nothing but what was lawful in defence of the property of their king whose policy towards the Portuguese they did not know. The Viceroy was pleased with the talk but told Timmayya that he could not spare time then in settling terms of agreement since he had to hurry to Cochin in order to send loaded ships to Portugal. He would, therefore, send his son with powers to settle the terms later on. Although Timmayya was satisfied with the Viceroy's words, he did not want to go away without being promised that he and the Muslims of Honavar could move safely in the Indian waters without being attacked by the Portuguese. The Viceroy made provisions for this safety and Timmayya departed.[14]

Correa records that the amount for the horses was 23,000 *xerafins* and that the Gersoppa chief sent his nephew, his sister's son, to Anjediv and he was to remain on the island as hostage until the amount for the horses was paid to the Portuguese, and the sum of the tribute was agreed upon. In due course the king paid the money for the horses. He also offered to pay an annual tribute of 1,000 *pardaus* on condition that Timmayya be allowed to move about freely with his fleet. The Viceroy did not accept the condition, nor the tribute. However, friendship between the two came to be established. Timmayya supplied provisions to the Portuguese at Anjediv by which he gained much, for he could procure these provisions almost for nothing.[15] Thus according to Correa no damage or tribute was charged by the Portuguese upon the Gersoppa chief, except the price of the horses for which the battle was fought.

Barros and Castanheda do not indicate how and when the actual treaty of peace was entered into between the Gersoppa chief and the Portuguese, and what were the terms of the treaty, though according to both, the Viceroy went to Cochin promising to send his son with powers to settle the terms of peace. However, from a letter written by the King of Portugal to the Archbishop of Braga on June 19, 1508, it appears that the Gersoppa chief gave to the Portuguese a place which was a sea-port busy with commercial activities. It was taken possession of by the Viceroy who appointed officials to collect the dues from the port. The Portuguese gained annually 1,000 *pardaus* from this.[16] Probably the place referred to in the letter is Mirjan, as can be gathered from another letter written by Albuquerque to the King of Portugal on April 1, 1512. The letter indicated that the Gersoppa chief gave Mirjan to the Portuguese and that the successor of this chief hardly paid the dues from the place.[17] Incidentally the second letter implies that the Portuguese did not have territorial possession of Mirjan, though both the letters say that the Gersoppa chief 'gave' them the place. What the Portuguese really got were the customs dues of Mirjan which amounted to 1,000 *pardaus* a year. Thus, from these two letters it appears that the Gersoppa chief not only paid for the horses on account of which the battle was fought but also agreed to pay an annual tribute of 1,000 *pardaus* in the form of customs dues from Mirjan.

It will be of interest to know more about Timmayya, who, in fact, played a significant role in the Portuguese conquest of Goa later on. The Portuguese knew him right from the year in which they arrived in India. As we know, Vasco da Gama stayed on the island of Anjediv for 12 days in September-October 1498, during the course of his return voyage from India to Portugal. A few days after he landed there, he saw two big boats, which appeared like *fustas*, and in which there were many people singing and playing musical instruments. The boats were being oared and had banners on the top of their masts. There were 5 more along the coast for protection. Da Gama, before the boats could reach his ships, inquired from the Malabaris whom he had captured at Calicut, about the people in them. He was told that he should not allow the boats to come near; that the men inside were thieves; and that they were coming in order to rob the Portuguese ships if possible. Being thus alerted, da Gama ordered his men to fire at the boats as soon as they reached within gun-shot range. The men in the boats cried out "*tambaram, tambaram*", perhaps requesting the Portuguese to stop firing. They began to retreat, however, when they found that the Portuguese would not understand them and would not stop firing at them. Nicolau Coelho, a Portuguese captain, chased them in a vessel to some distance until he was signalled to return.[18]

Castanheda says that da Gama learnt from the Malabaris that Timmayya was the leader of the thieves.[19] Barros adds that as soon as Timmayya had news of the Portuguese arrival at Anjediv he set out from Honavar with 8 ships which he fastened together and covered with boughs. The ships, therefore, appeared like a floating thicket. When they were within firing-range, they were bombarded and scattered by the Portuguese. Coelho who chased them took one of the ships in which there was rice and other provisions.[20]

Timmayya is thus referred to in the above Portuguese works as a pirate. Correa also calls him a corsair.[21] The author of the *Commentários* mentions that he had been of great service to the King of Portugal, but all the same he was "a man of low sort" and a pirate.[22]

Was Timmayya really a pirate and a man of low sort? He was neither. To be sure, he robbed ships but he did so as a servant of Vijayanagara whose orders he faithfully carried out. The Emperor sent 4 captains with Timmayya as captain-major to the Gersoppa chief with the command to compel all the mercantile ships to sail into the ports of Kanara, and to cause damage to those which persisted in going to Goa. He was not, therefore, a professional pirate. He attacked ships and emptied them of their goods in the service of his sovereign. He might have made over the spoils to the emperor, keeping a share of it for himself as a reward for his efforts, and a part for the king of Gersoppa in whose jurisdiction the ports lay.

Timmayya's marriage with a princess of Gersoppa is another proof of his high birth and status.[23] The Gersoppa chief would not have given the princess in marriage to one who was a mere pirate and a man of low sort. As Barros says, Timmayya's very bearing was noble and his behaviour refined,[24] befitting men of high birth.

It is said that Timmayya was a Maratha.[25] There does not seem to exist any basis for this supposition. The name 'Timmayya' is Kanarese. The Portuguese spelt it as Timoja, it being common to represent 'y' with 'j' in Portuguese. In fact, in one of the orders of Albuquerque, dated December 1, 1509, the name is spelt almost accurately as 'Timoya'.[26] Further, Correa and Tomé Pires record that Timmayya had his residence in Honavar, on the river bank, half a league from the coast.[27] By religion he might have been a Jain, since he married the princess of Gersoppa, whose rulers were Jains.[28]

Relations between Almeida and Timmayya continued to be cordial. They corresponded with each other. Timmayya wrote to the Viceroy from Honavar on November 9, 1508 in response to one from the latter: "Here they gave me your letter (in which you asked me) that I should send (messengers) to Diu to know how many were alive (there). I sent these two men by land, who brought a letter which I am sending to you. From it you will know who are (alive). The captain-major came here, spoke to me, and went away soon. I never heard of him anymore. A ship came from Gramus to Dabul, and brought the news that there were 66. Or is it only six (the word *seis* being repeated by the printer by mistake) ships in Hormuz?. The captain did not say what his name was. I inquire daily about you, and whichever ships come from Cannanore do not give me news about you. I think that you will come as early as possible, and let me know what I should do and all that I shall do, because I am at the service of the King of Portugal and of your lordship. Here there is news that the ships of Rumes will not come this year. Sir, these men who went to Diu, went a long way. I recommend them to be rewarded. I have a little (quantity) of cloves, camphor and black-wood. Let me know if you would like to have it ..."[29]

From the above letter it is evident that the Viceroy had asked Timmayya to find out how many were alive out of the 19 Portuguese who were taken prisoners[30] after the naval battle between Dom Lourenço and the combined fleets of the sultan of Turkey and the

Shah of Gujarat in 1507 in which the Portuguese were defeated and Dom Lourenço, the Viceroy's son, was killed. Timmayya sent his men who brought a letter from there, probably from one of the prisoners. The letter was forwarded to the Viceroy through the same men who had brought it to Timmayya. Dom Lourenço, on his way from Malabar to Diu, had a talk with Timmayya, as is mentioned in the latter's letter to the Viceroy. Timmayya also furnished the Viceroy with useful information about Hormuz. At the same time he did not forget trade and commerce, for the Viceroy was offered some articles of trade.

In February, 1509 the Viceroy went to Honavar to meet Timmayya. However, the latter was not there as he had fled away fearing the emperor of Vijayanagara who had come to the coast to weigh himself in gold at the temple of Gokarna. It is not clear why Timmayya was frightened of his sovereign. The king of Gersoppa came to the Viceroy with a tribute of 250 *pardaus* in addition to the 1,000 which he had given. There apparently was some misunderstanding between Timmayya and the king of Gersoppa also, which was removed by the Viceroy.[31]

In the following year, 1510, began the interesting collaboration between Gersoppa and the Portuguese to conquer Goa. Albuquerque, who succeeded Almeida, was proceeding from Malabar to the Red Sea Strait in February. On the way, Timmayya met him at Mirjan on the 24th of the same month and inquired where he was going. He responded saying that his intention was to go to the Red Sea and fight the fleet belonging to the sultan of Egypt. Thereupon Timmayya expressed his surprise that he should go so far as the Red Sea and fight the enemy when the latter was very near at hand in Goa. He informed him that one of the captains of the sultan had escaped from Almeida, the previous Viceroy, and had come to Goa with some Rumes; that the Muslim governor of Goa had received the captain well; that among the Rumes there were some carpenters and caulkmen who had built ships and galleys in the Portuguese manner; that the captain had written to the sultan requesting him to send men as he had decided to stay in Goa which was a land with many provisions, wood, and a good port; and that the captain hoped to use Goa as a base of operation to expel the

Portuguese from India and enable spices to reach Mecca and Cairo as before. Further, Timmayya told him that the king to whom Goa belonged (Yusuf Adil Shah) was dead and the successor was very young; that there were rebellions in the Deccan and therefore the defence of Goa was very weak; and that the time was ripe to attack Goa which could not withstand such a powerful fleet as his. Timmayya thought that the bar of the Mandovi river was three and a half *pathoms* deep at high tide and the whole of the Portuguese fleet could enter. Albuquerque thanked Timmayya for the advice and information. However, he said that he could not take such an important decision as to attack Goa without consulting his captains, especially since a decision to go to the Red Sea Strait had already been taken. Timmayya was therefore sent away with the assurance that he would be informed of the final decision.[32]

Castanheda writes that Timmayya sent a message to Albuquerque who was then in Bhatkaḷ, requesting the Portuguese governor to let him know where they could meet each other. Albuquerque and his advisors decided that the meeting should take place on an island off Honavar. In the actual meeting, Timmayya informed Albuquerque that the Adil Shah had ordered to build in Goa 20 ships of the Portuguese type, 5 of which were already finished. In addition some boats were also made. The purpose of all these was to have a large fleet to fight the Portuguese and their friends. In Goa there was artillery and many good soldiers who were all Turks. The successor of Yusuf Adil Shah had withdrawn a major portion of the garrison of Goa for his use elsewhere against rebels.[33] Goa was thus ill-defended and the Portuguese could take it with ease.

Correa too says that Timmayya met Albuquerque at Honavar with a gift of many provisions. About Goa, he told him that there was a garrison of 200 Rumes under a captain who was assisted by those who had escaped from Diu and Chaul after the battle of 1509 between Almeida and the Muslims in which the former inflicted a crushing defeat on the latter; that the people of Goa were not happy on account of the excesses of the Rumes; and that the Portuguese would be welcomed by the discontented people.[34]

A few questions naturally come up. Did Timmayya meet Albuquerque on his own accord or was he called for? If he met the latter on his own, why was he so eager that the Portuguese should capture Goa? Did the Vijayanagara emperor, whose servant he was, know of his invitation to the Portuguese?

As mentioned above, the author of the *Commentários* writes that Timmayya met Albuquerque, but does not specify whether he did so on his own or whether Albuquerque asked him to do so. Castanheda mentions that Timmayya sought an interview with him and met him at Honavar. Correa too records that Timmayya met Albuquerque without being invited to do so. Only Barros[35] and Faria e Sousa,[36] (who borrows heavily from the former) write that Albuquerque sent for Timmayya. However, the opinion of the first three authors that Timmayya met Albuquerque on his own initiative appears to be more acceptable. For several reasons Timmayya was eager that the Portuguese should capture Goa. First of all, he had not succeeded against the Muslim power of Goa even though he had fought against it before.[37] He now hoped that if the Portuguese succeeded in capturing Goa with his assistance, he could be made governor and he would thus gain by it.[38] Secondly, it seems that Timmayya had some inheritance in Goa which he was deprived of by his brother, Chidambara Timmayya (Cidabara Timoja).[39] It is quite likely that his forefathers were natives of Goa when it was under the jurisdiction of the Vijayanagara emperors. He thought that the inheritance would be restored to him if the Portuguese captured Goa with his help. Lastly, it is a fact that the emperor of Vijayanagara, Krishna Deva Raya, was desirous of ousting the Muslim power from Goa.[40] Once the Muslim power was curbed and Timmayya made governor of Goa, it could come under the influence of Vijayanagara. Friendship could be established with the Portuguese and commerce could be developed with them, especially with respect to horses from Arabia and Persia. Being aware of this, Krishna Deva Raya might have instructed Timmayya to set the Portuguese on the territory of Goa, or, at least, the emperor might have connived with what Timmayya was doing.

The effect of Timmayya's advice was positive on the Portuguese captains, nobles and pilots who, on being consulted by Albuquerque, came to the conclusion that Goa should be attacked and captured. Albuquerque, however, pointed out that there ought to be some motive for Timmayya to have given the information to the Portuguese, and this gave cause for some suspicion.[41] He therefore would not change his course until more concrete information about Goa was available.

On February 25, he sailed with his fleet from Mirjan. As he was emerging before the castle of *Cintacora* (Chitakul or Sadashivagad), Timmayya joined him with 13 large armed vessels with many soldiers. Albuquerque was happy to receive him. On being asked for news of Goa, Timmayya told him that he had received some messages and letters from important men of Goa from which he had learnt that Yusuf Adil Shah was dead; that the governor of Goa had 1,000 soldiers; that these soldiers, however, were discontented because of non-payment of their salaries; that many of them were dying of hunger; that the depth of the Goa bar was three and half *pathoms* as he had already informed; and that there was discontent among the people of Goa. Albuquerque asked Timmayya why he kept on coming to him and advising him to take Goa. His reply was that prominent Hindus of Goa had written to him saying that they were happy that the Muslim overlord of Goa was dead because he was robbing them and was tyrannical; that the whole of Goa was mutinous; and that if Timmayya desired to take Goa he could go there with his men and the Goans would hand over Goa to him willingly. Thereupon Albuquerque held another consultation with his captains in his ship, along with Timmayya, who promised the Portuguese that he would accompany them by sea with his vessels and would send more soldiers by land. He also opined that the governor of Goa would surrender it on the mere approach of the Portuguese.

Finally, it was decided that Timmayya should send his men by land in order to destroy places along the shore which belonged to the Muslims. He sent 2,000 of his men by land under the command of his brother-in-law and a Muslim, who had been a captain in the army of the Adil Shah but had deserted to Honavar. The defenders, however, took to flight at the approach of the Portuguese fleet. They fell upon the fortress of Chitakul which was being defended by a garrison. Timmayya's men pulled down a part of the fortress and burnt the houses inside. They also gathered a few guns.[42]

With this success the Portuguese sailed towards Goa. Timmayya, sailing along the coast in one of his vessels, captured a Muslim who was walking along the shore. He took him to Albuquerque who questioned him about Goa. The Muslim said that he was a poor *jogi*. However he had some news about Goa. He told him that Yusuf Adil Shah was certainly dead; that the successor was in the hinterland; that the people of Goa were seething with discontent; that they were praying that Goa be attacked and taken by the foreigner; that the captain of Goa did not have more than 100 Turks with him; that Goa had 12 ships, many large boats and *atalaias*; and that four ships were loaded with merchandise–two for Aden and two for Hormuz.[43]

It is rather strange that a *jogi* should know so many details, including facts and figures, about the situation in Goa. It is possible that he was actually one of the agents of Timmayya, who was eager to convince Albuquerque that it was the most suitable time to attack Goa. He seems to have still feared that Albuquerque might fall upon Goa, but might proceed towards the Red Sea, instead.

On February 28, Albuquerque sent António de Noronha, one of his captains, and a few pilots to fathom the Goa bar. Timmayya was sent with them and with two *atalaias*. The party discovered that the bar was two fathoms deep at low tide and three at high tide.[44] On the following day, March 1, the Portuguese attacked the castle of Panaji and captured it. Timmayya went to the north bank of the river where there was a bulwark with some artillery and about 30 soldiers; and as he was born a soldier, he "brought down his heavy hands upon them even as he sighted them".[45] His victory there was not less praiseworthy than that of the Portuguese on the south bank, for he defeated the enemy and captured the artillery.[46] With the fall of the castle the key to Goa was in the hands of the Portuguese.

The presence of Timmayya with the Portuguese in Goa was of great help to them. He rendered many services to them who were in a strange land and in the midst of strange people whose language they did not know. He acted as their linguist, collected information for them, acted as mediator between them and the natives, collected the revenues of Goa for them and fought on their behalf. He also advised them on various points.

After capturing the castle, Albuquerque was worried about the ways and means of taking possession of the city of Goa, too. That night he was told by a kinsman of Timmayya that the Muslim captain of the city had run away; that the fortress was deserted by the Turks and Rumes who did not want to fall into the hands of the Portuguese; and that the people of the city might indulge in looting.[47] It meant that the city could be taken by him without much fighting and it actually happened just as Timmayya had predicted.

Being in possession of the city of Goa, Albuquerque summoned Timmayya and informed him that he had received definite information that there were many Turks living in different parts of Goa. He requested him to help him to oust them from Goa. He consented to send his brother-in-law with large boats who would show the Portuguese the entrances of the various rivers of Goa of which they were ignorant.[48]

As a reward for his services to the Portuguese, Timmayya expected that Goa would be given to him as a *jagir*[49] in return for an annual payment. He had already informed Albuquerque that Goa had a revenue of 200,000 *cruzados* a year[50] and that he would pay that much if he were made the administrator of the territories of Goa. Albuquerque avoided giving him a definite answer in this respect. Timmayya then approached the Portuguese captains with his grievance and gained their support. This enabled him to wield more pressure on Albuquerque. Finally, the latter called a meeting of his captains and told them of how well Timmayya deserved an award for the great services he had rendered the Portuguese in conquering Goa. He also pointed out that he was an example for others of the land to come to the service of the King of Portugal. He asked the captains to advise him regarding the nature of a reward for Timmayya. The captains were of the opinion that he should be entrusted with Goa because he had a very good army with which he could defend and preserve it against the Turks and because he would pay an annual tribute. Albuquerque expressed his astonishment at the opinion of the captains and the reasons that they gave him justifying their contention. He pointed out that Goa was so important to the King of Portugal that it could not be given to Timmayya without securing it with a strong fortress. His intention was to make Goa the headquarters of the Portuguese empire in India. He thought that Goa should not be leased out without knowing its exact income and without studying how it should be administered. He concluded therefore that it would be better to consider Timmayya as a vassal in the service of the king in Goa and not as one on whom would depend the fate of all.

Realising the truth of Albuquerque's arguments the captains blushed for their early stand. Finally it was decided to make Timmayya the *Aquazil Mor* (chief judicial and administrative official), and the captain of the people of Goa. He was urged to be satisfied with this. As far as his desire to be made governor of Goa was concerned, Albuquerque told him that he could not do anything without writing to the King of Portugal and receiving his instructions. Timmayya accepted these offers though he was not very happy with them.[51]

Timmayya was given two houses near a tank at the entrance of the castle for his residence. Later on the tank came to be known as the "Timmayya tank".[52] Luckily for him the Portuguese did not know that the houses were well-stocked with merchandise, which he took with him to Honavar in two *zambucos*. He thus enriched himself.[53]

Three days after Timmayya's departure for Honavar some Hindus came to Albuquerque and told him that they would leave for ever if Timmayya were to remain away. Albuquerque pretended not to understand what they said. He thought it was a trick of Timmayya to get the governorship of Goa. Seeing that his scheme did not work, Timmayya sent one of his captains to Albuquerque with the message that after leaving Goa he had realised that he had left him without anyone who could tell him about the customs of Goa and that he would like to return to the service of the Portuguese. Albuquerque though aware that Timmayya was fretting and scheming for fulfilling his real desires, accepted his return. He came to Goa soon after.[54]

On Timmayya's arrival, Albuquerque assembled the prominent people of Goa and announced that he had appointed him as *Aquazil Mor* of Goa in the name of the King of Portugal and had given him all the power of justice over the Hindus as well as the Muslims and that all should obey him. The Hindus were very happy with this award and honour which was conferred on Timmayya whom they carried in a palanquin throughout the city with great festivity and music. Albuquerque rented out all the territories of Goa with the exception of the island itself to Timmayya for 100,000 *cruzados* a year on condition that he should pay for the army that was necessary for the defence of the territories farmed out to him. With all this Timmayya was satisfied and soon began the duties of his office.[55]

The native Muslims of Goa however, could not accept that they should subject themselves to the justice of Timmayya whom they hated. Some prominent Muslims therefore, went to Albuquerque and told him that they be allowed to leave Goa, for they "were very rich and honourable Muslims and they could neither bear nor suffer to be constrained by the justice of Timmayya who was a Hindu, much different in law and customs from the Muslims". Albuquerque sent them home promising that he would do what was proper in the matter. He took up the matter with Timmayya who readily and loyally agreed to abide by whatever decision taken by the governor. Accordingly he was relieved of the responsibility of administering justice to the Muslims which was entrusted to Cogebequi (Kwaja Beg), who was loyal and enjoyed the confidence of Albuquerque.[56] Barros, however, writes that Mir Kasim was made the judicial officer of the Muslims.[57] Timmayya continued to be the chief justice of the Hindus and to enjoy other favours which were conferred on him.

Timmayya seems to have been a little tyrannical and selfish in office, though generally of good service to the Portuguese. Albuquerque writes in a letter to the King of Portugal: "Timoji, who is more a tyrant, gives for it (Goa) 100,000 *cruzados*, and is obliged to have 6,000 or 7,000 men for defence. And further, though Timmayya was a friend of the King of Portugal he was "a very selfish man, and where it is possible, (for) good or bad, worked always for it (to meet his selfish ends); in our affairs I always received much benefit from him and very little damage".[58]

Timmayya discovered that the revenue to be collected was very heavy. When the Vijayanagara emperors were in possession of Goa the revenue was 150,000 *xerafins* a year; but the Muslim rulers had doubled this. Albuquerque, on being told by Timmayya and other prominent citizens, agreed to reduce the amount of revenue again to 150,000 *xerafins*.[59]

Next, Timmayya advised Albuquerque that new coins should be issued to facilitate administration and commerce, and that the price of gold and silver should be raised so as to prevent them from being exported. Albuquerque hesitated a little regarding coins. However, after a few days, when Timmayya pointed out that it was impossible to carry on the administration and trade without coins, he issued orders to mint Portuguese coins in Goa.[60]

The Adil Shah attacked Goa in mid-May in an attempt to retake it from the Portuguese. However, before the fight began there were attempts at a peaceful settlement. Albuquerque sent Mir Kasim as his envoy to the camp of the Adil Shah. Timmayya warned him that Mir Kasim should not be trusted. Albuquerque thought that Timmayya advised him as he did because of his hostility towards Mir Kasim. Ultimately, however, Timmayya was proved right. Mir Kasim turned out to be a traitor.[61]

In the meantime, the Adil Shah had apparently complained to Krishna Deva Raya, emperor of Vijayanagara, that the latter's feudatories were assisting the Portuguese against him. Timmayya was mentioned in the complaint. However, the emperor was in favour of the Portuguese as can be seen from the letter written by the chief of Gersoppa, Berforé, or Basavaraja, offering his services to them against the Adil Shah.[62] Timmayya was, in fact, an irritant to the Adil Shah since it was because of him that the Portuguese had captured Goa. The Adil Shah told Albuquerque, through envoys, that he had no complaint against the Portuguese because it was Timmayya and the Hindus of Goa who had surrendered it to them.[63]

Timmayya did not trust the Muslims of Goa. As the Adil Shah was preparing to recapture Goa the conduct of the Muslims of that place became an important aspect. Timmayya told Albuquerque that the Goan Muslims had never reconciled themselves to the Portuguese occupation. He showed him letters written by some prominent Goan Muslims to the Adil Shah and his replies to them. Albuquerque, however, thought that the letters might have been forged by Timmayya to avenge himself against the Muslims.[64] Timmayya, nevertheless, was right again and when Albuquerque consulted him about what was to be done in order to suppress and punish the guilty, he advised the Governor that the prominent Muslims as well as Hindus be summoned to reside in the castle so that they could be under vigilance.

He advised him about the summoning of the Hindu chiefs also because he thought that in those critical days none could be trusted. Albuquerque appreciated the advice, but felt that the first chief to gather his family into the castle should be Timmayya himself. If the people saw that such an important and powerful personage like Timmayya himself sent his family without any embarrassment there would be no ground for any suspicion or scandal and they could easily be ordered to bring their families to the castle. Timmayya weighed these words and then agreed to send his wife and a son who were with him to Goa. On the arrival of Timmayya's family in the castle, Albuquerque issued a notice that all responsible Hindus and Muslims should gather their families in the castle so as to avoid danger from the attacking forces of the Adil Shah. Though the people were worried a little at this notice, they readily obliged when they saw Timmayya's family in the castle. After this Albuquerque notified the Muslims who were moving in the camp of the Adil Shah that if they did not return within six days their wives and children would be seized and their property confiscated.[65]

Did Albuquerque doubt Timmayya? No doubt he gave good reasons justifying his action that the first one to send his family to the castle ought to be Timmayya. But the latter agreed to do so only after weighing what Albuquerque said. That Albuquerque had begun to have misgivings about him is discernible from the fact that an ambassador of the king of Gersoppa was appointed as the commandant of the soldiers at Augij Pass without the knowledge of Timmayya.[66] This was only the beginning of the disfavour which

Timmayya incurred of Albuquerque. By the end of the year, 1510, he began to consider Timmayya a man with undesirable qualities.

Albuquerque, being anxious for the safety of the Augij Pass through which the forces of the Adil Shah were expected to attack Goa, but having no faith in the ability of Timmayya's men to defend the Pass, sent Dom António de Noronha there. All was in vain, for the Adil Shah's army succeeded everywhere and the Portuguese had to withdraw and take shelter first in the castle and later in the ships, along with Timmayya and his men. However, one of Timmayya's captains, Menaique (probably Maha Naik), fought bravely in the clash and killed about 40 soldiers of the enemy.[67] Timmayya also fought valiantly along with his men.[68]

Before embarking Albuquerque ordered Timmayya to put to death all the Muslims (women and children) who had been gathered in the Panaji castle. Timmayya went with 50 of his men and executed the order though he took some women with him to his vessels. Later on, the women were taken by the Portuguese captains and soldiers in spite of Albuquerque's remonstrances.[69]

After being compelled to take shelter in his fleet in the middle of the River Mandovi in front of the Panaji castle, Albuquerque thought of spending the rainy season either in Anjediv or in Cochin, and wait there for the arrival of more ships and men from Portugal with the help of which he hoped to recapture Goa. However, it was already too late, it being the last phase of the month of May, and the mouth of the river being dangerous for sailing into the sea on account of the rains. It was, therefore, decided to spend the season in the river itself. In order to have sufficient stock of provisions, Albuquerque decided to send Fernão Perez D'Andrade, one of his captains to Anjediv and get provisions from there. Along with him, Timmayya was also sent with instructions to procure provisions from the various ports on the coast. However, when they approached the mouth of the river in their respective ships, they found the waters too rough there to enter the sea owing to a strong wind. They waited there that night, hoping that the waters would quieten the next day, but in vain. In the morning, D'Andrade decided to enter the sea. Timmayya advised him against the venture but was ignored with unfortunate consequences. His ship capsized while attempting to enter the sea. The crew and the equipment in the ship were saved only with great difficulty.[70] Thus the Portuguese fleet was confined to the river with a limited stock of provisions. It was only in the middle of the month of August that the fleet could sail into the sea.

While in the river, the Portuguese were subjected to a great deal of anxiety by the Muslims who fired at the fleet from the guns in the Panaji castle. Albuquerque wanted to silence the Muslim artillery, but none of his captains seemed to be ready to undertake the venture. It was in this critical situation that Timmayya offered his services. This enthused the Portuguese captains who then agreed to go with him to attack the castle. This task of putting out the Muslim fire from the castle was accomplished on June 14.[71]

There were peace moves by the Adil Shah. One of his ambassadors to the Portuguese, Mustafa Khan, suggested that the Muslims might consent to give Goa to the Portuguese if Timmayya were delivered to the Adil Shah. Albuquerque was so annoyed at this suggestion that he retorted sharply that Timmayya was always a loyal servant of the King of Portugal and for his services he deserved great reward and honour, and that the Adil Shah would see the day when Albuquerque would make Timmayya a great lord in the kingdom of the Deccan.[72]

In mid-July another attempt was made by Albuquerque to send some ships with the sick to Anjediv and Timmayya to Honavar for provisions. They could not enter the sea on account of a strong wind. They waited there hoping that the wind would subside sooner or later. Albuquerque, not knowing that these were stranded at the mouth of the river, sailed with the remaining fleet on 21st with a view to enter the sea. He only succeeded in joining them and returning with them to the original position.[73]

There was an acute shortage of food in the Portuguese fleet. Albuquerque sent his men in the middle of the night to a nearby island to fetch whatever provisions were available there. These men brought, among other things, some rice and few cows. They also captured two Brahmin girls. Five or six days later the girls' father apparently approached Timmayya and requested him to intercede on his behalf and get the girls released from captivity in return for a boatload of rice and other foodgrains for the Portuguese. When Timmayya approached Albuquerque, he agreed to the conditional release of the girls. That night the girls were sent along with Timmayya and some Portuguese captains to the island where the girls' father was agitatedly waiting for them. The girls were handed over to the Brahmin. The Portuguese got a boatful of rice. They also secured 50 cows from the island.[74]

Towards the end of July, Albuquerque realised that small ships could sail into the sea with little danger. Accordingly, he sent Timmayya to Honavar in order to procure as many provisions there as possible. This time Timmayya could sail into the sea and proceed to Honavar. A few weeks later, Albuquerque himself sailed for Anjediv reaching there on August 17.[75]

While in Anjediv, he received, through Diogo Mendez, one of the Portuguese captains, who had just arrived from Portugal with a fresh fleet, a letter which was addressed to Timmayya by the King of Portugal. In the letter Timmayya was instructed to supply pilots to Mendez who was to sail to Malacca. Albuquerque told Mendez that Timmayya had no pilots, but that the letter be delivered to him so that he would be happy that a letter was addressed directly to him by the King of Portugal.[76] Apparently Timmayya was being talked of highly in the court of the Portuguese king. This might have been due to Almeida who had been in frequent contact with Timmayya and who had been impressed by the personality of the important man from Honavar.

On August 19, Albuquerque left Anjediv for Cannanore. On the way he met Timmayya at Honavar. Mendez, who was with Albuquerque, gave Timmayya the letter of the King of Portugal. He was pleased with the letter and declared that he was always a vassal of the Portuguese king, and that he would be at his disposal. He told Albuquerque that the Adil Shah had left Goa within three days from the date on which the Portuguese fleet had sailed out of the River Mandovi, and that on the Adil Shah's departure the people of Goa had revolted and killed all the Muslim *thanadars*. Albuquerque was happy with this news. He requested Timmayya to encourage and maintain this state of affairs in Goa until he returned from Cannanore. He also entreated him to keep ready a good amount of provisions. Taking leave of him, he set sail for Cannanore where he reached on August 26.[77]

From Cannanore, Albuquerque sent a letter, dated apparently September 8 or 9, to Timmayya through Lourenço Moreno, one of the captains. In the letter, Timmayya was addressed as honourable *Aquazil Mor* and captain of the Hindus of Goa, and the chief of the lands of Chitakul. Albuquerque reminded him of his determination of recapturing Goa with his advice and help. He wanted him to help the enemies of Goa. He told him that he would send Lourenço da Silva and Fernão Vaz, who were good soldiers and captains, to command the soldiers marching in war; that the two captains, would be given befitting power because they were good soldiers and they would justify it; that he would himself join Timmayya very soon, and that he would be happy if he would send, by one of his large boats, news about Goa, particularly about its armed strength. He wanted to know how many soldiers Timmayya could send to assist the Portuguese in retaking Goa. He requested him to send, through Moreno, the provisions which had been requested to be kept ready. Besides, he requested Timmayya to compliment the king of Gersoppa on his behalf and secure additional help from him. He promised to assist the Gersoppa chief later on with his person, with soldiers, horses and arms, and to make him more powerful by getting for him the territories of the Muslims.[78]

From the letter it is evident that Albuquerque depended upon Timmayya to a considerable extent. He was very much in need of the information that the latter could collect and supply concerning the enemy, of the provisions he could provide, of the soldiers that he could give for fighting in Goa, and of his diplomacy.

Moreno went to Honavar with the letter and Albuquerque got all that he wanted. Timmayya was preparing to aid the Portuguese. He sent the provisions asked for.[79]

On his way back from Cannanore to Goa, Albuquerque anchored at the port of Honavar to take additional provisions and water. The king of Gersoppa and Timmayya, who were expecting his arrival there, went to talk to him. On being asked what news they had of Goa and of the Adil Shah, they said that Goa had three captains with a garrison of 4,000 men, all Turks, Rumes and Coraçanes, and some peons of Bhalagat. They added that the native Muslims might constitute another force of 4,000; and that if Albuquerque was determined to take Goa it was the most appropriate time, for the Adil Shah was busy fighting his enemies in the Deccan. The king of Gersoppa and Timmayya were ready with all their men to march against Goa by land. Albuquerque thanked them for the news and for their readiness to aid him.[80]

Timmayya and the king of Gersoppa had developed, in the meantime, a matrimonial relationship. The former was to marry the princess of Gersoppa. He invited Albuquerque to attend the marriage. In order to please his friend Albuquerque accepted the invitation. There was another factor also which enabled him to go to the wedding. There was the likelihood of a storm. In fact, the sea became rough after Albuquerque landed with many of his captains. He intended to return to the fleet soon after the wedding dinner, but he was held up in the land for three days on account of the storm which suddenly became furious. On the fourth day, when the force of the storm was less, he set out with the captains and their men for the fleet, but lost one boat with 30 men before he could make for the ships.[81]

Correa adds that Albuquerque landed with his men fully armed, telling Timmayya that his men did not have any more beautiful clothes than their arms and wanted the king of Gersoppa to see them in arms. Timmayya pretended to be pleased, but he understood the Governor well. Albuquerque had already put another condition that the dinner should be served in his boats.[82] Apparently all these were precautions on the part of Albuquerque against any foul play upon the Portuguese when they were on the land.

The king of Gersoppa promised to send 4,000 men with Timmayya by land.[83] The latter, on his part, sent one of his captains, Madhava Rao (Medio Rao), along with three ships to accompany Albuquerque. He promised to come himself by land with 6,000 men.[84] Albuquerque gave Timmayya, by way of payment for the men that he promised, cloth worth 5,000 *pardaus*.[85] After this he sailed to Anjediv.

In Anjediv, however, he was told that he should not believe in the promises of Timmayya and the king of Gersoppa. He was also informed that these two men were scared of the Adil

Shah with whom they did not want to be in worse relations, should the Portuguese fail to recapture Goa. Nevertheless, Albuquerque sailed into the River Mandovi and sent Manuel da Cunha with six ships to Old Goa and Agassaim to help Timmayya and his men who were expected to enter from that side. Cunha arrived at Agassaim via Banastarim, set it on fire and remained in the river quietly, expecting Timmayya with his men.

In the meantime, Albuquerque consulted his captains on whether they should wait until Timmayya arrived in order to recapture Goa or whether they should proceed to Cambay to capture that place. The captains were of the opinion that Goa should be taken forthwith. However, Albuquerque spent three days without taking any decision, still hoping that the promised help would come. Finally, he came to the conclusion that Timmayya and the king of Gersoppa were bribed by the Adil Shah. He also thought that Timmayya was delaying deliberately in order to avoid trouble and bloodshed which the latter knew would be necessary to take Goa, and that he might come after Goa was taken by the Portuguese without him. At any rate, Albuquerque did not wait any more for the help, attacked Goa and captured it on November 25, 1510.[86]

Madhava Rao, Timmayya's captain, who was sent with Albuquerque, played a prominent role in capturing Goa. Timmayya himself arrived at Goa, probably on November 26,[87] a day after Goa fell into the hands of the Portuguese. He brought with him not the promised 6,000 men but only 3,000. He apologised for the delay and pleaded that he could not come earlier than he did.[88]

Once again Timmayya was entrusted with the revenue affairs of Goa, with the exception of the island, as the letter of Albuquerque to the King of Portugal written on December 22 indicates. He was to pay for the defence forces that were necessary for him.[89] Barros writes that Timmayya was appointed captain of the Hindus over whom he was to administer justice according to their usage. His area, however, was limited. It did not include death, loss of property and other higher causes.[90]

Timmayya, however, did not enjoy the office for long. Albuquerque received a letter from Friar Luiz, whom he had sent to Vijayanagara as ambassador, in which the latter informed him that he should not trust the king of Gersoppa and Timmayya, for they were such scoundrels that they had written to the emperor of Vijayanagara that if the latter wanted to capture Goa, he should help them with foot soldiers, cavalry men and elephants and that they would take Goa for him before the Portuguese established themselves there.[91] This letter might have been one of the main factors which led to Timmayya's removal from office within five months of the appointment.

Another reason for his removal was Timmayya's attack on two merchant ships belonging to Chaul. He sailed with his own ships from Goa after telling Albuquerque that he was going to Honavar for which he was given permission. However, he proceeded towards Chaul and robbed the ships. Albuquerque arrested him and kept him in custody until the loot was made over to the governor of Chaul who was a friend of the Portuguese. Fortunately for Timmayya, Malhar Rao, his protector, undertook to pay for the damage.[92]

Albuquerque himself wrote to the King of Portugal that Timmayya secretly armed three *atalaias* which he possessed and sent them to rob merchant ships. Thus two ships of Chaul which were loaded with Indian cotton and one of Hormuz which was loaded with horses and pearls, were taken by his *atalaias*. All these ships were carrying passports issued by Albuquerque. The merchant ships were taken to Honavar and were not returned in spite of Albuquerque's repeated requests. On receiving a complaint from the governor of Chaul, he arrested Timmayya and put him under the guard of a captain with 20 men.[93]

Albuquerque reported that Timmayya helped the Portuguese for his own profit. His administration of revenue affairs was full of tyranny. And "if any one is to be condemned as a traitor, it should be Timmayya, because he allowed 300 unarmed Turks to enter the island of Goa even though he had 3,000 peons under his command,"[94] in May 1510. This statement of Albuquerque is quite in contrast to the heroic defence efforts attributed to Timmayya by Gaspar Correa,[95] who was also a contemporary writer, as he was the secretary of Albuquerque. Correa, however, adds that Timmayya has become very arrogant on account of the great service that he had rendered in taking Goa. He spoke to some of the Portuguese captains against Albuquerque. He said that the Portuguese lost Goa after its first occupation because of many mistakes that Albuquerque had committed. The latter knew all these, but did not take any action against him until a proper opportunity offered itself.[96]

Timmayya was removed from office when Malhar Rao offered to serve the Portuguese in Goa. Rao had been dispossessed of the throne of Gersoppa which was then being ruled by his younger brother. The former took shelter in Bhatkal whose chief was a relative of his. From there he tried to regain his throne but in vain. The king of Gersoppa, Rao's younger brother, sent a messenger to Albuquerque seeking the friendship of the Portuguese. He feared that Albuquerque would favour Rao. The latter, on coming to know that his brother was trying to secure the friendship of the Portuguese sent his own messenger to Albuquerque seeking his friendship. He offered his services to the King of Portugal. Albuquerque accepted the offer, not only because Rao was known as a brave soldier, but also because he was a captain whom the Hindus held in great esteem. Besides, Rao was born in Goa and had always fought the Turks. When in Goa which was under the Hindus and was twice encircled by the Turks, he fought in its defence as a great and valiant soldier.[97]

Knowing all this, Albuquerque sent galleys to fetch him from Bhatkal and also to bring his men and horses. Besides, he sent two Portuguese captains by land with 2,000 Hindu soldiers to receive him at Chitakul. The *thanadars* and the people of Goa were told to receive and obey Malhar Rao as their own. All did so with love because of the esteem they had for him and because they wanted to be governed by him.[98]

The king of Gersoppa who came to know that Rao was embarking for Chitakul, sent his army immediately to Karwar and Ankola in order to harass Rao's passage. He feared very much that Rao would be aided by the Portuguese in dethroning him. However, he reached Goa without any trouble in spite of his brother's watchfulness.[99]

Malhar Rao, who reached Goa, in the beginning of April 1511, was well received by Albuquerque who arranged for all that was necessary for him and for his men to stay in Goa.[100] The chief men of Goa were so happy with his arrival in Goa that they soon approached Albuquerque and requested him to make Rao their governor for all the people desired it. Apparently, these men did not know the real purpose for which Rao was in Goa. Albuquerque told them that on his part he was happy that they came to him with the proposal and that he would talk to Malhar Rao to know what he would say.

The next morning Albuquerque told Rao that he would like to farm out the lands of Goa to him and also to entrust the governance of the territories of Goa to him in return for 40,000 *pardaus* a year to be paid in four instalments to the King of Portugal or to his governors in India. Rao was happy. Having concluded and signed the agreement, Albuquerque summoned the chief men and announced the appointment. The people received the announcement with great rejoicing. There were festivities and music according to the local customs.[101] After two or three days, Rao proceeded to the mainland, taking with him 5,000 peons and 50 cavalry men and began to discharge the duties of his office.[102]

Timmayya was naturally aggrieved. He wrote to the King of Portugal from whom he expected a remedy. He also sought Albuquerque's permission to leave Goa for Honavar. Albuquerque, however, did not want that he should go out of Goa, for he feared that he would enter the services of the Adil Shah and thus become a formidable enemy. In order to appease him, he made him the 'receiver of all the money' of the land which Rao would collect, a post which satisfied him as he thought that he could enrich himself by it. Albuquerque also promised that after his return from Hormuz, where he proposed to proceed then, he would give him the position held by Rao. This, however, was not a sincere proposal and both of them knew it. Albuquerque secretly instructed Rao to be watchful of Timmayya's movements. He also gave orders to his officers that they should not allow him to go out of Goa.[103]

After making all these arrangements Albuquerque left Goa for Malacca. In his absence Adil Shah decided to attack and recapture

Goa. He sent in May 1511, one of his generals, Pulat Khan, to fall upon Rao and expel him from Goa. Timmayya, who was with Rao, was to be taken a prisoner. Being warned of Pulat Khan's attack, Rao awaited the enemy with his army. He sent Ishwar Rao (Iça Rao or Hicarrau) to a pass which the enemy had to use to enter Goa. However, Ishwar Rao was so late that, on reaching the pass, he found it in the hands of the enemy. He was defeated and killed. Pulat Khan then attacked Malhar Rao himself and defeated him. In the end, on the advice of Timmayya, Malhar Rao fled to Vijayanagara. He was too ashamed to show his face to the Portuguese captain on the island of Goa, Rodrigo Rebelo. Along with him Timmayya also went to Vijayanagara.[104]

While in Vijayanagara, Malhar Rao learnt that his brother was dead. He took the permission of the emperor of Vijayanagara and left for Gersoppa where he became king and always remained a faithful friend of the King of Portugal.[105]

While Albuquerque was on his way back from Malacca to Goa in 1512, he went to Honavar where Malhar Rao met him and told him that the Adil Shah was preparing to send a reinforcement of 20,000 men to Pulat Khan and, that therefore, he should hurry to Goa.[106]

Timmayya died in Vijayanagara on account of illness.[107] His wife and children went to Goa seeking Portuguese protection. By an order of Albuquerque, dated January 11, 1513, Timmayya's family was awarded 40 *pardaus* in memory of the services which Timmayya had rendered to the Portuguese during his lifetime.[108] Incidentally, the date of the order suggests that he died in December 1512. Albuquerque refers to his wife and children as those who had just come to Goa to live there. More than a fortnight had lapsed between the death of Timmayya in Vijayanagara, the transmission of the news of his death to Honavar where his family was, and the latter's arrival in Goa. Barros comments that the provision for the upkeep of Timmayya's family was not only for the sake of Timmayya's services but also to show the people of Goa that the wives and children of those who fought and died for the Portuguese would be protected.[109] A son of Timmayya probably became a captain of some armed ships under the Portuguese, as one may infer from another order issued by Albuquerque to the factor of Goa on February 5, 1513.[110] In 1515 again we hear of the provisions for five months, which were in arrears, being made over to the family of Timmayya by Albuquerque.[111] Thus Timmayya's services were not forgotten in spite of his subsequent dislike of the Portuguese.

Thus ended an interesting chapter of the Portuguese relations with Kanara. Timmayya and Malhar Rao played a prominent role in the Portuguese conquest and occupation of Goa, and its administration and defence. Though Timmayya lost Albuquerque's favour, his part in the first Portuguese conquest of Goa was immense. It was he who made Albuquerque change his decision of going to the Red Sea Strait and to attack Goa instead.

REFERENCES

1. *Lendas*, tomo I, pt. I, p. 289.
2. *Ibid.*, pt. II, p. 565.
3. *História*, II, p. 234.
4. *D-JB*, I. pp. 338-9.
5. *Ibid.*, p. 339.
6. *Lendas*, tomo I, pt. II, p. 565.
7. *História*, II, p. 236.
8. *D-JB*, I, p. 342.
9. *História*, II, pp. 236-7.
10. *Ibid.*, p. 237.
11. *Ibid.*, pp. 247-8; *D-JB*, I, pp. 243-6; *Lendas*, tomo I, pt. II, pp. 578-9.
12. *D-JB*, I, p. 346.
13. *História*, II, p. 239.
14. *D-JB*, I, pp. 246-7.
15. *Lendas*, tomo I, pt. II, p. 579.
16. *Cartas*, II, pp. 424-5.
17. *Cartas*, I, pp. 46-7.
18. Alvaro Velho, *Roteiro de Primeira Viagem de Vasco da Gama*, pp. 73-74.
19. *História*, I, p. 64.
20. *D-JB*, I, pp. 170-1.
21. *Lendas*, tomo I, pt. I, p. 289.
22. *Commentários*, II, p. 110.
23. *D-JB*, II, p. 227; *Lendas*, tomo II, pt. I, p. 141.
24. *D-JB* I, p. 346.

25. Dames Longworth, *The Book of Duarte Barbosa*, vol. 1, p. 186, footnote.
26. *Cartas*, IV, p. 205.
27. *Lendas*, tomo II, pt. I, p. 141; Tomé Pires, *The Suma Oriental*, tr. Armando Cortesão, p. 61.
28. *Gazetteer of the Bombay Presidency*, vol. XV, pt. II, Kanara, p. 1282.
29. *Cartas*, III, p. 203.
30. F. C. Danvers, *The Portuguese in India*, I, p. 130.
31. *História*, II, p. 441.
32. *Commentários*, II, pp. 110-111.
33. *História*, III, p. 19.
34. *Lendas*, II, pt. I, pp. 50-1.
35. *D-JB*, II, p. 186.
36. Manuel de Faria e Sousa, *Asia Portuguesa*, I, p. 291.
37. *D-JB*, I, p. 348; also II, p. 187.
38. *Commentários*, II, p. 139.
39. *D-JB*, II, p. 187.
40. *Commentários*, II, p. 183.
41. *Ibid.*, p. 112; *Lendas*, tomo II, pt. II, p. 51.
42. *Commentários*, II, pp. 112-7.
43. *Ibid.*, pp. 117-8.
44. *Ibid.*, pp. 118-9.
45. *D-JB*, II, p. 201.
46. Manuel de Faria e Sousa, *op. cit.*, I, p. 296.
47. *Commentários*, II, pp. 124-5.
48. *Ibid.*, pp. 135-6; *Lendas*, tomo, II, pt. I, p. 61.
49. P.S.S. Pissurlencar, "Colaboradores Hindus de Afonso de Albuquerque", *Boletim do Instituto Vasco da Gama*, no. 49, 1941, p. 31.
50. *Cartas*, I, p. 55.
51. *Commentários*, II, pp. 139-142.
52. *Lendas*, tomo II, pt. I, p. 62.
53. *Commentários*, II, p. 142.
54. *Ibid.*, pp. 142-3.
55. *Ibid.*, pp. 143-4.
56. *Lendas*, tomo II, pt. I, pp. 62-5.
57. *D-JB*, II, p. 207.
58. *Cartas*, I, pp. 22-23.
59. *Commentários*, II, pp. 167-8; *Lendas*, tomo II, pt. I, pp. 74-5. Correa records that the annual taxes of Goa amounted to 150,000 *pardaus* of gold under the Vijayanagara emperors.
60. *Commentários*, II, pp. 171-4.
61. *D-JB*, II, pp. 267-8.
62. *Commentários*, II, pp. 183-4; *Lendas*, tomo II, pt. I, pp. 80-1.
63. *Ibid.*, p. 191.
64. *Lendas*, tomo II, pt. I, p. 83.

65. *Commentários*, II, pp. 195-7; *Lendas*, II, pt. I, pp. 88-9.
66. *Commentários*, II, p. 198.
67. *Ibid.*, p. 206. Correa mentions Menaique as the brother-in-law of Timmayya; *Lendas*, tomo II, pt. I, p. 79.
68. *Lendas*, tomo II, pt. I, p. 93.
69. *Ibid.*, pp. 95-114.
70. *Commentários*, II, pp. 223-4.
71. *Ibid.*, pp. 229-30.
72. *Ibid.*, pp. 246-7; *Lendas*, tomo II, pt. I, p. 113.
73. *Ibid.*, pp. 251-2.
74. *Ibid.*, pp. 254-5; *Lendas*, tomo II, pt. I, pp. 118-9. Correa says that the Brahmin also was taken prisoner. He promised rice and other provisions if he and his daughters were released. He was taken to the place where the provisions were available.
75. *Commentários*, II, pp. 255, 258-9.
76. *Ibid.*, p. 260.
77. *Ibid.*, pp. 261-2.
78. *Ibid.*, pp. 294-5.
79. *Ibid.*, pp. 313-4.
80. *Commentários*, III, p. 2.
81. *D-JB*, II, pp. 227-8.
82. *Lendas*, tomo II, pt. I, pp. 141-2.
83. *Ibid.*, p. 142.
84. *D-JB*, II, p. 228.
85. *Lendas*, tomo II, pt. I, p. 142.
86. *Commentários*, III, pp. 3-4, 7, 9.
87. *Cartas*, V, p. 185.
88. *D-JB*, III, p. 235.
89. *Cartas*, I, p. 27.
90. *D-JB*, II, p. 237.
91. *Commentários*, III, p. 45.
92. *Cartas*, I, pp. 47-8; *D-JB*, II, p. 237.
93. *Ibid.*, pp. 165, 179. Two letters dated December 1 & 2, 1513.
94. *Ibid.*, p. 165.
95. *Lendas*, tomo II, pt. I, p. 93.
96. *Ibid.*, p. 160.
97. Goa belonged to the Hindus prior to 1469. If Malhar Rao was born in Goa and fought against the Turks when Goa was under the Hindus, within the Vijayanagara empire, then he was an old man of about 60 years in 1510, assuming that he fought against the Turks when he was about 20.
98. *Commentários*, II, pp. 33-5; *D-JB*, II, p. 237; *História*, III, p. 117; *Lendas*, tomo II, pt. I, pp. 160-1.
99. *Commentários*, III, p. 35.
100. *Cartas*, II, p. 90.

101. *Commentários*, III, pp. 35-6.
102. *Ibid.*, pp. 36-7.
103. *Lendas*, tomo II, pt. I, pp. 161-2, 178.
104. *Commentários*, III, pp. 229-30; *Cartas*, I, pp. 174-5; *D-JB*, II, pp. 294-5. Albuquerque mentions that Malhar Rao had 4,000 peons and 30 horses, whereas in *Commentários* the respective figures are 5,000 and 50. Barros writes that Malhar Rao was successful against Pulat Khan in the beginning, but the enemy's superior number began to tell upon him, and he was finally defeated.
105. *Cartas,* I, p. 136; *Commentários*, III, p. 230.
106. *História*, III, p. 216; *D-JB*, II, p. 324.
107. *Commentários*, III, 230.
108. *Cartas*, II, p. 107.
109. *Ibid.*, I, p. 179; *D-JB*, II, p. 295.
110. *Ibid.*, V, p. 404.
111. *Ibid.*, VI, p. 249.

4

THE PORTUGUESE ATTEMPTS TO TAKE OVER BHATKAL

In the last week of October 1505, Viceroy Francisco de Almeida, received at Cannanore an embassy from Vira Narasimha, the founder of the third dynasty of the Vijayanagara empire. Narasimha proposed an alliance of friendship between him and the Portuguese. He would aid them with ships and would allow them to build fortresses in his ports, except in Bhatkal, which was already given to some one else; he would supply all that was necessary for the construction of the fortresses; and for greater solidarity he would give in marriage his sister to the prince of Portugal. Narasimha also wrote a letter to the King of Portugal with all these proposals, and sent rich presents to the prince.[1] The embassy was well received, but the Viceroy did not send a reply, as he thought that it was not a proper time to do so.[2]

Did Narasimha send his embassy on his own initiative or was it in response to one, if any, from the Viceroy? To be sure, the latter had an instruction from the King of Portugal that he should send an envoy to Vijayanagara with presents. The King had also sent with him a letter addressed to the emperor. However, the Viceroy was given the option of not sending the envoy, if the Portuguese interest would be better served thus. In fact, there is no reference in Portuguese documents and chronicles to any embassy sent by the Viceroy to Vijayanagara until 1508.[3]

Thus, it seems probable that Narasimha sent his embassy before he received one from the Portuguese. There was good reason for him to endeavour to secure the alliance of the Portuguese whose naval achievements might have been reported to him. "His six year reign (1503-9) was almost wholly spent in fighting and success did not always reach him",[4] and, therefore, friendship and assistance were welcome from any quarter. Why not secure a Portuguese alliance? Both Vijayanagara and Portugal had a common enemy in the Muslims and the Adil Shah of Bijapur was intruding into the territories of Vijayanagara. It is also probably true, as the Portuguese believed, that the Franciscan friar, Luis Salvador, who was in Vijayanagara for some time prior to 1505, influenced Narasimha to seek the friendship of the Portuguese.[5]

The Viceroy, however, does not seem to have been satisfied with the proposals of the imperial embassy. Probably he had an eye on the port of Bhatkal, but Narasimha did not offer to allow the Portuguese to construct their fortress there. By now the Portuguese knew the commercial importance of Bhatkal. In 1501 and 1502 João da Nova and Vasco da Gama, commanding their respective annual fleets to India, had developed close contacts with the port.[6] While they were in Bhatkal the commandants might have noted mentally the numerous ships being loaded with great quantities of rice, iron and sugar. They might have been impressed by the commercial importance of the place, its good port, its easy accessibility from sea and its strategic defence possibility against attack from the hinterland. They might have reported all these to their sovereign and countrymen.

Thus, when Almeida came to India as Viceroy, he should have known the importance and usefulness of Bhatkal. However, he was not in a hurry to obtain the place for constructing a fortress. For one thing, the King of Portugal, in his instructions to him, did not include Bhatkal among the places of India where Portuguese forts were to be erected. Secondly, when the Vijayanagara embassy came to him in 1505, he was busy constructing fortresses in Anjediv and other places according to the royal instructions. In 1508, however, the situation changed. The Portuguese realised that their fort in Anjediv was incapable of being defended against enemy attacks and therefore it was demolished in 1506, hardly a year after it was erected. The Viceroy then thought of securing a suitable alternative place on the Kanara coast for constructing a fortress. Bhatkal was the place which attracted him. Accordingly, he sent Pero Fernandes Tinoco, along with Fr. Salvador as ambassador to Vijayanagara. The priest had been to Vijayanagara before and therefore he could be of much help to Tinoco. The Viceroy proposed to conclude a treaty of friendship as required by the emperor in his embassy of 1505, in return for permission to erect a Portuguese fortress in Bhatkal.

The embassy was not a great success. Tinoco could not fulfil its main purpose. The Vijayanagara emperor seems to have talked to him in general terms of peace and friendship without committing himself to anything concrete.[7] By this time Vira Narasimha had strengthened his position in Vijayanagara by driving the Adil Shah and putting down many a rebellion within his empire. He therefore did not need the Portuguese assistance in 1508 as badly as he did in 1505. He virtually ignored the Portuguese embassy, as he was not prepared to forego so valuable a port as Bhatkal.

The Portuguese, however, did not give up their effort to obtain the place. In 1509 Albuquerque suffered a mortifying defeat at the hands of the Zamorin of Calicut. The former, therefore, ardently desired to secure aid from the Vijayanagara emperor, Krishna Deva Raya, who succeeded Vira Narasimha in the same year, in order to wreck revenge on the Zamorin. He sent Fr. Salvador, the astute Franciscan, to Vijayanagara with the proposal that the Vijayanagara emperor, should march against the Zamorin by land while he himself would attack the enemy by sea; that he would assist Vijayanagara whenever necessary against their common enemy, namely, the Muslims; that he would undo the port of Goa and deprive the Muslim rulers of the Deccan of its commerce in Hormuz horses; and that he would direct all the trade in horses to Bhatkal or any other port of the Vijayanagara empire. Finally, he also proposed that if the Vijayanagara emperor allowed the Portuguese to trade and have a factory in any of the ports from Bhatkal to Mangalore; if he would order his men to give the Portuguese a place to build a strong house, meaning a fortress, all the commerce in horses and other articles of trade of Portugal would be secured for him.[8] The embassy was dispatched from Cannanore some time after February 7, 1510.[9]

From the letter which Fr. Salvador wrote to Albuquerque from Vijayanagara it is evident that the ambassador was instructed to obtain permission to build a fortress in Bhatkal. But when the ambassador put the subject before Deva Raya, the latter expressed his surprise that he should be asked to allow the Portuguese to build their fortress in that place.[10] Clearly, the emperor was not willing to concede the request.

Thus, the embassy did not meet with success. Fr. Salvador was received well by everybody in Vijayanagara except by the emperor,[11] who had no intention as yet to commit himself to anything. The ambassador was in fact murdered, probably on the orders of the emperor.[12] Virtually no concrete reply was given to this embassy. Instead, Deva Raya sent towards the end of 1510 his own ambassadors to Goa which was securely occupied by the Portuguese by then. Albuquerque refused to respond, excusing himself that he was not in a position to decide what to say since he had no response to his own proposals made through his ambassador, Fr. Salvador, a year before.[13] If Deva Raya could ignore Albuquerque's embassy of 1509, the latter was strong enough in 1510 to send back the former's without a concrete reply.

Albuquerque then began to make offers of friendship to the Adil Shah himself. This was a statesman-like move on his part. His desire was to develop friendly relations with his neighbour from whom he had snatched Goa, so that there would not be any more fights over the territory and that commerce in horses and other merchandise could go on smoothly. Deva Raya, on learning of Albuquerque's new policy, sent his ambassadors again to secure horses and prevent them from falling into the hands of his enemy, the Adil Shah.

However, Albuquerque had left for Malacca by the time the embassy arrived in Goa. On his return, he resumed diplomatic negotiations in October 1512. He sent Gaspar Chanoca with the proposal that, as all the kings of India had given the Portuguese sites in their ports to build fortresses in order to protect the Portuguese commerce, and as he very much desired friendship with Vijayanagara, the latter ought to have pleasure in giving Bhatkal for the erection of a fort (*casa forte*); that he desired that all the horses that come to Goa should go to Vijayanagara; and that though Fr. Salvador, the first of his ambassadors, had written that the emperor's words of friendship should not be trusted as long as the king of Gersoppa lived, he would ignore it, since his sovereign, the King of Portugal, had commanded him several times that he should endeavour to gain the emperor's friendship as the latter was a Hindu.[14]

The response to this embassy came in, apparently as late as January 1514.[15] Retelim Cherim (probably Ratna Shetty) arrived in Goa and presented to Albuquerque a letter in a folio of gold and told him that the emperor knowing the hostility between the Portuguese and the Adil Shah had decided to wage a war against the latter; that if Albuquerque was of the intention still to fight the Adil Shah, he should let the emperor know and that the combined forces could make a short work of the enemy. The ambassador also spoke concerning the horses.[16] No reference was made to Bhatkal either by the ambassador or by Albuquerque during the course of this negotiation. Probably the latter did not want Bhatkal any more, since he had firmly secured Goa by then, as has been pointed out by Castanheda.[17] In fact no conclusive agreement was reached between the Portuguese and Vijayanagara during the governorship of Albuquerque regarding either the horses, which Deva Raya required so much, or the construction of a fortress in Bhatkal, which the Portuguese wanted.

As these negotiations between the Portuguese and Vijayanagara were being carried on, the former kept up their direct relations with Bhatkal, which had begun in 1501. In that year, João Nova sailed into the port of Bhatkal with his fleet. The Portuguese were not strangers to the locals there, for all along the coast the Portuguese deeds were talked about. The owners of the ships which were anchored at the port, were anxious to know the intention of the Portuguese. They feared that the latter might cause damage to their ships. Some of the owners went in their boats to Nova with loads of rice and sugar, hens, oranges and figs. Some others went to the king of Bhatkal to request him to send his messenger to find out the objectives of the Portuguese. The latter, however, had peaceful intentions and soon commerce ensued between them and the local merchants, in which the Portuguese gained considerably.

Unfortunately, the money of the Portuguese was stolen. Though the money was recovered soon, the thieves escaped. Nova, after a consultation with his councillors, decided not to sail away until the thieves were caught and punished. He wanted to show the locals what would happen to those who behaved badly with the Portuguese. Accordingly, he (the captain-major) sent a messenger to the king of Bhatkal requesting him to arrest the thieves and entrust them to the Portuguese. He declared that he would not allow any local ship to move out of the port. He also threatened that he would burn all the ships anchored there if the culprits were not handed over. At first the king of Bhatkal excused himself from the responsibility of arresting the thieves, though the merchants told him that they would complain to the emperor of Vijayanagara, his suzerain, if no remedy was found by him against the Portuguese threat of burning the ships. But the king acted when Nova pressed further making a show of an attack. The thieves were found and handed over to the Portuguese. Nova ordered that they be hanged after their hands were cut off. He then sent a present to the king of Bhatkal and it was reciprocated. The Bhatkal chief told the Portuguese that they were always welcome to his port for trade.[18]

In the following year, Vasco da Gama, after burning ships in the Honavar river and a part of the city of Honavar itself, proceeded to the port of Bhatkal where there were many Muslim ships, which had come there for rice, iron and sugar. Being aware of his atrocities in Honavar the locals of Bhatkal were determined to defend themselves and had assembled some small guns on a rampart on a hill at the entrance of the river. Da Gama sent his brother, Estevão, with men and boats to effect a landing. The defenders hurled stones from the hill at the boats as they entered the river, but the Portuguese succeeded in landing. And as they were marching to take the rampart some Muslim envoys met Estevão and said that they were going to his brother with a message from the king of Bhatkal who was prepared to declare obedience to the Portuguese. Estevão sent a Portuguese soldier with the Muslims to his brother and awaited his orders. Da Gama told the envoys that he did not come with the intention of causing harm to Bhatkal but that he had ordered his men to fight as he had confronted hostility from the natives; that his sovereign, King of Portugal, was the lord of all seas and, therefore, all the ports where there was navigation should obey the King of Portugal and pay tributes to his men who moved about in his fleet; that this was a symbol of obedience, by which alone the ports would be free and secure in their trade and commerce; that the ports should neither trade in pepper nor admit Turks nor ships from Calicut; that if the king of Bhatkal was prepared to abide by those conditions of tribute and trade he should soon send his word of consent, lest the ships and the port be burnt not only then and there but also every year so that no trade could be carried on in Bhatkal.

Being told about what da Gama had declared, the king of Bhatkal proposed to give an annual tribute of 1,000 bags of ordinary rice to the Portuguese soldiers and 500 bags of fine rice for the captains. He could not give more as he was a tenant of the emperor of Vijayanagara to whom Bhatkal belonged nor could he give tribute in gold or silver. After verification, da Gama accepted these terms of peace and obedience, whereupon the king of Bhatkal sent his letter of obligation and the rice due. Da Gama gave the king the safe conduct and proceeded to Cannanore.[19]

In 1508, Almeida was invited by Timmayya to help against Bhatkal but on reaching the port he found the belligerents at peace.[20] He went to the port again on February 25, 1509 on his way back from the Konkan coast to Malabar. The Bhatkal chief met the Viceroy and declared himself a vassal of the King of Portugal. He bound himself to pay every year 2,000 bags of good rice (*giraçal*) and paid immediately for that year.[21]

One does not know what made the Bhatkal chief to submit to the Portuguese and pay tributes. Probably it was in consequence to the Viceroy's readiness to aid the Gersoppa chief against Bhatkal. The Bhatkal chief might have done so to secure his neutrality in case hostilities should break out again between Gersoppa and Bhatkal.

The Bhatkal chief seems to have considered this treaty valid only as long as Almeida was the Viceroy in India. For in the following year a messenger from the chief went to Albuquerque who was in Goa after its occupation. He was told that Condanechatim (Gundanna Shetty) and Naodaquiçar (Nanda Kishore), administrators of Bhatkal, desired friendship with the Portuguese and would subject themselves to the King of Portugal. Albuquerque did not respond to this message immediately as he did not have any ship to spare for the purpose of sending his reply to Bhatkal. However, in September 1510, he sent Lourenço Moreno to come to an agreement with Bhatkal. Moreno was given the services of a Muslim of Cannanore, Porcassem by name, who was to act as his interpreter and to help him in the negotiations. He was instructed to propose to the administrators of Bhatkal that the Portuguese should be provided with a house in which a factor could store his merchandise securely; that the house should be of stone and mortar; constructed at the cost of the Bhatkal administrators and that an annual tribute of 2,000 bags of rice should be paid to the Portuguese.

On reaching Bhatkal, Moreno found that the administrators had changed their minds. They told him that they could not take any decision without knowing what their sovereign, Deva Raya, would command in this matter.[22] The Bhatkal chief might have sent his messenger to Albuquerque in Goa in keeping with his sovereign's policy of empty offers to the Portuguese. Or he might have done so when it was thought that the Portuguese were a power to reckon with on the Konkan and Kanara coasts and that it would be safer to be on friendly terms with them. But they were defeated and driven away from Goa by the Adil Shah, and therefore, they were not very strong after all. Accordingly, when Albuquerque revived the negotiations before capturing Goa, the Bhatkal chief did not consider it necessary to provide any concrete answer. Besides he might have received instructions from his sovereign, in the meantime, not to commit himself to anything specific, for the sovereign himself was dealing with the Portuguese embassy under Fr. Salvador, who too had brought the proposal, among other things that the Portuguese be allowed to have a fortress in Bhatkal.

By the end of 1510 the situation changed again. The Portuguese proved their strength by recapturing Goa. The Bhatkal chief, as well as the emperor, sent their respective ambassadors to seek Portuguese friendship. The Bhatkal chief paid the arrears of tribute which he had agreed to pay in 1509 and offered the Portuguese a site for constructing a fortress in Bhatkal. The Portuguese Governor accepted the tribute and friendship, but rejected the offer concerning the fortress since he had no need of it now that Goa was secure.[23] It is difficult to say whether this rejection is true or not, because Albuquerque included in his embassy of 1512 to Vijayanagara the demand for a site in Bhatkal for the erection of a fortress.

At any rate after the second occupation of Goa, Albuquerque was no more in a mood to play second fiddle in his negotiations with Vijayanagara. He wanted to have his own terms regarding horses and, what is more, he was determined to undo the commerce of Bhatkal. He sent some captains to sail along the coast to compel all the merchant ships to go to the port of Goa.[24] In 1513 he sent António Raposo to the port of Bhatkal with orders to demand the surrender of a ship from Aden. Dama Shetty, administrator of Bhatkal, complied with the demand.[25] This policy deprived the Bhatkal port of its commerce of horses and other articles of trade. Thus though Albuquerque failed to secure a site for the construction of a fortress or even a factory in Bhatkal he succeeded in damaging the trade and commerce of the place.

Early in 1516, soon after the death of Albuquerque a quarrel appears to have taken place between the Portuguese and the local merchants of Bhatkal. Simão de Andrade, one of the Portuguese captains, assisted by a factor, Aleixo, was loading a large ship of provisions, including rice, sugar, and iron, to be taken to Hormuz. While the work was being carried on, a quarrel arose between the native merchants and the Portuguese in which 24 of the latter were killed and many were wounded. The Portuguese were robbed of goods worth 10,000 *pardaus*.

Lopo Soares de Albergaria, successor to Albuquerque, learning of this murder and robbery, emerged at the Bhatkal port later on with a view to avenge the damage. However, the Bhatkal chief immediately sent a messenger with boats full of refreshments, rice and sugar for the Portuguese governor. The messenger told him that the incident had taken place in the absence of his chief at a place 10 leagues away from Bhatkal. And that therefore he was not responsible for the incident. The real culprits were three old Muslim merchants whom the chief handed over to Albergaria advising him to hang them. He was also ready to give similar punishment to the wives and children of the guilty Muslims. However, none of these were punished, for Albergaria pardoned the three old guilty men when they fell at his feet and prayed for mercy with much weeping. What was the use of killing these three for would it compensate for the 24 murdered Portuguese? He also requested the Bhatkal chief not to punish their families. But at the same time he warned the chief that if such an incident and robbery recurred he would hold the chief responsible and would reduce Bhatkal to ashes. Thus, no punishment was inflicted on Bhatkal for the damage. Pleased with the outcome of the negotiations the Bhatkal chief allowed Albergaria to load his ships with all the provisions that were required.[26]

The cause of the unfortunate incident is not known. However, the Portuguese chroniclers note that it was all a matter of an experiment by the locals, particularly by Muslims, to find out the strength of the new Portuguese Governor, Lopo Soares. If they were to find him weak-kneed they would always flout the Portuguese authority and hinder their commerce. The experiment was not a great success.[27]

In the following year, 1517, the Governor ordered João Gonçalves de Castelo Branco, captain of a caravel, to sail along the coast from Cochin to Diu and take Bhatkal and other places on the way. He was instructed to leave at Bhatkal a factor to procure all the saltpetre that was available there.[28] However, it is not known to what extent Castelo Branco executed this order.

Towards the end of 1518 there was a skirmish once more between the Portuguese and the Bhatkal chief who seems to have refused to pay the annual tribute of rice which was agreed upon in 1509. Governor Lopes, sent Afonso de Menezes with three ships ordering him to remain at the bar of the Bhatkal river and prevent the entry and exit of any ship until the governor himself joined him with a view to punish the Bhatkal chief for his contumacy. And reaching Bhatkal early in 1519 the Governor brought the rebel back to obedience and obtained from him the payment of tributes due. He also imposed other "satisfactions" upon the chief for his rebellious conduct.[29] The other "satisfactions" were probably in the form of 1,000 *pardaus* as compensation for the expenses incurred by the Portuguese fleet.[30]

For about two decades after this, the Portuguese-Bhatkal relations seem to have been normal. However, in 1542 there was a major clash between the two, the cause of which was two-fold: non-payment of the annual tribute by the queen of Bhatkal for some years prior to 1542; and the protection which she gave to pirates who used to cause damage to the Portuguese commerce. The governor, Martim Afonso de Sousa (1542-5), sailed from Goa with a large fleet and many men. Reaching the Bhatkal river, he sent a message to the queen demanding the payment of the arrears of tribute and the surrender of all the pirate-ships which had taken shelter in her port. The queen took recourse to delaying tactics, knowing very well that the Governor was in a hurry to go to Cochin and therefore would not tarry at Bhatkal for long. She responded to his message by saying that she was ready to do all that he required; that she was preparing to pay the tribute; and that she would surrender all pirate ships. On the following day she sent two large boats, old and worn out. Two days later two more ships were sent. All these were purported to have been pirate ships. Seven or eight days passed this way due to the queen's subterfuge, and no tribute arrived in the meantime. Fed up with the her duplicity the Governor decided to punish her by launching an attack. Accordingly, 1,400 soldiers, divided into two equal squadrons, one under the command of Fernão de Sousa de Tavora, and the other under the Governor himself, landed. Tavora led the attack and marching smartly he reached the city which was being guarded by many artillery men who faced the attackers bravely. There was stiff resistance and all the local soldiers fought well for the defence of their city, of women, children and goods. But the Portuguese succeeded in putting them to flight in spite of the latter's spirited and courageous defence.

The Portuguese then entered the city. The Governor, who joined the victorious squadron soon after, allowed his men to sack the city. They did so to their satisfaction, putting to death many residents irrespective of sex and age. After the sack the Portuguese set the city ablaze, cut down palm-trees and destroyed the farms. Finishing these vindictive and cruel punitive measures, the Governor returned with his men to the fleet and sailed away to Cochin. The Portuguese atrocity on Bhatkal and its people caused so much fear among the local people that they began to say: "Beware of Martim Affonso", wherever he anchored along the western coast of India.[31]

Castanheda adds that the Portuguese fleet consisted of 40 ships and 1,500 men. The Governor sailed with it from Goa towards the end of October 1541. There were seven pirate ships which had taken shelter in the Bhatkal port. Only four of them surrendered to the Portuguese. In the battle, the Portuguese lost about 12 of their men but the enemy suffered a heavy loss. On withdrawing his men to the fleet the Governor did not sail away immediately. Instead, he waited for four days expecting some response from the queen. During the period he sent his soldiers each day to cause more and more damage to the city and the surrounding fields and groves. At last the queen surrendered the remaining three pirate ships, paid the arrears of tribute and begged for peace which was conceded.[32]

Correa's account of the Portuguese-Bhatkal clash of 1542 is interestingly different. There seems to have been only one cause which led to the quarrel. Many corsairs, who bothered the Portuguese, had taken shelter along with their ships in Bhatkal. The Portuguese fleet, comprising 70 ships and 2,000 men in arms, sailed to Bhatkal. On reaching there the Governor sent a message to the administrator of Bhatkal to the effect that he would not burn the port, or wage a war, if the pirate ships surrendered immediately, and an assurance was given that the pirates would neither be sheltered nor be allowed to arm themselves in Bhatkal in future. The administrator announced his readiness to do the Portuguese bidding, saying, however, that it was subject to the approval of the chief of Bhatkal.

As these negotiations were going on some of the Portuguese seem to have been busy trading in the market. Unfortunately, however, a quarrel arose there and two Portuguese were killed and eight or nine were wounded. Thereupon all the Portuguese who had landed gathered themselves in the Portuguese factory there. They could not return to their fleet owing to the presence of many armed men of Bhatkal who came to the market as soon as the skirmish arose. It was a common practice among the local people to ask for the protection of armed men as soon as any Portuguese fleet arrived at the port, because the Portuguese were known to indulge in malpractices and misdeeds on such occasion, being sure to be protected by the fleet should the locals attack them. From the factory the Portuguese managed to send a message to the fleet, seeking the Governor's help. The latter made preparations to land his men immediately.

In the meantime, the administrator sent his own message to the Governor saying that the trouble started when some of the Portuguese forcibly took some cloth from a local merchant; that in the skirmish that followed some Muslim mercenaries joined hands and killed some of the Portuguese; that truly speaking the latter themselves were responsible for the incident; that in spite of all this he held his men answerable; and that he had arrested some of the Muslim mercenaries whom he would hang if the Governor so ordered. He also requested him not to harm Bhatkal by landing his men. The Governor pretended to accept the explanation of the administrator and sent a deceivingly good reply. At night he landed his men who placed themselves in the factory which was near the sea. In the morning he himself joined his men with many rifles. There was no resistance, however. The city was deserted as soon as the Portuguese landed. The latter sacked the city and procured much rice, sugar and linen. The royal mansions themselves were not spared. However, there was no much scramble among the Portuguese for sharing the royal belongings that the Governor, annoyed at the behaviour of his men, destroyed all the things so that none could have anything.

While the Portuguese were thus fighting over the booty, they were attacked by the locals. From a rocky elevation nearby they began to shoot at the Portuguese. The Governor ordered that the enemy be driven away from the strategic position. The nobles and the captains urged their men to attack the enemy but the soldiers responded: "You who are nobles should go there for the Governor rewards you much and you have horses and silken dress, we wish to go in search of cloth for shirts which we do not have". And none went to fight the local soldiers! The Governor ordered Garcia de Sa to go to the hill. The locals fled when he marched against them. But when he returned they retook their former positions and revived their attack with greater vigour. Many Portuguese soldiers were wounded. Once again Sa went to the hill and once again the locals fled. They returned again when he marched back. Finally, the Portuguese were compelled to return to their fleet. But even while embarking there was much disorder and confusion and many were drowned. Every one wanted to be the first to embark, lest he should be the last and become a victim of the attacking soldiers.[33]

The incidents of the day upset the Governor considerably. He declared that his soldiers were not those brave and good ones whom he had known some years before; that he never dreamt finding so much of treachery among the Portuguese; and that he now feared the Rumes should they come because in India there were so many nobles and honoured men with so much treachery. An experienced and intelligent knight responded: "Sir, the men do not have more bravery than (is warranted by) the favours and rewards that are conferred on them for their good deeds; the king and the governor confer rewards and favours as they please and not as they ought; the men who fight do not steal, and on account of this they die of hunger; and not only do they endure this evil, but are spiritually hurt for being unable to receive (benefits) without pleasing those who never fight". The Governor did not say anything in reply. That night he caught fever and had to be treated by being bled. The following day he could not come out though he wanted to attack the city of Bhatkal again.

The next day, however, he sent Sa and Tristão de Ataide to the city with orders to destroy it. The men landed and, no doubt, caused much damage to the city but in the process they were again taken to task by the locals and many a Portuguese soldier was wounded. Yet, the governor did not give up his attempt at causing the maximum damage to the city. Everyday for a period of eight days he sent men to cut trees and set fire to the houses in the city. Finally, the administrator of Bhatkal sought peace which was granted. The Portuguese got the arrears of tribute and the pirate ships. They were promised that no pirate would either be allowed into the port or to harm himself in Bhatkal. The amount of the annual tribute for 1542 was doubled. These terms were confirmed by the Bhatkal chief and witnessed by his administrators. The Portuguese factory was allowed to function as before.[34]

The Bhatkal chief apparently did not observe these terms for long. In the first quarter of 1547, Governor João de Castro (1545-6), sent a captain, Francisco de Siqueira, to Bhatkal to request the queen to entrust to him the horses and the cloth which were robbed at the port from two Portuguese *fustas* by thieves who then took shelter in Bhatkal. Should the queen refuse to oblige, the captain was to recall the Portuguese factor from Bhatkal and then wage war in all her ports. She apparently did not comply with the request. The captain then commenced hostilities against her so vigorously that he got back all that was robbed.[35]

The queen probably did not pay the tribute also regularly. For a fresh treaty was entered into between her and the Portuguese in 1548 covering both the issues of pirates and tributes. She sent her ambassador, Poka Nayaka, to Goa, with full powers to enter into a treaty on her behalf. Governor, Garcia de Sa (1548-9), received the ambassador well. In the treaty of peace and perpetual friendship that was signed on September 17, 1548, the queen agreed: (a) to pay the annual tribute, including the arrears; (b) to prevent the exit, entrance and armament of pirates in the ports within her jurisdiction; (c) to confiscate the robbed Portuguese articles should they be brought to Bhatkal by outside pirates for selling them there, (and probably to restore the articles to the Portuguese); if she did not confiscate the articles she would pay compensation to the Portuguese for all the loss and damage that might be caused to them and their vassals on account of the piracy; and (d) to hand over to the Portuguese all the pirate ships that might be there in her territories.[36] The only obligation on the Portuguese side was not to attack Bhatkal as long as the queen observed the terms of the treaty.

Simão Botelho notes in 1554 that the amount of the yearly tribute was 2,000 bags of good rice. The ruler allowed in the port of Bhatkal a Portuguese factor who was to issue *cartazes* (passports or permits) to the ships sailing out of the port, as well as to sell the Portuguese articles of trade there. The factor received an annual salary of 100,000 *réis*. He had a writer to assist him, with a salary of 30,000 *réis*.[37]

Thus, during the course of about 50 years of the Portuguese-Bhatkal relations from 1510 to 1560, the former dealt with the latter from a position of strength, particularly after the death of Albuquerque in 1515. The latter failed to secure a site in Bhatkal for the construction of a fortress there but he succeeded in damaging the commerce of that port. His successors compelled Bhatkal to pay tributes and at the slightest provocation attacked her mercilessly with sword and fire.

REFERENCES

1. *História*, II, pp. 241, 249.
2. *Lendas*, I, pt., II, pp. 618-9.
3. *APO-BP*, tomo IV, vol. I, pt. I, p. 70.
4. K. A. N. Sastri, *A History of South India*, p. 266.
5. *Documentação*, V, p. 399.
6. *Lendas*, I, pt. I, pp. 238, 289.
7. *D-JB*, II, p. 112.
8. *Commentários*, II, pp. 99, 101-4.
9. *Cartas*, II, p. 74; *Documentação*, I, pp. 88-9.
10. *Commentários*, III, p. 47.
11. *Ibid.*
12. R. Oruganti, *Studies on Krishna Deva Raya of Vijayanagara*, p. 83.
13. *Commentários*, III, p. 49. Barros and Castanheda do not refer to the embassy of Fr. Salvador. They (*D-JB*, II, p. 204 and *História*, III, pp. 27-8), however, speak of an embassy that was sent by Albuquerque in March 1510, soon after the first occupation of Goa. The ambassador was, according to both, Gaspar Chanoca. Castanheda adds that the priest was sent with this ambassador. These statements, however, do not seem to be correct. The embassy of Chanoca was sent in 1512. Fr. Salvador was murdered in 1510 and, therefore, he could not have accompanied Chanoca in 1512.
14. *Commentários*, III, pp. 300-1; *História*, III, p. 230.
15. *Lendas*, II, pt. I, p. 376.

16. *Commentários*, IV, pp. 156-8.
17. *História*, III, p. 116.
18. *Lendas*, I, pt. I, pp. 238-43.
19. *Ibid.*, pp. 289-91.
20. *Supra*, p. 18.
21. *História*, II, p. 441.
22. *Commentários*, II, pp. 291-3, 313.
23. *História*, III, p. 116.
24. *Commentários*, III, pp. 50-1; IV, p. 79.
25. *Cartas*, I, p. 30; *História*, III, pp. 288-9.
26. *Lendas*, II, pt., I, pp. 469-70; *D-JB*, III, p. 15; *História*, IV, pp. 384-5.
27. *D-JB*, III, p. 15; *História*, IV, p. 384.
28. *História*, IV, p. 433.
29. *D-JB*, II, pp. 239-41.
30. *História*, V, p. 4.
31. *D-DC*, *Década Quinta*, pp. 560-2.
32. *História*, IX, pp. 575-7.
33. *Lendas*, IV, pt. I, pp. 257-60.
34. *Ibid.*, pp. 261-2.
35. *Lendas*, pt. II, p. 618.
36. J. F. J. Biker, *Collecção de tratados e concertos de pazes*, I, pp. 130-1; Simão Botelho, "O tomo do Estado da India", in *Subsidios*, pp. 242-3.
37. Simão Botelho, *op. cit*, p. 243.

5

THE PORTUGUESE FORTRESSES ON THE KANARA COAST

The Portuguese had decided, in 1505, to strengthen themselves on the western coast of India by building forts at various places and by appointing a resident viceroy to look after their interests in the East. They began with a fortress at Anjediv. It was built in 1505, but was destroyed the following year. However, in 1682 they erected another on the island. At Mangalore, Honavar and Basrur they built their fortresses between 1568-9 and had them till Shivappa Nayaka of Ikkeri captured them in the 1650s. Another fortress was built at Gangolly in 1630-33, but was lost to the powerful Nayaka.

Anjediv

The task of constructing the first Portuguese fortress at Anjediv, off the Kanara coast, was entrusted to the first Viceroy, Francisco de Almeida. He landed on the island on September 13, 1505 and commenced the work of fortification on the following day.[1]

Gaspar Granadim (Gaspar of India), whom Vasco da Gama had taken prisoner at Anjediv in 1498, and who had been in the service of the Adil Shah of Bijapur, seems to have advised the King of Portugal to fortify the island. Gaspar's argument was that from the fortified Anjediv the Portuguese could easily acquire control over the Goa bar.[2] The island was situated in the middle of the whole of the western coast of India; it was close to the mainland; the Portuguese ships could find there fresh water for their men;

and, above all, it was a good haven for ships in the rainy season.[3] The island was virtually a no man's land in those days, though it was within the jurisdiction of the Gersoppa chief who had neglected its development.[4] The Portuguese fortification of the island was not challenged by him. On the contrary he sought their friendship.

The fort, which was named 'Santa Justina' was constructed in 20 days. Lime, prepared out of burnt shells, was secured from the locals who came to sell provisions to the Portuguese. Whatever quantity of lime was needed for preparing mortar was thus procured.[5] The locals, who were treated well by the Portuguese, also supplied them with timber, canes and palm-leaves for building houses within the fort. Stone was available on the island in plenty. However, the required quantity was taken from a temple on the island, which the Portuguese razed to the ground.[6]

Houses of canes and palm-leaves, adequate for 70, were built inside the fort. Manuel Paçanha was appointed its captain and Rodrigo Rebelo, a nobleman, was made the commandant of the ship assigned for the defence of the island. Duarte Pereira was installed as factor. In addition, writers and other necessary officials were appointed. The required pieces of artillery and ammunitions were also provided. Merchandise was supplied for the payment of the soldiers.[7]

The neighbouring rulers showed a mixed reaction to the construction of the fort. The Muslim governor of Goa became particularly uneasy. He and his co-religionists of Chitakul and Ankola tried to prevent the locals from trusting and helping the Portuguese.[8]

The fortress, nevertheless, was not retained by the Portuguese for long. It was soon discovered that the island was vulnerable to attack and could not be easily and effectively defended. During the rainy season of 1506 the island was besieged by Muslims who put Paçanha, the captain of the fortress, under great pressure. Nevertheless, he sailed forth several times and attacked the enemy successfully. Sending news of this subsequently to the Viceroy, who was then at Cochin, Paçanha told him that there was no advantage in maintaining the fortress and that he and his advisers had come to the conclusion that he should be requested to order the destruction of the fortress. The Viceroy received the message in

September 1506 and concurring with Paçanha, he instructed his son, Dom Lourenço, to effect the destruction. He seems to have executed this order in the same month.[9].

The Portuguese continued to use the island, however, for sheltering their ships whenever necessary, in the rainy season or when there were storms, and for taking water and other supplies when required. As long as they were sure to enjoy these facilities unhindered they did not think of fortifying the island again. But in April, 1682 they learnt that Sambhaji, the Maratha ruler, intended to occupy the island and fortify it. This was considered by the Portuguese as dangerous to their commercial interests, particularly to the rice-supply from Kanara. Cargo ships carrying this vital commodity from the ports of Kanara had to pass by the island, and Sambhaji, entrenching himself there, could capture these ships. Thus, in a meeting of the Council of State, held in Goa on April 27, 1682 a decision to build forthwith a new fortress at Anjediv was taken. The necessary materials were to be sent to the island from Goa. It was also decided that the fort should be equipped with six pieces of artillery; that a fleet of ships (*manchuas* and *sanguiceis*) should guard the island; and that food supplies sufficient to last during the rainy season of that year should be made to those who were to be sent to the island.[10] On July 2, the fortification was commenced and within six months the fortress was ready. Amaro Simões Pereira was its first captain who oversaw the construction.[11]

Mangalore

The first important Portuguese fortress on the mainland coast of Kanara was built at Mangalore in 1568. However, before considering the circumstances under which the fortress was built it may be useful to review the Portuguese relations with Mangalore.

In 1513, Albuquerque sent a ship with soldiers under the command of Fernão Gomez de Lemos to Mangalore where two vessels belonging to the Zamorin of Calicut, with whom the Portuguese were at war, were anchored. The governor of Mangalore was to be asked to entrust these vessels to the Portuguese. If the governor were to refuse to oblige, the navigation of the port was to be prevented until the Calicut ships were made over. Lemos did not face any obstruction and the vessels were secured.[12]

In the first quarter of 1525 the Portuguese arrived at Mangalore with a fleet of four vessels and placing themselves at the mouth of the river prevented a hundred or more ships of the Muslims, which were in the river, from coming over. Nevertheless, the Muslims tried to sail forth several times, but in vain. As the Portuguese were guarding the mouth of the river, some Calicut ships came there, a few days later, to take goods from the port. When they saw the Portuguese fleet they realised that the Muslim ships were in the river. They gave the Portuguese a fight in which those in the river also fought against the latter from behind. The Portuguese decided to sail out into the sea to attack the Calicut ships. As soon as they did so, most of the Muslim ships, which were inside the river also sailed out and reassembled in the sea. The battle was not a great success for the Portuguese. However, some Muslim ships which could not come out of the river in time were chased further up to the river and destroyed.[13]

Five years later in 1530 the Portuguese caused great destruction to Mangalore. In that year Governor Nuno da Cunha (1529-38) learnt that a rich Hindu merchant of Mangalore, a tenant of the emperor of Vijayanagara, and popularly known as the Shetty (Chatim) of Mangalore, had clandestine commercial dealings with the Zamorin of Calicut, an enemy of the Portuguese, which caused considerable damage to the Portuguese trade interests. The Shetty was the richest merchant on the whole of the western coast of India from Goa to Cape Comorin. He was also a friend of the Portuguese who allowed his merchant ships to ply about freely. The Zamorin, finding it impossible to export his spices from his ports to the Strait of the Red Sea on account of the Portuguese vigilance, sent the spices to Mangalore probably by land with an understanding between himself and the Shetty. From Mangalore the spices were exported to the Red Sea Straits in the ships of the Muslim merchants of Mecca who were allowed by the Portuguese to load at Mangalore, the port of a friend. The merchants paid the Zamorin for the spices. The Portuguese were not aware that the spices actually belonged to the Zamorin, until they discovered the fact in 1530. The Zamorin had such great profits that he aided the Shetty to fortify Mangalore, supplied with artillery, and at his own cost maintained a garrison to defend the city and the fort. Cunha decided to punish the Shetty for his league with the Zamorin. Diogo da Silveira, captain major of the Portuguese fleet of Malabar, was sent with two galleys, one caravel and three *bargantins*, with about 400 men against the Shetty.[14]

The Shetty had been warned of the Portuguese attack. He, therefore, prepared himself well and awaited the Portuguese fleet with a determination of defending himself. Silveira reached the mouth of the river perhaps on March 26, 1530. On the following day he landed 440 men of whom 120 were gunners. The landing was made at a spot which was outside the range of enemy fire from the stockade. Simultaneously, the remaining men were to sail in *bargantins* and bombard the fortress, the galleys and the caravel being at the mouth to guard it. It was expected that the bombardment from the river would divide the enemy forces and would minimise the pressure on the Portuguese soldiers attacking by land. Silveira's brother João, led the attack by land with riflemen. Proceeding towards the stockade, the Portuguese confronted about 2,000 enemy soldiers in a palm grove. With a loud battle cry the Portuguese fell upon the enemy shooting with rifles and also with bows. Their attack was so vigorous that they killed some of the Shetty soldiers and compelled the rest to retreat to the stockade. Having retreated, one of their firemen decided to light the artillery on the stockade. However, as God would have it, one of the Portuguese noticed him in action and quickly killed him with a gunshot. The Portuguese then rushed in before the artillery could go off. The Shetty's forces retreated further into the fortress. João da Silveira, with about 70 of his men, marched along the river towards the fortress, and on the way he came across a mosque wherein were gathered-many of the enemy whom he attacked. The defenders fought so well that many of the Portuguese were wounded. As this fight was going on, a Portuguese named Francisco de Souza placed himself alone at the entrance of the mosque, seized a Muslim by the arm and killed him with a dagger thrust. Seeing this, those who defended the entrance retreated a little inside, which left a little space for the

Portuguese to enter. Finally, all the Shetty's forces within the mosque were killed. In the meantime, those who had remained with Diogo da Silveira massacred the residents of the city. None was spared. And with great enthusiasm the Portuguese marched to attack the fortress in which they soon faced stiff resistance, because there were many enemy soldiers on the galleries from where they vigorously discharged potfuls of explosives, hurled numerous stones and some gunshots, with which they wounded some of the attackers. However, they did not last long, as the Portuguese gunners killed some and forced others to retreat. Thus finding themselves free from pressure from above, the Portuguese began to force their ways into the fortress.

With a few cannon shots they broke open one of the doors and entered in spite of the defenders within. Soon the Shetty men fled in great confusion. Some of them plunged themselves into the river in order to assemble on the other bank. However, many were killed while fleeing both inside the fortress and in the river, where the Portuguese were in action. In the confusion the Shetty was also killed with a gunshot. None of the Portuguese was killed.

Having thus cleared the fortress of the enemy Diogo da Silveira commanded his brother João and Manuel da Vasconcelos to guard the entrances of the fortress so that the enemy could not return while the Portuguese robbed and took them by surprise and entrusted the task of embarking the artillery belonging to the enemy to João da Souza Lobo, Diego Alvarez, Martim Vaz Pacheco and Francisco Barros de Paiva, respectively. There were 70 cannons of which many were large ones and three were of quarter size. In the meantime the fortress was sacked. A lot of copper, coral, mercury, grains, velvet and many other rich articles of trade from Mecca, and also many explosives and countless provisions were gathered. A major part of these spoils were burnt as the Portuguese did not have sufficient space in their ships to carry all the spoils.

After the embarkation of the artillery Diogo ordered the fortress to be set on fire and it was burnt totally with the exception of the walls on the banks of the river as they were very strong but they were pulled down to their very foundations. The city was also burnt. 13 ships which had anchored at the port, were sunk. The gardens were ruined and reduced to ashes. All this was done in such a manner that it appeared that there was never a habitation in Mangalore.[15]

In 1539 Alvaro de Noronha, son of the then Viceroy, confronted off Mangalore, 25 ships belonging to Calicut. On seeing the Portuguese fleet the Calicut ships entered two estuaries. Noronha chased them and gave them a fight in which some local people helped the enemies of the Portuguese. He defeated and killed many of the enemy and burnt their ships.[16]

Mangalore experienced another devastating fury of the Portuguese in 1555. Alvaro da Silveira burnt the city and killed many residents. A rich temple with its idols was also destroyed.[17] The cause of this wanton cruelty is not told.

In 1558 once again, the Portuguese exhibited their brutality to the people of Mangalore. In that year Luiz Mello da Silva, captain major of the Portuguese fleet of the Malabar coast learnt that a ship belonging to the Muslims of Cannanore was anchored at Mangalore. Placing himself at the mouth of the river, he sent two of his captains with orders to force the Muslim ships out of the river into the sea. While the captains were engaged in this task they found that some people of Mangalore assisted the crew of the Muslim ship. Silva decided to chastise the Mangaloreans for aiding the enemy, though Mangalore belonged to the emperor of Vijayanagara with whom the Portuguese were at peace. He sailed up the river, landed his men in good order, entered the city and put to sword all those whom he confronted, without discriminating between men and women, old and young. In all these proceedings the Portuguese were akin to bloodthirsty hounds and they thought that these atrocities were necessary to terrorise the enemies.

The city was set on fire. The captain major posted himself with some of his men at the entrance of a street. A host of Muslims fleeing from the fire and destruction caused by the Portuguese, came along the street to break through the lines where the captain major was. An old man, with his hair long and loose, carrying a dagger two spans long, and an armour of iron which covered his breast to the middle, marched straight up the captain major and stabbed him on an arm and engaged him in a hand-to-hand fight.

Silva seized him by his hair and pushed him into the hands of his soldiers saying: "Take this devil". The old man and others who followed were captured. The fire was widespread by then, and it consumed the city with its houses and goods of all sorts. A grand and beautiful temple was also burnt. The brass and copper that covered the roof and the tower of the temple and fine works of gold that were inside, were taken by Silva. The Portuguese lost Gonçalves Sanches, one of the captains, who was killed along with some of his men. The Muslim ship which was the cause of the trouble, was burnt, as also some others lying at the port.[18]

In 1568, the Portuguese constructed a fortress at Mangalore. At first a site on the southern bank of the river Netravati, at its mouth, was examined. However, it was found that the ground there was not firm and could be eroded by the sea. Finally, therefore, the Viceroy, Antão de Noronha, decided to erect the fortress on the north bank of the river at Mangalore, a region under the Bangar chief who was an ally of the Portuguese. The chief met the Viceroy off Mangalore and offered to supply all the materials and services necessary for the construction of the fortress and to pay the workers. A treaty was entered into between the chief and the Portuguese whereby he declared himself a brother-in-arms to the King of Portugal, binding himself to help defend the fortress with his person and men whenever necessary.[19]

Paulo de Trindade gives us an interesting account of the causes which made the Bangar chief concede the site to the Portuguese. There was a market at the site dominated by Muslims who did not obey the chief. They insulted him in several ways. For instance, they insisted that he should walk and not be carried in a palanquin, whenever he passed by the market. This, of course, he did not do but he decided to set the Portuguese on them by giving the site to the former, for he knew that there was little love lost between the Portuguese and the Muslims.[20]

The site was on a high plateau overlooking the river. The Viceroy and his men worked tirelessly and within 15 days the foundations were ready. The first stone of the edifice was laid by the Viceroy himself on January 20, 1568, the day of St. Sebastian, whose name was given to the fortress, not only in honour of that saint but also in honour of the then reigning King of Portugal whose name also was Sebastian. The fortress was speedily completed with a residence for its captains, a factory, a warehouse, and a chapel. António Pereira, the Viceroy's brother-in-law was appointed captain with 300 men under three flag commanders. Provisions to last for six months were stocked. Having arranged all these, the Viceroy sailed for Goa on March 20.[21]

From the ordinance that was issued by the Viceroy it appears that the defence forces of the Mangalore fortress consisted of only 200 men and their officers. Out of these 100 were riflemen who were divided into four groups of 25 each under a commandant. The four commandants were under the chief of the whole contingent of riflemen. The latter were locals who enjoyed the confidence of the authorities.[22]

Describing the fortress of Mangalore in 1582 or thereabout, the unknown author of the *Livro das Cidades e Fortalezas* says that the fortress was built on the north bank of the river at its entrance in a region which belonged to the Bangar chief whose city was about one falcon shot from the fortress. The Portuguese built their fortress at the site where there was a Hindu temple. The site was on a spot controlling the port and entrance of the river. The Portuguese secured iron from the lands which belonged to the temple[23] which was retained until 1620.

Bocarro, writing in 1635 or thereabouts, says that the fortress was about a falcon shot from the bar of the Netravati river and was built on solid ground by the river bank. It was a square structure with four bulwarks in the four corners. Each wall of the fortress was 22 metres long, 8.8 metres high and 6 palms wide. Inside the fort there was a chapel, and a residence for the captain and his family by the north wall. The bulwark was a little dilapidated and required repairs.[24]

There were 35 Portuguese *cazados* whose habitation was outside but close by the fortress. The habitation consisted of houses built of stone and lime and having tiled roofs. It was surrounded by a wall, 4.4 metres high, with many watch towers and bulwarks of circular shape. The wall was a little higher on the side of the mainland and had a small moat.[25]

Within three years of its construction an attempt was made by the Zamorin's forces, in 1571, to capture the fortress of Mangalore. The queen of Ullala, who was then hostile to the Portuguese, told Catipocra (probably Kutti Pokre), admiral of the Zamorin's fleet, that the fortress could be taken easily. Without a warning he suddenly attacked the fortress one night. While his men were scaling the wall, a servant of the captain of the fortress was awakened. Seeing the enemy he threw out of the window the first thing that he could seize, which happened to be chest filled with silver belonging to his master. The chest knocked down the men on the ladder. In the meantime, hearing the noise, the captain and the garrison also woke up, fought the enemy and forced them to retreat. The chest was carried away by the fleeing enemy to their ships. However, off Cannanore, Kutti Pokre was confronted by another Portuguese fleet which defeated and killed him. The chest, with its silver, was recovered and made over to its owner.[26]

After this, until the second decade of the 17th century, the Portuguese fortress of Mangalore was free from any attack.

Honavar

The next fortress that the Portuguese came to possess on the Kanara coast was at Honavar. The relations between the Portuguese and Honavar seem to have been peaceful from the days of Albuquerque down to 1538. In that year, however, the Viceroy, Garcia de Noronha, sent his son, Alvaro, with a large fleet to Honavar where a ship belonging to Turks was known to have been loading. The Turks had erected a stockade along the river and had well-equipped it with artillery. However, as soon as the Portuguese fleet approached the river, the Turks fled without a fight. Alvaro took possession of their artillery and burnt their ship.[27]

A different version of this incident is given by Faria e Sousa. Nuno da Cunha, predecessor of Garcia de Noronha, sent Gonçalo Vaz Coutinho, to Honavar where a ship belonging to Suleiman, king of Sofala, an enemy of the Portuguese, was suspected to be aiding the queen of Gersoppa who was not constant with regard to the terms of peace which she had agreed to with the Portuguese. The queen told Coutinho, when he arrived to Honavar, that Suleiman's ship was in her port against her wish; that she could not drive it away; and that she would be glad if the Portuguese captured it. Coutinho then attacked it and in the long drawn fight lost 15 of the 80 men he had brought. One of the dead was his own son, Diogo. The enemy ship slipped away. The queen was suspected to have aided the enemy of the Portuguese and Coutinho angrily refused to accept certain presents that were sent by her for the wounded. She, however, justified herself and offered the terms of peace anew which were acceptable and sworn. She agreed to allow some of the Portuguese to come and observe how she laboured to expel the Turks from her port.[28]

Thirty one years later, Luiz de Ataide, who was the Viceroy then (1568-71), intended to wage a war against the Zamorin of Calicut. Since the latter procured the necessary provisions from Kanara, Ataide determined to deprive him of these provisions by closing the ports of Kanara to his ships. He thought that he could achieve his objective by building several fortresses on the coast of Kanara. There was already one at Mangalore. He decided to have two more, one at Honavar and another at Basrur.[29]

Besides, the Viceroy desired to punish the chiefs of Gersoppa and Barkur, under whose respective jurisdictions Honavar and Basrur lay, as they were not paying the due tributes for five or six years prior to his assumption of office. The Portuguese believed that the Malabaris instigated these chiefs to disobey them and not to pay them the tribute. Already, in 1568, António de Noronha, predecessor of Ataide, had gone to Honavar to secure the tribute but the chief had 'arrogantly' refused to pay. Noronha wanted to chastise the chief for his stand. The occasion, however, was improper, for the rainy season was about to begin and, besides, he did not have sufficient forces with him then. He did not forget to tell his successor, Ataide of the need to punish the chief for his arrogant behaviour.[30]

In the beginning of December, 1569, Ataide set sail from Goa with a large fleet consisting of 113 ships and 3,000 soldiers and reached the Honavar river within a few days. He went up the river towards the fortress built by the Gersoppa chief. The fortress was on the north bank of the river, built on the summit of a hill and surrounded the walls. The Viceroy landed his men who assaulted the fortress. The defenders hurled stones on the attackers, but they could not prevent the latter from forcing their ways into the fortress. On entering, the Portuguese found very little resistance. Some imagined that the Viceroy had an understanding with the captain, Lavarná who escaped with goods without much of a fight. The Viceroy got the fortress consecrated and named it after St. Catharina. He appointed Jorge de Moura its captain, giving him 200 soldiers and providing him with ammunitions, provisions and funds.[31]

According to António Pinto Pereyra it was on November 12, 1569 that the Viceroy set out from Goa with a fleet of more than 130 sails, 70 of which were warships, the rest being merchant and other vessels. There were more than 2,500 Portuguese soldiers in the fleet. On reaching Honavar 2,100 to 2,200 men landed. The fortress of Honavar appeared to have been impregnable. It was hard indeed to reach it owing to the height of the hill on which it was located. It was well-defended by 400 to 500 soldiers and was well-supplied with provisions. Some bullets were fired by the defenders in order to disorganise the attackers as the latter were climbing, but in vain. The city, which was rich and had beautiful edifices, but which was now deserted, was sacked and then reduced to ashes. The Portuguese encamped near the fortress and bombarded it incessantly for four days until November 24. At last the garrison surrendered, losing all hope of being relieved, for the reinforcement that was sent by the queen would not dare to attack the Portuguese. The garrison, led by Kantappa Naik, was allowed to go out without arms. There was very little to plunder inside the fortress, except 13 pieces of artillery and some other war materials. In the battle the Portuguese lost 20 men. On the feast of St. Catharina, November 25, 1569, a mass was held in the fortress. Jorge de Moura was appointed captain of the fortress, with a garrison of 400 soldiers, half of whom were Portuguese and the other, Christians of Goa.[32]

The queen of Gersoppa to whom Honavar belonged was asked to pay the arrears of tributes and bind herself to pay the annual tribute regularly thereafter. She was also asked to give pepper every year, sufficient for a ship-load, at the rate of 22 and 1/2 *pardaus* a *khandi*. A war compensation of 20,000 *cruzados* was also demanded of her forthwith. She hesitated to give it. The Viceroy did not wait until she gave him a definite reply. He proceeded to Basrur in order to take that place also. Ultimately, she refused to accept the conditions.[33]

In the beginning of 1570 the Viceroy had to urgently send a strong fleet to Honavar, for he was informed that the queen of Gersoppa was planning to attack the Portuguese fortress of Honavar. She plotted to administer to the Portuguese soldiers in the Honavar fortress the fruit of a plant known as *duturo*, mixing it with their food. The fruit was known to have the power of causing loss of memory to the one who ate it and one would not know what one was eating and not sense any pain even if wounded. However, she did not succeed in her plot. The people who were to execute her scheme were discovered and hanged. And the Portuguese fleet sent by the Viceroy reached Honavar. There were four ships under four captains each with able soldiers.[34]

The queen had been instigated by the Adil Shah of Bijapur to wage war against the Portuguese in Honavar. However, in spite of the great pressure on his limited resources by the combined forces of the Adil Shah, the Nizam Shah and the Zamorin, the Viceroy sent effective relief to Honavar to the great astonishment of the enemy who thought that he did not possess enough forces even to defend Goa. Thus, Honavar was saved for the Portuguese for the time being.[35]

The Adil Shah, however, did not give up his effort of setting the queen against the Portuguese. By July 1571 he again prevailed upon her to attack the Honavar fortress. He sent her a contingent of 2,000 men, to which she added 3,000 of her own, and with these combined forces she besieged the fortress. The Viceroy received this news in the middle of July and speedily dispatched a fleet of ten ships which reached Honavar and gained in a trice a thumping victory against the queen. She lost many of her forces and fled, leaving behind all her cannons which fell into the Portuguese hands.[36]

The author of the *Livro das Cidades e Fortalezas* mentions that the Honavar fortress was within the jurisdiction of the queen of Gersoppa. It was located on the bank of the river of Honavar, a gun-shot distance from its mouth. The fortress was erected on a hill which was encircled on the sea side by steep rocks, thus making the fortress inaccessible from that side; on the land side, wherever necessary, walls of stone and lime were built, with a bulwark surrounded by a moat overlooking the city of Honavar which was about a gun-shot distance from the fort.[37]

Bocarro writes that the fortress was a quarter league away from the bar. The circumference of the fortress was 880 metres. In 1635 there lived inside the fortress some *cazados* and other Portuguese, who numbered 30 in all. There were 11 bulwarks, which were circular in shape, to protect the habitation of the Portuguese. Some of the bulwarks were roofed.[38]

Basrur

Basrur was known to the Portuguese from the days of Albuquerque. They had peaceful commercial contacts with that region. However, in December, 1569 it was attacked in accordance with the decision of Viceroy Luiz de Ataide in order to have a fortress there. He entered the river with his fleet on the south bank of which Basrur was situated. He led the vanguard himself sitting in a brocaded chair in his ship. Near him a musician played notes on a harp. He addressed his men grandiloquently: "Enter, O! Greeks in Troy, three by three and four by four". As the fleet approached the fortress some shots began to fly hissing about the ships. The musician became uneasy, but the Viceroy was undisturbed. He told him to go ahead and to bother him not. Some nobles and captains approached him and urged him not to risk his life proceeding ahead under the bombardment from the enemy but he was unmoved.

However, Luiz Mello da Silva, who was near the Viceroy, said: "Let him go, gentlemen; if he is killed I shall govern India; and if I am also killed you gentlemen shall govern". The Viceroy was pleased with his words.[39]

The fortress of Basrur was erected on the summit of a hill about a quarter league inside the coast, on the south bank of the river. It was surrounded by walls and bulwarks and was equipped with some pieces of artillery. It was maintained by the merchants or Shettys of Basrur. The city was governed like a republic. It paid tribute to the emperor of Vijayanagara.[40]

Arriving at the fortress the Viceroy landed his men. Silva was given the command of the vanguard. He marched towards the fortress bravely under the enemy fire and reaching there cleared it of the enemy who fled for life from another side. He sent the message of his victory to the Viceroy who joined him soon after. António Botelho, the Viceroy's cousin, was appointed captain of the fortress with 300 soldiers. The Viceroy ordered the strengthening of the fortress with the help of the workmen and materials that he had brought with him for the purpose.[41]

António Pinto Pereyra informs us that Ataide had sent Francisco Mascarenhas to Basrur in advance in order to secure the place by a negotiated settlement. But the government of Basrur was not prepared to allow the Portuguese to have a fortress there. There seems to have been a prompt exchange of communications between the government of Basrur, on the one hand, and the chiefs of Tolar and Gangolly, on the other. These three had an agreement to aid each other against each other's enemies. The queen of Gersoppa, whose influence was predominant among these, also consented to provide 3,000 soldiers to defend Basrur against the Portuguese.[42]

Faria e Sousa says that the Viceroy, before proceeding there himself, sent to Basrur one of his captains, Pedro da Silva e Menezes, with a fleet of 13 vessels. The reason for the decision to take Basrur was the Tolar chief's disobedience. Probably Faria e Sousa thought that Basrur was within the jurisdiction of the Tolar ruler. The Viceroy secretly won over the captain of the fortress of Basrur who agreed to surrender it to the Portuguese. Thus, when Menezes reached there the fortress was handed over to him as promised. It was night and the Portuguese, entering the habitation, killed or captured more than 200 residents. However, the chiefs of Tolar and Gangolly speedily collected 1,500 men that night and began to attack the Portuguese.

On the following day they gathered 5,000 more. They fought the foreigners bravely, but lost many soldiers. The Portuguese lost five. Menezes and his captains came to the conclusion that the fortress could not be sustained. They, therefore, abandoned it, but not without causing heavy damage to the fortress and taking 20 cannons, a lot of ammunition and various other arms.[43]

The Viceroy, after capturing the fortress of Honavar, proceeded to Basrur. Its fortress was now being guarded by 11,000 men. He succeeded, after a hard fight in which he lost nine of his men but killed 200 of the enemy, in capturing a stronghold from where he could block the entrance of the fortress. That dispirited the defenders so much that they gave up fighting and allowed the Portuguese to enter. However, the chiefs of Tolar and Gangolly collected an army of 6,000 and attacked the Portuguese who were in possession of the fortress then. It was a dark night and the Portuguese captain of the fortress, Pedro Lopes Rebelo, fought vigorously with his 200 soldiers. The chiefs lost 300 men and the Portuguese, five. At last, losing all hope of success, the chiefs sought peace which was granted.[44]

A treaty of peace was signed with the following terms and conditions: (i) The Portuguese could erect a fortress at a site of their choice at Basrur; (ii) The latter would pay a certain quantity of rice tribute every year, probably 500 bags, for the sustenance of the fort; (iii) All the pepper of the land should be supplied to the Portuguese at a 'common' price; and (iv) The signatories should be friends of their friends and enemies of their enemies.[45]

The Viceroy issued an interesting but long ordinance, dated March 30, 1570, in which there is a reference to the construction of a new fortress by the Portuguese at Basrur. Probably the old fortress which the Portuguese had just conquered was not strong enough and was open to easy attack. The new fortress was at a more secure spot.[46] The Viceroy spent about 40 days in supervising its construction.[47]

The captain of the fortress and other officials were instructed to treat the people well and commit no offence against them. The Viceroy pointed out that it was the surest way of maintaining peace there and carrying on gainful trade in the port, from which he expected a considerable income not only to maintain the fortress but also to supplement remittance to Portugal.[48]

Writing about the Basrur fortress the autnor of the *Livro das Cidades e Fortalezas* indicates that it was 16 leagues south of Honavar. It was at the entrance of the river on its south bank. It was built on the top of a hill about a gun-shot distance from the mouth of the river and another shot from the city. Basrur bordered the principality of Tolar and that of Gangolly. There was a treaty of friendship between the people of Basrur, on the one hand, and the chiefs of Tolar and Gangolly, on the other, all of whom declared themselves to be friends of friends and enemies of enemies. The Portuguese got an annual tribute of rice from the people of Basrur, with which they sustained the fortress.[49]

Bocarro also states that the Portuguese fortress of Basrur was on the bank of the river, built on a hill and half a league from the bar. As one entered the river one found the fortress located on the right hand side. It was a structure, almost square in shape. Its walls measured 6.6 metres high and 5 palms thick. There were four circular bulwarks at the corners. It had no moat. The circumference of the fortress was 220 metres. Inside, by the wall, was located the captain's residence.[50]

In 1635 there lived 35 *cazados* outside the fortress at a distance of a gun-shot. Each *cazado* had a slave who accompanied him, carrying his master's arms. The habitation of the *cazados* was surrounded by a mudwall, 3.3 metres high, with watch towers in the form of bulwarks. The *cazados* possessed some rice fields and palm-trees outside the habitation. When there was peace they enjoyed the produce of their possessions, including about 96 loads of black rice.[51]

Ahead of the fortress of Basrur, a little less than a league, by the side of the river, there was a habitation of the Hindus, called Shettys of Upper Basrur, who paid the Portuguese a customary tribute of 500 loads of rice for allowing them to carry on their commerce and to transport their goods by the fortress.[52]

Subsequent to the fortification of Basrur by the Portuguese foreign merchants stopped trading with its port owing to the cupidity of the Portuguese captains who summoned to the fortress those merchants who entered the river and compelled them to sell their goods at a very low price. Many a time the merchants fought the

Portuguese in order to free themselves from this kind of oppression at Basrur.

In 1583 Francisco Mello de Sampaio was the captain of the fortress and he, like his predecessors, worked to enrich himself so much that the local merchants of Basrur, who stood to lose their trade and income by his proceedings, decided to take the fortress by treachery. They negotiated with some Christians, who were in the service of the fortress and who were known to be ready to enter into a plot, promising them grand rewards if a way to take the fortress was suggested. Finally, the doorkeeper of the fortress was won over by the plotters. He told them that the days of Holy Week were approaching; that on those days the Portuguese would be occupied in penitential sacrifices; that on the night of Friday there would be a grand procession from the fortress to the habitation of the Christians; that on that night the plotters could send some of their soldiers to the fortress the door of which would be opened to them by him from within; and that the remaining soldiers of the plotters could suddenly attack the procession and kill all. Fortunately for the Portuguese the plotters were disappointed on the day fixed. Gileanes Mascarenhas, a captain, arrived at Basrur with a strong fleet on the very Friday on which the fortress was to be attacked. He remained there the whole day and night and left for Goa only on the following day. The plotters dared not to attack the fortress as long as the fleet was present.[53]

Though the merchants of Basrur lost a golden opportunity they began to plot again as soon as Mascarenhas sailed away. They approached the very Christians who had cooperated earlier and prepared a plan. The men who were in charge of the key of the fortress were bribed and won over. It was agreed that in the night about 50 men should scale the wall by ladders to be thrown from the fortress and set fire to the artillery inside. 3,000 men-of-arms were to be ready to assault. At a suitable time, the men who had the key had to open the doors from within. If, however, it was impossible to open the doors, all the soldiers of the plotters were to use the ladder and scale the walls. Once again the merchants were disappointed. As God would have it, the captain of the fortress suspected some treachery on the eve of the Easter when he saw the familiarity with which some of his men, namely, those who were in league with the plotters moved among the locals. He arrested the suspects and put them to torture whereupon they confessed everything. Afterwards they were hanged publicly.

The captain wrote to the Viceroy informing him of the situation and requested for reinforcements. He began in the meantime to be more careful, particularly, about the keys of the fortress. The merchants, having thus failed twice in driving the Portuguese by treachery decided to fight them openly. They secured aid from the chief of Tolar, their neighbour, and the two allies collected between them 5,000 men of arms. They intended to capture the *cazados* who were living outside the fortress. However, before they could carry out their intention the *cazados* were gathered inside the fortress. The Portuguese captain set the cannons ready for defence, informed the Viceroy again of the situation, collected as much provisions as possible and repaired the fortress wherever possible. The local soldiers set the habitation of the *cazados* on fire, though it was already deserted, and encamped near the fortress but outside the range of the enemy fire. From there they launched attacks on the fortress from time to time. The Portuguese found themselves in short supply of ammunitions. The captain requested thereupon the captain of the fortress of Honavar, which was the nearest Portuguese fortress to Basrur to help him out. The Honavar captain sent immediately a large boat with gunpowder, bullets and some soldiers.

In the meantime, the Viceroy received a message from Basrur and he also sent relief under the command of André Furtado de Mendonça who hastened to Basrur and reached there within two days from the date of his departure from Goa, that is on April 15. The first thing that he did on reaching Basrur was to supply provisions to the besieged. The locals raised their siege on learning that substantial relief had arrived. Mendonça sent some ships up the river to launch continuous attacks upon the merchants of Basrur in all the villages along the banks. Finally, the native camp itself was attacked and subjected to much damage.

On the following day, he assaulted the temple Condansur (the temple of Kodandeshwara?), inside which some local soldiers were gathered. It was set on fire and those who were inside were burnt. The temple too was reduced to ashes, which caused much sorrow to the locals as it was greatly venerated. Later on, no doubt, it was rebuilt by the natives at the cost of considerable money and time.[54]

On May 15 two more ships arrived from Goa at the request of Mendonça. He then intensified his attacks on Basrur, destroyed and burnt its habitations. The whole of that rainy season was spent by him in these destructive activities. A nearby island, called the Great, in which the local people had erected *palisades* and had dug ditches, was attacked when the Portuguese came to know that articles of trade were stocked there. After a hard fight the island fell into the hands of the Portuguese who killed everyone alive with sword and fire. Later, Upper Basrur was attacked twice; its habitations were burnt and palm trees were cut down. Being thus subjected to continuous onslaughts and atrocities, the merchants of Basrur finally sought peace but Mendonça did not concede it, as he was not prepared to do so without orders from the Viceroy. In August he sailed into the sea in search of a ship belonging to the merchants of Basrur and expected from Mecca. However, the ship seems to have been warned of the trouble at Basrur and went to Hormuz.[55]

The three fortresses of Mangalore, Basrur and Honavar were considered by the Portuguese as very important. Says the author of the *Livro das cidades e fortalezas*[56]: "these fortresses are of great importance and are very necessary for the conservation of those ports from which (being in the possession of the enemies) can ensue very grave damages and losses to the state of India because in them are loaded every year many ships to the Strait of the Red Sea and many other parts; on account of this region of Kanara having great quantity of pepper, ginger, iron, coir, wood, saltpetre, and other articles, and above all, the great abundance of foodgrains of all sorts of which the whole of India is supplied, particularly, Malabar which suffers much scarcity of foodgrains, go out from there the greatest supply of them; and not only this but also explosives, artillery, gunpowder, ammunitions, and all other things with which the war is sustained are supplied from here".

"And, these ports of Honavar, Basrur and Mangalore, the Malabaris had their chief ports where they traded; and some were nests of thieves in which all the ships and pirates of Malabar had some shelter of certainty in which they deposited the plunder they made. From all of which resulted many and great damages to the State of India, very prejudicial to the Portuguese, the Malabaris being their first and major enemies with whom they always had, and have, continuous war from the beginning of the conquest. All these were stopped with these fortresses, which we have at these ports, with which not only were the Malabaris deprived of those shelters, but also were they impeded in the commerce of the province so fertile and so near and from where they derived so much profit; and the great commerce and trade, which was extant from them to Mecca, India and many other parts, was impeded".

Gangolly

At Gangolly, which the Portuguese called Cambolim, they built their last fortress in Kanara. Its construction was begun probably in early 1630 and was completed in 1633 during the vice-royalty of Count of Linhares. It was located in a peninsula formed by the sea and the river Gangolly, and was just opposite to their fortress of Basrur. It distanced a stone-throw from the river and less than a league from the river mouth. In front of the fortress the river was 13.2 meters deep, where all kinds of embarkations, including cargo ships, could sail in. The fortress was a square structure with four bulwarks at the four angles. Each wall of the fortress was 41.8 metres long, 10 palms wide at the base, 6 palms wide at the top, and 25 palms high. The bulwarks were triangular in shape, two of them being large and the other two, small. In 1635 or thereabout the fortress had an artillery consisting of five pieces of bronze of 8 to 12 pounds calibre, ten falcons and many cradles. The head of the fortress was a captain who was also the captain-major of the garrison. He lived in one of the three bulwarks covered with tile, the fourth bulwark having no roof.[57]

The first effect of the construction of this fortress was the control it secured to the Portuguese over the island of Gangolly.

The island yielded 30,000 bags of rice with which the fortress could be sustained as also all other fortress of Kanara. The fortress could receive relief by sea as well as by river any time of the year.[58]

From the minutes of a meeting of the Council of State held in Goa on November 22, 1629 it is evident that the Portuguese had a desire to possess the peninsula of Gangolly since long. They intended to transfer the fortress of Basrur to the peninsula and convert the latter into an island by digging a canal between the sea and the river Gangolly.[59] But Venkatappa Nayaka, the powerful ruler of Ikkeri, who was the master of the territories of Kanara, seems to have been in the way of the fulfillment of their desire. The opportunity to gain the place offered itself, however, when he died on November 10, 1629. All those chiefs whom he had subjugated revolted against his grandson and successor, Virabhadra Nayaka. Under these circumstances the 'possessors and dwellers' of Gangolly, who were also in revolt, offered the peninsula to the Portuguese who were quick to avail of this opportunity. They fished successfully in the troubled waters.

Towards the end of November the Viceroy sent Diogo de Sousa e Menezes to take possession of the place. He was authorised to negotiate with the municipality of Upper Basrur to whom the peninsula of Gangolly belonged. He was instructed to secure a legal title for the possession of the place. After constructing a fortress in Gangolly the establishment of the fortress of Basrur was to be transferred to the new fort.[60]

On January 3, 1630 Menezes who was at Basrur wrote to the Viceroy that he personally went by night to measure the Gangolly pass which was 80 paces from the river to the sea; that a canal could easily be cut across this pass, the land being sandy; that with 500 workers the canal could be finalised in 8 days; that in order to do this work he would require additional soldiers whom he requested the Viceroy to send.[61] From these statements it is clear that the Portuguese were not yet in possession of the place. But in a letter dated February 20, written to the King of Portugal, the Viceroy says that Menezes "began to fortify with stockades and to open the bar to join the river with the sea, a task in which labour at present 1,000 spade-men and for which I have ordered much stone and lime, miners, masons and carpenters, and the two engineers (Torral and Frias) with many big and small baskets, much gunpowder and ammunitions, 70 or so sea-faring firemen ...[62] From this one can conclude that the Portuguese took possession of the place by February 1630 and soon after began to fortify it.

The task of converting the peninsula of Gangolly into an island seems to have been beset with difficulties. On November 4, the Viceroy wrote in a letter to the King of Portugal that Menezes had completed digging the canal but the sea waves deposited sand in it continuously and that he had given up the work. He also changed the site of fortification to the one where finally the fortress (São Miguel) was erected. The Viceroy complained that the change was made without his order. Menezes was recalled to Goa soon after, as he fell ill.

Francisco de Moura, who was then sent to Gangolly, continued the work of fortification by building two bulwarks and one wall of the fortress and by erecting stockades. In the rainy season the Viceroy sent reinforcements to Gangolly, as the Ikkeri forces used to attack the new fortification. At the time of writing the letter he was still ordering stone and lime, with the instruction that the work should not be stopped until the fortress was completed.[63] From this letter it is evident that the Portuguese were in effective possession of Gangolly but its fortification was not yet complete. Even by March of the following year the fortress does not seem to have been ready in spite of the Viceroy's order that the work should not be stopped before completion. In a treaty of peace entered into between the Portuguese and Virappa Nayaka of Ikkeri on March 7, 1631 there is a clause which says that the Viceroy and his successors "can order" construction of fortresses in Gangolly.[64] The clause is in the future tense and there is no reference to any existing fortress. This implies that the Portuguese completed the construction of their fortress only after this date. Probably they did finish it only in February 1633, for a letter of the Viceroy of the 2nd of the same month says: " ... the walls and bulwarks, in order to be completed, require a few courses of stones in one of them, which will be finished within this month of February".[65] Thus the Portuguese took more than three years to complete their fortress of Gangolly. The cause of this delay was Virabhadra Nayaka of Ikkeri.

The administrative and defence arrangements in the fortress

As soon as a fortress was established, the Viceroy (or the governor) usually issued an ordinance making provisions for the appointment of various officials, their salaries, their functions and the procedure that they should adopt in discharging their functions. The ordinance took into account the defence needs, commercial activities and religion, and included provisions for them.

Officials

***Captain*:** Each fortress was in the charge of a captain. The choice seems to have been made by the king himself, at least in the early days. For instance, Manuel Paçanha, the captain of the Anjediv fortress (1505-6), was sent by the king for this purpose along with the Viceroy.[66] Later on, however, the Viceroy seems to have been given the power to appoint captains. Thus, António Lopes de Siqueira, who was captain and factor of Honavar in 1574, was appointed by the Viceroy.[67] Normally, the candidate for the post of captains was a nobleman who had rendered much service to the King of Portugal and who enjoyed his confidence. Generally the term of office was three years but it could be extended.

***Factor*:** Every fortress contained a trading centre or factory. To look after it, a factor was usually appointed. The Viceroy could fill this post. The factor's term of office was also three years and the candidate was generally one who had rendered valuable service to the King of Portugal. Thus, Bartholomeu Rodrigues de Sora was appointed factor of Basrur for a term of three years by the Viceroy in 1585, having regard for the 19 years of service that the former had rendered in India in taking the fortress of Basrur where he had received two wounds from lance-thrusts; in the taking of the fortress of Honavar; in the siege of Chaul where he was wounded; and in other battles waged by the Portuguese in India.[68]

Some time the functions of the major and of the inspector of the magazines and food supplies were also entrusted to the factor.[69] By an order of the King of Portugal, Dom Sebastião (1557-1578), the posts of captain, factor, and inspector of the treasury, came to be combined in one person. This was no doubt an economy measure. Thus, in 1582 or thereabouts, the captains of Honavar and Mangalore were also factors and inspectors of treasury. The captain of Basrur was also factor, and inspector of the treasury.[70] In 1635 or thereabouts, the captain of Mangalore was factor in addition but at Basrur there were two individuals occupying the posts of captain and factor separately.[71] Thus, the captain who was primarily a military official, looked after civil functions too.

***Writer*:** Every factor had a writer. He was appointed by the viceroy for a term of three years. The writer was attached to the magazines and food supplies as well. He had also the function of assigning lodging to guests or to those who had the right to such accommodation in the fortress.[72]

***Judge*:** One or two judges were appointed in every fortress to administer justice. Thus, there was a judge of the rank of *ouvedor* and another of the rank of *meirinho* in the fortress of Basrur in 1570.[73] The *ouvedor* was perhaps the head of the judicial tribunal in the fortress. The *meirinho* was inferior in rank to *ouvedor*. The former was probably in charge of sentinels, summons and conducting of prisoners. The common practice was to appoint a *meirinho* only in a fortress. In Basrur the *meirinho* was assisted by a writer and four footmen in 1570.[74] This writer was different from the writer attached to the factory. The armed peons or footmen were to move about with the *meirinho* and assist him in discharging his duties. In Honavar the *meirinho* was also the *alcaide* of the sea in 1582.[75] The judicial officials were appointed by the viceroy from among those poor soldiers who had rendered good service to the state.[76]

***Surgeon*:** A surgeon was generally appointed in each fortress. Preferably he was to be a physician too. There were such surgeons in Basrur and Mangalore in the early days.[77] Probably surgeons could be appointed by the captain.

***Interpreter*:** An interpreter, who knew Portuguese and the local language, was invariably appointed in each fortress. He served the captain as well as the factor. He was a man who enjoyed the confidence of the authorities.[78] The captain and the factor dealt with the local authorities, chiefs, merchants and other locals in general, whenever necessary, through the interpreter.

Chief of artillery : Among the military officials there was a chief of artillery. He was much inferior in rank to the captain of the fortress, as their respective salaries would indicate.[79] He commanded the firemen.

Doorkeeper: Every fortress had another military official in the person of a doorkeeper. He was a Portuguese national of much alertness.[80] Perhaps he was in charge of the keys of the doors of the fortress too.

Superintendent of sentinels (sobre-rolda): In Mangalore there was a special military post known as *sobre-rolda* or superintendent of sentinels.[81]

Chief of peons (Naik): A number of local peons were appointed in every fortress. They were under the command of a chief or *Naik* who was also a local. In 1570 the *Naik* at Basrur had 12 peons under his charge,[82] in 1635 the *Naik* of Mangalore had 40 peons and that of Honavar 33.[83]

Church Officials: A church was generally headed by a vicar under whom there were several other officials. Thus at the Basrur fortress the church had a vicar, two clergymen, a choir boy, a treasurer and some ordinaries.[84] The choir boy was normally a Portuguese. In the Mangalore fortress also there were chapels with vicars at their head in 1635.[85]

Salaries

The ordinances provided for the salaries of the various officials. The salary of an official did not remain constant. It varied according to the importance and income of the fortress. In addition to cash payments some officials were allowed residential quarters and provisions.

Captain: The captain's salary was normally 400,000 *réis* a year. But the captain of Honavar had 100,100 *réis* a year in 1574, 1582, and 1635, respectively, because the fortress did not have much income.[86] The captain of Gangolly had 180,000 *réis* in 1635.[87] The captain of Mangalore had 400,000 *réis* in 1568,[88] but only 100,000 *réis* in 1574 and 1582 respectively.[89] However, it was raised again to 400,000 *réis* in 1635.[90] The captain of Basrur alone seems to have enjoyed a steady salary of 400,000 *réis* a year. In addition to the salary the captain got residential quarters for himself and his family within the fortress.[91] He was allowed the services of 20 Portuguese servants who attended upon him.[92] When the captain was factor in addition, he did not get any additional salary for it.

Factor: The factor's salary was invariably 100,000 *réis* a year.[93] He was allowed two Portuguese servants.

Writer: The writer of Mangalore had a salary of 40,000 *réis* a year,[94] and that of Basrur, 50,000,[95] and this was the salary of the writer of Honavar as well.[96] A writer was allowed one servant.[97]

Judge: The *ouvedor* of Basrur had an annual salary of 60,000 *réis* in 1570.[98] The subordinate *meirinho* usually got 18,000 *réis*; [99] but at Honavar he got only 12,000 *réis* in 1574 and 1582 respectively.[100] The *meirinho* was generally assisted by some peons. Thus, at Basrur he had four peons to move about with and to help him carry out his functions.[101] Each of these peons of Basrur got one *pardau* a month and provisions in 1570,[102] and one *xerafim* a month in 1635.[103]

Surgeon: The surgeon's salary varied according to his qualifications and nationality. In 1570 the surgeon and physician of Mangalore got 720 *réis* a month but if he was a Portuguese he got in addition the salary and provisions due to men-of-arms.[104] In 1635 he got 720 *réis* a month and 1,200 a year if he was a Portuguese.[105] The surgeon and physician of Honavar got 30,000 *réis* in 1574 and the surgeon and bleeder of the same place got 36,000 *réis* in 1635.[106] At Basrur the surgeon got 30,000 *réis* a year in 1570 and 1635 respectively.[107]

Interpreter: He usually got 14,000 *réis* a year but at Honavar his salary was 12,000 *réis* a year (in 1574).[108]

Chief of Artillery: He had varying salaries. At Mangalore it was 24,000 *réis* a year (in 1568)[109] and 1635 respectively.[110] At Basrur it was 46,000 *réis* in 1570.[111] In addition to the salary, he got provisions.

***Doorkeeper*:** He received invariably 600 *réis* for provisions. In addition to this he got the salary and provisions due to men-of-arms,[112] which was probably 12,000 *réis* a year as at Mangalore in 1635,[113] and in all it came to 19,200 *réis* a year.[114]

***Church Officials*:** The vicar's salary was 30,000 *réis* a year plus provisions, the total coming to 46,320 *réis* a year.[115] The *beneficiado* got 20,000 *réis* and provisions.[116] The choirman got 400 *réis* a month.[117] The ordinees received for the year wine, oil, meal, etc.[118] The treasurer earned 6,000 *réis* a year as salary plus 6,000 *réis* for provisions, and a salary and provisions due to men-of-arms.[119]

***Other Officials*:** The superintendent of Sentinels got 18,000 *réis* a year at Mangalore in 1568 and 1635 respectively.[120] The writer who assisted the *meirinho* got 12,000 *réis* a year including his salary and provisions due to a man-of-arms.[121] The fireman had a salary and provisions as agreed upon at the time of enrollment.[122] A peon's salary was 3,600 *réis* a year.[123] The *Naik* of the peons got double the salary of a peon under him.[124]

Mode of Payment

The factor was to make quarterly payments to the above officials, including himself. The payments were to be entered in a register kept for the purpose. Only those who resided in the fortress and served there were to be paid. Each one was to receive his salary personally and no one was allowed to receive it on behalf of another. The payee and the writer were to sign each payment. As the man in charge of the accommodation in the fortress, the writer would know who was eligible for receiving payments and, therefore, he was held responsible for unauthorised payments and was made liable to pay the government double the amount that he paid out illegally. At the end of all quarterly payments the factor was to sign the register which was then sent to Goa for being scrutinised by the inspector of the royal treasury to see if it conformed to the viceroy's ordinance.[125]

Maintenance of accounts, records and warehouses

A book of receipts and dispatches was maintained by the factor. It was to be certified, numbered and signed by a royal accountant. If it was not possible for the accountant to do so for some reason, it was to be done by an official of the royal treasury. In the book all that was received by the factor from the royal treasury, or all that was entrusted to him by any other mode, was to be entered under the factor's receipt which was to be prepared by the writer of the factory and was to be signed by the factor. What was received, the officials from whom they were received, the person by whom it was delivered, and the day, month and year of receipt, were to be entered in the receipt. After that information, an account of it was to be given to the official concerned; the account was to be signed by the writer and the official, and was to contain the number of the folio of the book wherein the receipt was written. There were to be different heads of entries in the book, one concerning all the trade, foodgrains, ammunitions and goods that might be entrusted to the factor; matters pertaining to artillery and other materials of the magazine; for taxes if the King of Portugal had right for any in the fortress or the port or its lands, to show what was levied or what was received from the levies; expenses incurred at the factory; and receipts by purchase.

The factor could purchase whatever was necessary to promote the interests of the King of Portugal and provide the fortress. But he was to make purchases with the captain's approval, and actually purchase what was approved in the presence of the writer as an eye-witness. The sales of all royal merchandise and other articles was to be entered too. The selling was to be executed in the presence of the writer who, with the knowledge of the captain, was to prepare a receipt for the money received against sales.[126]

The expenses in cash and kind, which the captain incurred from the receipts of the factory, were to be entered by the writer in the book under the appropriate title. The writer was authorised also to verify the expenses by collecting information from the receiver of cash or goods. If any excess payment was made the illegal portion of it was not to be taken into account. The book of receipts and dispatches was to be kept in a locked box and the factor was not permitted to make any entries in it without the presence of the writer, both of them having two separate keys to the box.[127]

All the articles of trade, ammunitions, food supplies, or any other goods received by the factor from the royal stocks or by way of purchases for providing the fortress, were to be stored by him in the locked warehouses which were to be opened only in the presence of the writer who also had a key different from that of the factor. The latter was responsible for any damage that might befall the stored goods on account of his negligence, particularly in the rainy season when roofs were likely to leak for want of timely repairs.[128]

Cash box

A coffer with two separate lockers was to be maintained at the factory. All the money received by the factor from the royal treasury was to be deposited in it. The factor and the writer were to have two separate keys for the coffer and thus neither could open it without the knowledge of the other.[129] It was a good arrangement for minimising the incidents of misappropriation of funds.

Financing the fortress

Diogo Velho's financial statement of 1574 gives us a good account of the income and the expenses of the fortresses of Honavar, Basrur and Mangalore. The unknown author of the *Livro das Cidades e Fortalezas* also furnishes some useful information for 1582 or thereabouts. Falcão supplies a statement of income and expenses at the turn of the 16th century. António Bocarro provides a similar statement for the year 1635 or thereabouts.

In 1574 the fortress of Honavar had no income. The expenses incurred therein came to 2,984,980 *réis*, the amount being supplied from Goa. The income of the fortress of Basrur was 2,100,000 *réis* and its expenses, 3,132,200 *réis*, the deficit being 1,032,200 *réis*. The income was from the duties levied on horses of Hormuz, which came there, 5,000 *cruzados* or 1,800,000 *réis*, and upon the goods exported from the port, 1,000 *cruzados* of silver or 300,000 *réis*.

The fortress of Mangalore had a small income of 600,000 *réis* but its expenses amounted to 3,383,800 *réis*, the deficit being 2,783,800 *réis*. The income included revenues from the land belonging to the temple in which the fortress was established. The main items on which expenses were incurred in all these fortresses were the salaries of the officials, soldiers and others, and the maintenance of the fortress. The deficits were made good by the government at Goa.[130]

The author of the *Livro das Cidades e Fortalezas*, writing in 1582 or thereabouts, makes no reference to any income at Honavar. But at Basrur the Portuguese got tributes in rice with which the fortress there was maintained. Besides this they got supplies of pepper at a reasonable price. At Mangalore they had some income from iron from the land belonging to the temple.[131]

At the beginning of the 17th century, Mangalore had an income of 930,000 *réis*, but its expenses came to 1,155,300 *réis* a year. Honavar and Basrur, however, had no income but expenses only. The former spent 990,000 *réis* and the latter, 1,386,680 *réis* a year.[132]

In 1635, according to one account, Mangalore had an income of 999,904 *réis* and an expenditure of 238,360 *réis*.[133] Thus, there was a credit balance of 761,544 *réis*. According to another account, in the same year or thereabouts, the fortress of Mangalore earned 750,000 to 900,000 *réis* and spent 620,720 *réis*,[134] leaving a credit balance of 129,280 to 279,280 *réis*. Both accounts show no income at Honavar, Basrur and Gangolly. There were only sources of expenses. According to the former account the expenses of these fortresses were 421,980 *réis*, 376,900 *réis* and 375,200 *réis*, respectively.[135] The other account indicates the corresponding expenses as 907,280 *réis*, 1,028,500 *réis* and 2,185,299 *réis*.[136] The expenses were met with funds or merchandise sent from Goa.

Advisory Council

If the captain needed anything which was not provided for in the ordinance he had to write to the viceroy. However, a lot of time was involved in exchanging communications between a fortress on the Kanara coast and the viceroy at Goa owing to the distance between the two places. If, therefore, the captain had reason to believe that it was dangerous to await a reply from Goa he was to go ahead doing what was necessary. But before acting he had to consult the factor and the writer of his fortress. A minute of the consultation was to be kept. The reason for not waiting for the viceroy's instructions was also to be recorded.[137] The factor and the writer, thus, formed the advisory council of the captain. This was, in a way, on the model of the Council of State that existed in Goa to advise the viceroy.

REFERENCES

1. *História*, II, p. 228.
2. *Lendas*, I, pt. II, p. 561.
3. *D-JB*, I, p. 337.
4. *supra*, p. 19.
5. Barros, however, writes that lime could not be procured by the Portuguese. The stone walls of the forts, therefore, were erected with the help of clay (*D-JB*, I, p. 338).
6. *Lendas*, I, pt. II, p. 562.
7. *Ibid.*, pp. 562-3. According to Barros the commandant of the ship was João Serrão (*D-JB*, p. 338). Faria e Sousa notes that the captain was given 80 men for the defence of the fort. (*Asia Portuguesa*, I, p. 190).
8. *D-JB*, I, p. 338.
9. *História*, II, p. 282.
10. *Assentos*, IV, pp. 388-90.
11. A. C. Teixeira de Aragão, *Descripção geral e história das moedas*, III, p. 261.
12. *Commentários*, IV, p. 79; *Cartas*, I, p. 242.
13. *História*, VI, p. 291.
14. *Ibid.*, VIII, pp. 211-2.
15. *Ibid.*, pp. 213-4. Barros agrees with Castanheda in many of these details, but writes that the Shetty threw up bulwarks at the mouth of the river and placed artillery on it to cause damage to the enemy fleet entering the river; and that in the battle more than 1,000 of the Shetty's men were killed and 13 of the Portuguese too. (*D-JB*, IV, pp. 192-4).
    Correa also gives similar details. He agrees with Barros that 13 of the Portuguese soldiers were killed. (*Lendas*, III, pt. I, pp. 350-3).
16. *História*, IX, p. 532.
17. Manuel de Faria e Sousa, *Asia Portuguesa*, III, p. 267.

18. *D-DC*, VII, pt. II, pp. 61-3.
19. *Ibid.*, VIII, p. 127.
20. *CEO*, II, pp. 229-30.
21. *D-DC*, VIII, pp. 128-30. Bocarro, in his "LPFCP", mentions that the fortress was constructed in 1569 by Luis de Ataide. This seems to be wrong in view of the ordinance issued by Dom Antão de Noronha who was the Viceroy up to September 1568 only. (*Regimentos*, pp. 494-8). Besides, Bocarro was writing about 65 years after the event. (LPFCP, in *APO-BP*, tomo IV, vol. II, pt. I, p. 318).
22. *Regimento*, pp. 496, 498.
23. *LCF*, fl. 42.
24. "LPFCP", in *APO-BP*, *op. cit.*, p. 318.
25. *Ibid.*, p. 320.
26. Faria e Sousa, *op. cit.*, IV, p. 124; F.C. Danvers, *The Portuguese in India*, I, pp. 569-70; G. M. Moraes, *Mangalore*, pp. 12-3.
27. *História*, IX, p. 532.
28. Faria e Sousa, *op. cit.*, III, pp. 19-20.
29. *D-DC*, VIII, p. 272.
30. A.P. Pereyra, *História da India no tempo em que a governo o viso rei Dom Luis de Ataide*, p. 51.
31. *D-DC*, VIII, pp. 273-8. According to Bocarro, the Honavar fortress was established in 1568. "LPFCP", in *APO-BP*, *op. cit.*, p. 307.
32. A.P. Pereyra, *op. cit.*, pp. 55-61. Also see Manuel de Faria e Sousa.
33. A.P. Pereyra, *op. cit.*, pp. 63, 65.
34. *Ibid.*, pp. 150-1; Manuel de Faria e Sousa, *op. cit.*, IV, pp. 66-7.
35. *Ibid.*, p. 151; Manuel de Faria e Sousa, *op. cit.*, IV, p. 82; F.C. Danvers, *op. cit.*, p. 556.
36. Faria e Sousa, *op. cit.*, IV, pp. 92-3; F.C. Danvers, *op. cit*, I, pp. 559-60.
37. *LCF*, fl. 41.
38. "LPFCP", in *APO-BP*, *op. cit.*, p. 307.
39. *D-DC*, VIII, pp. 278-9.
40. *Ibid.*, p. 279.
41. *Ibid.*, pp. 279-80.
42. A. P. Pereyra, *op. cit.*, p. 66.
43. Faria e Sousa, *op. cit.*, IV, pp. 56-7.
44. *Ibid*, pp. 62-3.
45. A. P. Pereyra, *op. cit.*, p. 73.
46. *Regimentos*, pp. 427-8.
47. A.P. Pereyra, *op. cit.*, p. 75; Henry Heras, *The Portuguese fortress of Barcelore*, p. 3. Fr. Heras locates the ruins of this new fortress in the centre of the modern town of Kundapur.
48. *Regimentos*, pp. 428-9.
49. *LCF*, fls. 41-2.

50. "LPFCP", in *APO-BP*, *op. cit.*, p. 313.
51. *Ibid.*, p. 315.
52. *Ibid.*, p. 316.
53. *D-DC*, X, pt. I, pp. 381-3.
54. *Ibid.*, pp. 385-9.
55. *Ibid.*, pp. 390, 417-9.
56. *LCF*, fls. 40-1.
57. "LPFCP", in *APO-BP*, *op. cit.*, pp. 311-2.
58. *Ibid.*, p. 312.
59. *Assentos*, I, p. 249.
60. *Ibid.*, pp. 249, 257-8.
61. *Ibid.*, p. 257.
62. *Ibid.*, p. 248.
63. *Ibid.*, pp. 513-4.
64. *Ibid.*, p. 537.
65. *Ibid.*, pp. 561-2.
66. *Lendas*, I, pt. II, p. 562; *D-JB*, I, p. 338.
67. *Orçamento*, p. 95.
68. *APO-CR*, V, pt. III, p. 1103.
69. *Regimentos*, p. 432.
70. *LCF*, fls. 41, 42.
71. "LPFCP" in *APO-BP*, *op. cit.*, pp. 313-14, 319.
72. *Regimentos*, p. 432.
73. *Ibid.*
74. *Ibid.*, pp. 432-33.
75. *LCF*, fl. 41.
76. *Ibid.*, fls. 41, 42.
77. *Regimentos*, pp. 433, 495.
78. *Ibid.*, pp. 433, 496.
79. *Ibid.*, pp. 432, 496.
80. *Ibid.*, pp. 433, 496.
81. *Ibid.*, p. 495.
82. *Ibid.*, p. 433.
83. "LPFCP" in *APO-BP*, *op. cit.*, pp. 308, 320.
84. *Regimentos*, pp. 433-4; "LPFCP", in *APO-BP*, *op. cit.*, p. 315.
85. "LPFCP", in *APO-BP*, *op. cit.*, pp. 308-9, 320.
86. *Orçamento*, p. 95; *LCF*, fl. 41; "LPFCP", in *APO-BP*, *op. cit.*, pp. 307-308.
87. "LPFCP", in *APO-BP*, *op. cit.*, p. 312.
88. *LCF*, fl. 42.
89. *Ibid.*; *Orçamento*, p. 103.
90. "LPFCP" in *APO-BP*, *op. cit.*, p. 319.
91. *Ibid.*, pp. 312, 318.
92. *Regimentos*, pp. 434, 496; *Orçamento*, pp. 95, 99, 104.
93. *Regimentos*, p. 432; *Orçamento*, p. 100; "LPFCP" in *APO-BP*, *op. cit.*, p. 314.

94. *Regimentos*, p. 494.
95. *Ibid.*, p. 432.
96. *Orçamento*, p. 95; *LCF*, fl. 41; "LPFCP" in *APO-BP*, *op. cit.*, p. 308.
97. *Regimentos*, p. 434.
98. *Ibid.*, p. 432.
99. *Ibid.*, pp. 432, 494; *LCF*, fl. 42.
100. *Orçamento*, p. 96; *LCF*, fl. 41.
101. *Regimentos*, p. 433.
102. *Ibid.*
103. "LPFCP", in *APO-BP*, *op. cit.*, p. 314.
104. *Regimentos*, pp. 495-6.
105. "LPFCP", in *APO-BP*, *op. cit.*, p. 319.
106. *Ibid.*, p. 319; *Orçamento*, p. 96.
107. "LPFCP", in *APO-BP*, *op. cit.*, p. 315; *Regimento*, p. 432.
108. *Orçamento*, p. 95
109. *Regimentos*, p. 495.
110. "LPFCP" in *APO-BP*, *op. cit.*, p. 319.
111. *Regimentos*, p. 432.
112. *Ibid.*, pp. 433, 496.
113. "LPFCP", in *APO-BP*, *op. cit.*, p. 319.
114. *Orçamento*, p. 96.
115. "LPFCP" in *APO-BP*, *op. cit.*, pp. 308-9.
116. *Ibid.*, p. 315; *Regimentos*, pp. 433-4.
117. "LPFCP" in *APO-BP*, *op. cit.*, p. 315; *Regimentos*, pp. 433-4.
118. *Ibid.*
119. *Ibid.*
120. "LPFCP" in *APO-BP*, *op. cit.*, p. 319; *Regimentos*, p. 495.
121. *Regimentos*, pp. 432, 495.
122. *Regimentos*, pp. 432-3, 496.
123. "LPFCP" in *APO-BP*, *op. cit.*, pp. 308, 314; *Regimentos*, p. 433.
124. *Ibid.*
125. *Regimentos*, pp. 434-5, 497-8.
126. *Ibid.*, pp. 429-3.
127. *Ibid.*, pp. 430-1.
128. *Ibid.*, p. 431.
129. *Ibid.*, p. 431.
130. *Orçamento*, pp. 98, 99, 102, 103, 106.
131. *LCF*, fls. 41-2.
132. Falcão, *Livro de Toda a Fazenda*, quoted in *Subsidios para a História Militar Marítima da India*, (vol. I, pp. 638, 640) by Botelho de Sousa. Falcão does not indicate the precise year to which these figures belong, but Botelho de Sousa suggests, taking into consideration the context of Falcão's writings, that the figures might pertain to any one year between 1598 and 1607.
133. *APO-BP*, *op. cit.*, pt. V.

134. "LPFCP" in *APO-BP*, *op. cit.*, p. 320.
135. *APO-BP*, *op. cit.*, pt. V.
136. "LPFCP" in *APO-BP*, *op. cit.*, pp. 309, 312, 315.
137. *Regimentos*, p. 440.

6

THE PORTUGUESE AND THE NAYAKAS OF IKKERI - I (1499-1629)

The Portuguese relations with the Keladi chiefs, better known as the Nayaks of Ikkeri, form an interesting chapter in the history of Kanara. The dynasty of these Nayaks was established in 1499. There were in all 18 members of this family who ruled for about 260 years from 1499 to 1763.

The founder of this ruling house was Chauda Gauda of Keladi, a village in the district of Shimoga. He was a farmer who became rich and influential owing to a treasure that he discovered. Vira Narasimha, the then emperor of Vijayanagara, bestowed upon him the title of Nayaka in 1499. He thus became Chaudappa Nayaka. Keladi and its neighbourhood were entrusted to his care. He ruled as a feudatory of the Vijayanagara emperor for 14 years from 1499 to 1513[1] though only one inscription of the year 1506[2] belonging to him has so far been discovered.

Chaudappa was succeeded by his son Sadashiva Nayaka, who ruled for a long period up to 1565.[3] In 1554 or thereabouts, Sadashiva was appointed governor of Barkur and Mangalore. Aliya Rama Raja, the *de facto* ruler of Vijayanagara, conferred on him this award in appreciation of his military services to the empire. By 1563 Araga, Gutti, Tuluva, Barkur and Mangalore were under Sadashiva.

Dodda Sankanna Nayaka, Sadashiva's elder son, was the next ruler.[4] Sankanna accompanied Vitthala, Aliya Rama Raja's cousin, in a campaign against the Portuguese. It is said that the Portuguese governor of Goa was captured during the course of this campaign.[5] However, no confirmation of this statement can be found in Portuguese sources.

Chikka Sankanna Nayaka and Rama Raja Nayaka were the next two rulers.

During the reign of Venkatappa Nayaka,[6] the sixth ruling member of the dynasty, the kingdom of Keladi was expanded considerable to include the territories from the river Mirjan in north Kanara to the river Chandragiri in Kasaragod. Venkatappa seems to have rejected the suzerainty of the Vijayanagara emperor but only to become a tributory of the Adil Shah of Bijapur. His expansion naturally attracted the attention of the Portuguese as their position on the Kanara coast was very much affected by his conquests.

In a letter to the Viceroy, dated November 21, 1598[7] the King of Portugal instructed the former to watch carefully the doings of Venkatappa Nayaka and to countermine his designs. Wrote the king: "You say that the queen of Bhatkal (who was also the queen of Gersoppa) has not paid for many years the tribute which she owes, because a Nayaka (Venkatappa), who was a vassal of the king of Vijayanagara, but who is now in revolt, demonstrating his intention to subjugate the neighbouring kings, has placed her in a difficult situation; and this being a matter of greater danger for the fortress of Honavar, you shall keep yourself informed of all his doings, countermining his designs." However, neither Francisco da Gama, the Viceroy to whom the letter was addressed, nor his successors could do anything to prevent Venkatappa from becoming the master of practically the whole of Kanara and other territories.

It seems that Venkatappa and Bhaira Devi, queen of Gersoppa, were already at war by 1595. The queen seems to have solicited help not only from the Portuguese but also from the Adil Shah, to both of whom she was paying tributes. The King of Portugal wrote to the Viceroy on January 28, 1596: "You also say that the Adil Shah sent some of his captains against the kings and lords of Kanara at the instance of the queen of Bhatkal (also of Gersoppa) and that the captains would have taken two fortresses at the Ghat had not the revolt of the Adil Shah's brother obliged (the former) to recall them."[8] The Adil Shah's preoccupation with his own affairs gave a free hand to Venkatappa to carry on his expansion wars in north Kanara.

Pietro Della Valle gives an interesting account of what Venkatappa did to Bhaira Devi and his kingdom: "the last Queen of Gersoppa fell in love with a mean man and a stranger, into whose power she resigned herself, together with her whole kingdom. In which act, setting aside her choosing a lover of base blood, upon which account she was blamed and hated by the Indians (who are most rigorous observers of nobility and maintainers of the dignity of their ancestors in all points) as to giving herself up as prey to her lover, she committed no fault against her honour; for in these countries it is lawful for such queens to choose to themselves lovers or husbands, one or more, according as they please. But this man who was so favoured by the Queen of Gersoppa, having thought as ignoble as his blood, instead of corresponding with gratitude to the Queen's courtesie, designed to rebel against her and take the kingdom from her; which design for a while he executed, having in process to time gained the affection of most of her most eminent vassals'.

"The Queen, seeing herself oppressed by the traitor, had recourse to the Portugals, offering them her whole state on condition they would free her from imminent ruins. But the Portugals, according as they had always in India done by their friends (whereby they have been many times the ruins of others and themselves too) did not succour her till it was too late and then very coldly. On the other side the traitor (as his ill fate or rather God's just anger, would have it) called to his assistance against the Queen and the Portugals his neighbour Venktapa Naieka, now Master of those countries. Venktapa Naieka, taking advantage of the occasion, entered suddenly into the kingdom of Gersoppa with great diligence and force, so that, shortly becoming master of the whole country and the city royal, and having driven out the Portugals who came to defend it, he took the Queen prisoner and carried her to his own court; where being kept although honourably, she ended her days in an honourable prison. But the traitor underwent the punishment of his crime, for Venktapa Naieka caused him to be slain; and, for more secure keeping that State in his power, caused the city and royal palace of Gersoppa to be destroyed, so that at this day that lately flourishing city is become nothing but a wood, trees being already grown above the ruins of the houses, and the place scarcely inhabited by four cottages of Peasants."[9]

This decisive war between Venkatappa and Bhaira Devi might have taken place early in 1606 for a letter dated January 16, 1607 written by the King of Portugal to the Viceroy, Martim Affonso de Castro, refers to the kingdom of Gersoppa as already in the possession of Venkatappa.[10] The Portuguese policy at this time was to dissemble with those who sought their assistance. Venkatappa himself asked for their help when he was attacked by the Adil Shah in 1606 or thereabouts, soon after the fall of Gersoppa; so also did the Adil Shah. The Portuguese, however, merely pretended to be responsive but concealed their real intention of not giving actual help to any. In the letter of January 16 (referred to above), the King of Portugal approved the Viceroy's policy of dissemblation saying that it did not suit the Portuguese interest to declare in favour of any of the belligerents.

Now that the kingdom of Gersoppa which extended from Bhatkal to Mirjan, fell to Venkatappa, the Adil Shah became hostile to the Nayaka, particularly because Bhaira Devi was a vassal of the Adil Shah and was paying tributes to him. Venkatappa was not ready to continue to pay this tribute for the territories of Gersoppa, which was a definite loss to the Adil Shah. Besides, the borders of the kingdom of Venkatappa and that of the Adil Shah became coterminous now along the coast. The two, therefore, were drawn into a conflict which lasted until 1611 when Venkatappa was compelled to acknowledge the Adil Shah's overlordship and pay tribute. Though the Portuguese did not want to involve themselves in the conflict they desired Venkatappa's friendship, for pepper and foodgrains which they needed so much came from his territories. Thus, from a letter[11] of the King of Portugal we learn that the captain of Basrur, Luiz de Mendonça, met Venkatappa and offered him whatever assistance possible, pointing out "how convenient it would be for his (Venkatappa's) conservation" to be obedient to the King of Portugal.

Venkatappa was urged to confirm his friendship towards the Portuguese by issuing a declaration, to be proclaimed all along the coast within his jurisdiction, to the effect that the captains of his fortresses should neither allow provisions to pirates, nor admit pirate ships into his ports, and that even if the pirates happened to possess passports, they should be captured and put to death.

Though nothing concrete seems to have been agreed upon, Venkatappa demonstrated friendship towards the Portuguese. However, the latter found it difficult to carry on their pepper trade in Kanara with much profit, as Venkatappa hoped to demand for himself gratifications from the contractors whereby the price of pepper went up. He impeded embarkation of that commodity if his demands were not met with. Learning of this the King of Portugal commanded the Viceroy to consider how best he could remedy the situation without breaking peace with Venkatappa. If he found it impossible to have a solution by himself and got pepper at the old rate, he was instructed to approach either the emperor of Vijayanagara whose vassal Venkatappa was still considered to be, to bring pressure on him, or the Adil Shah of Bijapur, who might be persuaded to wage a war against him. But in approaching the Adil Shah he was to be careful so as not to be discovered in the act.[12]

Whether it was owing to the Portuguese instigation or otherwise, there actually seems to have been an encounter between the forces of the Adil Shah and Venkatappa Nayaka in 1608 and the Viceroy was instructed not to do anything that would bring about peace between the belligerents.[13] But in 1611 or thereabouts, Venkatappa and the Adil Shah entered into a treaty of peace to the great chagrin of the Portuguese. The Viceroy was ordered to continue his efforts to bring the two to the battlefield again.[14] It suited the Portuguese to keep the native powers at war with each other.

Being free from anxiety from the north as a result of peace with the Adil Shah, Venkatappa planned to extend his territories in the south. Luckily for him an opportunity offered itself when the Bangar chief invoked his assistance against the 'king of mountain' (probably the king of Cannanore), who was waging a war against the chief. Venkatappa eagerly extended his help , but in such a manner that the Bangar chief was made his feudatory. He also built a fortress at Bolar, not very far from the Portuguese fortress of Mangalore. This happened probably in 1612.[15] The Bangar chief then turned towards the Portuguese for help.

At this stage, one can review the Portuguese relations with the Bangar chief and the relations of both of these with the Chauter chiefs of Ullala. The Portuguese established friendship with the Bangar chief as early as 1568. They obtained from him not only the site where they built their fortress of Mangalore but also cultivable lands in the neighbourhood of the fortress.[16] These fields seem to have extended in the north up to a rivulet at the distance of a musket-shot from the fortress and the rivulet was considered as the boundary of the Portuguese jurisdiction.[17] The Bangar chief gave them certain trade privileges also, such as non-payment of tolls for articles carried by boats in the rivers within his jurisdiction.[18] The temple, which was within their jurisdiction, seems to have had an annual income of 5,000 *pagodas* which went to them.[19] The Portuguese documents refer to the Bangar chief as always a loyal friend and brother-in-arms to the King of Portugal. Frequently the chief sought Portuguese assistance against his enemies and obtained it, though in varying degrees.

Before the Bangar chief's offer of the Mangalore site for the construction of the fortress the Portuguese had intended to build one within the territories of the kingdom of Ullala. It was a means of safeguarding their own interests against the queen who was not only irregular in paying tribute to the Portuguese but also helped their enemies in Malabar. With these factors in mind the Viceroy, Antão de Noronha, had sailed there with a strong fleet with 3,000 soldiers. At the mouth of the river Netravati, on its south bank, the queen had erected a wall, ten or eleven spans wide, with some watch-towers in which she had placed a few small pieces of cannon. She had stationed 500 soldiers to guard the wall. All along the river as far as the city of Ullala she had deployed about 11,000 soldiers for defence.[20]

The attack was commenced on January 4, 1568. António Pereira, the Viceroy's brother-in-law was entrusted with the task of attacking the city. He was given 500 soldiers. The rest were divided into six contingents. The landing was effected late that evening. The captains and their soldiers took up positions. However, there was no order or discipline among the Portuguese. In the night, which was very dark indeed, Francisco Mascarenhas, one of the commandants, and his soldiers took supper and indulged in revelry, lighting the tent with torches and candles. The enemy, observing this carelessness of the Portuguese, decided to fall upon them suddenly. 2,000 soldiers of Ullala gathered together. 1,500 of them remained at the stockades and 500 descended like an avalanche upon Mascarenhas' camp which was a little more than 100 paces from the wall. The surprise was complete and the Portuguese did not have time even to arm themselves. More than 50 of those who were outside the tent were killed in a trice. However, recovering from the shock, the Portuguese fought back bravely including Mascarenhas who received five wounds. There was much confusion and chaos. The soldiers commanded by other captains ran helter-skelter in the darkness, being unable to distinguish between friend and foe. Mascarenhas lost most of the 600 men whom he commanded. The Viceroy quickly sent 70 men under a captain to relieve Mascarenhas. During the course of this disastrous fight a nobleman suggested to the Viceroy that all should retreat to the fleet, because everything was lost and the enemy was triumphant. The Viceroy was not taken in. Instead, he rallied his men and marched towards the centre of the battlefield. On hearing the trumpets the enemy retreated. In order to prevent the foe from surprising for a second time the Viceroy caused ditches to be dug up, which were completed by one in the morning.[21]

At first the Viceroy decided to attack the city of Ullala on the very next day and made arrangements for it. But later on he decided to postpone the attack to the second day, which caused disappointment to those who were eager to avenge the previous night's insult and disaster. These enthusiastic captains and soldiers, who numbered more than 200, commenced the assault without his orders. Finally, therefore, the Viceroy was compelled to involve the whole army in attacking Ullala on January 5 itself. The Portuguese entered the city and bazaar, killing many of the 6,000 soldiers of the queen who fought in defence, and putting the rest to flight. The palace was set on fire, as also some parts of the city.

Many trees and palm groves were cut down and destroyed. All this lasted only a little over half the day. However, as the Portuguese were returning to the ship, with the wounded, a fresh attack was made upon them by the soldiers of Ullala but no considerable damage befell the Portuguese except the death of one of their brave nobles. The battle of this day cost the Portuguese 35 or 36 lives, but the queen lost more than 300 of her men.[22]

After this successful attack the Viceroy examined the ground on the south bank at the entrance of the river with a view to construct a fortress there. But being dissatisfied he crossed over to the north bank to Mangalore, where finally the fortress was erected with the co-operation of the Bangar chief.

Soon after the Portuguese fortress of Mangalore was constructed the Bangar chief and the queen of Ullala found themselves in hostility. A situation of war did not suit the Portuguese trade interests in the region. Therefore, the Viceroy, Luiz de Ataide, went personally to Mangalore in 1569 to establish peace between the two parties. He found the belligerents ready to accept his mediation and his efforts were crowned with success.[23] (Fr. Heras suggests[24] that the marriage, which was mentioned by Pietro Della Valle,[25] between the queen of Ullala and the Bangar chief, might have taken place after this incident in order to establish the friendship and peace on a firm basis).

However, the queen referred to in 1569 seems to have been a different person from the one whom Della Valle met in 1623. If both the queens were one and the same person, then Della Valle should have found an old woman of about 70 as the queen of Ullala, but Bukka Devi Chautar whom he met was about 40. In fact, between the queens of 1569 and 1623 the kingdom of Ullala seems to have been ruled by a king.[26] Besides, there were some more occasions after 1569 when the chiefs of Ullala and Bangher quarrelled.

Though the queen of Ullala agreed in 1569 to be on friendly terms with the Bangar chief she remained secretly hostile towards the Portuguese. She sought an opportunity to free herself from the tribute which the Portuguese had imposed upon her. That is why she took advantage of the troubles in which the Portuguese were placed in 1570-4, as a result of the confederacy organised against them by the Adil Shah. She had instigated the Zamorin's admiral to attack the Portuguese fortress of Mangalore and with much success.[27]

By 1589 the Bangar chief and the ruler of Ullala, who was now king, fell out again. The latter gained an upper hand. From a letter dated January 12, 1591, written by the King of Portugal to the governor, we learn that the king of Ullala had deprived the Bangar chief of almost the whole of his kingdom. The Portuguese made some intrusions into the territories of Ullala, probably on behalf of the Bangar chief. The king of Ullala professed to be a friend and vassal of the Portuguese. However, he built a fortress, probably in the rainy season of 1589, not far from the Portuguese fortress of Mangalore, on the opposite bank of the river. The Portuguese could not block the construction owing to the rains. For its defence the king of Ullala employed 30,000 men. The governor ordered the captain-major of the Malabar fleet to go personally to Mangalore and endeavour to make peace between the ruler of Ullala and the Bangar chief. The new fortress was to be destroyed. If the king of Ullala did not come to terms the captain-major was to wage a war on him.[28]

An account of what the captain-major, Thome de Souza Coutinho, did to the king of Ullala is given in a document dated August 22, 1591, and signed by the captain-major himself. He departed from Goa on December 1, 1589, with three galleys and 30 ships. Arriving at Mangalore he informed the king of Ullala that he had come there at the instance of the Governor in order to bring the belligerents to peace on the basis of just terms, particularly the restitution of territories captured from each other. He invited the king for a talk. After a delay of many days the king met the captain-major off the fortress of Ullala. He promised that he would destroy the fortress the following day and would enter into a just peace. However, he did not keep up the promise. Thereupon the major declared war against him on behalf of the Bangar chief. Many palm trees in Ullala were cut down. A temple, much venerated and well defended, was captured and entrusted to the Bangar chief who compensated the Portuguese with 1,000 *pagodas* and a piece of cannon. The major then set sail along the coast and captured Bedrette and other places. All together more than 1,000 palm trees were cut down during the course of these attacks. Many people were put to death. Later on, he provided the fortress of Mangalore with whatever it needed, including 90 soldiers.[29]

However, the fortress of Ullala escaped destruction on this occasion. For in a letter of February 15, 1593, the King of Portugal was still expressing his displeasure at the existence of the fortress, in spite of his orders of 1590 and 1591 to his governor to get it destroyed.[30] The Viceroy continued to endeavour to make friends with the ruler of Ullala (now a queen) and the Bangar chief but he was instructed by the King of Portugal by a letter dated March 1, 1594 that no peace should be concluded without a provision for the destruction of the fortress.[31] In case the queen was not to agree to such a term, the Viceroy was instructed to capture the fortress whenever an opportunity offered itself.[32]

Moreover, it seems that the fortress was at last demolished by the queen in 1594. This was probably because she was involved in a war against 'the king of the mountain'. Yet the King of Portugal was informed that the destruction of the fortress was not effective, because the foundations were intact and that with a few days' labour and very little material it could be reconstructed. The Viceroy, therefore was ordered to secure complete destruction of the foundations also.[33]

After the destruction of the fortress there was peace not only between Ullala and the Portuguese but also between the queen of Ullala and 'the king of the mountain'. The latter was at peace with the Portuguese. The Governor requested the Bangar chief to compose the differences between the belligerents but not to help 'the king of mountain' at any rate against the queen.[34]

When the Bangar chief asked for Portuguese assistance in 1612 against Venkatappa they were not ready to extend it. They hesitated because Venkatappa was a powerful chief, unlike the rulers of Ullala against whom they rarely hesitated in aiding the chief. In the territories of Venkatappa they had commercial interests; they had several fortresses there; food supplies required for their Kanara fortress and for Goa, Hormuz and Muscat came from his regions; above all those were the days when they had Europeans rivals in India and elsewhere. Considering these they were not willing to help the chief openly but they were ready to encourage and advise him and personally aid him in an indirect manner.

Thus, they endeavoured to form a confederacy against Venkatappa. The Bangar chief, the 'king of the mountain' and the queen of Karnad were to be allied. The Portuguese themselves were to be out of it. The Viceroy sent Henrique de Noronha, captain-major of the Portuguese fleet of Malabar, to forge this alliance. Noronha, on reaching Mangalore, invited these three chiefs to the fortress of Mangalore where he tried to impress upon them the necessity of a united front against the common foe. He assured them of whatever help the Portuguese could give. His effort was rewarded with success. The three chiefs declared themselves allied and swore to help each other. The captain-major received thanks from them for this labour.[35]

This alliance was joined later on by three more chiefs, namely, those of Ajilara, Condegare and Ullala. The Bangar chief, acting on behalf of the allies, wrote to the Viceroy seeking Portuguese aid in the form of a fleet to take the fortress of Mombalão (?) and the bazaar of Ullala, which were apparently in the possession of Venkatappa. He also informed him that the queen of Ullala would pay an annual tribute of 3,000 loads of rice if she was allowed 30 Portuguese soldiers for her fortress at Torotale (?). The Portuguese were caught in a dilemma. On the one hand, Venkatappa was becoming more and more powerful and should the allies be defeated by him the Portuguese fortresses in Kanara would all the more be in danger and the Bangar chief, leader of the allies, and the chief of Karnad were always loyal, paying the Portuguese regularly the tribute they owed and it would be a discredit to the Portuguese not to help them in their need.

On the other hand, the territories of Venkatappa provided the Portuguese 2,850 quintals of pepper which might not be available to them if he was antagonised by their help to his enemies; besides he would attack their fortresses at Honavar, Basrur and Mangalore. The whole matter was considered by the Viceroy-in-Council and it was finally decided that the allies should be helped, but in such a way that there was no risk with regard to procuration of pepper in Venkatappa's territories; that pepper should be gathered on the arrival of the fleet from Portugal; that the allies should be entreated and encouraged, help being offered when time permitted; that it was undesirable, as long as there was professed friendship between the Portuguese and Venkatappa, to write and urge him not to wage war against the allies, because it was well-known that he would not desist from attacking the allies merely because the Portuguese did not want to find them in a helpless position.[36] In short, no open aid was to be given to the allies, but encouragement, lest the pepper supplies and the fortresses of Kanara be endangered.

In 1615, the Bangar chief wrote directly to the King of Portugal informing him how Venkatappa and other enemies had leagued themselves to oust the chief from the kingdom. In spite of the Portuguese efforts to the contrary Venkatappa was becoming the master of Kanara. The Viceroy was instructed by his king to help the chief in such a way that Venkatappa did not prevail against the chief. The King of Portugal also sent a reply to the chief urging him to go ahead against his enemies.[37] The Portuguese realised that if Venkatappa wanted to attack their fortresses he could do so, causing them considerable damage. The King therefore ordered the Viceroy to adopt a cautious policy to see that Venkatappa did not become all-powerful in Kanara.[38]

Early in 1616 Bernardo, a Portuguese captain on his way to Malabar, anchored his fleet at Mangalore for a brief time. The Bangar chief immediately met him and sought aid against Venkatappa. The captain merely offered to come with his fleet precisely when it was necessary. The Bangar chief pleaded that it was the proper time to aid, but Bernardo excused himself saying that he had to proceed to Cochin urgently and that other Portuguese fleets of the coast might help him. The chief understood very well that the Portuguese intention was to contemporise with everyone; but did not give up all hope of getting assistance from the Portuguese.[39]

In the same year the chief and the queen of Ullala seem to have fallen out once again and the latter allied herself with Venkatappa. The chief, with the assistance of the king of Cannanore, deprived the queen of her territories until at last she was left with only one fortress which he boasted he could take easily. Writing of these to the Viceroy the chief urged the former to aid him with a fleet to defend and maintain his newly acquired position, fearing, no doubt, that Venkatappa would soon come to the rescue of the queen. He also approached the captain of the Portuguese fortress of Mangalore requesting him to send men to enable him to build a fortress in Ullala. The captain responded by saying that he could do nothing without the Viceroy's orders. At the same time the former wrote to the Viceroy who ordered the captain not to commit himself to any help, pointing out that though the Bangar chief was a brother-in-arms to the King of Portugal, the queen of Ullala was on friendly terms with the Portuguese. To the Bangar chief, the Viceroy wrote encouraging him against his enemies and promising him all help, should the time and occasion arise. The chief was, however, urged not to build the fortress which be planned to erect in Ullala. The chief was extremely disappointed with these replies. Soon the scales of fortune turned against him in the war,[40] for Venkatappa joined hands against him.

On November 29, 1616, the chief once again wrote to the Viceroy complaining of the little help given by the Portuguese, but this letter also had no effect. The Viceroy did not send any assistance. By this time he had lost most of his kingdom to Venkatappa. Early in 1617 the latter demanded the Bangher fortress itself which was located at Codial Bail. He also declared his intention of erecting a fortress there nearby. The chief cleverly handed over the keys of the fortress to the captain of the Portuguese fortress of Mangalore and replied to Venkatappa saying that he should ask the Bangher fortress from the Portuguese.

Being informed of these developments from the chief as well as the captain of Mangalore, the Viceroy-in-Council decided that the Bangar chief ought to be aided for enabling him to defend and sustain and also for not allowing Venkatappa to become all powerful; that the aid must, however, be given by dissimulation so as not to break with Venkatappa completely; that the Viceroy should send to Mangalore 70 soldiers under two captains, all to obey the captain of Mangalore; that these should defend the fortress of Bangher, but only if Venkatappa began to attack it and if the queen of Ullala, his ally, proceeded to rebuild her fortress which had been destroyed in 1594; that as long as Venkatappa and the queen did not do so the Portuguese should continue their friendship; that in the meantime no open war should be declared against Venkatappa, but that the Viceroy should send to the chief some pieces of cannon, as the latter had lost all of his; and that a letter should be sent to Venkatappa requesting him to desist from molesting the Bangar chief. The Viceroy actually sent the men and the pieces of cannon decided upon, together with gunpowder, ammunitions and also 500 *xerafins* to construct a bulwark. A letter was sent to Venkatappa as decided.[41]

It seems that the Bangar chief was not without successes against his powerful enemy, Venkatappa. We learn from a letter of February 1619 written by the Viceroy to the King of Portugal that the Bangar chief 'took' from Venkatappa the fortress of Bangher on February 20, 1618 after a siege of two months. It is probable that Venkatappa had taken the fortress some time in 1617 and that the Bangar chief, with the aid of the Portuguese, succeeded in regaining it. The Portuguese had in fact kept on sending assistance to Mangalore. Towards the end of 1617 they had dispatched ten soldiers under the command of António de Saldanha with gunpowder and explosives. Later, on March 16, 1618, they had sent Gaspar Pita de Almeida with 93 soldiers. On regaining his fortress the Bangar chief once again desired to entrust it to the care of the Portuguese, no doubt, being fully aware that Venkatappa would soon attack the fortress with greater vigour.

The Portuguese seem to have realised by now that it was impossible for them to defend the fortress against Venkatappa. Accordingly, António de Saldanha to whom the keys of the fortress were offered by the chief, refused to accept them. Instead, he advised the chief to dismantle and pull down the fortress. If it was not possible to do so within a month, then it was to be defended until the rains set in.[42] In the rainy season it was, of course, easier to demolish it, particularly because Venkatappa could not be in a position to attack it effectively then.

However, Venkatappa seems to have returned to the attack much earlier than expected. By April or May, 1618, he pressed upon the Bangar chief so much that the latter was obliged to leave the fortress entirely to the care of the Portuguese who could not avoid the responsibility now. The chief retired to Kasaragod from where he wanted to approach the king of Cannanore and other royals in order to get assistance from them and then to return to attack once more. However, he did not get any aid from those quarters and did not venture to attack Venkatappa again.[43]

After the departure of the chief the fortress of Bangher was assaulted several times by Venkatappa's men. Besides, the latter began to build a fort in Mangalore. The queen of Ullala openly assisted Venkatappa's men. Receiving information regarding those developments the Viceroy "was forced to deploy 500 soldiers, rather more than less", who were led from Goa by Francisco de Menezes, who had just come from Bassein, probably to live in Goa in retirement. He was an experienced but aged noble who had participated, with credit, in many a battle at Bassein. In the meantime Venkatappa's men launched many attacks upon the fortress of Bangher but were repulsed vigorously every time. During the course of these assaults the Portuguese lost only ten or eleven men, but caused more loss to the enemy.[44]

Nevertheless, Venkatappa's men seem to have gained an upper hand. For in July, 1618 Menezes repeatedly sought relief from Goa, informing the Viceroy that Venkatappa was investigating every means of investing more effectively men and money in the siege of the Bangher fortress in order to take it before the Bangar chief returned from Kasaragod. The Viceroy dispatched Francisco de Miranda Henriques with a fleet of 8 ships.[45]

From Kasaragod the Bangar chief wrote to the Viceroy complaining that the king of Cannanore was delaying in giving help, either because he had no means to extend the actual help or because he had no intention of keeping his promise. However, Adda Raja, probably a feudatory of Cannanore, explained in another letter to the Viceroy that the king of Cannanore was not in a position to help the chief at the moment as he was engaged in settling some domestic troubles. The chief at any rate seems to have lost all hope of receiving help and therefore requested the Viceroy to intervene as a third party between him and Venkatappa and reconcile them as best as he could. So also Kamanna, the chief's minister or *adioar* who as in the Bangher fortress along with the Portuguese, wrote to him in similar terms.

The Portuguese captains in Mangalore suggested that a peace treaty might be arranged between Venkatappa and the Bangar chief in which the latter would pay an annual tribute to the former. Taking into account these matters, the Viceroy-in-Council decided that the Viceroy should forge an understanding between the belligerents, but with the caution that Venkatappa did not come to know that he had initiated the negotiations. It was, therefore, decided to use João Fernandez Leitão, captain of Honavar, who seems to have written to the Viceroy already concerning the possibility of establishing peace with Venkatappa. Diogo Lobo, captain of the city of Goa and member of the Council of State, who was also a relative of Leitão, was asked to write to the latter to find out an opportunity to begin peace talks.[46]

Salvador Ribeiro Marinho, captain of Mangalore, reported that the Portuguese fortress was without artillery as the eight pieces that were there were destroyed, no doubt, by Venkatappa. All the Portuguese commandants who were in Mangalore agreed that under no circumstances should the Bangher fortress be allowed to be taken by Venkatappa, because being its master he would attack the Portuguese fortress of Mangalore, since the latter contained a temple. Better defence and offence arrangements, therefore, were to be made at Mangalore. The palm groves and other trees around the fortress were to be cut down so that explosives could be discharged from the fortress unobstructed to cause greater damage if the enemies besieged it. The owners of the trees were to be paid the value of their property. The expenses on this count were calculated to be less than 35,000 *xerafins*. Six pieces of cannon were to be sent. Both the fortresses of Mangalore and Bangher were to be staunchly defended. The construction of the fortress at Mangalore by Venkatappa was also to be obstructed.[47]

There seems to have been much disorder and lack of discipline in the Portuguese camp at Mangalore. The captain general of the war of Mangalore, Francisco de Menezes, fired thrice at his own men led by Francisco de Miranda Henriques, captain-major of the Portuguese fleet of Malabar, creating a scandal. The mistake seems to have happened partly owing to the old age and infirmity of the captain general. He himself realised this and wrote to the Viceroy requesting him to relieve him of his position. The request was granted and Luiz de Brito e Mello was appointed his successor.[48]

On December 26, 1618 Mello sailed forth from Goa in a ship with 30 soldiers and six pieces of cannon. Soon after his arrival at Mangalore he and Henriques decided to take the fortress which Venkatappa had erected by now between the Grand Tank and the Portuguese fortress. An attack was launched upon on January 7, 1619, with unfortunate results for the Portuguese. Brito and Henriques were killed, together with 20 other captains and nobles. Among their soldiers more than 200 were killed, 20 or so were taken prisoner and more than 30 took to flight. The disaster occurred because Brito and Henriques proceeded without the Viceroy's orders and contrary to his instructions which he had given them at the time of their departure from Goa. The latter who had been to Malabar before the arrival of the former at Mangalore was unwilling to stay at Kasaragod for a day or two for the Bangar chief who would have been then ready with his forces to come with Henriques to fight Venkatappa. Besides, the Portuguese commanders at Mangalore were known for their mutual distrust and lack of cooperation. Brito and another captain quarrelled over the issue as to who should carry the flag. This led to the delay of one day in commencing the attack and the enemy was not only informed of the imminent attack but also got time to prepare for the defence. Further, Christovão de Brito, captain of Bangher, and Adigar, captain-major of the forces of the Bangar chief there, had warned that the Portuguese should not come out of their fortress of Mangalore.[49]

After these disastrous defeats the Portuguese position in Mangalore became very precarious. To send substantial reliefs, the viceroy did not have sufficient money. Gomes da Silva, who was escaping from Mangalore with merchandise valued at 8,000 *pagodas* was robbed on the way to Goa. However, some generous nobles and captains offered their services and to sail forth at their own cost to defend Mangalore. The Viceroy accepted the services of three of these generous ones: Francisco de Manuel, Manuel de Andrade Berenguer and Francisco Pinto Pimenta.[50] Salvador Ribeiro Marinho, who was sincere and able continued to be the captain of the Mangalore fortress. Gaspar de Mello e Sampaio was appointed captain-major of the war of Mangalore.

While this difficult situation continued at Mangalore, Venkatappa approached the English for selling them his pepper. In February 1619 he sent his messenger to Swally where the English were. The latter were told that Venkatappa could provide pepper enough for two 'good' ships. The English decided to send to Ikkeri two representatives to see the commodities and fix the price. Venkatappa's messengers left at Swally some of their companions as hostages and returned with the English representatives.[51] It is not possible to say what happened to this negotiation. Probably, the English procured pepper from Venkatappa that year. But in March 1620, by which time a peace treaty between the Portuguese and Venkatappa was signed, we find Venkatappa approaching the Portuguese and the latter agreeing to purchase the commodity from him.[52] Besides, elsewhere we are told that in October of the same year four English ships were moving about the coast of Kanara with a view to secure pepper, but Venkatappa did not want to receive them.[53]

In the meantime the Portuguese desired to reconcile Venkatappa with the Bangar chief and to free themselves from the fruitless expenses involved in the defence of the Bangher fortress. But the chief does not seem to have been so eager to accept peace, though he had written to the Viceroy requesting him to intercede as a peace maker. In March, 1619, the Portuguese sent a fleet to Kasaragod to take the Bangar chief from there to Cannanore where he still hoped to get succour with which he intended to recover his lost kingdom from Venkatappa. The fleet was to be at his disposal only up to the middle of May. There was, however, no sign of any assistance coming to him as he was poor and was not in a position to pay even to a few soldiers who were with him. His neighbouring rulers were not eager to come to his rescue.

Considering all these the Viceroy-in-Council came to the conclusion on April 5 that the Portuguese should disentangle themselves from the conflict between Venkatappa and the Bangar chief; that instead of spending money ungainfully in assisting the chief it should be employed to strengthen the fortress of Mangalore and to pay the soldiers; that at the end of the rainy season an effort should be made to reconcile the belligerents; and that the Bangher fortress should be given up, but in such a way that the Portuguese benefited by doing so.[54]

Gaspar Afonso de Mello de Sampaio, captain-major of the war of Mangalore, wrote to the Viceroy on April 2, 1619, giving him an account of his meeting with the Bangar chief who was brought to Mangalore from Kasaragod. The chief seems to have insisted upon the formalities and honours due to a king, which the Portuguese captains seem to have extended, though not whole-heartedly. He did not wish to land at Mangalore, but remain in the ship in which he was brought; nor did he consent to go to the Portuguese fortress. Finally, he agreed to go to Sampaio's house. At night he desired to return but was ultimately prevailed upon to go to Bangher to enthuse his men there, though he had declared that he would not set his feet in Bangher until he became its ruler again.

The next morning there was a meeting between him and the Portuguese captains in Sampaio's house. Sampaio pointed out that the Portuguese had always extended to him whatever assistance was possible for them right from the beginning of the hostilities between the chief and Venkatappa; that the Portuguese continued to extend this favour in the form of men and money as before, trusting in the chief's promises that he would attack Kumbala today, Manjeshwara tomorrow and Ullala thereafter; that the chief, however, was inactive and unenthusiastic; and that he did not trust the Portuguese who were his loyal supporters, but had repugnance towards them. He was asked to say what was his plan which he would really execute. He was urged to pay the three years' arrears of tribute to Venkatappa who was too powerful for him. At the same time the Viceroy would send him 500 local soldiers of Goa, as those 500 who were already at Bangher were tired. The only response that came from the chief was a question whether the Viceroy had sent him the 20,000 *xerafins* which he had asked for. The chief apparently had said before that if the Portuguese would send him a fleet he would secure the services of the Nairs of Malabar but when a fleet was actually sent to be at his disposal for two months not a single Nair or any other soldier came with him.

He was now urged to stay at Bangher and enthuse his people. It was better, he was told, to live in his own fortress rather than in a cottage in Kasaragod. However, his female relatives would not allow him to do what he wanted to do. Apparently, the temple within the Portuguese fortress had an annual endowment of 5,000 *pagodas* which the chief asked for his own maintenance. Concerning peace terms with Venkatappa, the chief said that he could go only to the Portuguese for help, as all were friends to Venkatappa who was very powerful, whereas he himself was poor and disgraced, unfit to be favoured by anyone. Sampaio, however, promised him all friendly co-operation by the Portuguese.[55]

Sampaio suggested to the Viceroy that there was no alternative but to negotiate for peace, more on Venkatappa's terms than on the terms of the Bangar chief; and that the Adil Shah, to whom Venkatappa paid an annual tribute of 36,000 *pagodas*, could be requested to instruct the latter to raise the siege of Bangher and to conclude a treaty with the chief.[56] Meanwhile, Puttappa, one of the ministers of Venkatappa, had sent an envoy with letters to Goa. Therefore, on receiving Sampaio's letter, the Viceroy-in-Council, who were disillusioned with the Bangar chief, decided to give up the cause of Bangher and to go ahead with Puttappa's envoy. However, the Portuguese fortress of Mangalore, which needed money and materials, was to be strengthened at the same time.[57]

The negotiations for peace were initiated by the captain of Honavar, João Fernandez Leitão, at the instance of the Viceroy. Leitão sent Simão Leal with a letter to Puttappa who was the most favourite administrator whom Venkatappa trusted. Puttappa was told that if he was to send a man of good understanding to Goa the Viceroy would negotiate for peace and friendship. He reacted to this favourably and requested Leitão, through Leal that the Viceroy be informed that he would send a messenger to Goa. Later on, he actually sent Nagoji Pandita with a letter to the Viceroy. He pointed out that the Portuguese were not justified in sheltering the Bangar chief against Venkatappa because the latter was merely bringing a rebel to the right path by chastising him.

The Viceroy was requested to withdraw the assistance which was still being extended to the chief, so that one obstacle on the path of friendship between the Portuguese and Venkatappa would be removed. Pandita was commissioned to say that the fortress of Bangher, which belonged to the Bangar chief, and not to the Portuguese, should be ceded to Venkatappa, overlord of the chief; that the Portuguese, should withdraw their help which they had sent to Bangher; that Puttappa was aware that Bangher was virtually in the hands of the Portuguese, who had paid for it with men and money, and therefore they might not find it easy to give it up; but that Puttappa was helpless, it being the wish of his master, Venkatappa, that he should get the fortress; and that the latter could be induced to begin peace talks if the Bangar chief was made to give him money, good elephants and other things.[58]

On studying these statements the Viceroy-in-Council decided to respond amicably to Puttappa's mission. He was told clearly that the Portuguese had no intention to wage any war against Venkatappa, but only to defend their less powerful neighbour and friend, the Bangar chief, from his enemies; and that the Viceroy would rejoice to mediate between their two friends, Venkatappa and the chief, and bring about an honest settlement in which Venkatappa would not lose what was his and the chief would not remain shorn of his kingdom. Leitão, who had initiated the negotiation with Puttappa, was chosen to continue the peace talks. He and Puttappa were to settle mutually where they should meet. Leitão was instructed to endeavour to secure restoration of the kingdom of Bangher to its chief, who would pay Venkatappa his due, after which the two would resume friendly relations which they had before. If these terms were not acceptable either to Venkatappa or to the Bangar chief, he was to negotiate then for getting Venkatappa's consent for the chief to dismantle the Bangher fortress, as it was not in the interests of the Portuguese to allow the fortress to be.

The Viceroy-in-Council decided upon a third alternative of which Leitão was not informed at the moment. If neither of the first two alternatives was acceptable to the belligerents, the Portuguese were to hand over the keys of the Bangher fortress either to the chief himself or to his minister and then withdraw their troops and artillery, telling the chief to defend his fortress as best as he could. The chief was to be informed of their intention to hand over the keys some days in advance. Finally, it was decided that Sampaio should be kept informed of the developments in peace negotiations so that he could consult the Bangar chief from time to time in order to obtain the latter's views in the matter.[59]

Leitão found Venkatappa rather unenthusiastic about peace talks. Puttappa did not come down for a meeting, though he was expected to. Leitão then sent Rama Krishna, interpreter of the fortress of Honavar, who was a practical Brahmin of good qualities, to Ikkeri, with a letter addressed to Venkatappa. Rama Krishna reached Ikkeri, presented the letter to Venkatappa and awaited for days for an answer. Ultimately, Venkatappa told him curtly that time was not yet ripe for negotiations. The envoy, however, learnt from Puttappa that the Nayaka expected a war compensation of 100,000 *pagodas* from the Bangar chief if he wanted to be restored.

Nevertheless, Puttappa suggested that Venkatappa might agree to any one of the following alternatives: (1) The fortress of Bangher should be ceded to him and he would compensate the chief with some lands; (2) The fortress should be destroyed in which case the chief would be compensated too; or (3) If neither of these was acceptable the Portuguese should give up Bangher fortress and Venkatappa would be friendly towards them. At any rate, Venkatappa was not prepared to restore the kingdom of Bangher to its chief. However, he was willing to provide the chief with the means of livelihood if he agreed peacefully to cede the fortress of Bangher. On being told of these by the envoy, Leitão made them known to the Bangar chief, his minister and Sampaio. Of course, he informed the Viceroy also through a letter dated June 15. The latter, in consultation with his Council, decided that Leitão should continue to negotiate with Venkatappa on the basis of the latter's offer to compensate the chief if he consented to dismantle the fortress of Bangher. Besides, Venkatappa was to be told that the soldiers of Bangher should not be subjected to any damage. Instead they should be given freedom to go wherever they wanted to go in order to earn their livelihood.

In the meantime the chief seems to have gone to Kasaragod once again. Venkatappa tried to pressurise the Portuguese by hindering their trade at Honavar where Leitão was not permitted to transport the timber sold to him.[60]

The second series of negotiations showed signs of better results. Venkatappa agreed to give the Bangar chief the territories of Nandavara and Mogarnar (?), both together yielding 2,400 *pagodas* and 8 *fanams*; of Sazapú, yielding 764 *pagodas* and 8 *fanams*; and of Belur, yielding 473 *pagodas* and 2 *fanams*. These lands fetched additional income in the form of customs. All together the lands were worth 4,925 *pagodas* and 7 *fanams* a year. The chief was to destroy the Bangher fortress at Codial Bail.

This was to be followed by the destruction of two more fortresses which Venkatappa had newly erected at Nandavara and Parangary (Uppinangady) within the territories to be given to the chief. So also all the stockades that were erected during the course of the war were to be pulled down. Finally, the chief was to give to Venkatappa an elephant, named Padmanabha. Rama Krishna secured these terms which were soon made known to the Viceroy. Venkatappa wrote to Leitão appreciating his untiring labours in the negotiations. He also asked Rama Krishna to write in Kannada to the Bangher chief informing him of the terms, which was done. The Viceroy-in-Council commanded Leitão to accept the terms offered by Venkatappa even if the Bangar chief was not prepared to consent to them. The Portuguese contention was that they were not obliged to defend Bangher which was abandoned by its chief who was away in Kasaragod and was doing nothing to relieve it in spite of repeated requests by them.[61]

The chief was disappointed when he saw the terms offered by Venkatappa. He considered the territories and their income to be given to him as inadequate to his station and insufficient for even one month's expenses. He became bitter when he learnt that the terms were accepted without his consent. He was also informed to his great chagrin that the Portuguese garrison, which was defending Bangher, was required for services elsewhere. He complained to the Viceroy that he was kept out of the process of arriving at the decision, particularly with regard to the destruction of his fortress, though the subject of negotiations was his. However, he told the Viceroy that he was helpless and therefore would accept the terms offered, emphasizing that he did so because the Viceroy wanted him to do so. He lamented that he had lost his kingdom and had no place to set his feet. Yet, as long as the Portuguese had means to support him he could remain without his kingdom, because he was sure that the Viceroy would restore him his kingdom one day, as his brother-in-arms, King of Portugal, would require him to do. In reply to all these the latter told him curtly that there was nothing more to be done and that the chief need not write to him any more on the subject.[62]

Ishwara Shenoy, the Bangar chief's envoy at Ikkeri, wrote to Leitão complaining that he was not informed, when he was in Honavar, that the destruction of the Bangher fortress was one of the conditions of the peace treaty with Venkatappa. He contended that peace negotiations were not only his business but his as well, since he was also to participate in them actively, talking face to face with Venkatappa, according to his master, the Bangar chief's orders.[63]

Though the chief wrote to the Viceroy as well as to Leitão, expressing his readiness to accept the terms offered by Venkatappa and to abide by what the Viceroy commanded him, he seems to have endeavoured to secure better terms by sending independent instructions to Shenoy. He seems to have desired particularly to secure more compensation than what was offered. Learning of this Leitão began to censure the chief's communications to Shenoy. He did not allow the chief's messengers free movements until the chief was compelled to desist from his course. Besides, the latter was very slow in responding the communications from the Portuguese. Sampaio had to employ a ship with 90 men in order to find out where he was and to bring him to Mangalore for negotiations. Leitão feared that such delays might enrage Venkatappa who might withdraw from peace talks. The Viceroy wrote to Sampaio saying that the chief was out with fresh excuses to delay the execution of the treaty, since he had instructed his man at Ikkeri in terms which did not conform to what he had written to Leitão; that Sampaio should complain of this to the chief who should clearly be told not to expect any aid from the Portuguese with regard to the restoration of his lost kingdom.[64]

Leitão also wrote curtly to the chief saying that if the latter was not satisfied with what he was doing he should look after the fortress alone as best as he could. Nevertheless, the Portuguese successfully tried to secure more concessions to the chief. At this stage it was felt necessary that the queen of Ullala, who had sided with Venkatappa, should also be a partner in the final treaty. Leal, Leitão's envoy to the court of Venkatappa, was instructed on this matter.[65]

After his further audiences with Venkatappa, Leal gave Leitão an account of the talks and the results thereof. Of course, Leal had tried to proceed about his work speedily. Thus, as soon as he had received fresh instructions he had sent a messenger to the camp of Venkatappa, who was at Belur waging a war against its chief, in order to find out whether it was possible to have an audience with Venkatappa there. The messenger returned with the intelligence that it was of no use to go to Belur, since Venkatappa was too busy dealing with the Belur chief. Instead, it was suggested to him that he should proceed to the fortress of Durga where Venkatappa was expected to go soon.

Accordingly, Leal went to Durga where he reached on November 3. Venkatappa came there on the 8th but as he arrived late and tired Leal did not talk to him on that day. On the following day a messenger came from Mangalore carrying two letters, one from Sampaio and the other from the Bangar chief. Sampaio probably urged that the peace treaty should be concluded as speedily as possible in order to have regular supply of foodgrains from the territories of Venkatappa who had prevented such supply to pressurise the Portuguese. The Bangar chief seems to have indicated his readiness to accept the terms offered by Venkatappa, provided additional monetary concessions were obtained for him. On being presented Leitão's letter Venkatappa responded, after reading it, that nothing more ought to be given to the chief than what he had already agreed to give. With this answer he sent Leal away.

The latter, however, sought the intervention of Puttappa who took him to the palace where Venkatappa was urged to concede 3,000 *pagodas* more to the chief. Finally, Venkatappa consented to give an additional sum of about 2,000 *pagodas,* thus making the total about 7,000 *pagodas*, with the conditions that the Bangher fortress should be destroyed, though the inner circle was to be left intact if the population desired so; that the Bangar chief should come to live in the fortress of Nandavara or any other place in the territories of Venkatappa; that the latter would never erect a fortress at Bangher nor would he raise an army there to wage war against the Bangar chief, and that Venkatappa as well as the queen of Ullala would destroy the fortresses and stockades erected during the course of the war. Leal urged that the site of the Bangher fortress be left to the chief. Venkatappa flared up at this suggestion and ordered him to leave forthwith. With great difficulty Leal managed to secure another audience with him and urged him to grant six days' time to let Leitão know of the term in dispute. The king refused to grant even half an hour. Whereupon Leal begged for a quarter of an hour to consult the interpreter. This was conceded.

Leal and the interpreter decided to signify acceptance of the terms, fearing that if they were rejected the Portuguese as well as the Bangar chief might land in trouble and risk a war with Venkatappa. On hearing the decision Venkatappa agreed that Leitão be informed of these terms. At first it was decided that the interpreter should carry the message to Leitão but finally Venkatappa sent one of his *amaldars* along with one of Leal's men. Answer was to be brought within six days. Venkatappa also agreed that the fields near the Portuguese fortress of Mangalore should be left to the Portuguese; that the embarkations belonging to the *cazados* and the residents of Mangalore should be permitted as before; and that Puttappa should go to Gersoppa to sign the treaty of peace and friendship. The revenue of the cultivable lands conceded to the Portuguese was to be deducted from the sum to be given to the

Bangar chief. Leal wrote to Sampaio and the Bangar chief informing them of these developments.[66]

On November 11, Venkatappa himself wrote to Leitão, saying that he had decided in the beginning not to give anything to the Bangar chief, taking into account what the latter had done against him but subsequently he changed his mind and conceded lands yielding a total income of about 5,000 *pagodas*. However, the chief was not satisfied with the sum and Leitão had written on behalf of the chief asking for more. Knowing that the latter and his ancestors were loyal formally, Venkatappa decided to grant him an additional sum of 2,000 *pagodas* with the following conditions: (1) The fortress of Bangher should be destroyed, (2) The chief should give to Venkatappa the elephant named Padmanabha, (3) Venkatappa would destroy the two fortresses erected in Nandavara and Uparangary (Uppinangady), (4) He would also instruct his administrator in Codial Bail to destroy all his stockades, (5) If the Bangar chief was not prepared to accept these terms Venkatappa would no more deal with him for peace and Leitão should no more write about it, (6) The Portuguese garrison in the Bangher fortress should then be withdrawn. Venkatappa also specified in his letter the various territories and the yields thereof which he proposed to give the chief. Leitão was asked to send a reply within four days, because Venkatappa was tired of the delays which were caused so far.[67]

Leitão saw no objection to the terms offered by Venkatappa since they were in keeping with the Viceroy's instructions. However, he had some doubts regarding Venkatappa's demand that the land and the habitation of the Bangher fortress, after its destruction should belong to him. It was a new matter upon which the Viceroy had given no instructions. Accordingly he decided to inform him about it before writing to Venkatappa concerning the acceptance of the terms. At the same time he feared that Venkatappa would come down upon Mangalore since no answer was sent to him within the specified time and cautioned the Viceroy to this effect.[68]

The Viceroy-in-Council decided to instruct Leitão to accept Venkatappa's terms. If the Bangar chief did not care to accept them Sampaio was instructed to hand over the keys of the Bangher fortress to the chief or his minister and to withdraw from it the Portuguese soldiers and artillery. After all, it was of great importance for the Portuguese to be on friendly terms with Venkatappa in whose territories they had fortresses at Basrur, Honavar and Mangalore and from whose regions they secured supplies of foodgrains to sustain not only these fortresses but also Goa, Hormuz and Muscat. They had done for the chief whatever was possible for them to do during the course of his war with Venkatappa and they had lost, fighting on his behalf, many captains, nobles and soldiers. They had also spent much money for him. Now the chief was doing virtually nothing to defend his fortress, but was staying away. There was no objection in allowing Venkatappa the land and the habitation of Bangher after razing the fortress to the ground. Leitão was ordered to conclude the treaty as speedily as possible so that the Portuguese would be relieved of the anxiety and expenses.[69]

However, there were still some more hurdles to be overcome. Either because of the Bangar chief or because of the queen of Ullala, the Portuguese and Venkatappa were not in a position to conclude the treaty as early as they wished. Concerning the queen, Leal secured Venkatappa's consent to include her as a party to the treaty. She was to resume her former friendly relations with the Portuguese. However, if she was required to destroy the stockades, which she had constructed, the ship that had been taken from her by the Portuguese during the conflict was to be returned to her along with the cargo and the Portuguese were to destroy those which they had in their habitation in the neighbourhood of their fortress of Mangalore. On the other hand, the latter were to retain their stockades and were not to return the ship if the queen were allowed to retain hers. Ultimately, the second alternative of retaining their respective stockades was accepted by the signatories of the treaty.[70]

In the meantime the situation in Mangalore was becoming unbearable for the Portuguese. On November 24, 1619 Sampaio wrote to the governor explaining this situation. The Portuguese were dying at the rate of six a day because Venkatappa's general Basavappa Naik, would not allow any food supplies. Sampaio and his captains were without shirts and collars, for they had sold or mortgaged them. What used to cost four formerly cost ten now and yet one did not find anything to purchase. The fleet was desperate for there was neither a coin of copper nor a grain of rice. The soldiers wanted to flee along with Sampaio. The captains and the priests impeded them and yet some soldiers were gone. If those 1,000 Christian souls among the *cazados*, soldiers and women were not helped by the governor in time, a great disaster was certain to follow. The governor was warned not to be complacent thinking that peace negotiations were afoot. The enemy knew the condition in which the Portuguese were in Mangalore. Sampaio pointed out that he should not be blamed if any disaster occurred after this report was sent to the governor. The soldiers had been paid only up to September 5, though money was sent to him for paying them up to November 5. Out of the 4,000 *xerafins* that were sent to him he had given 2,000 to the merchants of Basrur for sending him additional fleet.[71]

Sampaio proceeded to say that the greatest enemies that the Portuguese then had were the Bangar chief and his *adigar*. The peace talks could have been speeded up, but for the Bangar chief who ran to Kasaragod every now and then, thus necessitating 20 days to consult him and send a reply to the governor or to Venkatappa. Sampaio concluded by saying that he feared the enemy would begin a war in two days.[72]

This precarious situation in Mangalore forced the Portuguese to accept the terms offered and hasten the conclusion of the treaty with Venkatappa. The latter had written by now to the governor through Leitão. The substance of the letter was that he had no intention of accommodating the Bangar chief or to negotiate with him, considering what the chief had done against his interests; that he had ultimately negotiated because the Portuguese had interceded on behalf of the chief; and that the governor should soon signify his acceptance and arrange for signing the treaty of peace and friendship, the terms of which he sent along with the letter by a separate note.[73]

These terms included the names of the territories and the yields thereof, which were the same that Venkatappa had already agreed to give. The rest of the terms and conditions were: (1) On receiving the sum the Bangar chief should order the destruction of the Bangher fortress. This article referred also to the places where the chief was to live but the document is unfortunately unreadable here, (2) The ground and the habitation of Bangher should belong to Venkatappa who would neither erect in it a fortress at any time nor raise any wall nor have men of arms there, (3) The chief should give the elephant named Padmanabha to Venkatappa, (4) The latter would order the destruction of the fortresses erected in Nandavara and Uppinangady, (5) He would also order his administrator at Bangher to destroy all the stockades that were erected during the course of the war and also those which existed near the Portuguese fortress of Mangalore, (6) The *cazados* of Mangalore should pay Venkatappa customs and other duties for the rice which they brought to the fortress from his territories, except for 500 bags a year meant for their own consumption, (7) the possessions at the river and the temple Ossadual (?), which the Bangar chief had given the Portuguese, would remain with them, the income from the cultivable fields near the river being discounted from the sum to be given to the chief, (8) The queen of Ullala should be associated with the treaty and Venkatappa would declare for himself and on behalf of the queen that both would be on friendly terms with the Portuguese as before and that the queen would begin to pay the annual tribute to the Portuguese which she used to pay formerly. The queen should be allowed to retain the stockades which had been built in her territories. There was a condition to this which is not clear as the document is damaged here, (9) If the Bangar chief was not prepared to conform to these terms the Portuguese should no more favour him and the governor should withdraw the Portuguese soldiers and artillery, which were in the Bangher fortress, the keys of which should be handed over to the chief; doing this there would be friendly relations between the Portuguese, on the one hand, and Venkatappa and the queen of Ullala, on the other, on the basis of the terms except those pertaining to the chief.[74]

Considering the above terms and conditions the Viceroy-in-Council decided that they should be accepted for the following reasons: (a) Venkatappa was sure to continue to prevent food supplies from his territories if the terms were not accepted. There was a great scarcity of rice already at the Portuguese fortress of

Mangalore, Muscat, Hormuz and other Portuguese fortresses also were experiencing shortage of this commodity, (b) Accepting the terms would release the Portuguese from the burden of expenses on the Bangher fortress. The captains, the soldiers and the artillery employed in the defence of Bangher could be used for other and more advantageous purposes, (c) Refusal to accept the terms was most likely to endanger the security of the Portuguese fortresses within the territories of Venkatappa who might attack them any time, (d) Pepper, the principal article of trade, could also be secured in large quantity from Venkatappa's territories after concluding the treaty, (e) The Bangar chief, with his illusions and tactics of delay, was now more an enemy than a friend to the Portuguese. He was doing nothing to defend his fortress. He did not even want to stay at Bangher, but by compulsion. He virtually deserved nothing considering his inactivity. The terms offered were good enough to him, though he had asked for more, (f) From the Portuguese point of view the terms of the proposed treaty were in keeping with their own interests and requirements. The *cazados* were to be allowed 500 bags of duty free rice a year, which was not bad, though the quantity was not as large as the Portuguese wished it to be. They were not called upon to return to the queen of Ullala the ship which they had taken from her, nor were they expected to destroy their own stockades, provided she was allowed to retain hers and that the latter was to begin to pay tributes as before.[75]

Leitão was to sign the treaty on behalf of the Bangar chief as well as the Portuguese.[76] It seems to have been signed by January 1620. Sampaio wrote to the governor on January 8, that he had completed the withdrawal of soldiers and artillery from the fortress of Bangher; that the treaty had been signed; and that since he had nothing more to do at Mangalore he might be permitted to go to Goa. On considering the letter the Governor-in-Council came to the conclusion that he should be allowed to leave Mangalore only after: (a) the conditions of the treaty were actually carried out, and (b) Venkatappa withdrew all his troops from Mangalore. At the time of his departure from Mangalore Sampaio was to leave behind 40 or 50 soldiers for the defence of the fortress under the command of its captain.[77]

Soon after the conclusion of the treaty Venkatappa began peaceful commercial dealings with the Portuguese. Thus, his ambassador in Goa was instructed to find out whether the governor was prepared to take from him every year 1,000 quintals of pepper which was customarily taken from him by the Portuguese contractors according to the price fixed by agreement, the contractors being free to purchase as much additional quantities of pepper from his subjects as was needed. The Governor-in-Council readily agreed on March 7, 1620 to send their contractor for the pepper offered for sale, with the condition that the contractor be permitted to purchase more pepper in Venkatappa's territories, as suggested by the latter himself.[78]

The Bangar chief was unfortunate. After the conclusion of the treaty fresh obstacles cropped up and the chief did not get the promised sum of 7,000 *pagodas* a year. He seems to have insisted upon residing in Kasaragod, whereas Venkatappa commanded that he should come and live either in a place within Venkatappa's territories, but which did not belong to the chief formerly, or in Goa. The chief feared that he might be murdered at the instance of Venkatappa if he were to obey the latter. Venkatappa was apprehensive that the chief, living outside his control, might foment trouble against him once again. The chief wrote to the Viceroy complaining of the non-fulfilment of the terms on the part of Venkatappa and urging him to get the payment of the sum from the Nayaka. The Viceroy-in-Council decided on January 30, 1623 that an embassy should be sent to Venkatappa for securing the compliance of the treaty. Even though he might cause certain amount of discredit to the Portuguese by not responding favourably to the embassy, the Council thought of satisfying their friend and ally, the Bangar chief, by sending an embassy to Ikkeri. Leitão, who had played such an important role at the peace negotiations and who had access to Venkatappa, was chosen to lead the embassy.[79]

The decision to send the embassy was not executed until October. In the middle of that month Leitão, with his entourage, sailed forth from Goa to Honavar from where the land route to Ikkeri was taken. Vittala Shenoy, who was Venkatappa's ambassador to Goa, and who spoke Portuguese very well, was also with the embassy. And, it was this embassy led by Leitão that Pietro Della Valle, accompanied to Ikkeri. He gives an excellent account of the proceedings of this embassy.[80]

While receiving advance news from Vittala regarding the Portuguese embassy Venkatappa did not react to it with any enthusiasm, knowing the purpose for which it was being sent. There was another cause for his coldness. He knew very well that the Portuguese had no money to pay for the pepper which they had to take from him that year and for a great part of the quantity of the commodity taken in the previous year. As a result, the reception accorded to the embassy, which reached Ikkeri on November 6, was rather poor.[81]

Della Valle regarded Venkatappa as more a royal than a king, because he paid an annual tribute to the Adil Shah who himself was a feudatory of the great Mughals. Besides, the conditions at the court of Ikkeri also were such that they did not befit a real king. However, he noted that the people in India as well as the Portuguese considered Venkatappa a king. The Portuguese did so for their own glorification, he thought.[82]

Della Valle did not approve some of the proceedings of the embassy. Leitão sought Vittala Shenoy's intervention to secure a letter from Venkatappa to the King of Portugal to the effect that he might get additional remuneration. Della Valle laughed at this behaviour of the ambassador seeking the recommendation of an alien prince, who was virtually regarded as an enemy by the Portuguese, to secure favour from the ambassador's own master. So also, his impression regarding the competence of the embassy was poor. The Portuguese were generally ignorant of what was happening around them. They often indulged in rumours. For instance, Venkatappa was told that England was made Catholic by the public command of its king.[83]

During the course of fifteen days after his arrival at Ikkeri, Leitão had several audiences with Venkatappa. On one occasion a letter from the King of Portugal was presented to him. The former thanked the latter for refusing to sell pepper to the English and the Dutch who had approached him to buy the commodity. He also expressed hope in the continued friendship between the Portuguese and Venkatappa. Concerning the affairs of the Bangar chief, the Portuguese monarch merely said that the ambassador would present the case on behalf of the chief. Venkatappa's answer regarding the last particular was that he would pay 7,000 *pagodas* a year to the chief only if he came to live in the Nayaka's territories or at Goa and that it was his final verdict. He gave a letter of promise to this effect. Venkatappa pointed out that the chief was not reliable because once he had written repenting for what he had done owing to evil counsel and saying that he would come to live in Venkatappa's kingdom and be obedient, receiving the annual sum from him but that later on the chief had changed his mind.[84]

The King of Portugal seems to have written to the Viceroy ordering him to wage a war on Venkatappa, if necessary, in order to restore the kingdom of Bangher to its chief. However, he was to do so only if the circumstances permitted such a course of action. In fact, the Portuguese position in India and elsewhere was not sound in those years. Their European rivals, particularly the Dutch, were creating troubles for them in different parts of the world. Therefore, the Viceroy had to satisfy himself with the answer given to Venkatappa. At the same time it was contended that the embassy would show the Bangar chief that the Portuguese did whatever was possible for them to do to secure the fulfillment of the terms of the treaty on the part of Venkatappa.[85]

The chief wrote to the Viceroy, a couple of months after the result of the embassy was made known to him, saying that he had been to the king of Cannanore who had received and treated him well and had again promised to help him in retaking his lost kingdom. He sought a similar favour from the Viceroy also when he requested to provide him 20 *sanguiceis*, 10 ships, one big boat and one galley. If he was not to have these immediately the Viceroy was urged to provide him with money for maintenance to give him the land of old Mangalore; and to grant him four passports every year for free sea trade. Recalling what the Portuguese had done to the chief with such great damage to themselves the Viceroy-in-Council decided on March 22, 1624 merely to tell him to come to the territories which Venkatappa had affirmed to give him. If the chief did not consent to do this and went ahead with his novelties and agitations instead, the Portuguese were to have nothing to do with him anymore.[86]

The King of Portugal was always interested in restoring the Bangar chief to his former kingdom. He wrote to the latter towards the end of 1625, apparently assuring him help to this effect, and sent the letter to the Viceroy to forward it to the chief. The Viceroy-in-Council decided on January 20' 1626, not to send it to him. Instead, the Viceroy himself was to write a few consoling words to the chief.[87] Ultimately, the latter derived no benefit from the peace treaty of 1620. He seems to have remained without his kingdom, a fugitive in Kasaragod, until the death of Venkatappa on November 10, 1629.

We need to look at the conquests of Venkatappa and the extent of his territories as evident in Portuguese documents. Venkatappa had annexed the territories of :

(1) Gersoppa.

(2) Bangher. The kingdom of Gersoppa comprised the regions from Bhatkal to Mirjan. The total yields of this kingdom were 25,000 *pagodas* from Gersoppa and 300,000 *pagodas* from Ankola. The kingdom of Bangher yielded 125,000 *pagodas*.[88] The following were the other conquests and annexations made by Venkatappa.

(3) The kingdom of Basavapattana ruled by Amappa Nayaka, son of Kenge Gauda. Venkatappa attacked Basavapattana probably in 1620 and took territories worth 50,000 *pagodas*. These territories were perhaps Lukkuhalli, Gajanur and Shimoga.[89]

(4) Bellare, located in Puttur Taluka in South Kanara district. Venkatadri, king of Bellare, had given his sister in marriage to Venkatappa's son, Bhadrappa. However, the marriage does not seem to have been a happy one, but forced by Venkatappa who also secured territories worth 40,000 *pagodas* from Venkatadri. Bhadrappa died soon after the marriage. At the death of Venkatappa the king of Bellare tried to regain his territories from the successor of Venkatappa, namely, Virabhadra Nayaka.[90]

(5) From the kingdom of Sonda, ruled by Ranganatha, territories worth 12,000 *pagodas* were extracted by Venkatappa.[91]

(6) Gantaorer (?), king of Bilgi, ceded territories worth 100,000 *pagodas*.[92]

(7) The queen of Ullala was yet another ruler in South Kanara whom Venkatappa brought under his control. She had joined the league formed against Venkatappa at the instance of the Portuguese in 1612. However, by 1616 she fell out with the Bangar chief, her husband and the leader of the league. In the battles they fought against each other the husband began to gain an upper hand. Under this circumstance she seems to have sought Venkatappa's help. The latter did give it in the form of a large army which attacked the Bangar chief who sought Portuguese aid. The combined forces of the Portuguese and the Bangar chief could not withstand Venkatappa to whom the chief ultimately lost everything. The queen of Ullala, to whose aid Venkatappa had gone, was compelled to acknowledge his overlordship and cede a considerable part of her territories, including Bedrette, the best of her cities,[93] all worth about 10,000 *pagodas*.[94]

(8) The queen of Karnad in South Kanara district was also subjugated by Venkatappa. She too was a member of the league formed against Venkatappa in 1612. The latter, however, brought her under his control and imposed an annual tribute on her. This he did in 1618 or thereabouts. The Portuguese were not in a position to help her against Venkatappa. As Della Valle says, her defeat was due not only to her own weakness but also due to "the bad fortune and weakness of the Portuguese, her defenders, to whom she had always been a faithful friend".[95]

(9) The chief merchants of Basrur were forced to cede territories worth 50,000 *pagodas*.[96]

(10) King Honna of Gangolly ceded territories worth 100,000 *pagodas*.[97]

In addition to the above, a number of minor chiefs were also subjugated by Venkatappa. They were the king of Palpare in South

Coorg; Ramanatha Hari, chief of Kumbala; the king of Nerenki, in Puttur taluka; the king of Ajilara near Mulki in Udipi taluka; the king of Vamanjur in Mangalore taluka, who paid an annual tribute of 800 *pagodas*;[98] the Ballalas of Guedumardady, Manipary, Doltady, Kulur, Panambur, Pedanar, Mudibidri, Yerumal, Kapu, Katpadi, Nidambur, Chittupadi, Belor, Konnara, Mudradi, Hebri, Hiretor, Tomboso, Anaji, Tagrette, Herar, Gololer, Agumbe, Muttur, Malor, Modicar, Adolly, Muloly and Vitala; the queen of Saura; and the people of Baguanor, Kelenar and Kanduli.[99]

REFERENCES

1. *KNV*, p. 28.
2. N.L. Rao, "The Nayakas of Keladi", *VSCV*, p. 256.
3. *Ibid.*, p. 257. But according to *KNV* (p. 42), Sadashiva Nayaka ruled for about 32 years from 1513 to 1545.
4. *KNV*, p. 64 mentions 1545-1558, about 13 years as the reign period for Dodda Sankanna Nayaka whereas an inscription dated 1566, belonging to him has been discovered (N.L. Rao, *op. cit.*, p. 259).
5. N.L. Rao, *op. cit.*, p. 260.
6. *KNV*, p. 90 assigns nearly 47 years reign for Venkatappa Nayaka, from 1582-1629; but inscriptions belonging to him are available only for the period from 1592-1629 (N. L. Rao, *op. cit.*, pp. 261-2).
7. *APO-CR*, vol. III, p. 916. Fr. Heras, *The Aravidu Dynasty of Vijayanagara*, I, p. 423, refers to this letter but he wrongly identifies the Keladi chief referred to in the letter as Chikka Sankanna. Fr. Heras, no doubt, is aware that Venkatappa began to rule at least from 1592, as he himself mentions. Since the Portuguese letter in question is of 1598 it cannot be considered as referring to Chikka Sankanna but to Venkatappa.
8. *APO-CR*, vol. III, p. 591.
9. Pietro Della Valle, *The Travels of ....*, ed. Edward Grey, II, pp. 218-220.
10. *DRI*, I, p. 74.
11. *Ibid.*, pp. 167-8. Letter dated 2.1.1608 addressed to the Viceroy.
12. *Ibid.*, p. 254, II, pp. 159-60. Letters from the King to the Viceroy, dated 29.10.1609 and 13.2.1612.
13. *Ibid.*, II, pp.89-90. Letter from the King to the Viceroy dated 11.3.1611.
14. *Ibid.*, pp. 160, 350-1. Letters from the King to the Viceroy dated 13.2.1612 and 1.3.1613.
15. *Ibid.*, p. 294. Letter from the King to the Viceroy dated 16.1.1613.
16. *Assentos*, I, pp. 97, 109.
17. Valle, *op. cit.*, p. 302.
18. *Assentos*, I, p. 97.

19. *Ibid.*, p. 35.
20. *D-DC*, VIII, pp. 111-2.
21. *Ibid.*, pp. 113-22.
22. *Ibid.*, pp. 123-6.
23. Manuel de Faria e Sousa, *Asia Portuguesa*, IV, pp. 64-5.
24. Henry Heras, I, *op. cit*, p. 298.
25. Valle, *op. cit.*, p. 313.
26. Thome de Sousa Coutinho, *Certidão*, 22.8.1591, p. 1; *APO-CR*, vol. III, p. 244.
27. *supra*, pp. 94-5.
28. *APO-CR*, vol. III, pp. 243-4.
29. Coutinho, *op. cit.*, pp. 1-3.
30. *APO-CR*, vol. III, pp. 370-1.
31. *Ibid.*, p. 427.
32. *Ibid.*, p. 426.
33. *Ibid.*, p. 503.
34. *Ibid.*, p. 677.
35. *D-AB*, I, p. 40-1.
36. *Ibid.*, pp. 182-3; *DRI*, III, pp. 229-30.
37. *DRI*, III, p. 478.
38. *DRI*, IV, p. 132.
39. *D-AB*, II, p. 471.
40. *Ibid.*, p. 701.
41. *DRI*, IV, pp. 196-8. Letter of the Viceroy to the King dated 28.3.1617. This date seems to be erroneous. The letter seems to have been written by João de Coutinho (Count of Redonda) who became Viceroy with effect from 18.11.1617. Probably the letter was written soon after his assumption of office.
42. *DRI*, V, pp. 236-7.
43. *Ibid.*, p. 237.
44. *Ibid.*, pp. 238-9.
45. *Ibid.*, p. 241.
46. *Assentos*, I, pp. 15-16, 18-19.
47. *Ibid.*, pp. 17-19.
48. *Ibid.*, pp. 17-18; *DRI*, V, p. 244.
49. *DRI*, V, pp. 244-6; *CEO*, II, pp. 240-1.
50. *Assentos*, I, p. 20.
51. *EF*, 1618-1621, pp. 69-70.
52. *Assentos*, I, p. 115.
53. Alfredo Botelho de Sousa, *Subsidios para a história militar marítima da India*, III, p. 145.
54. *Assentos*, I, pp. 30-1.
55. *Ibid.*, pp. 33-5.
56. *Ibid.*, pp. 35-6.

57. *Ibid*., p. 32.
58. *Ibid*., pp. 37-9.
59. *Ibid*., pp. 39-40.
60. *Ibid*., pp. 45-8.
61. *Ibid*., pp. 61-4.
62. *Ibid*., pp. 65-6.
63. *Ibid*., p. 99.
64. *Ibid*., pp. 66-68, 70.
65. *Ibid*., pp. 92-3.
66. *Ibid*., pp. 95-7.
67. *Ibid*., pp. 97-9.
68. *Ibid*., p. 94.
69. *Ibid*., pp. 99-100.
70. *Ibid*., p. 102.
71. *Ibid*., pp. 104-5.
72. *Assentos, I,* pp. 105-6.
73. *Ibid*., p. 107.
74. *Ibid*., pp. 107-110.
75. *Ibid*., pp. 101-03, 110.
76. *Ibid*., p. 110.
77. *Ibid*., pp. 111-2.
78. *Ibid*., p. 115.
79. *Ibid*., pp. 146-7.
80. Valle, *op. cit*., I, p. 191; II, pp. 202-89.
81. *Ibid*., II, pp. 212-13.
82. *Ibid*., pp. 243-4.
83. *Ibid*., p. 255.
84. *Ibid*., pp. 285-7.
85. *Ibid*., pp. 287-8
86. *Ibid*., p. 201.
87. *Assentos*, III, p. 639.
88. Henry Heras, "The Expansion Wars of Venkatappa Nayaka", pp. 1-2.
89. *Ibid*., p. 1, 10-11.
90. *Ibid*., p. 1.
91. *Ibid*.
92. *Ibid*.
93. Valle, *op. cit*., II, pp. 314-5.
94. Heras, *op. cit*., p. 1.
95. Valle, *op. cit*., p. 353.
96. Heras, *op. cit*., pp. 1-2.
97. *Ibid*., p. 2.
98. Valle, *op. cit*., pp. 305-6.
99. Heras, *op. cit*. The identification of names is on the basis of that of Heras.

7

THE PORTUGUESE AND THE NAYAKAS OF IKKERI - II (1629-1645)

Venkatappa Nayaka was succeeded by his grandson Virabhadra Nayaka,[1] who ruled from 1629 to 1645. Virabhadra had to face a threefold danger at his accession. In the first instance, the Adil Shah and the other neighbouring rulers showed hostility towards him. Secondly, all those chiefs of Kanara, whom Venkatappa had subdued and had made vassals, revolted as soon as they heard the news of his death. Thirdly, a kinsman of Virabhadra, Virappa Nayaka, necessitated a war of succession to the throne of Ikkeri. He confronted all those troubles bravely.

The Adil Shah demanded from Virabhadra 9,000,000 gold pieces valued at 2,700,000 *pagodas*, five elephants and 200 Arab horses. In addition, an arrear of two years' tribute, calculated at 80,000 *pagodas* was also claimed. Further, Virabhadra was told to evacuate all the territories taken from kings, queens and *ballalas* on the Kanara coast. These, no doubt, were impossible demands. Virabhadra responded by saying that he would pay in all 300,000 *pagodas* provided the Adil Shah would aid him against those chiefs who were already in revolt. The Adil Shah was not satisfied with this reply and the hostility continued[2] until October 1630, when the two came to terms. Virabhadra paid 500,000 *pagodas* to the former.[3]

The king of Sonda invaded the territories of Virabhadra who sent his army to defend. Both sides lost heavily in men. The chief of Bilgi allied himself with Sonda. So also the rulers of Basavapattana and Belur jointly invaded his territories and took one of his fortresses. The 'king of the mountain,' (king of Cannanore), who was a distinguished captain, marched personally against Virabhadra and defeated and wounded the latter's general, Virappa Naik, killing many of his men and capturing an elephant and 30 horses. Virappa fled from the battlefield and took shelter in a fortress at Baguanor. Virabhadra sent another army under the command of Siddhalinga Naik against the 'king of the mountain'. But the latter defeated the former too. These setbacks damaged the strength of Virabhadra considerably. The Bangar chief, the queen of Ullala and Karnad, as well as all those subjugated kings, *ballalas* and peoples rose up in arms in South Kanara. Thus, practically the whole of Kanara was in revolt against the authority of the new king of Ikkeri. However, the latter was able to withstand all, since he was rich and could afford to wait until an opportune moment offered itself to strike against his enemies effectually, particularly when the latter might be divided owing to internal differences.[4]

The Portuguese decided to fish in the troubled waters. They desired particularly to take the peninsula of Gangolly and build a fortress there. They had a fortress in Basrur nearby. But as decades rolled by the force of winds had filled the river on the side of the fortress with sand. Thus, the bar at the fortress became shallow, but at the same time the river became deep on the side of the peninsula. Large and heavy ships could not reach the fortress except during the high tide. At times it so happened that their ships carrying merchandise had to take shelter at the peninsula of Gangolly awaiting the high tide in order to go to the fortress. While at Gangolly the ships used to be attacked by pirates of Malabar and the Portuguese captain of the fortress was not in a position to send effective relief to such ships. This situation of loss and danger led the Portuguese to covet the peninsula itself, where they thought of building a fortress.[5] The suggestion to fortify Gangolly was made to the King of Portugal as early as 1617, for in his letter of February 5, 1618 to the Viceroy, the King refers to this suggestion and commands him to consult the Council of State on this matter and report to him.[6] However, the Portuguese did not get an opportunity to take the peninsula as long as Venkatappa lived.

Not only Gangolly but also other lands of Kanara were coveted by the Portuguese. Francisco de Souza Alcoforado, captain of Honavar, writing to the Viceroy on November 18, 1629, proposed that the fortress of Honavar should be strengthened and that certain islands nearby, which yielded 3,000 *cruzados* or more, might be captured. In fact, an attempt seems to have already been made to capture these islands. Nuno da Cunha, a Portuguese captain, had sailed forth with his fleet in order to occupy the islands but he could do nothing "by reason of the great power which the king of those territories (namely, Venkatappa Nayaka) had". Now that the latter was dead and every one was in revolt against his successor, Alcoforado suggested that the Viceroy should authorise him and send assistance to occupy these islands. He pointed out further that everyone was trying to grab at whatever was possible, that the Adil Shah intended to occupy some lands of Kanara and that he would be more dangerous than a Hindu ruler as a neighbour. Deliberating upon the suggestion of Alcoforado, the Viceroy-in-Council decided on November 22, 1629 to order the repairing and strengthening of the fortress of Honavar and to send 30 soldiers. So also 50 soldiers were to be dispatched to Basrur and 30 to Mangalore for the defence of the fortresses there. Regarding the occupation of the islands near Honavar, more information was to be collected before taking a decision.[7] In fact, the Portuguese did not seem to have occupied the island at all.

In the same Council meeting, the question of Gangolly was also considered. It was recalled that since several years the King of Portugal had intended to change the fortress from Basrur to Gangolly and to convert the latter peninsula into an island by digging a canal between the sea and the river. As soon as Venkatappa died the merchants of Upper Basrur, to whom the peninsula had probably belonged formerly, seem to have offered it to the Portuguese. The merchants apparently needed Portuguese protection in view of the prevailing disturbances. The Portuguese also thought that the peninsula, fortified and made into an island, would be a safer place than Basrur for themselves. They could defend themselves better and at the same time carry an offensive action against Virabhadra by encouraging and animating his enemies. They had another anxiety too. The Adil Shah was trying to dominate at least some of the territories which belonged to Ikkeri and the Portuguese did not want this to happen. The Viceroy-in-Council chose Diogo de Sousa e Menezes, experienced soldier and member of the Council, as captain-general of the armed forces of land and sea of Kanara, who was to visit the various fortresses and communicate with the local chiefs promising them assistance against Virabhadra. He was to start from Goa with four ships (*manchuas*), two meant for Honavar and two for Basrur. All the captains of the Kanara fortresses were to be under his command; so too the captains-major of the fleets of Malabar and Kanara. He was to pay particular attention to the Basrur fortress and study the peninsula of Gangolly. He was to see that the Adil Shah did not become master of any territory in Kanara.[8]

On reaching the Basrur fortress, Menezes found it in disorder. The soldiers disobeyed their captains. A vicar had been murdered and many other offences had been committed. The culprits were mostly unpunished and even those who were awarded sentences like exile, were still residing in the fortress. Reporting of these to the Viceroy on December 22, Menezes sought judicial powers to clean the fortress of its offenders, homicides and exiles. The Viceroy-in-Council empowered him to do so.[9]

Menezes also visualised shortage of rice, should Virabhadra prevent its supply from his lands as a result of hostility. Provision to secure rice worth 50,000 *xerafins* from the North was therefore to be made. The municipality of Upper Basrur was to be requested not to revolt until the necessary supply of rice was taken out.[10]

On January 3, 1630 Virabhadra declared the Portuguese his enemy and ordered the blockade of rice supplies from Basrur as expected. Menezes suggested in his letter of the same date to the Viceroy that the latter too should reciprocate by a similar declaration. The municipality of Upper Basrur and all the people within the boundaries of Basrur were now in revolt and in league with other kings and *ballalas* of the Kanara coast. Menezes considered it a golden opportunity to secure the peninsula of Gangolly. He personally measured by one night the width of the land between the sea and the river at the north and of the peninsula. It was 80 paces and a canal could easily be dug up as the land was sandy. After the conversion of the peninsula into an island, he thought 10 *manchuas* were sufficient to defend it at times of war. The fortress of Basrur also needed explosives and firemen. He urged the Viceroy to send him all these in eight *manchuas* as quickly as possible, warning that delayed relief would be of no avail.

The Viceroy-in-Council decided that Menezes should arrive at a settlement with the municipality of Upper Basrur by which the latter would give the Portuguese the peninsula of Gangolly as a gift, thus providing a legal right to possess the place. It seems that Venkatappa had imposed on the Portuguese, in order to maintain two temples at Basrur, a tax in the form of 200 bags of rice every year on the rice supplies they took from Basrur. He was instructed to secure the discontinuation of this provision in the new settlement with the municipality. On the contrary, the latter was to be induced to give the Portuguese a good quantity of rice, in addition to the customary tribute for the sustenance of the Basrur fortress. So also the municipality was to be urged to agree to give the Portuguese every year an appreciable quantity of pepper at 56 *xerafins* a *khandi*. Besides, Menezes was to endeavour to secure as much other useful concessions from the municipality as possible. The latter's reward was to be Portuguese assistance against Virabhadra and later on the protection of the Portuguese fortress to be built on the peninsula. A fleet with men of arms and mariners to dig the canal was sent to Menezes and 4,000 *xerafins* were also furnished for his expenses. In addition, he was authorised to spend the income of the Basrur fortress in the rice trade.[11]

By February, Menezes took possession of the peninsula, as a letter from the Viceroy to the King of Portugal dated February 20, indicates. Regarding the utility of the place he wrote to the Viceroy: "This island of Cambolim (Gangolly) is two leagues in length and one-third of a league in breadth. It has lovely paddy-fields which certainly yield a yearly crop of 20,000 bags of rice, as also many beautiful palm groves. It will be of great use to the State if this island comes into the possession of His Majesty where this fortress, which is not quite safe, may be transferred, for in case the enemy sets up a bulwark at the point where this river is narrowest, it will be impossible for anyone to enter it, or to bring reinforcements to this fortress, except by very light and small boats, whereas, in case this fortress stands on this island it will be possible at any moment to send it aid by the deserted coast. In this way it will also be possible to secure better the provisions that go from this harbour to that city (Goa), a thing very essential to it, and it will also be possible to take from this harbour a yearly load of 1,500 *khandis* of pepper at a moderate price, as formerly ...".

"And there will be found on this island also many sailors for the royal fleets of the State, which will make it possible to dispense with those of the metropolis, this will prevent the Malabaris from having these sailors for their ships, for it is well known that they come here to take them".

"And if from this harbour they should sally forth, in September 12, in armed *sanguiceis*, and scour the seas between Cannanore and this fort, till the month of May, it will be the best kind of war that could be waged against the whole Malabar, by cutting off from it the provisions that go to it from these places, as also by preventing them from securing the said sailors".

"His Majesty will have from this island an income of 10,000 being proceeds of the quit-rent and other sources sufficient for the maintenance of the said fortresses and in future this income will greatly increase, especially if the customs house is transferred there".[12]

Soon after taking possession of the peninsula, Menezes began to fortify the place with stockades and to dig the canal to link the river with the sea. At the time of writing the letter of February 20, 1630 the work was in progress with 1,000 workers. The Viceroy sent stone and lime together with skilled carpenters, masons and engineers.[13] The peninsula was in fact converted into an island by March,[14] when Menezes fell ill and was permitted to go to Goa. But the canal was filled with sand. And the dream of converting the place into an effective island never seems to have been fulfilled.[15] However, the place was fortified by February 1633.[16]

As the work of fortification was in progress the forces of Virabhadra seem to have attacked the Portuguese at Gangolly as well as at Basrur. He caused a stockade to be erected near those of the Portuguese at Gangolly and endeavoured to take the half completed fortress, with two bulwarks, one wall and some stockades, from the Portuguese. The latter, however, defended well and killed many of the Ikkeri forces. The Viceroy sent reinforcements. And the work continued until the end of the rainy season without much trouble. In August, the captain-major of Kanara, with a fleet of 16 ships, approached Basrur. Virabhadra's men were dismayed at the sight of the powerful fleet.

In the meantime, Virabhadra had to face a civil war.[17] His uncle, Virappa Nayaka, who was in prison for 33 years, escaped and declared himself king of Ikkeri. The nobles and the feudatories of Ikkeri were now divided, some supporting Virabhadra and others, Virappa. Both sides came to have more or less equal strength. The Viceroy decided to favour Virappa, thinking that he was the just heir and that Virabhadra was already hostile towards the Portuguese. Virappa seems to have soon gained successes at Basrur against his rival. It resulted, at any rate, in regular rice supplies to the Portuguese from Upper Basrur. Besides, the stockade that was built by Virabhadra's men in front of the Portuguese fortress of Gangolly was destroyed at the instance of Virappa. The latter also made overtures of peace through Vittala Shenoy who had been for some time the envoy of Ikkeri to Goa. The Viceroy was not satisfied with the terms proposed and therefore he sent his own ambassador with Vittala Shenoy, with new and modified proposals to Virappa.[18]

Finally, a treaty of peace and friendship was actually signed between the Portuguese and Virappa Nayaka[19] on March 7, 1631. Its terms and conditions were as follows:[20] (1) Virappa and his successors should always be loyal and faithful friends of the Portuguese, having mutual friends and enemies. They should give all the assistance and favour to the Portuguese in their wars, whenever requested. The Portuguese also should give similar assistance and favour to Virappa and his successors. (2) Virappa should cede to the Portuguese the peninsula of Gangolly, extending from the point up to the small temple of Marsamy (Kumaraswamy ?), the Portuguese being allowed to possess and enjoy the place forever with its customary privileges. But the income of the temple of Gufaçar (Guheshwara?) and that of Marsamy should belong to these temples as before. The people of the peninsula should be allowed to live according to their law and customs. The Viceroy and his successors should be permitted to erect fortresses on the island. (3) Virappa and his successors should allow the Portuguese every year to cut and take away timber from the lands of Ikkeri. No duty should be imposed upon such timber. The Ikkeri rulers should instruct their administrators to give necessary guards to the timber, the guards being paid by the Portuguese. (4) The Ikkeri rulers should not admit into their ports the two *Babeas* (probably pirates of Malabar), nor any other embarkations of the Malabaris to take sailors or foodgrains from their ports and lands. (5) The navigation of Honavar should be free as before. (6) The rulers of Ikkeri should pay a tribute of 500 loads of rice with all punctuality in the future, as well as that which was due. (7) The taxes, imposed on articles sold and purchased by the Portuguese and which were in force during the course of the previous eight years should be discontinued. So also no duties should be imposed upon the ships of Muscat. (8) The lands and the palm groves belonging to the *cazados* and other Portuguese residents near the fortress of Basrur should be ceded to Virappa. In return for these the latter should give, to the greater advantage of the former, land and income in Gangolly. Assessors should be appointed to settle the value of the four villages promised; and if it was insufficient additional income should be given to the *cazados* and residents. (9) All the pepper of Gersoppa and other places belonging to the Ikkeri rulers should be sold freely without any obstruction to the purchasers or the sellers. The Viceroy should have no obligation to purchase any pepper from Virappa; so also the latter should not be obliged to sell any to the former. However, if the Viceroy wished to purchase pepper and Virappa wished to sell it, it should be done according to the price fixed by free agreement between the two parties. (10) Virappa and his successors should refer to him for his decision any dispute with any of the allies of the Portuguese and should abide by the decision given.

The above clauses referred to the terms and conditions applicable to Virappa. The following applied to the Portuguese: (1) The Viceroy,

Count of Linhares, and his successors should be friends of Virappa and his successors and vassals, friends of their friends and enemies of their enemies. If any of the allies disobeyed the sentence given by the Viceroy with regard to a dispute referred to him by Virappa, he should declare the disobedient ally an enemy, and the obedient, a friend. (2) Virappa and his successors should be allowed to take from Goa every year ten horses free of all duties, as long as the treaty of peace was maintained. (3) The Viceroy should hand over to Virappa two ships that were captured from Virabhadra during the course of the hostility between the latter and the Portuguese.

A fine of 10,000 *pagodas*, equivalent to the Goan currency of 35,000 *xerafins*, should be paid by the party that failed to fulfill the terms and conditions of the treaty in full or in part, to the other party which abided by them. The treaty should not be renewed unless the violating party paid the prescribed fine to the other.

The treaty was signed at Basrur by the Viceroy and by Vittala Shenoy and Tirumalayya, ambassador of Virappa respectively. The latter, was pleased with the treaty, rewarded the captains of the Portuguese fleets with 21,450 *xerafins*, which was distributed among those who had taken out ships at their own cost. He also issued a notice to the people of Gangolly on April 18, that he had given the land to the Viceroy whom they should obey and to whom they should pay the customary revenues. If they were offended by the Portuguese, complaints were to be sent to Virappa. He assured them to request the Viceroy not to offend anymore.[21] In virtue of the treaty and the notices, a deed of possession was drawn on May 12, whereupon the Portuguese took actual possession of Gangolly.[22]

A couple of months after the conclusion of the above transactions, Virappa died[23] and Virabhadra, his nephew became the unrivalled king of Ikkeri. Simultaneously with Virappa, Virabhadra too had made his own proposals for a treaty of peace and friendship with the Portuguese. However, the Viceroy had preferred to deal with Virappa.[24]

Virabhadra renewed his negotiations with the Portuguese in October or thereabouts. Vittala Shenoy, who was also Virappa's ambassador, presented the proposals which were substantially different from the terms and conditions of the treaty with Virappa. Virabhadra wished that the Portuguese should purchase pepper from him at the old rate and that they should destroy their fortress of Gangolly. These terms were not acceptable to the Portuguese, and Vittala was told that Virabhadra should agree to a treaty with the same terms and conditions of the treaty with Virappa. He reported this to Virabhadra. Though about a fortnight had passed, no response came from the latter. Thereupon the Viceroy-in-Council deliberated upon the matter anew on November 18.[25]

In the meantime, the rulers of Bangher, Karnad, and the 'mountain' requested the Portuguese their ally, to assist them against Virabhadra. In return for the help the Portuguese were promised substantial supplies of pepper, wood, iron, and rice and also carpenters, blacksmiths and other skilled workers for the fortifications of Gangolly. The captain-major of the fleet of Kanara, Domingos Ferreira Beliago, suggested to the Viceroy in a letter of November 13, that a quick resolution should be taken regarding the negotiations with Virabhadra who was being attacked anew by the Adil Shah, as Virabhadra had not paid the latter the customary tribute which a vassal, at his succession and coronation, paid to his lord. Beliago further mentioned that the Muslim captain of Ponda also had sent his forces to the frontier of the kingdom of Ikkeri; that in addition to the rulers of Bangher, Karnad and the 'mountain', the merchants of Basrur also sought Portuguese aid against Virabhadra; and that if the latter tried to postpone the conclusion of a treaty, in terms of the previous treaty with Virappa, until he came to terms with the Adil Shah, so as to be able to impose his own terms upon the Portuguese, the Viceroy should decide in favour of the allies against him. Taking all these into account the Viceroy-in-Council came to the conclusion that their allies should openly be assisted against Virabhadra.[26]

It seems that Virabhadra had to fight against his enemies at several points at once. He led his army personally against Kenge Gauda of Basavapattana. He sent troops against the revolting merchants of Upper Basrur. By March, 1632 he settled terms with Kenge Gauda and prepared to send reinforcements to Basrur. By this time the Mughals also appeared in the Deccan. This was a common danger for all, the Portuguese, the Adil Shah and Virabhadra. The Viceroy thought of negotiating for a truce between Virabhadra and his revolting feudatories who were being aided by the Portuguese. Further, if Virabhadra was found willing to aid the Adil Shah against the Mughals, the Viceroy thought of favouring Virabhadra.

Accordingly, Baltazar Marinho, who was experienced and well-versed with the affairs of Kanara, was dispatched as ambassador to Virabhadra.[27] He was instructed to congratulate Virabhadra on his succession to the throne of Ikkeri; to secure his permission for the fortification of Gangolly at the site of the *Pao*[28]; to agree upon reasonable prices for rice and pepper; and to prepare a survey of the peninsula of Gangolly on his return journey. At Ikkeri, Baltazar found Virabhadra firm in not allowing the Portuguese to fortify Gangolly. Being informed of this, the Viceroy-in-Council, meeting on May 25 decided to dissemble. Marinho was instructed to demonstrate friendship towards Virabhadra by saying that the Portuguese would erect a fortress at the *Pao* only when Virabhadra permitted it, though they were certain that he would never allow this. He was also instructed not to decide anything regarding the prices of rice and pepper, as the price of rice was very high, and as pepper trade could be carried on in the manner provided for in the treaty with Virappa.[29]

Meanwhile, the Portuguese strengthened the defences of their fortresses in Kanara and favoured and animated Virabhadra's enemies, the Tuluvas, under the sly. On the surface they appeared to be neutral.

Writing of this to the King of Portugal on November 4, 1632 the Viceroy said, "It appeared to me convenient to send Baltazar Marinho as ambassador with instructions ... and meanwhile I provided and furnished with doubled garrison and arms all the fortresses which Your Majesty possesses in Kanara, and, under the sly, I animated the Tuluvas, who offered me grand advantages, with the condition that aid be given them, and as the said king, Virabhadra Nayaka, is so powerful in these parts, I was happy to make myself conveniently neutral in appearance, so that I am more free to choose for agreement of friendship one who emerges victorious, without falling out with the other party".[30]

Virabhadra emerged victorious. He gained Upper Basrur in due course. He did not permit the Portuguese to be complete masters of Gangolly. The Viceroy, however, thought of dominating the whole of Gangolly by erecting another fortress at the point where the peninsula was separated from the mainland; but did not get an opportunity to do so. Virabhadra offered fresh terms of peace; but the Viceroy considered them unbecoming of the Portuguese to accept. One of the conditions was that the Portuguese should give up or dismantle their fortress of Basrur. *Prima facie* the conditions were harmless, for the fortress in question has been virtually useless. But this condition would be accepted only if Gangolly was given to the Portuguese with permission to fortify it. Gangolly had an income of 5,000 *xerafins* a year and the Viceroy hoped to increase it to 50,000 in due course. He also visualised the day when the peninsula could be populated with Christians from Goa. Further 20,000 loads of rice of the *giraçal* variety, which the people of Gangolly sold every year, could always be secured for Goa. But Gangolly was not offered by Virabhadra.[31]

As the Viceroy was considering the above, news reached Goa towards the middle of November, that Virabhadra was erecting a fortress in Gangolly, about a cannon-shot from the Portuguese fortress there. By this time he had already finished two walls each, 6 to 7 spans wide and 2.3 meters high with four bulwarks of the same height, all of stone. Many armed men and 400 labourers were being employed and the work was being carried on with great speed so that the fortress could be completed before the Viceroy sent a fleet from Goa to hinder the work. António de Azevedo, captain of Gangolly, and Mallasena, general of the 'king of the mountain', who reported this development to the Viceroy, opined that Virabhadra would violate peace as soon as fortress was completed half way. Mallasena offered the Portuguese 1,000 men-of-arms to obstruct the fortification. Deliberating on these developments, the Viceroy-in-Council decided to demand the destruction of the fortress under construction. Accordingly, Beliago, the captain-major of Kanara, who was on his way to Cochin, with a fleet of 16 ships and who was to stop at Honavar for wood, was instructed to meet Vittala Shenoy at Honavar and say that if Virabhadra wanted war before peace, the Portuguese were prepared for it; but that if he wanted peace, the fortress must be demolished forthwith and the soldiers be withdrawn from Gangolly. If Vittala agreed to secure the destruction of the fortress, Beliago was to see it done and then proceed to Cochin. If Vittala refused to do so, the captain-major was to suspend his voyage to Cochin and to communicate instead with Mallasena, the king of Karnad and the ruler of Bangher in order to induce them to send their soldiers to Gangolly, which they always wished to do in order to capture Upper Basrur from Virabhadra, and to allow this they had requested the Viceroy several times with the offer that they would secure Gangolly for the Portuguese.

The major was to leave six ships at Honavar to fetch wood and with the remaining ten ships he was to attack the vessels at the ports of Kanara. He was also to keep on encouraging and favouring the enemies of Virabhadra. If Vittala was to say, as a third alternative possibility, that he would proceed to Goa for peace talks, the major was to ensure that he actually sailed for Goa and then proceed on his own voyage to Cochin.[32]

The Portuguese wondered why Virabhadra insisted upon preventing them from entrenching themselves in Gangolly which they had secured by two 'good' titles: (1) by way of gift from the municipality of Upper Basrur to whom the peninsula originally belonged; (2) by the treaty between them and Virappa Nayaka. They were surprised also to be asked to destroy their fortress of Basrur, without compensation in the form of Gangolly. The King of Portugal ordered the Viceroy not to give up the Basrur fortress without his express command, even if Gangolly was secured and fortified.[33]

Vittala Shenoy came to Goa with the following proposals of peace and friendship: (1) The Portuguese should destroy their fortress at Basrur and cede all their lands there to Virabhadra who would then cede to them the whole of the peninsula of Gangolly, with the condition that the Portuguese would never erect a fortress in Gangolly in addition to the one which they had there already. (2)

Virabhadra would grant the *cazados* as much other lands in Gangolly as they had in Basrur. (3) The Portuguese could collect the customary land revenues from the subjects of Gangolly but the lands belonging to the temple *Gufeçar* should be free. (4) The price of pepper could be decided largely by the Viceroy. (5) There should be a perpetual treaty of peace between the Portuguese and Virabhadra, as friends of friends and enemies of enemies. (6) The Portuguese should assist Virabhadra against the Tuluvas, whenever necessary. (7) Virabhadra should be allowed every year twelve horses, or as many more as possible without taxes. (8) He should be given three passports every year for three embarkations to the Strait of Mecca, Muscat, and to Kishin. (9) He would release rice and wood from his territories as before for the Portuguese. (10) He would not admit any pirates into his lands. (11) He would not impose more taxes on the Portuguese than was customary. (12) The Portuguese should return the two ships captured from him. Vittala Shenoy was not empowered to agree to any modifications in these terms.[34]

The Viceroy-in-Council, in a meeting on December 21, considered the first provision the most offensive to the prestige and reputation of the Portuguese. Virabhadra himself "did not inherit fortresses from his forefathers to give them up". The Portuguese, therefore, would not dismantle their fortress of Basrur, not even by agreement, and not even though they knew very well that it was of no use once the island of Gangolly was fortified, unless the King of Portugal wished to dismantle it on his free will. Finally, it was decided to tell the ambassador that the question of dismantling the fortress would be left to the King of Portugal and that no terms regarding pepper and other matters were acceptable to the Viceroy, on the basis of which negotiations could be continued.[35]

Nothing concrete was concluded until March 31, 1633, by which time Virabhadra completed the construction of the fortress in Gangolly. Vittala, however, was back for peace talks. The Viceroy-in-Council considered whether they should conclude a treaty with Virabhadra even though the latter had completed the fortress and had collected the revenues of Gangolly. Their conclusion was that they should purchase from him every year 350 *khandis* of pepper, but 500 *khandis* in the first or current year, at the rate of 22 *pagodas* a *khandi*, provided that Gangolly was left by him in the same condition in which it was at the time of commencing peace talks, and also provided that its revenues were left to them.[36]

At last, on April 5, 1633 a treaty of peace and perpetual friendship was signed in Goa between the Portuguese and Virabhadra. Its terms and conditions were as follows: (1) No change or modification should be made with regard to the Portuguese fortresses of Gangolly and Basrur, everything being left in the state in which it was when Virabhadra wrote to the Viceroy through Vittala to conclude the treaty, until the Viceroy received further orders from the King of Portugal. This meant that the Portuguese and Virabhadra were to retain their respective fortresses in Gangolly and Basrur, until the King of Portugal agreed to dismantle the Basrur fortress. (2) There should be perpetual friendship between the Portuguese and Virabhadra, both being friends of friends and enemies of enemies, and helping each other against each other's enemies to whatever extent possible. Virabhadra should not admit pirates or Malabaris into his ports. (3) Virabhadra and his successors should release all the rice and other foodgrains from the lands of Ikkeri and its ports of Goa and other Portuguese fortresses, as was always the custom. He should instruct his *thanadar* at Upper Basrur that the rice should by right be released for the Portuguese. (4) He should command the merchants of Upper Basrur to pay the customary annual tribute of 500 loads of rice to the Portuguese. (5) The latter should compulsorily purchase from Virabhadra every year 350 *khandis* of pepper at the rate of 22 *pagodas* a *khandi*. In payment for this pepper he should accept the exchange rate of 102 old *São Tomés* for 100 *pagodas* of Ikkeri. If the Portuguese wished to purchase more pepper it should be at a price fixed by agreement between them and Virabhadra as between merchant and merchant. (6) Virabhadra should be allowed to take from Goa, every year, twelve horses of Arabia free of duties; in return he should release every year 24 masts by the river of Gersoppa or by the waters of Sangari (?) for the Portuguese ships. (7) The Portuguese should give Virabhadra three passports every year for his three embarkations to Mecca, Muscat and Kishin, as was the custom before. (8) The Portuguese should be allowed to cut down and bring all the necessary wood from his territories, without any payment, for their shipyard; and he should aid them in the process of cutting and transporting the wood. (9) He should instruct his tax-collectors of the Kanara coast not to collect from the Portuguese more taxes than those imposed by his grandfather, Venkatappa, at the commencement of the latter's reign. (10) The Portuguese should return the two ships captured from Virabhadra. (11) If either party violated any of the terms and conditions of the treaty, the violating party should pay the other all the losses and damages caused.[37]

Virabhadra wrote to the Viceroy after the conclusion of this treaty and assured him of the supply of iron and saltpetre at a reasonable price. He thanked the Viceroy for the latter's present consisting of a horse and the saddle, and a sword and a spear, saying: "I did not expect these things from Your Excellency except pure friendship, but as Your Excellency sent them with love, I accepted them with great pleasure".[38] No doubt, he also had sent a present of 300 loads of fine rice to the Viceroy before the treaty was signed. In the letter of credentials given to his ambassador, Virabhadra had sought a gunner, a master of horses, a physician and a cook from the Viceroy.[39] It is not indicated whether these were supplied or not.

With all these, Virabhadra was accused of violating the terms and conditions of the treaty. We learn from the minutes of the Council of State held on November 18, 1634 that he demanded 28 *pagodas* for a *khandi* of pepper, whereas the treaty provided for 22 *pagodas*. However, 28 *pagodas* was the price charged formerly by Venkatappa. It seems that the Viceroy had deliberately included the low rate of 22 *pagodas*, taking advantage of the proposal of Virabhadra that the price of pepper should largely be decided by the former. Virabhadra prohibited the supply of even a single load of rice to the Portuguese so that they should be compelled to pay the raised price of pepper. The Viceroy-in-Council decided to insist upon the terms of the treaty and to warn Virabhadra not to force new hostilities by violating the treaty. Baltazar Marinho, procurator, who had been sent to secure the pepper, was instructed accordingly. If the Nayaka refused to abide by the treaty, Marinho was to withdraw quickly from his kingdom. Hostility was then to be commenced by hindering Virabhadra's embarkation.[40]

By February 1635, Virabhadra subdued all the rebels. The Viceroy wrote to the King of Portugal on February 6: "King Virabhadra Nayaka has overpowered all the kingdoms which, at the death of his grandfather, Venkatappa Nayaka, had rebelled, because he (Venkatappa) conquered them tyrannically, and the lands under his (Virabhadra's) control border upon those of the king of Cannanore. However, Virabhadra did not lack in enemies, particularly his neighbours in the hinterland, against whom he sent several armies, some of which he led personally. The Viceroy considered him "arrogant by inclination and deficient in keeping promise". This, no doubt was a reference to Virabhadra's demand for more than the contracted price for pepper. His threat of war seems to have resulted in Virabhadra's retreat from the position he had taken. The Portuguese were given pepper at 20 *pagodas* a *khandi* as per the treaty. They were also allowed to take rice as before.[41]

In the following year Virabhadra again demanded a higher price for pepper. He also seems to have hinted that the Portuguese should dismantle their fortress of Basrur. In order to pressurise the Portuguese he blockaded rice supplies to them from his territories as in the previous year. Considering these factors in a meeting of January 17, 1636 the Viceroy-in-Council came to the conclusion that under no circumstances should a higher price be conceded and that the Basrur fortress be not destroyed. They decided to purchase foodgrains from the ports of Manjeshwara and Kumbala. Though these ports belonged to Virabhadra, the people there sold their rice to anyone who paid for it.[42] By April, Virabhadra sent an ambassador, Devarasa Shenoy, to Goa with certain proposals of general character. During the course of the discussion in the Council meeting concerning the embassy, some members suggested that the embassy should be taken advantage of to negotiate for the destruction of the fortress built by Virabhadra in Gangolly. They also opined that if this was agreed to and if Gangolly was given to the Portuguese with the right to fortify it, they might consent to dismantle their fortress of Basrur. However, the last mentioned issue was to be mooted only if Devarasa expressly referred to it. So also they thought that the issue of the price of pepper should come first from Devarasa. The Viceroy, however, decided to respond to the embassy by merely saying that the Portuguese were prepared to abide by the treaty already concluded and that certain complaints made by Virabhadra against the previous Viceroy, Count of Linhares, would be referred to the King of Portugal.[43]

The document that Devarasa submitted to the Viceroy is of considerable interest. It traces the relations between the Portuguese and Ikkeri from the days of Venkatappa, saying that there was always friendship between the two, and that Venkatappa, at his death, had advised Virabhadra to continue friendly relations with the Portuguese. But, "Count of Linhares, Viceroy, sent a fleet of which Diogo de Sousa e Menezes was the captain-major, in order to negotiate with the merchants and *ballalas*, vassals of the king my lord, and on the other hand sent ... Baltazar de Araujo to king Virabhadra Nayaka my lord to say that the fleet which the Count sent was in his favour", thus deceiving Virabhadra who intended to be on friendly terms with the Portuguese in keeping with his grandfathers's advice. The document continued to say that when the Viceroy began to fortify Gangolly, Virabhadra told him that it belonged to the king of Ikkeri and therefore he should not fortify it. But the fortification was continued. While Virabhadra was absent from Ikkeri, being engaged in a battle against the `king of the mountain', some captains revolted and proclaimed Virappa as king of Ikkeri. Virabhadra fought against the latter for six months at the end of which Virappa was defeated and his supporters were punished. The kings of Sonda and Bilgi, two important supporters of Virappa, were captured. While Virabhadra and Virappa were at war the Count of Linhares went to fortify Gangolly. The Viceroy was told that Virappa was only a figurehead, and not the rightful king; but the Count concluded a treaty with him, setting aside the peace proposals of Virabhadra, from whom only the presents were accepted. Virappa gave the Count 10,000 *pagodas* of gold and agreed to whatever the latter told him.

In concluding the document pointed out that it was found impossible to have friendship with the Portuguese, in spite of the treaty of 1633, as long as the Count of Linhares remained the Viceroy; but hope was expressed that the new Viceroy, Pero da Silva, would be amenable to friendly relations.[44] As this document was considered as containing no concrete proposals, Devarasa made another statement in which he declared that Virabhadra did not wish to allow the Portuguese both the fortresses of Basrur and Gangolly, but only one, and that the rest of the terms and conditions could be settled after the destruction of one of the two fortresses.[45]

A special meeting of the Council of State was held on April 25,[46] to consider the clarifying declaration of Devarasa. Three former captains-major of Kanara were invited and asked to give their opinions. The proposition before that was: what advantages the Portuguese could get by having the fortress of Gangolly or by not having it; and which of the two fortresses of Gangolly and Basrur was of more utility than the other. One of the captain-majors opined as follows: (1) At the time of war the fortress of Basrur could be better defended with less number of soldiers, because it was small, well-constructed and more amenable to defence than that of Gangolly. (2) The fortress of Basrur was the gateway of Upper Basrur from where nothing could go out, and to which nothing could come, except by way of the fortress by the river. That was why the merchants of Upper Basrur paid an annual tribute. (3) Whenever the Ikkeri rulers blocked rice supplies the *cazados* of Basrur could go to city by night in order to purchase the commodity which the local merchants sold them. This facility would not be available at Gangolly which was encircled by water. (4) Even if Virabhadra gave the peninsula to the Portuguese on his own free will, or it was gained by force, the existing fortress was of no use for defence as it was far away from the pass from the mainland. A wall with a bulwark would have to be built at the *Pao* guarding the pass, and then alone the Portuguese could gain by the products of Gangolly and its population could be converted to Christianity as in Goa. (5) Notwithstanding the impediment that the Basrur fortress depended heavily upon help by the river in times of war, and that heavy and large embarkations could not reach the fortress at low tide, the fortress could always be relieved with the help of small fast moving ships and *sanguiceis*. This defence had always been provided with great effect. In fact, André Furtado, the then captain-major of Kanara, sailed up the river and caused such damage to the enemy whom he compelled to seek peace.

For these reasons he thought that the Portuguese should retain the Basrur fortress on a permanent basis. The existing fortress of Gangolly should be destroyed, as it was nothing but a source of expenses and vexations. The Christians, who were at Gangolly were being insulted by the natives with impunity. They broke, for instance, a cross that was placed at the distance of a stone throw from the fortress. He also pointed out that if the Basrur fortress was given up, Virabhadra would certainly entrench himself there and thus gain control over the river and Upper Basrur, which would result in the loss of the tribute to the Portuguese from the latter city. Besides, the advantages from Gangolly depended much upon Upper Basrur which was a centre of much trade.

The second captain-major had a different opinion. It was true that the Basrur fortress was of better build, was on a better and more elevated site, and was more convenient to defend than the fortress São Miguel of Gangolly; but there were many difficulties in relieving it in times of war, because it was away from the mouth of the river and the enemies, placing themselves along the bank, could bombard the Portuguese ships navigating the river. Besides, cargo ships and other heavy vessels could not reach the Basrur fortress except at high tide. It was also known that the current was depositing more and more sand at the bar of the Basrur fortress. Further, it was impossible to aid the fortress by land. Defence and security of the fortress were always important, but the position of the Basrur fortress was very weak indeed from this point of view. On the other hand, Gangolly could be relieved anytime by landing soldiers by the sea shore. If Virabhadra gave Gangolly to the Portuguese, a fortress could be erected at the *Pao* and the place could become impregnable to the enemy. However, with the existing fortress of São Miguel alone Gangolly could not be controlled effectively, particularly because of the existence of an enemy fortress at the distance of a gunshot. If Virabhadra destroyed this fortress first and gave Gangolly to the Portuguese, the Basrur fortress could be destroyed.

The third captain major agreed with the second, but pointed out that São Miguel too was away from the bar and aid by land was not easy.

The consensus therefore appeared to be that Gangolly was better than Basrur, provided the former was given wholly to the Portuguese and a fortress was erected at the *Pao*. Accordingly, the Viceroy-in-Council came to the conclusion that the Basrur fortress could be destroyed provided Virabhadra destroyed his fortress in Gangolly first, and gave the whole of the peninsula to the Portuguese with the permission to erect their fortress at the *Pao*. The destruction of the Basrur fortress was to be effected only after fortifying Gangolly at the *Pao* and other necessary points and not before. This resolution was made known to Devarasa who, however, said that he was not commissioned to agree to the ceding of additional territories in Gangolly. He therefore sought permission to return to Ikkeri to present the case before Virabhadra for his further orders. The Viceroy-in-Council was not prepared to permit him to go immediately, fearing that Virabhadra might create fresh troubles. They decided to wait until news was received from the captain-major of Kanara concerning the situation there, and then send their own ambassador to Ikkeri along with Devarasa.[47]

By the latter half of October, Devarasa was back with practically the same proposals from Virabhadra. The latter was not prepared to undo his fortress of Gangolly, nor was he prepared to allow the Portuguese to erect another of theirs at the *Pao*. But he insisted that one of the Portuguese fortresses of Basrur and Gangolly must be destroyed. The Portuguese could not take any decision in the face of this firmness.[48]

Virabhadra did not give up trade relations with the Portuguese. In March, 1637 he wrote to the Viceroy demanding again 28 *pagodas* a *khandi* of pepper. He wrote that the English had offered him 30 *pagodas* and that they would make him the payment in the form of lead at the rate of 22 and 1/2 *pagodas* a *khandi*. The Viceroy decided to respond by saying that the English were deceiving the Nayaka; that the former sold the very lead to the Portuguese at the rate of 20 *patacas* a *khandi*, which came to about 12 *pagodas*; and that if Virabhadra was prepared to purchase lead from the Portuguese at the rate quoted to him by the English, he would pay Virabhadra 30 *pagodas* for a *khandi* of pepper. This was a good commercial trick of the Portuguese. They decided to keep Virabhadra in good mood so that he would not block rice supplies. At the same time they made an arrangement to purchase additional pepper in Cochin.[49]

Martim Teixeira de Azavedo, captain-major of Kanara, was sent as ambassador to Virabhadra. He was to be assisted by Sancara da Gama, probably a Hindu converted to Christianity, who was apparently a good merchant. Azavedo was instructed to complete his mission as speedily as possible and be at Cannanore by the beginning of July. He was to secure as much pepper as possible in Virabhadra's territories, paying a higher price than 22 *pagodas* a *khandi* if absolutely necessary, but under the condition that an additional quantity should be given at a cheaper rate, so that on the whole the price paid for all the pepper would be equivalent to the current price. This shows that the market rate of pepper was higher than the contracted price; but the Portuguese were reluctant to pay it; yet they did not hesitate to accuse Virabhadra of violating the terms of treaty. There was another matter to be settled with Virabhadra. One of his ships was captured by the Portuguese off Muscat. The Viceroy learnt from Gama that the cargo was worth about 2,500 *pagodas*. Virabhadra demanded satisfaction. In response, the Viceroy wrote to him saying that he was prepared to give satisfaction provided wood was supplied to the Portuguese. Azavedo was now instructed to see that this affair was settled on the line indicated and that the satisfaction given did not go much beyond 2,000 *pagodas*. Further, Azavedo was to urge Virabhadra to throw out of his ports and lands all the English merchants who had gone there. The commercial activities of the rival merchants were highly disadvantageous to the Portuguese and the Viceroy told Azavedo that if the English were permanently debarred from the territories of Virabhadra it would the greatest of the services he would have done for the King of Portugal.

He was to endeavour to get a written promise from Virabhadra regarding the exclusion of the English as well as regarding continued sale of pepper to the Portuguese. The Viceroy visualised that before conceding these requests of the Portuguese Virabhadra would ask for the destruction of the Basrur fortress. However, Azavedo was to say that he had no instruction in this respect; but that he would urge the Viceroy to agree to it if Virabhadra consented to destroy his fortress of Gangolly first, and not to erect there any other in the future.[50]

By June, 1637 Bangher, allied with others, revolted against Virabhadra again. So also the king of Sonda fought against the latter. Virabhadra's administrator of Upper Basrur and other territories in the neighbourhood sought permission from the captain of the Basrur fortress to allow the residents of these territories to take shelter in the fortress whenever necessary. The captain wrote to the Viceroy on June 24, seeking his orders in this respect. The Viceroy-in-Council meeting on July 29, came to the conclusion that the Portuguese should be neutral, not favouring any of the belligerents openly; and that the request of Virabhadra's administrator should be conceded to a certain extent in view of the existing friendship between the Portuguese and Virabhadra, the people being allowed to gather outside the fortress, but not inside, so that the security of the fortress could remain unimpaired.[51]

The queen of Bangher wrote to the Viceroy on January 25, 1638 recalling the good old friendship between Bangher and the Portuguese and seeking Portuguese aid against Virabhadra. She also complained that the former captain of Mangalore, Diogo Tavares, had taken two pieces of artillery belonging to her. The Viceroy decided to return the artillery and reprimand the captain. As for assistance against Virabhadra, nothing concrete was to be given.[52]

The Portuguese were well-disposed towards Virabhadra Nayaka in those months. In February 1638 Vasudeva, Virabhadra's administrator-in-chief in Barkur, sought explosives from the Portuguese who agreed to send the war material readily under the pretext that it was being carried to Basrur for the defence of their own fortress there. Further, Azavedo, ambassador to Virabhadra was instructed to write to the latter that the Portuguese had no intention of putting pressure upon him or of meddling in his affairs and that they did not want Gangolly unless it was given freely after peace was established.[53]

By this time, the Adil Shah also had entered the fray against Virabhadra. The latter wrote to the Viceroy in February informing him that the Adil Shah had already taken some of his fortresses and his very capital, Ikkeri, where all his war provision were also lost. He, therefore, requested the Viceroy to send him some explosives, guns and gunpowder. He also dispatched to Basrur two envoys, Devarasa Shenoy and Rama Pai. The latter was empowered to concede to the Portuguese whatever they wished regarding Gangolly. In fact, in the beginning of February, Vasudeva, chief administrator of Barkur, had suggested to the captain of Basrur, Manoel Rois (Rodrigues) Bravo, that the Portuguese should quickly send 2,000 men-of-arms, who were natives of Goa, and some workers to fortify the peninsula of Gangolly, if the Portuguese wanted to ensure the place for themselves before the forces of the Adil Shah occupied it. Taking these factors into account the Viceroy-in-Council decided as follows in a meeting of March 2, 1638: (1) to send 50 barrels of explosives, though in an earlier meeting of February 20, the Council had decided to send only 30 barrels on the request of Vasudeva; and to send, in addition, 100 cans of gunpowder and some guns. A responsible man like Azavedo was to carry these war materials to Basrur to be delivered there to Virabhadra. Utmost secrecy was to be maintained regarding the real destination of the materials, for the Adil Shah also had sought a similar favour from the Portuguese through the *havaldar* of Ponda, Mahamad Razak, but was refused. The materials, therefore, were to be carried with the declared purpose of providing the Portuguese the fortress of Basrur. (2) Not to send 2,000 native soldiers of Goa to Gangolly, as it was not possible to assemble so many. The captain of Basrur was to say merely that the Portuguese would fortify Gangolly after it was given to them by Virabhadra of his own accord.[54]

Some secret letters seem to have been exchanged between the Viceroy and Virabhadra. One was written by the former on December 14, 1638. Probably, Virabhadra had sought the mediation of the Viceroy between him and the Adil Shah. He agreed to do the office. He wrote in the letter just mentioned: "And to my ambassador to the court of the Adil Shah, I have written, and I have to write anew that he should cooperate (*corra com amizade*) with the ambassador of Your Highness and that he should help in the negotiations which have been ordered by your Highness to the very Adil Shah and in all other matters I shall always do the office of a good friend ... [55]

António Borges da Costa, *cazado* of Basrur, who was sent as the new ambassador to Virabhadra, wrote to the Viceroy on February 24, 1639 giving an account of his proceedings with Virabhadra. The latter's father-in-law seems to have been obstructing the transfer of Gangolly to the Portuguese but Virabhadra was now ready to cede the places, though he complained that Count of Linhares had written to him saying that the King of Portugal would soon order the abandonment of the Basrur fortress, but nothing had actually been done in this respect until Rama Pai was authorised to conclude matters concerning the cession of the peninsula. Costa found Virabhadra ready to sell pepper as merchant to merchant. The former was also hopeful in excluding the rival merchants, the English, from Bhatkal with the assistance of Siddha Lingappa, a general of Virabhadra, who preferred the Portuguese to the English. Already, in December 1638, Virabhadra had refused entrance to an English ship into the Bhatkal port.[56] Siddha considered the Portuguese better friends as they had helped Virabhadra with war materials. He convinced the advisors of Virabhadra of this and Costa was determined to leave the court only after achieving the destruction of the English factory at Bhatkal. However, he noticed that the English were doing their best to retain their trading centre by spending a lot on presents and bribes to important men in Virabhadra's court. They had solicited personages like Pramodji Baniane to plead their case before Virabhadra. Costa discovered that Vasudeva, chief administrator of Barkur, was a great enemy of the Portuguese, because he had once told Virabhadra that he would take one of the two fortresses of the Portuguese in Basrur and Gangolly. Besides, Vasudeva allowed the Dutch to embark at Basrur where they remained nearby the Portuguese fortress for four or five days. He even urged Virabhadra to permit the Dutch to establish their factory in an island named Bogapatão (?) near Barkur.[57]

The English factory at Bhatkal was destroyed soon, as we learn from a letter written by Virabhadra to the Viceroy on March 6, 1639.[58] However, in 1642 the English were again settled in the same place and they were also allowed to trade at Basrur.[59]

Virabhadra awaited a reply from the King of Portugal concerning Gangolly. The reply came by November 1639. The King of Portugal was not ready to destroy his fortress of Gangolly; instead he commanded it to be strengthened as it was (1) more secure than Basrur for sheltering war ships as well as cargo ships which went there for rice and other goods; and (2) open to ships throughout the year, and thus capable of being relieved any time in case the enemies in Kanara should besiege the place. However, he agreed to dismantle the Basrur fortress and transfer the materials to Gangolly, provided the whole of the peninsula of Gangolly, or at least that much part of it which was equivalent to the lands possessed by the Portuguese in Basrur, was ceded to him. Virabhadra's ambassador was, of course, informed that the whole of Gangolly should be ceded. It was in keeping with the usual trick of asking for more so that the lesser was secured.[60]

In the meantime, the Adil Shah seems to have put Virabhadra under greater stress. Costa informed the Viceroy-in-Council on November 12, that Virabhadra sought to be sheltered along with his family in any of the fortresses of the Portuguese in Kanara, in case he should have the worst success against the Adil Shah. He also sought additional guns and ammunitions.[61] It is not known what decision the Viceroy took in this respect.

Virabhadra and the Portuguese did not come to any decision regarding Gangolly even by the beginning of 1640. The Portuguese in fact were not prepared to take any decisions until after fresh instructions came from the King of Portugal in September of that year. Virabhadra was not prepared to cede the whole of Gangolly. He was also not agreeable to the condition that he should destroy his fortress in Gangolly first.[62] Pero da Silva (1635-39), successor of Count of Linhares, was not very much impressed by Gangolly. In a letter to the King of Portugal dated September 10, 1638, he pointed out that it cost the Royal Treasury 14,000 *pardaus* a year but had no income of its own; and that Virabhadra was retaining even the revenues of the temple. He in fact was in favour of giving up the fortress of Gangolly. The King of Portugal, in his letter of February 18, 1640 instructed António Telles de Menezes, successor of Pero da Silva, to consult the Council of State and let him know the different opinions of its members in this connection.[63]

From the same letter of the King of Portugal we also learn that the Adil Shah demanded exorbitant tributes from Virabhadra and that the latter complained to the Mughal emperor, overlord of the Adil Shah, offering him to pay the very tribute which he was paying to the Adil Shah. Virabhadra probably thought that the emperor would protect him against the Adil Shah if he became the direct feudatory of the emperor. Virabhadra's own vassals adopted the same strategy. The queens of Ullala and Bangher and the king of Gersoppa approached the Adil Shah for protection, offering him to pay the tribute that they owed to Virabhadra. In these circumstances the Viceroy was instructed to follow a cautious policy of aiding some with ammunitions in utmost secrecy so that none would be extinguished completely and none became too powerful in Kanara. Outwardly he was to be neutral "encouraging and entertaining" the belligerents.[64]

By the end of November 1643 Virabhadra recovered Ikkeri and much of the other territories lost to the Adil Shah. He remained friendly towards the Portuguese.[65] However, his war with the Adil Shah was not yet over. By December 20 of the same year the latter again marched against Virabhadra. The queen of Bangher apparently aided his enemy. The Portuguese favoured Virabhadra, since they thought that the Hindu king was a better neighbour than the Muslim ruler.[66]

Towards the middle of 1644 Virabhadra's affairs took another unfortunate turn. His uncle, Shivappa Nayaka, turned against him. In June, Manoel Viera, captain of Basrur, informed the Viceroy that Shivappa had encircled the fortress of Canarcota (Konnara in Karkal taluka ?) with 7,000 or 8,000 men of whom, 1,000 were cavalrymen; that Virabhadra had taken shelter inside; that he was being attacked by land as well as by sea; that Shivappa had come with the pretext of asking for money which was promised by Virabhadra to the Mouro, namely the Adil Shah; that Virabhadra, however, knew that he had actually come to take the very kingdom from him; and that Shivappa was also known to be planning to attack Gangolly. Bravo requested the Viceroy to send reinforcements to Gangolly and also send him instructions what he should do in case Virabhadra desired to take shelter in any of the Portuguese fortresses. The Viceroy-in-Council met on June 20 and decided as follows: (1) Since it was the rainy season no ammunition and explosives could be sent to Gangolly immediately. (2) The Portuguese should give shelter to Virabhadra in any of their fortresses, if he sought such a favour. He should not be charged, as he was a friendly neighbour. (3) However, it would be of convenience in avoiding dissensions with Shivappa, if Virabhadra left, as soon as possible, the fortress where he might be given shelter.[67]

What befell Virabhadra thereafter cannot be gathered from the extant Portuguese documents. Probably Shivappa defeated and killed Virabhadra in 1645 as indicated in *Chikkadevarayavamshavali*.[68]

REFERENCES

1. At his accession, Virabhadra was a young man of 20 or 24, addicted to luxury and bad habits (Henry Heras, "The expansion wars of Venkatappa Nayaka of Ikkeri", pp. 1-3, 5)
2. Henry Heras, *op. cit.*, p. 5.
3. *Assentos*, I, p. 303.
4. Heras, *op. cit.*, pp. 5-7.
5. *CEO*, II, p. 234.
6. *DRI*, IV, pp. 305-6.
7. *Assentos*, I, pp. 245-8.
8. *Ibid.*, pp. 249-50.
9. *Ibid.*, p. 253.
10. *Ibid.*, pp. 252-4.
11. *Ibid.*, pp. 256-8.
12. Heras, *op. cit.*, p. 7.
13. *Assentos*, I, p. 248.
14. *Ibid.*, p. 264.
15. *Ibid.*, p. 513.
16. *Supra*, ch. 5.
17. *Assentos*, I, pp. 513-4.

18. *Ibid.*, pp. 389-90.
19. Virappa Nayaka, son of Ramaraja Nayaka, was a rival of Virabhadra for the throne of Ikkeri and not a joint ruler with Virabhadra as suggested by N.L. Rao ("The Nayaks of Keladi", *VSCV*, p. 263).
20. *Assentos*, I, pp. 536-41. In clause (5) of the treaty the word '*taurim*' means a local boat. From this I have interpreted it to mean the navigation of such boats.
21. J.F.J. Biker, *Colecção de Tratados e Concertos de Pazes*, I, p. 276.
22. *Ibid.*, pp. 277-9.
23. Virappa might have died early, in August 1631, for the viceroy wrote about the death to the King of Portugal on August 11 (*Assentos*, III, p. 641).
24. *Assentos*, I, p. 390.
25. *Ibid.*, pp. 390-1.
26. *Ibid.*, pp. 391-3.
27. *Ibid.*, p. 411.
28. '*Pao*' or '*pau*' means wood. The site of *Pao*, therefore may be taken to imply a site where there was wood.
29. *Assentos*, I, pp. 426-7.
30. *Ibid.*, pp. 554-5.
31. *Ibid.*, pp. 555-6.
32. *Ibid.*, pp. 448-50, 559-60.
33. *Ibid.*, p. 449.
34. *Ibid.*, pp. 456-7.
35. *Ibid.*, pp. 458-9.
36. *Ibid.*, pp. 469-70.
37. *Ibid.*, pp. 569-71.
38. *Ibid.*, p. 571.
39. J. F.J. Biker, *op. cit.*, pp. 302-3.
40. *Assentos*, III, pp. 12-3.
41. *Ibid.*, pp. 528-9.
42. *Ibid.*, pp. 54-6.
43. *Ibid.*, p. 73.
44. *Ibid.*, pp. 75-8.
45. *Ibid.*, pp. 78-9.
46. *Ibid.*, pp. 79-83.
47. *Assentos*, III, p. 84.
48. *Ibid.*, pp. 116-7.
49. *Ibid.*, pp. 167-9.
50. *Ibid.*, pp. 543-5.
51. *Ibid.*, pp. 173-4.
52. *Ibid.*, p. 202.
53. *Ibid.*, p. 202.
54. *Ibid.*, pp. 202-4.
55. *Ibid.*, pp. 555-6.

56. *EF*, 1637-1641, p. 115.
57. *Assentos*, III, pp. 650-3.
58. *Ibid.*, pp. 654-5.
59. *EF*, 1642-1645, p. 109.
60. *Assentos*, II, pp. 271-2.
61. *Ibid.*, p. 270.
62. *Ibid.*, p. 277.
63. *Ibid.*, p. 562.
64. *Ibid.*, pp. 561-2.
65. *Assentos*, III, p. 657.
66. *Ibid.*, p. 658.
67. *Ibid.*, pp. 24-5.
68. N. L. Rao, *op. cit*, p. 263. Writes Rao: "The *Chikkadevarayavamshavali*, however, informs us that Shivappa Nayaka murdered his chief Virabhadra Nayaka and ascended the throne and hence Chikka-devaraja, the Yuvaraja of Mysore rejected the presents offered to him by such a traitor. Though there is no apparent reason for doubting the veracity of this statement, *no other evidence in support of it is available from any other source* (italics mine). The Portuguese document just referred to, namely, the minutes of the meeting of the Council of State, containing the substance of Manoel's letter.and the decision thereof (footnote 67 above), may be considered as supporting the statement of the *Chikkadevarayavamshavali.*

8

THE PORTUGUESE AND THE NAYAKAS OF IKKERI - III (1645-1660)

Shivappa Nayaka (1645-60),[1] the greatest of the Nayakas of Ikkeri, proved to be the destroyer of the political power of the Portuguese in Kanara. In 1650s he captured from them all of their fortresses on the Kanara coast. He promised afterwards to allow them to establish their factories in some of his ports; but nothing definite was concluded in this respect until his death. No doubt, circumstances were favourable to Shivappa in his wars against the Portuguese. The latter were hard pressed by the Dutch who waged wars against them all around and obstructed their trade and commerce so much that Portugal suffered considerably in wealth and power. The King of Portugal was not in a position to send sufficient help to India in order to fight Shivappa. Nature too was unkind to the Portuguese. In May, 1652, just before Shivappa commenced hostilities against them, they lost many ships in a storm. This does not mean that Shivappa's successes were due only to these circumstances. To be sure, he was a very enterprising and energetic king who achieved successes not only against the Portuguese but also against several of his powerful neighbours. The Portuguese did have opportunities to gain his friendship which would have been of great help to them in their war efforts against their greatest enemy, the Dutch; but they were too slow in appreciating his strength and power. They sought his friendship when it was too late to seek, as we shall see in the following pages.

At his accession Shivappa faced grave difficulties. The Adil Shah, who had captured many lands belonging to the kingdom of

Ikkeri, continued to be hostile. In this circumstance he began with peaceful relations with the Portuguese. He indicated his willingness, through an envoy, to negotiate a settlement with them regarding the peninsula of Gangolly. The Viceroy-in-Council, meeting on February 12, 1646, and recalling that Gangolly was always considered important to promote Portuguese interests in Kanara, particularly to prevent the Adil Shah from mastering the Kanara coast, decided to negotiate so as to secure the 'island' with the right to erect a fort at the site of the *Pao* or any other better spot. At the same time they were not to consent to destroy the Basrur fortress, if Shivappa proposed such a course. The usual tactic of delay was to be taken recourse to by saying that the destruction would depend upon the will of the King of Portugal to whom the proposal would be reported.[2]

In keeping with this decision, the Viceroy sent a letter to Shivappa through the latter's envoy. Shivappa was told that it would be in his own interest to give Gangolly to the Portuguese. He was urged to erect a new fortress at the site of the *Pao* and allow the Portuguese to station their soldiers and artillery therein, so that Gangolly would be safe from Shivappa's enemies. He was assured that he could come into this fortress with his men whenever necessary and from there endeavour to recover his lost lands. The Viceroy cited the example of the Bangar chief and others who always trusted the Portuguese and received their protection. He disclosed that the Adil Shah, who always desired to capture Kanara, had requested the Portuguese several times in the past to permit him to take his army through Portuguese territories in Kanara, but was not granted this permission. He continued to say that the fortress of Basrur could be destroyed after the erection of a fortress at the site of the *Pao*. Shivappa was assured that the Portuguese had no pretensions over his lands, but expected only what was necessary to shelter themselves.[3] The letter was thus polite in tone, though the Portuguese might have been aware that Shivappa was not strong enough then to have his own way. However, it was in their own interest that he was not discouraged and weakened vis-a-vis the Adil Shah. Nevertheless, they were anxious to secure Gangolly for themselves, as the Viceroy's letter of February 14, to his King would indicate. He wrote: "what suits us better is to fortify Gangolly well, and with this the fortress of Basrur, which has inherent drawbacks, can be given up ..." But he pointed out that His Majesty had not given any decisive order in the past as to what should be done to get Gangolly. The prevailing opportunity in Kanara, he continued should not be lost by delays.[4]

In response to the Viceroy's letter, Shivappa seems to have sent an ambassador to Goa, but no agreement was arrived at until the beginning of 1647. Writing to the King of Portugal on February 7, the Viceroy said that he could not consent to destroy the Basrur fortress as Shivappa's offer to give only a part of Gangolly was not satisfactory. He thought that the whole of Gangolly alone would be of any use to the Portuguese and accordingly be sent another envoy to Shivappa. The latter was not willing to cede that part of Gangolly where there were temples. He expressed his inability to use force to acquiring Gangolly, because he knew that Shivappa would send his army to occupy the Portuguese fortresses of Kanara if provoked, and because the supply of foodgrains from his territories would be stopped. Besides, the Dutch were already in contact with Shivappa and were ever ready to set him against the Portuguese. The Dutch were also trying to secure his favour for allowing them to trade at his ports and establish their factories at suitable places belonging to him.[5]

It is not possible to say what transpired between the Portuguese and Shivappa during the course of the next four years. Towards the middle of 1651 the Portuguese sent Fr. António Correa as ambassador to him. From the instructions given to him on May 6 of that year we learn that there was some disturbance in Gangolly, though what exactly the disturbance was, is not clear. Apparently, the Portuguese received some damage at the hands of Shivappa's officials, for the instruction asked the ambassador to urge Shivappa to punish "the *thanadar* or whosoever was guilty". Shivappa, like his predecessor, seems to have quoted a higher price for pepper but the ambassador was instructed to agree to purchase only 200 *khandis* at the rate of 25 *pagodas* a *khandi*, more was to be purchased only if it was offered at a lower price. Again, Shivappa had apparently sought Portuguese assistance against the Muslims and in this respect the ambassador was commanded to say that the

Viceroy was always ready to extend it, provided it was not against the king of Cannanore who was a friend of the Portuguese; but if the king of Cannanore brought pirate ships, the Portuguese would aid against such ships.

Another interesting development that can be deduced to have taken place during 1647-51 was Shivappa's offer to give the Portuguese lands in Kasaragod or in those territories conquered by him from the Nairs of Malabar, in lieu of Gangolly. But the ambassador was to turn a deaf ear, if the offer was repeated, pointing out to Shivappa that the Portuguese were not conquerors in Kanara, but had fortresses there from olden days. Of course, the Viceroy conveniently forgot that the fortresses had been established by conquest. The ambassador was to point out that rice and pepper, which were secured in Gangolly, were not available in Kasaragod; and that the Portuguese had spent much in building and garrisoning the fortress of Gangolly. The ambassador was next instructed to impress upon Shivappa's envoy, who was in Goa and with whom he was to proceed to Kanara, how ill-advised Shivappa was not to secure Portuguese friendship, particularly when he was surrounded by enemies — the Nairs, the Mysoreans and the Adil Shah. Fr. Correa was also instructed to get Shivappa's permission for the captain of Honavar to cut some timber for masts. On his way back the ambassador was to tell the captain to have timber yards at Honavar. Further, the captain was to be told not to trust Shivappa, for the latter might cause much loss to the Portuguese who were friendly with the king of Cannanore, Shivappa's enemy.[6]

From a letter of the Viceroy to the King of Portugal dated December 27, 1651, we learn that Shivappa gained some victories against his enemies and thus became more powerful and animated. However the Adil Shah restrained his ambition. And, yet, the Portuguese were apprehensive that he might attack their ill-defended fortresses of Kanara.[7]

The embassy of Fr. Correa seems to have achieved nothing and another ambassador, Duarte de Figueiredo de Mello, was apparently sent. The latter too returned empty-handed by June 1652. In the meantime the Portuguese were involved in a war in Kanara as noted in the minutes of the Council of State, which met on June 3.[8] However, it is not clear from the minutes who their enemy was. It was, in fact, Shivappa himself who commenced hostilities against them in May. The main cause of his hostility was the Portuguese refusal to purchase pepper and pearls from him. The Portuguese believed that the Dutch instigated him against them.[9] Their fortresses of Kanara needed much relief, but it was rainy season. However, the Viceroy-in-Council decided to send at once *almadias* with as many soldiers as possible and with explosives and ammunitions. This was to be followed by additional relief in August,[10] which was actually done on the 8th of the month by sending additional soldiers, ammunitions and explosives. On the 11th a fleet of five ships was sent and again another similar in September.[11] In due course 70 ships were engaged to send regular supplies of soldiers, money, explosives and foodgrains to the defence of the four fortresses in Kanara.[12]

The month of May was an unlucky one for the Portuguese. On the very first day of that month they lost their fleet of Kanara, consisting of 14 warships, in a storm off Gangolly. About 140 embarkations carrying people and merchandise were also lost along with the fleet at the very place. It was the gravest of the losses suffered by them in that month owing to storm. A boat and a galley alone were salvaged. The Viceroy believed that this shipwreck, which took place in Shivappa's jurisdiction, benefited the latter greatly and that it induced him to begin hostilities against the Portuguese. At the Goa bar also some ships were lost. The Viceroy, writing of these losses, urged the King of Portugal to send reinforcements to India.[13]

In August Shivappa sent Vittala Malo an ambassador to the Portuguese. Vittala dispatched, before reaching Goa, a letter to the Viceroy through Fr. Ignacio de Arcamone, who was in Bednur. The letter was written at the instance of Venkatappa, Shivappa's younger brother (*rei pequeno*), with the consent of the former. Its essence was that the Portuguese should purchase pepper from Shivappa, probably at a higher rate than that proposed by the Portuguese, and also perhaps more quantity than what the latter were prepared to purchase. The Viceroy-in-Council, meeting on August 14, decided to purchase 250 *khandis* at the rate of 28 *pagodas*; if Shivappa was not satisfied with this, 25 *khandis* more were to be purchased, 20 in honour of Venkatappa and 5 in honour of the prince, Bhadrappa. The Portuguese came to this decision so as to avoid greater hostilities from Shivappa.[14] However, it was not substantial enough to satisfy the latter.

On the same day Fr. Arcamone was sent back as ambassador to Bednur with instructions regarding his mission there: (1) he was to complain of Shivappa's hostility under the guise of friendship, (2) before proper peace talks were begun, the priest was to propose cessation of all hostilities and fighting on the part of Shivappa whose soldiers were to be withdrawn to a reasonable distance from the Portuguese fortresses. If this was agreed to, the priest was to inform the captains of the fortresses and the captains-majors of the fleets to suspend hostilities on their part, (3) he was to agree to purchase 250 *khandis* of pepper at the rate of 28 *pagodas* a *khandi*. This quantity, and no more, was to be purchased every year. Probably, he was instructed to increase the quantity by 25 *khandis* as per the decision of the Viceroy-in-Council, though it is not indicated in the instructions proper, (4) if Shivappa talked of Gangolly, the ambassador was to say that the matter was under consideration by the King of Portugal who was then at war with Castile. A decision was to be assured within three years, (5) it seems that the Portuguese had captured a ship belonging to Shivappa, probably as soon as the hostilities commenced. In this connection the ambassador was to say that António Carneiro Salema, who had taken the ship, had died in prison before he was tried. However, the ambassador was to agree upon the satisfaction to be given if Shivappa consented to restore to the Portuguese the wood, which came from Cannanore, but which apparently had been captured by him as a retaliation. The satisfaction to be agreed upon was to be low, not because the Portuguese would gain by it, but because the captured ship was small and had very little on board, (6) if Shivappa were to propose that a treaty of peace be concluded, the ambassador was to insist that the terms and conditions should be similar to those agreed to during the vice royalty of Pero da Silva, (7) the ambassador was not to negotiate with Shivappa without the Viceroy's express orders if Shivappa happened to have taken any of the Portuguese fortresses of Kanara by the time the ambassador reached Bednur.[15] This anticipation of the Viceroy was what actually happened, as we shall presently see.

In September a good deed of relief was sent from Goa to the fortresses of Kanara. Three fleets (2 of 6 ships each and the third of 10 ships) were dispatched with soldiers, mariners, money and provisions. 200 native soldiers of Goa, who were mercenaries, were also recruited.[16] In October the Viceroy-in-Council decided to send the fleets of the North and Muscat to Kanara.[17]

However, all these were too late. On October 28 the Viceroy received the news that the fortress of Basrur had been abandoned on August 29. Fr. Correa, who returned from Kanara, explained to the Viceroy-in-Council that the Portuguese garrison was compelled to give up when Shivappa's men besieged the fortress, launched frequent assaults, mined and destroyed a part of the fortress, entered the Portuguese settlement and caused shortage of foodgrains and ammunitions. He also disclosed that the relief sent from Goa in August went mostly to Mangalore, and not to Basrur and that the garrison of Basrur crossed over to Gangolly which was also being besieged vigorously by the enemy. He added that the fortresses of Honavar and Mangalore too were experiencing similar distress at the hands of Shivappa's men. The Viceroy-in-Council were surprisingly late in receiving the news of the loss of Basrur. They decided to do their best to preserve the remaining fortresses by dispatching as much reinforcements as possible and as quickly as permissible. Fr. Correa was also sent back to Kanara.[18]

The captain of Basrur, Miguel de Figueiredo, was accused of negligence and of having surrendered the fortress even though he was in a position to defend it. The charge sheet drawn against him on December 15 states the case as follows: Shivappa began to attack the fortress on June 14, 1652. He had with him six or seven pieces of artillery and many soldiers. He mined and destroyed a bulwark and two earthworks attached to it but all were repaired. Shivappa's battery did not do much damage to the walls of the fortress. Yet the captain proposed to his assistants, and others that the fortress be dismantled and abandoned, and all of them go to the Gangolly fortress, which was done on the night of August 29. During the course of the fight from June to August, only eight of the Portuguese soldiers, black and non-blacks, were killed. The captain pretended to have no explosives, though in one of the bulwarks thirteen cans of the material was abandoned. The captain of Gangolly, hearing of Shivappa's attack, offered the captain of Basrur four embarkations with mariners, saying that he would pay for four and Miguel should pay for the remaining; but the latter pretended that he did not have money for the payment. Francisco de Lux, who had been sent from Goa with four vessels to relieve Basrur, was also accused of not providing the relief, though he could have in fact provided it. However, having reached the bar on August 9 or 11, and finding it undesirable to enter the river owing to strong winds, he probably proceeded to Mangalore, though he could have awaited at St. Mary Islands for an opportune moment to go to Basrur when the winds subsided.[19]

The Portuguese endeavoured to weaken Shivappa by setting the king of Cannanore against him. The Viceroy instructed the captain of the Portuguese fortress of Cannanore to induce the king to march against Shivappa. The captain was provided with some money to pay the Nair soldiers, if necessary. He succeeded in the mission assigned to him. Soon the king of Cannanore wrote to the Viceroy expressing his desire to fight Shivappa and seeking Portuguese assistance in the form of a fleet, ammunitions and gunpowder, and also some Portuguese soldiers to accompany his men by land. The Viceroy-in-Council met on October 30, 1652 and decided to respond positively.[20]

The situation in Gangolly was now very precarious. The Viceroy learnt that Shivappa, after gaining Basrur, had sent more men to capture Gangolly which was very weak. Shivappa employed many diggers and miners, whom the Portuguese feared most. Francisco de Castelo Branco, who had been in Basrur, advised the Viceroy-in-Council to send relief, substantially and quickly. He also felt it desirable to accept peace offers, if made by Shivappa. He opined that it was not feasible to be at war with the neighbouring kings in India, particularly because the Dutch had declared war against the Portuguese. The Viceroy-in-Council, who met on November 5, decided to send some boats full of foodgrains of all available sorts,

100 barrels of explosives, 200 *morrões* of Portugal, cotton and herbs, 100 firearms (*arcabuzas*) with their shots, 200 tins of gunpowder, a cannon with 200 appropriate grenades, 20 boxes of explosives for firearms and muskets, and 100 shots (*lanças*) of fire. Carpenters and masons were also to be dispatched. All these were to be carried in the fleet of the North, which the Viceroy-in-Council had already decided to send to Kanara.[21] In another meeting of December 9 the Viceroy sought the opinion of the councillors whether it was advisable to enter into peace negotiations with Shivappa before the rainy season, as the three Kanara fortresses were very weak and the Dutch were waging war at Manar and Jaffnapatnam. As the advice sought was on an important matter the councillors asked for time to consider.[22] The ultimate decision of the Viceroy-in-Council in this matter seems to have been to open peace negotiations. For towards the middle of the month Fr. Miguel de Almeida was sent as envoy to Gangolly to initiate peace talks. The following instructions were given to him on December 13.[23]

(1) Shivappa might be expected to complain that the Portuguese (a) did not purchase pepper from him, (b) did not destroy either the fortress of Basrur or that of Gangolly, and (c) did not restore the galley taken from him by António Carneiro Salema. Regarding (a), Fr. Almeida was to say that the Portuguese did not purchase pepper because the fleet did not come from Portugal for it, and because Shivappa demanded exorbitant prices. Concerning (b), the envoy was to point out that the Portuguese possessed Gangolly legitimately by virtue of the treaty with Virappa Nayaka, who gave it as a gift, that in spite of this gift of the whole place, the Portuguese possessed there nothing but the ground on which their fortress was erected, the rest of the territory being always in Shivappa's hands, and that the King of Portugal did not take a quick decision regarding the destruction of the Basrur fortress or that of Gangolly, because he was engaged in wars, and also because he thought that Shivappa would be friendly and, therefore, there was no need of any hasty decision. In respect of (c), Fr. Almeida was to submit respectfully that Shivappa ought not to speak of so small

an embarkation with such an insignificant cargo; that Salema was a rebel and was arrested and imprisoned for his crimes and that he died in prison.

(2) If Shivappa was satisfied and was prepared to treat of peace, the envoy was to insist upon a truce as a precondition for negotiations. If the truce was agreed upon, talks were to be commenced on the basis of the terms and conditions proposed by the former Viceroy, Pero da Silva (1635-39), with some modifications suggested by the Count of Obidos, author of the instructions under consideration.

(3) The envoy was to say that the Portuguese were ready to purchase every year 300 *khandis* of pepper from Shivappa at the rate of 28 *pagodas* a *khandi.* However, the ambassador was empowered to vary the quantity to the extent of 350 *khandis* if necessary.

(4) On the question of abandoning the fortress of Gangolly, the ambassador was to point out that it was a matter which required consideration, especially (a) because of the changed conditions in which the Portuguese were; (b) because the King of Portugal should be informed of it for his orders; and (c) because Shivappa himself had asked on previous occasions for the abandonment of only one of the two fortresses of Basrur and Gangolly. In view of these the ambassador was to suggest that the fortress of Basrur be returned to the Portuguese who would then certainly destroy one of the fortresses in question, preferably that of Basrur itself, in return for the gift of Gangolly from Shivappa.

(5) Settlement of the value of the loaded embarkation taken from Shivappa was to be offered provided the latter agreed to release the wood that he had blocked.

(6) Shivappa had demanded, through Fr. Arcamone that the Portuguese should give up all the articles that were washed ashore to his territories as a result of the shipwreck of the Portuguese fleet off Gangolly in May. He also demanded the galley and the ship that were salvaged by the Portuguese. The

ambassador was instructed to admit Shivappa's right to have the articles, as the shipwreck had taken place within his jurisdiction but regarding the salvaged vessels, he was to point out that the demand was unjustified, because they were saved by the grace of God and the efforts of the Portuguese.

(7) In conformity with the above the ambassador was commissioned to conclude a treaty. The Viceroy's ratification was to follow, with the declaration that both the parties to the treaty ought to exchange the soldiers, ships and embarkations captured during the war.

The ambassador was instructed to fulfill his mission as quickly as possible. He was to take with him Fr. Arcamone who had Shivappa's permission to return to Kanara and who was expected to be of great assistance to the ambassador.

Fearing that Shivappa might not agree to some of the above terms and conditions and being in acute need of peace in Kanara, the Viceroy gave another set of instructions[24] to the ambassador to be utilised in case the latter's effort at peace settlement on the above basis did not succeed. The second document was deliberately undated and unsigned. For greater security against leakage, it was prepared in Latin. There were many Kanarese and other Indians, who knew Portuguese, but very few who knew Latin in those days. It was most probably issued on the very day on which the first document of instructions were given to the ambassador. The following were its important instructions:

(1) If Shivappa insisted that the Gangolly fortress should be destroyed and if he was found unprepared to change his stand, the ambassador was instructed to agree to the condition. However, no written contract or agreement was to be entered into in this respect, so that total damage was not done to the prestige of the Portuguese; but assurance was to be given that the destruction would be effected. In return Shivappa was to be urged to allow the Portuguese to re-edify the Basrur or to erect a new fortress on the same side of the river, where they were to be given lands equal in area to those possessed by them at Basrur, (2) again, if Shivappa insisted that

the offer to purchase every year 300 or 350 *khandis* of pepper was inadequate, the ambassador was authorised to offer to purchase 400 *khandis* at the rate of 28 *pagodas* a *khandi*.

The rest of the terms were to be in accordance with the first set of instructions. The ambassador was instructed to speak to Venkatappa, Shivappa's younger brother, who was known to be well-disposed towards the Portuguese and was fighting against them rather reluctantly. So also the ambassador was to meet Vittala Malo who was also amicable. These two were to be urged to help the Portuguese to get favourable terms from Shivappa.

Nothing concrete seems to have resulted from this embassy. In the latter half of December, Shivappa sent Rama Pai to Goa to fathom the Portuguese attitude towards a peace treaty with him. Pai did not have powers to conclude anything specific. In fact, he came under the guise of being the envoy of the people of Bednur rather than of Shivappa. After listening to him, the Viceroy-in-Council, meeting on December 26 decided as follows: (a) the Portuguese would purchase 500 *khandis* of pepper immediately and 300 *khandis* every year, in both cases at the rate of 28 *pagodas* provided Basrur was restored, (b) if Shivappa agreed to this condition, a peace treaty was to be negotiated, (c) André de Lima, well-informed of the Kanarese situation, should be sent as ambassador with Pai. He should be instructed to begin peace talks after obtaining a cease-fire, (d) a letter should be addressed to Shivappa. The substance of the letter, which was subsequently written, was that Shivappa as well as the Portuguese should suspend fighting so as to create a proper atmosphere for peace talks.[25] The Portuguese were so eager for a peace treaty with Shivappa that the Viceroy considered the arrival of Pai at Goa as a godsend; it was "not a small mercy from the heaven".[26]

However, all those were not helpful to the Portuguese. In January 1653, they abandoned the fortress of Gangolly after taking out the artillery and mining the fortress to destruction. Writing of this to the King of Portugal on January 26, the Viceroy pointed out that the Gangolly fortress was a source of expenses and that to defend it he had to divide his limited armed forces at the cost of lesser defence for the more important and useful fortresses of Honavar and Mangalore.[27]

Having captured the Basrur and the Gangolly fortresses from the Portuguese, Shivappa sent an ambassador again. Vittala Malo, the ambassador, went to Honavar and from there sent a letter to the Viceroy, saying that he would be there for eight days and that he should send an envoy with powers to conclude peace. Taking into account the war against the Dutch in Ceylon, which needed all concentration, the Viceroy-in-Council, meeting on February 19, decided that peace talks should be continued; that Fr. Gonçalo Martins should be sent as ambassador with clear instructions and powers to conclude peace, provided Basrur and Gangolly were restored; that the offer to purchase 500 *khandis* of pepper immediately at *pagodas* a *khandi* and 300 *khandis* every year at the same rate, should be repeated.[28] To assist him, two more men of experience were sent with him. They were Ramoji Sinai Kothari, a dealer in horses, who had gone to Kanara often, and who was the trusted interpreter of the Portuguese and João Roiz (Rodrigues) Viegas.[29]

Fr. Martins was given more or less similar instructions which had been given to former ambassadors to Shivappa. Regarding pepper, he was to say that the Portuguese offer to purchase immediately 500 *khandis* of pepper and 300 *khandis* every year thereafter at 28 *pagodas* a *khandi* was still valid. He was made aware that this offer was being made in spite of the fact that the King of Portugal was not in a position, unlike former years, to send capital to India and that the price offered was much higher than that which existed in Cochin and Ceylon, thus being of great loss to the royal treasury. Yet the offer stood in order to secure peace, which was so necessary in Kanara. The ambassador was to insist upon the restoration of Basrur and Gangolly. Compensation for the losses and damages thereof were also to be demanded. Permission to erect a new fortress at a convenient place at the bar, where Shivappa was to give lands equivalent to the lands possessed by the Portuguese at Basrur formerly, was to be secured. Shivappa was to be asked to destroy the fortresses which he had erected in the meantime at Basrur and Gangolly. After all these, Shivappa was to be asked to agree that the Portuguese be free to decide whether they should destroy their fortress of Gangolly or not. However, if Shivappa were not to agree to restore Gangolly, the ambassador was to get an assurance from him that he would destroy the new fortress which he had started constructing in Gangolly at the mouth of the river. Regarding the embarkation which had been captured by António Carneiro Salema, the ambassador was to endeavour to pass it off, so that Shivappa did not ask for any satisfaction; but if he insisted on satisfaction being given, the ambassador was to agree to it, provided that Shivappa consented to release the timber which he had suppressed while the Portuguese were bringing from Cannanore and provided also that he agreed not to admit into his ports the embarkations of Malabar and of the native enemies of the Portuguese. Further, Shivappa was to be urged to agree not to admit nor to have any trade dealings with the Arabs, nor to send his ships to Arabia, the Portuguese being permitted to seize the contraband. Next, Shivappa was to be asked to allow the Portuguese to cut and take away whatever wood they needed for their shipyards and for repairing fortresses and houses. Of course, all these negotiations were to be preceded by a cease fire.[30]

Fr. Martins' mission was a failure. On reaching Honavar he found Vittala Malo making excessive demands. He was invited to go to Bednur to meet Shivappa. However, he had no order to proceed to Bednur and besides Shivappa was reported to be ill and, therefore, was not in a position to treat of peace. He was commanded to return to Goa with Rama Pai. The Portuguese decided in the meantime to strengthen the defences of Mangalore and Honavar.[31] On April 28, 1653 the Viceroy-in-Council decided to sent Constanço Fialho Ferreira as captain-general of war with four regiments to Mangalore. These soldiers were to go by two or three ships as far as Honavar where they were to change to small embarkations and proceed to Mangalore. From Honavar the ships were to return to Goa.[32]

Ferreira was not in a position to prevent Shivappa from causing damage to the Portuguese fortress of Mangalore. On July 28, Shivappa's men mined two walls of the Portuguese settlement of Mangalore, entered the settlement, killed many of the residents and soldiers, captured some and forced the remaining to retreat into the fortress. Ferreira wrote to the Viceroy saying that there were hardly a hundred soldiers left for defence, and asking for speedy relief. In this desperate condition the king of Cannanore extended great help to the Portuguese. He not only allowed them to take foodgrains, fish and meat from his territories, but sent 5,000 Nair soldiers to Kumbala in an attempt to divert Shivappa's attention and thus mitigate pressure on Mangalore. The king of Cannanore, however, wrote to the Viceroy to pay the Nairs who were in fact disobedient owing to non-payment. The financial condition of the Portuguese was really pitiable owing to their war expenses in Ceylon against the Dutch, coupled with the reduced income from trade which was being hindered by the European rival. Nevertheless, the Viceroy-in-Council decided on August 27 to send whatever money that was possible to the king of Cannanore and to thank him for his invaluable assistance. They also decided to send immediately to Mangalore 4 *almadias* with a captain and 4 soldiers each, with ammunitions, explosives and food supplies, drugs and sweets for the wounded and the sick, and materials required for repairing the fortress. Six warships were also to be dispatched as quickly as possible.[33]

The decision to send the relief was too late. Seven days earlier, on August 20, Shivappa had taken the fortress of Mangalore.[34] The Portuguese garrison abandoned the fortress, leaving behind the artillery. Only the fortress of Honavar remained now. Shivappa stepped up his attacks on this fortress and by January 1654 took control of the main entrance to the fortress and encircled it, the Portuguese being left with only one entrance from the river to a bulwark which they defended.[35] The Viceroy kept on sending relief but Shivappa was too powerful for the Portuguese. As Leonardo Pais says, Shivappa was rich with territories extending from Mirjan to Kasaragod, and possessed 40,000 to 50,000 excellent men-of-arms.[36]

By January the king of Sonda offered to assist the Portuguese. He himself was of little strength, but he proposed to urge the Adil Shah, his suzerain, to march against Shivappa. The governor, Bras de Castro, welcomed the proposal, but nothing concrete seems to have followed.[37] So also Vitoji Vishwasa Rao, Nayaka Varymor (?) of Ankola, probably an official of the king of Sonda, offered to mediate between the Portuguese and Shivappa. Rao was a friend of the Portuguese and was providing food supplies to their fortress of Honavar. The governor-in-council decided on February 19 to accept the offer and to send an envoy to Ankola to meet Rao.[38]

The Portuguese tried to hinder the commerce of Shivappa. They did not issue passports to the merchants of the kingdom of the Zamorin, who used to go to the ports of Kanara for securing food supplies. The Zamorin, however, did not appreciate this policy and wrote to the governor demanding passports for his merchants. The Portuguese, of course, were not in a position to have another enemy and therefore decided to issue four passports a year.[39]

In February, Francisco de Sousa Alcoforado, captain of the Honavar fortress, held peace talks at Honavar with Mallappa Malo, son of Vittala Malo, whom Shivappa sent for the purpose. The talks were a failure. Shivappa demanded that the Portuguese should purchase from him immediately 1,000 *khandis* of pepper at 28 *pagodas* a *khandi*, and thereafter 500 *khandis* every year at the same rate. Alcoforado could not accept this. However, he secured a truce of 15 days with effect from February 22 promising to obtain in the meantime orders from Goa concerning Shivappa's demand. On being informed of these, the governor-in-council meeting on February 27, decided to adhere to the former offer to purchase 500 *khandis* immediately and 300 *khandis* every year, provided all the fortresses captured by Shivappa were restored. No envoy was to be sent, but Malo was to be informed by means of a letter that Shivappa should send his envoy to Goa if he really wanted to conclude peace. The Portuguese had sent several ambassadors before but as the negotiations were being held Shivappa had captured the fortresses.[40]

Nevertheless, by a resolution of the governor-in-council dated March 5, Fr. António Nunes, Alcoforado and Pero Pinto de Mello, captain-major of the fleet of Kanara, were authorised to continue negotiations on the basis of the decision of February 27. They were given the following instructions by means of a document dated March 6: (1) Concerning pepper, talks should be commenced with an offer to purchase only 200 *khandis* at 24 or 25 *pagodas* a *khandi*, pointing out that even when the Portuguese had all their Kanarese fortresses, they were willing to purchase only this much from Ikkeri rulers. If an offer to purchase more had been made in the past it was because of the insistence on the part of the latter. Now that only one fortress was left in their hands, they were not in a position to offer more. However, the envoys were to increase the quantity of 250 *khandis* at 26 *pagodas* a *khandi*, after the first offer was rejected. Further, increases were similarly to be made, always with a show of great reluctance. At any rate, the quantity specified in the decision of February 27 was not to be exceeded. (2) Restoration of the captured fortresses was to be insisted upon; but peace talks were not to be abandoned even if this demand was not accepted by Shivappa. He was to be told, however, that he would not gain much even if he captured the Honavar fortress as well, for he would lose their commercial dealings with him and besides, they might hinder his dealings with other nations through his sea ports. (3) The captain of Honavar was authorised to go to Bednur, if necessary, for negotiating a treaty; but Shivappa was to be told that the finalisation of the treaty would be done in Goa where he should send his ambassador with the commission to conclude the treaty.[41]

On March 13 the Adil Shah wrote to the governor informing him that he had sent an order to Shivappa, commanding the latter to raise the siege of Honavar and to restore the three fortresses to the Portuguese. The Adil Shah promised to take positive action against Shivappa if he did not obey the order. The Adil Shah apparently acted on his own accord, though the king of Sonda, who had offered to urge him to march against Shivappa, might have played some role in asking him to issue the order. The governor sent Fr. Martins to Bijapur with a present to the Adil Shah, "as the Muslims do not act and do favours, except for gain". Fr. Martins was not sent as ambassador, but because the Adil Shah had expressed a desire in his letter just mentioned that he be sent to his court.[42] However, he was given certain instructions on April 16 to guide him in his audiences with the Adil Shah. The latter was to be thanked for the order that he had sent to Shivappa and for his promise to punish the latter should he disregard the command. Fr. Martins was made aware that the Adil Shah might find it easy to send his army against Shivappa, for the king of Mysore had also sought the Adil Shah's intervention against Shivappa. Should the Adil Shah offer to mediate for peace between Shivappa and the Portuguese, he was instructed to urge him to make Shivappa to reduce the quantity of pepper, which he insisted that they should purchase from him.[43]

On April 28, Mello, the captain-major of the men of war at Honavar, reached Goa and reported to the governor that Shivappa had insisted upon his own terms regarding the quantity of pepper to be purchased from him and that on the rejection of his terms he had stepped up assaults on the Honavar fortress. The Governor-in-Council decided on the same day to send Pero Pinto back to Honavar with relief consisting of soldiers, food supplies and medicines, so that the fortress could be defended until the rainy season. Regarding the future action, decision was to be taken in keeping with the help that was expected from Portugal in September. It was hoped that in the rainy season Shivappa would not be able to cause such damage to the fortress.[44] However, this hope of holding on up to September was soon shattered. News reached that it was impossible to defend the fortress that rainy season, for the soldiers were worn out and a great part of the walls and bulwarks of the fortress was already destroyed by the enemy. Besides, the only defence wall that was left was in a precarious condition. In order to avoid the loss of 1,000 soldiers, 300 white and 700 non-whites who were defending the fortress, and a considerable amount of artillery therein, and also to avoid diversion in Kanara in September when it was expected that there would be a severe fight with the Dutch, the Governor-in-Council decided on May 4 to accept the terms offered by Shivappa. Effort, no doubt, was to be made to induce him to lower the quantity of pepper and its price as much as possible. They were to offer to purchase 700 *khandis* in September or October and 300 *khandis* every year thereafter, at 28 *pagodas* a *khandi*, if not at 27 *pagodas*. In the meantime the fortress was to be repaired and some 'honest' excuses were to be found to impress upon Shivappa their inability to purchase all the quantity agreed upon.[45]

In fact, all were eager in Goa by the middle of May to conclude peace with Shivappa at any cost. The municipality of Goa submitted a memorandum on May 9, urging the Governor to conclude peace "with the greatest speed that is possible". The document expressed the awareness of the municipality that Shivappa was guilty of violating peace and that the Portuguese were justified in defending. However, the document pointed out that the food supplies of his territories were important for the sustenance of Goa and for the Portuguese soldiers waging war against the Dutch at Ceylon and other places, and, therefore, peace with Shivappa was of great significance. Gilianes de Noronha, a respected member of the Council of State, but who was not attending its meetings on account of illness, expressed himself in favour of peace. He wrote to the Governor on May 12, in response to the decision of the Governor-in-Council of May 4, which was referred to him for opinion, saying that he always considered peace with Kanara as desirable owing to its food supplies and particularly desirable now because the Dutch were obstructing food supplies from the North. Apropos the Adil Shah's order to Shivappa, Noronha opined that it was in vain to expect much from the Muslim. Therefore, he suggested that peace should be concluded with Shivappa immediately by accepting his demand concerning pepper, promising him to purchase 1,000 *khandis* in September or October and 5,000 *khandis* every year thereafter. During the truce that would prevail between the date of this agreement and October, the Honavar fortress could be repaired. Noronha proceeded to say that during the truce an attempt should be made to convince Shivappa by sincere efforts of the inability of the Portuguese to purchase that much quantity of pepper. He was sure that Shivappa would then be considerate. He also pointed out that peace with him would save the men and artillery of the Honavar fortress and these could be employed against the Dutch.[46]

Finally, the Governor-in-Council appointed to conduct negotiations. On May 16 a set of instructions was sent to him. He was authorised to agree to purchase 700 *khandis* of pepper immediately and 300 *khandis* every year, both at 28 *pagodas* a *khandi*. Of course, he was to begin with an offer to purchase at the rate of 27 *pagodas* a *khandi*, one more *pagoda* being offered only if absolutely necessary. Further, he was instructed to insist upon the restitution of the fortresses, at least, of Mangalore and Basrur. Gangolly too was to be demanded, pleading the right of possession granted by Virappa Nayaka. Even if Shivappa refused to return these fortresses, the negotiations were to be continued to ensure peace.[47]

Alcoforado achieved nothing. Shivappa refused to talk unless the Portuguese agreed unconditionally to purchase from him 800 *khandis* of pepper at once and 300 *khandis* every year thereafter. Alcoforado and Pero Pinto sent the factor of Honavar, Gonçalo Vas de Morais, to Goa to report to the government there the miserable condition in which Honavar was. Morais reached Goa on August 9 and spoke to the Council on the very day: many soldiers were dead, more by hunger than by wounds, the sufferings of those who survived were immense; the bare necessities for the sick were exhausted; the greater part of the wall, the fortifications that were erected within and a great part of *cuirass* were destroyed with mines; in front which the enemy had constructed a fortress from where it attacked the anchorage, thus rendering it difficult for the fleets to enter and help the place; and if the help was attempted, there was manifest danger as was experienced in reality in the rainy season; the fortress, in fact, had no defence and no repair was possible; Shivappa's besieging army was 11,000 to 12,000 strong and was incapable of being repulsed except by a strong Portuguese army which should be prepared to attack his camp; the Governor-in-Council should either issue orders to dismantle the fortress after removing the artillery or send forthwith 1,000 Portuguese soldiers, together with some non-white men-of-arms.[48]

Alcoforado, in his letter of August 2, informed the Governor that more than 70 soldiers had died of hunger during the course of the month; that there was such a shortage of food supplies in the fortress during the rainy season that "rats and cats" were eaten; that more than 100 soldiers were sick; that there was no money with him, nor rice; that the Dutch were in league with Shivappa and that the latter had erected a fortress at the entrance of the river.

Pinto added that no soldiers, Portuguese or native, was in a condition to fight the enemy.[49]

Meanwhile, rumour was rife that the Adil Shah, instead of sending a punitive expedition against Shivappa as he had boastfully declared, was planning to commence hostilities against the Portuguese themselves. Taking into account all these developments, the Governor-in-Council decided to send as much provisions as possible immediately and to take the final decision to dismantle the fortress as soon as ships arrived from Portugal.[50]

In the second half of August the Adil Shah actually sent his troops into Goa. The Portuguese believed that the Dutch were behind this hostility of the Bijapur ruler. The Governor also received the news that Shivappa's men had further damaged the Honavar fortress by mining it on August 24. Under these circumstances, the Governor-in-Council decided on September 5 to issue orders forthwith to dismantle the fortress of Honavar, so that the men and the artillery of that fortress would be available for the defence of Goa against the Adil Shah.[51] The Portuguese had to muster all their available forces in India as no ships as yet arrived from Portugal. The decision to dismantle the fortress was probably carried out in the month of September itself. They took out almost all the pieces of artillery and destroyed the fortress by means of explosives.[52]

After the loss of their fortresses of Kanara the Portuguese naturally continued to consider Shivappa their enemy and stopped trade relations with him and his subjects. We learn from the minutes of the Council of State, which met on October 6, 1655 that two *parangues* of Kanarese merchants, carrying rice, had entered the Goa bar on the previous day, under the plea that they were being permitted to come formerly and therefore they had come again. This was a surprise for the new Viceroy, Rodrigo Lobo da Silveira, who thought it abominable that enemy merchants should enter the Portuguese port as if they were friends. The Viceroy-in-Council however, decided that the two *parangues* should not be seized as the merchants seemed to be innocent, but that they should be allowed to go away after selling the rice at the port. It was also decided that in future any embarkation that came from Kanara should be captured with the cargo and the men. It may be noted that the merchants of Goa too were eager to proceed to the ports of Kanara in order to secure food supplies. The Viceroy-in-Council decided against them, announcing that if any embarkation of theirs was found dealing with Kanara, it would be confiscated with its cargo.[53]

However, within two days the decision regarding the *parangues* from Kanara was altered. On October 7, 12 more such boats came to Goa with foodgrains. Considering the matter again on the following day it was decided that all these boats be allowed to go back after selling their cargo at Goa. It was pointed out by some members of the Council that Goa was experiencing shortage of food supplies; that it was difficult to secure supplies from the North owing to the Adil Shah's hostilities; and that there was no harm in carrying on trade with the merchants from enemy territories, as was being done formerly when Venkatappa was at war with the Portuguese in Mangalore, and it was being done now in Portugal where the Dutch merchants came to the port of Lisbon for trade.[54]

In November, the prince of Cannanore sought Portuguese assistance against his own enemies. In return, he promised to fight against Shivappa by land, paying his soldiers from his own treasury. The Viceroy-in-Council decided on December 11 not to assist the prince, since he was not powerful enough to wage war against Shivappa, nor was he always reliable as far as his promises were concerned.[55]

We are not in a position to know what transpired between the Portuguese and Shivappa for nearly three years afterwards. However, from a letter written by the Governor of Goa to the King of Portugal on December 17, 1658 we learn that Shivappa had promised the Portuguese in the meantime to allow them to establish factories at Basrur and Mangalore. The letter further informs that the Portuguese fleets and *cafilas* were allowed to enter and come out freely at these ports; that merchant ships were permitted at Honavar also; that these movements were allowed by toleration, and not by any specific agreement; that the Christians, who lived in Shivappa's territories, were being treated well; that some Portuguese nationals had become residents therein and that food supplies from his territories came to Goa.[56] Thus, Shivappa and the Portuguese were in good terms by 1658.

However, in September or a little earlier, 1659, Shivappa detained at Basrur a fleet of seven *periches*. The efforts of its captain-major, Luis de Costa, did not succeed in getting the fleet released. Being informed of this, the Governor-in-Council decided to send a present worth up to 500 *xerafins* to Shivappa and urge him to free the fleet.[57] In accordance with this decision, instructions were sent on October 3 to Fr. Francisco de Espinola who was already at Bednur. A beautiful mirror valued at 250 *xerafins* and a piece of damask valued at 200 *xerafins* were sent as presents to Shivappa, Fr. Espinola being instructed to give them as from himself, and not as from the Governor, for the presents were too small to be given as from the latter. A silken carpet of Persia valued at 100 *xerafins* was also sent as a present to Venkatappa, Shivappa's younger brother. Fr. Espinola was instructed to say that the fleet had entered the port of Basrur in good faith, as Shivappa had always permitted the Portuguese ships into his ports; and, therefore, the detained fleet should be released.

If Shivappa were to say that the Portuguese had captured at Cochin one of his ships with three horses and they should give satisfaction for it, the ambassador was to respond by pointing out that it was captured at a time when Shivappa was waging war against them and that it was therefore unfair to ask for satisfaction. Besides, Fr. Espinola was also to point out that the value of the ship and its cargo was not even 1,000 *xerafins* whereas Shivappa had taken 12,000 *xerafins* from the factor of Jaffnapatnam who was proceeding from Cochin to Goa. Thus, the ship was more than well paid by means of this sum of 12,000 *xerafins* as well as by means of the goods and artillery that he had captured along with the fortresses. If Shivappa inquired whether Fr. Espinola had commission to negotiate for peace, the latter was to present the letter of credence that was sent along with the instructions; but it was to be presented, not readily, but as a last resort.

Apparently, the Portuguese were not ready as yet to enter into a treaty with Shivappa. Fr. Espinola was instructed to talk on general peace, exchange of articles of trade, mutual liberty of entrance for merchants, ships and fleets into the ports of Kanara and Goa and issuance of passports for Shivappa's ships. If he were to talk of pepper, he was merely to say that the Portuguese would purchase the commodity from him when things improved and when there was unhindered voyage between India and Portugal. In case he were to inquire why the Portuguese did not send an ambassador to him before, if they really desired peace, he was to respond that the authorities were too busy dealing with the Dutch who were creating trouble at the Goa bar. If Shivappa was not satisfied with any of the above clarifications and refused to release the fleet, he was to urge him to permit the captain-major, the captains and the soldiers of the fleet to leave for Goa or Cannanore.[58]

Two days later on October 5, the Governor-in-Council decided to send an ambassador, Fr. Pero da Costa with greater powers to negotiate with Shivappa. This was a result of a letter written by Luis da Costa, captain-major of the interned fleet. Probably, Costa indicated in his letter that Shivappa was entertaining the Dutch. Fr. Costa's task was therefore to wean Shivappa away from the Dutch. To please him, presents worth 3,000 to 4,000 *xerafins* were to be sent to him through Fr. Costa. So also presents worth 500 *xerafins* were to be given to Venkatappa. Fr. Costa was to endeavour to get the interned fleet released from Basrur and also ensure food supplies to Goa.[59]

Shivappa's reign came to an end in 1660. It is not possible to say when Fr. Costa reached Bednur and to what extent he succeeded in his mission of weaning away Shivappa from the Dutch. As far as the interned fleet was concerned, it remained in that condition until after Shivappa's rule.

The Portuguese thus lost whatever hold they had over Kanara, never to recover it any time, though attempts were made subsequently to re-establish themselves as a political power in the region. Perhaps, they could have retained some of their Kanarese fortresses. They had only to concede in the beginning itself what they conceded when it was too late, namely to purchase from Shivappa a substantial quantity of pepper every year. Instead, they followed a childish policy, offering to purchase 200 *khandis* in the beginning and then slowly raising the quantity by 50s and 100s until they reached the figure of 700 for the current year and 300 for year to year thereafter. It is true that their position was tight financially.

However, they would have gained much more in the long run by conceding his demands, regarding pepper as well as regarding the destruction of either of the fortresses of Basrur and Gangolly in the very beginning. They would have earned thereby his friendship and could have retained the remaining fortresses. There would have been peace in Kanara. This peace would have been of great value in their troubles against the Dutch.

REFERENCES

1. *KNV*, p. 116 assigns this reign period of nearly 15 years. This period is accepted by N.L. Rao, "The Nayaks of Keladi", *VSCV*, p. 264.
2. *Assentos*, III, pp. 100-01.
3. *Ibid.*, pp. 101-02.
4. *Ibid.*, p. 478.
5. *Ibid.*, p. 481.
6. *Ibid.*, p. 522. K.D. Swaminathan, *The Nayaks of Ikkeri*, pp. 261-2 refers to this document in Appendix no. 6 of his book. However, he gives no date. Though the translation gives the impression that it is of the whole document, it is not. Many sentences are omitted. The arrangement of paragraphs also is not in accordance with the original. The translation of the last paragraph is incorrect. There is no reference in the original to "ships made out of the wood that would not be bought by the aforesaid king nor by that of Cannanore".
7. *Assentos*, III, pp. 526-27.
8. *Ibid.*, pp. 197-8.
9. Letter of Fr. António de Conceição quoted by M.A.M. Fitzler, *O Cerco de Columbo*, p. 135.
10. *Assentos*, III, pp. 197-8.
11. *Ibid.*, pp. 202-03.
12. Letter of Fr. Conceição quoted by Fitzler, *op. cit.*, p. 135.
13. *Assentos*, III, pp. 543-4.
14. *Ibid.*, pp. 199-200.
15. *Ibid.*, pp. 523-5.
16. *Ibid.*, pp. 206-7.
17. *Ibid.*, pp. 208-9.
19. *Ibid.*, pp. 211-2.
10. *Ibid.*, pp. 541-2.
20. *Ibid.*, pp. 212-3.
21. *Ibid.*, pp. 213-5.
22. *Ibid.*, p. 218.
23. *Ibid.*, pp. 530-3.
24. *Ibid.*, pp. 533-5.
25. *Ibid.*, pp. 219-21.

26. *Ibid.*, pp. 540-1. The Viceroy's letter to the King of Portugal, January 20, 1653.
27. *Ibid.*, pp. 544-5.
28. *Ibid.*, pp. 229-30.
29. *Ibid.*, pp. 230-1.
30. *Ibid.*, pp. 546-9.
31. *Ibid.*, p. 239.
32. *Ibid.*, p. 249.
33. *Ibid.*, pp. 270-1.
34. Francisco de Sousa, *Oriente Conquistado*, pt. II, Conquista, I, Div. I, p. 32. K. D. Swaminathan's account *op. cit.*, pp. 96-9 of the series of the wars that led to the fall of the Portuguese fortress in Kanara is not chronological; it is confused and unconnected. His difficulty is understandable, though. With the few Portuguese documents badly translated for him, he could not give a clear picture of the events that took place one after another. Speaking of Mangalore, he says that the Portuguese abandoned it in August. True enough. However, what is not true is that it "was the only fort left to the Portuguese". The fortress of Honavar was still in their hands and it was given up by them only in September 1654. He says about this fort of Honavar that it was the "only fort that had not surrendered" and does not say whether the fort was surrendered to Shivappa at all. Further, he writes (p. 97) that Shivappa "concentrated his forces on Cambolim with reinforcements amounting to 80,000 men". If reinforcements alone amounted to 80,000, Shivappa must have had many thousands more of soldiers employed elsewhere. This fantastic figure does not appear to be correct. In the first instance, Swaminathan does not quote any source from which he secured this figure. Secondly, Leonardo Pais, whom Swaminathan himself quotes (p. 98) says that Shivappa's whole army consisted of 40,000 to 50,000. Thirdly, even in the siege of the important fortress of Honavar, Shivappa seems to have employed only 11,000 to 12,000 men according to the Portuguese themselves (*Assentos*, III, p. 350).
35. *Assentos*, III, pp. 558-9.
36. Leonardo Pais, quoted in *Assentos*, III, p. 559.
37. *Assentos*, III, p. 559. Letter of Viceroy to the King of Portugal, January 20, 1654.
38. *Ibid.*, pp. 307-8, 559.
39. *Ibid.*, p. 311.
40. *Ibid.*, pp. 319-22.
41. *Ibid.*, pp. 565-7.
42. *Ibid.*, pp. 326-8
43. *Ibid.*, pp. 569-70.
44. *Ibid.*, pp. 329-30.
45. *Ibid.*, pp. 331-3.
46. *Ibid.*, pp. 333-7.
47. *Ibid.*, pp. 571-3.

48. *Ibid.*, pp. 350-1.
49. *Ibid.*, pp. 355-7.
50. *Ibid.*, pp. 351-5.
51. *Ibid.*, pp. 357-60.
52. *Ibid.*, pp. 581-2. Governor's letter to the King of Portugal, February 2, 1655.
53. *Ibid.*, pp. 395-7.
54. *Ibid.*, pp. 397-8.
55. *Ibid.*, pp. 419-20.
56. *Ibid.*, p. 624.
57. *Assentos*, IV, p. 10.
58. *Assentos*, III, pp. 510-2.
59. *Ibid.*, pp. 11-12.

9

THE PORTUGUESE AND THE NAYAKAS OF IKKERI-IV (1660-1763)

Shivappa Nayaka's brother, Venkatappa Nayaka II, became the next ruler. His reign was short (1660-61). The Portuguese followed an unwise policy in their relations with him, though they could have taken advantage of the new king, who was favourable to them as their own records show, to gain definite trade and other concessions. Instead, in December, 1660 they annoyed him by capturing one of his ships along with its equipment and crew. Some of the crew were converted to Christianity. Coming to know of this, Venkatappa detained a European priest proceeding from Cochin to Goa and decided not to release their fleet of seven *periches* that had been detained at Basrur during Shivappa's rule. This compelled the Portuguese to renew their negotiations with Bednur. In January 1661, they sent Ramoji Sinai Kothari with a present and a letter to Bednur. Kothari had two audiences with Venkatappa on February 5 and 10, respectively. On the second occasion he was told to carry on negotiations with four ministers of Venkatappa's council. In accordance with the instructions[1] he was given in Goa, he negotiated regarding the release of the fleet detained at Basrur and regarding the money taken from Manoel da Costa, in return for Venkatappa's ship. The ministers were ready to urge their king to release the fleet, but were unprepared to talk of the money. Kothari bribed them with 40 *pagodas*, whereupon they agreed to place before Venkatappa the question of the money also.[2] Besides, he probably succeeded in getting the European priest released.

Writing of these matters to the governors on February 20, Kothari disclosed that without monetary or other promises the authorities in Bednur did not do anything. The Governor-in-Council, meeting on March 4, decided to authorise him to promise the ministers further bribes to the extent of 500 to 1,000 *xerafins* provided they secured Venkatappa's order for restoration of the money. Concerning the fleet, its restitution was to be accepted only if its artillery and arms were also returned. If only the skeletons of the ships were offered, Kothari was to inform the governors for further instruction.[3]

Unfortunately, no further records are available to know the final outcome of the embassy. Probably, the fleet and the money remained with Venkatappa. The Portuguese themselves were to be blamed for their ill success and Venkatappa's subsequent inclination towards the Dutch who had approached him towards the end of 1660.[4]

Bhadrappa Nayaka (1660-64), son of Shivappa Nayaka, succeeded Venkatappa. In September, 1663 the Adil Shah invaded the territories of Bhadrappa. Soon, the latter lost a major part of his dominions, including the capital, Bednur, which the Adil Shah destroyed.[5] Bhadrappa sought aid from the Dutch and the Portuguese. The Dutch, probably promised help but did not give it in time. The Portuguese sent word saying that they were willing to help him secretly. However, what assistance they actually gave is not indicated. In fact, it was a hypocrisy. In the meantime, Bhadrappa and the Adil Shah came to terms. The former bought peace by paying more than 3 million, probably *xerafins*.[6]

While Bhadrappa was being hard pressed by the Adil Shah, the Portuguese decided to pressurise the former and try to regain at least some of the lost grounds in Kanara. Accordingly, the Viceroy instructed all those Portuguese nationals, who were in his territories, to assemble at a place from where they could be gathered to security. This was a show of threat to Bhadrappa who was anxious to get their assistance against the Adil Shah. The Nayaka sent messengers proposing to compose his differences with the Portuguese. The Viceroy was requested to send his ambassador for this purpose. Recalling how former Portuguese ambassadors had returned empty-handed and disappointed on several occasions, the Viceroy responded insultingly that if Bhadrappa had anything to negotiate he should send his ambassador to Goa. At the same time he sent a fleet of 10 ships, under the command of Simão Gomes da Silva, to procure rice from Kanara. Silva was instructed to demonstrate lack of confidence in Bhadrappa by not entering the ports of Kanara. The fleet was also a threat to him, for it could be used to fight him, if necessary. It could also be used to block the sea trade at his ports. Apparently the Viceroy's policy brought about the desired result. Bhadrappa sent Mallappa Malo as his ambassador to Goa in February 1664.[7] A present of 6,000 bags of rice was also sent. Bhadrappa proposed to restore to the Portuguese their former fortresses of Honavar, Basrur and Mangalore.[8]

As Malo was engaged in the negotiations in Goa, Bhadrappa was probably murdered by some Brahmins,[9] and his young brother, Somashekhara Nayaka (1664-71), ascended the throne. There was confusion in Bednur, but Narayana Malo, Mallappa's brother[10] took control of the situation and normalcy was established. Mallappa's embassy began to show results by October. A navy comprising eleven ships, two *galliots* and one *pataxo* carrying ammunitions and arms, was sent from Goa.[11] Manuel Lobo da Silveira was its captain-major. He was to take possession of Gangolly which was apparently to be returned to the Portuguese. At Basrur the fortress was to be dismantled and its materials were to be transferred to Gangolly.[12] The Portuguese were to get Mangalore also. However, no agreement was as yet finalised.

Silveira reached Honavar on October 26 and sent a message to Narayana Malo. The latter asked him to go to Basrur where the two could conclude the negotiations. On the 29th, the two actually met in Silveira's *galliot* off Basrur. Apparently, Narayana had expected certain presents from the Portuguese. He expressed his hope to get presents for king Somashekhara, for the king's brother-in-law and for others. He required 500 barrels of explosives also. Silveira excused himself saying that the expected explosives and other things could not be brought in the *pataxo* which was sufficient to carry only those things which were necessary for his fleet. Regarding the fortresses to be ceded, Malo who seems to have been absent from Bednur for some time, said that nothing definite could be concluded unless he once again consulted the king. He took this stand probably because the Portuguese did not give what was expected to them in the form of presents and explosives. He also disclosed that Somashekhara was prepared to cede a site on the southern bank of the river Netravati, and not the former Portuguese fortress of Mangalore itself. He and a representative of the Portuguese, Domingos da Guerra, went to Bednur, promising to return in five days.[13] Writing of these to the Viceroy on October 30, he opined that he could easily take Gangolly by force if Somashekhara refused to cede it. He also boasted that he was with his fleet just in front of Malo's house, ready to capture him and his uncle, should he indulge in delaying tactics. He requested the Viceroy to authorise him to do so, pointing out that if the two were captured, all the Portuguese demands would be conceded.[14] Apparently Malo was so eminent and powerful in Kanara.

A few more interesting events are referred to in the same letter. Some time before Silveira's arrival at Honavar there was great danger for the very existence of the kingdom of Ikkeri. Two powerful men of the kingdom, namely, the brother-in-law of the king and Govayya, the king's secretary, were so hostile towards each other that the one desired to get rid of the other. The governor of Mangalore who was Govayya's brother, was taken in chains to Bednur. The queen of Bangher and the Chautar chief of Ullala besieged the fortress of Mangalore. She was reported to have secured the services of 2,000 Nairs for the purpose. Sheriza Khan and Badul Khan, two generals of the Adil Shah, were marching triumphantly against Somashekhara who fled from Bednur and took shelter in a strong fort called Andrug (Anedurga). As the king was a child, all the feudatories were in revolt. These wars and revolts continued and Silveira thought it was a good occasion to knock out concessions from Somashekhara.[15]

On November 10 Malo returned to Basrur with a positive answer. The Portuguese were to get the fortresses of Basrur, Gangolly and Mangalore. The ships, which had been taken from the Portuguese during the rule of Shivappa and Bhadrappa, were to be returned with all the artillery and ammunitions. The Portuguese were to be free from the obligation of compulsory purchases of pepper from the Ikkeri kings. They were to get regular supplies of rice.[16]

On November 13, Silveira took possession of Gangolly. However, on the following day while preparation was being made to take possession of Basrur, two Dutch ships appeared on the scene and surrounded the Portuguese *pataxo*. In order to discover their real intention, Silveira ordered the *pataxo* to be removed from the place where it was. While this order was being executed, the Dutch captain sent a message saying that the treaty between the Portuguese and the Dutch entered into on November 12, 1663 laid down that wherever the Dutch had a factory the Portuguese should neither have a fortress nor a factory, and that the Dutch were permitted by Somashekhara to have a factory at Basrur and therefore the Portuguese should not take possession of the fortress of Gangolly or Basrur. Silveira responded saying that the Viceroy alone knew what the provisions of the treaty were and that the fortresses which were being taken possession of by him were those which the Portuguese had in Kanara formerly and which Somashekhara had agreed to return. The Dutch captain pointed out that the Portuguese had lost these fortresses in a clean battle, and after the loss, the Dutch were the first to have been given the right to establish a factory at Basrur. He therefore, informed him to leave the fortresses as they were and also the *pataxo* where it was, until his superior, who was expected there in three or four days time, decided the issue. Silveira dared not disregard the suggestion. The Viceroy was informed of this development.[17]

Silveira thought that Malo and others, who feared both the Portuguese and the Dutch, had invited both of them, so that the Kanarese would be free from oppression from either, for the European rivals were bound to be busy opposing each other there. This suspicion, however, was not well-founded, for English sources tell us that the Dutch had already warned Malo that he should not deliver the fortresses unless his master intended to fight the Dutch; but he had responded that he would be failing in his duty if he did not deliver the fortresses to the Portuguese for his master had ordered him to do so.[18] Silveira feared also that the Dutch were looking out for excuses to wage a fresh war on the Portuguese. He pointed out further that Somashekhara had a net gain of 200 barrels of explosives which the Viceroy had sent in the meantime and which was entrusted to Malo a day or two before the arrival of the Dutch.[19]

The Dutch were bent upon preventing the cession of the Mangalore fortress too.[20] They placed four ships there for the purpose. Silveira was helpless; he dared not divide his fleet and send relief to Mangalore. Besides, he was aware that Somashekhara's garrison of Mangalore would not cede the fortress unless it received the king's order to that effect. In the meantime, Malo went away from Basrur. In his absence Silveira saw the end of negotiations for getting both the lost fortresses.[21]

On November 25, 1664, Malo addressed a letter to the Viceroy informing him that the Dutch were threatening to invade the kingdom of Ikkeri with 20,000 Nairs, together with the rebel feudatories of Somashekhara, if Mangalore was not ceded to them. Malo had urged that what was done could not be undone, whereupon Rickloff, the Dutch commander, had sent his factor to the court of Somashekhara. Malo had ordered his men to delay the factor's affairs until the Viceroy's response to the latter arrived. The Viceroy was told that the fortress of Mangalore was besieged by the rebel feudatories encouraged by the Dutch and that the family of Locayya, an important man of Bednur and relative of Govayya, was within the fortress. The Viceroy was, therefore, urged to send a fleet to Mangalore and take possession of the fortress and rescue Locayya's family.[22]

The Viceroy and Malo exchanged several letters. The latter always emphasized that he had done for the Portuguese whatever he had promised, particularly regarding the return of the Kanarese fortresses; and that he was always a friend of the Portuguese. In one letter he wrote that he considered the Dutch as "women" whereas the Portuguese were "men".[23] In another he said that Somashekhara had agreed to return the fortress to the Portuguese "because I had told him that you, the Portuguese, were powerful, and that without your help and of your Excellency (the Viceroy) we would not be able to live".[24]

Lobo also wrote to the Viceroy on December 12, 1664 informing him of Malo's visit to him at Gangolly a couple of days earlier. Malo once again mentioned that he had spent money and had laboured hard for the sake of the Portuguese, and how sorry he was not to see the fulfillment of his efforts on account of the Dutch. He told Silveira that the Dutch had sent their representative, a factor, to Bednur along with Babusa Pai and Ishwara Kamath, both brahmins and influential at the court of Somashekhara; that the two brahmins solicited on behalf of the Dutch, urging the king to give them Mangalore and grant other requests of theirs; that the representatives had threatened that the Dutch would take Somashekhara's territories from Mangalore to Mirjan, within eight days, with the help of 20,000 to 40,000 Nairs, the queen of Bangher and the Chauter chief of Ullala, if Mangalore was not given; that if, on the other hand, the Dutch request was granted, they promised to protect his kingdom from the rebel feudatories and to purchase all the pepper and rice available in his territories; that Malo himself was considered a traitor for having sided with the Portuguese and thus being the probable cause of the ruin of the kingdom of Somashekhara; that on being summoned to the court, Malo found every one turned against him and he, therefore, decided to run away to the coast; that he was allowed to get away when he pretended to go to warn the Portuguese not to meddle in Somashekhara's affairs; that he was in fact a fugitive and might be arrested any time; and that as long as the Dutch continued to influence the court with threats and promises, there was no hope of anything being gained for the Portuguese. However, the fortress of Gangolly, which was virtually in the hands of the Portuguese, could continue to remain with them. Lobo concluded that it would be better to sail away to Goa, leaving João Pereira de Vasconcelos in charge of the Gangolly fortress. The Portuguese were not willing to break with the Dutch and invite a fresh war.[25]

Writing of these developments to the King of Portugal on January 29, 1666, the Viceroy suggested that he should take up the question with the government of Holland, protesting that the Dutch hindered the Portuguese from taking possession of the fortresses which were willingly given by a local ruler.[26] In the meantime, the execution of the agreement between the Portuguese and Somashekhara regarding the restoration of the fortresses was suspended and Lobo was permitted to return to Goa.

In November 1666, the question of taking possession of the fortresses of Kanara was reconsidered. On November 17, the Viceroy-in-Council appointed João de Sousa Freire, captain-major of the fleet of Malabar and dispatched him to the south with instructions to open negotiations with Somashekhara.[27] The fortress of Gangolly, was in Portuguese possession. However, its garrison was not paid for the previous seven months. Arrangements were now made to pay through Freire who was ordered also to procure pepper, rice and other provisions from Basrur through Vasconcelos, captain of the Gangolly fortress.[28] He was further instructed to secure the whole of the 'island' of Gangolly for the Portuguese and hinder the Arab trade with Basrur.[29] However, from two letters of the Viceroy, Count of St. Vicente written to the King of Portugal on January 26 and 27, 1667 respectively, we learn that Somashekhara did not consent to cede the fortresses. He was prepared only to allow the Portuguese to trade in his territories.[30] The Viceroy then instructed Freire to open hostilities against Somashekhara in August. While this order was being carried out, Shivaji invaded Goa towards the end of November and the Viceroy recalled Freire to Goa where he reached in January 1668. As soon as the Portuguese fleet withdrew from Kanara, Somashekhara captured all the Portuguese nationals and Christians who resided in his territories, and took possession of the fortress of Gangolly.[31] Malo who was so favourable to the cause of the Portuguese, now took up the cause of the Dutch.[32]

In 1671 Somashekhara reopened peace negotiations. On February 14 he wrote to the Governor of Goa offering the following terms and conditions: (1) the Portuguese would be given sites for establishing factories and timber yards at Mangalore, Basrur and Honavar. Each factory would be assigned surrounding lands to the extent of a handgun shot. No stone wall, single or double, should be constructed at the site; nor were there to be bulwarks, parapets and ditches. The Portuguese should not try to secure more than the specified area; (2) the Portuguese should not establish oil mills at the sites; (3) they should use weights and measures of his kingdom; (4) they should not convert anyone to Christianity by force; they should neither take orphans nor kill cows and brahmins; (5) the fugitive slaves of the Portuguese could be taken back freely by the latter; (6) necessary explosives and gunpowder could be kept by the Portuguese at each factory for defence against thieves and enemies; (7) he would order the merchants to pay the Portuguese factors the customary dues of anchorage and import and export duties. He would also order his custom officers to give the Portuguese the rice tributes; (8) the loading and unloading at the ports should be without unnecessary delay. The loading should be done in the presence of the customs officers. The relations between his officials and the Portuguese factors should be orderly and peaceful. The Portuguese merchants, who sold goods at the ports, should pay him taxes; (9) the articles, which might be taken from his lands and which were meant for consumption at the factory would be exempt from taxes; (10) the boats, ships and *menchuas* of the merchants of the Portuguese lands, which came into his ports and sold their goods there, would be given free passage to go back provided the sales tax was paid to him; (11) the ships carrying Portuguese passports should not be searched but allowed free navigation; (12) the boats and ships belonging to the pirates, who oppressed the Portuguese merchants, would be expelled from his territories; (13) the embarkations of his territories would take passports from the Portuguese and pay them the taxes. His own ships, carrying pepper, should be given passports as of old days; (14) the Portuguese should assist him with their fleet, ammunitions and shots against his enemies–Muslims, Nairs, and others. The Portuguese should not aid his enemies; (15) the embarkations of his lands should have free access into Portuguese ports, giving the embarkations good passage, but collecting due taxes from them. In case of storms, the embarkations should be allowed shelter in their ports without any attack; and (16) his own ships carrying rice should not be subjected to pay any Portuguese taxes.[33]

Malo and later, Vittala Malo were entrusted with the task of carrying on negotiations with the Portuguese on the basis of the above proposals. The Viceroy-in-Council meeting on April 20, 1671 decided to accept the terms, provided Somashekhara gave 70 *khandis* of pepper in satisfaction of the *periches* that were captured by Shivappa Nayaka but never returned. There was another suggestion in the Council that Somashekhara should be asked also to compensate for the money taken from Manoel da Costa Botelho. However, the final decision in this respect was to take up the matter with Somashekhara after the conclusion of the treaty.[34]

The treaty was signed on the same day namely April 20, 1671. With some modifications, all the proposals contained in Somashekhara's letter were incorporated in the treaty. The following were the changes made: (1) a single wall could be built around the factory for defence; (2) Somashekhara's ships carrying pepper were not to go to the ports of the enemies of the Portuguese; (3) the latter would assist him against his enemies, provided they were not the friends of the Portuguese; (4) he was to pay 70 *khandis* of pepper as a compensation for the captured *periches*, and (5) if either of the parties to the treaty violated its terms and conditions, the violating party should pay all the losses and damages caused thereby to the other party.[35]

In December Somashekhara was murdered.[36] His wife, Chennammaji (1671-1696) succeeded him, though an unsuccessful attempt was made to enthrone one Shivappa Nayaka, son of Andhaka Venkatappayya, and also another kinsman.[37] The supporters of Shivappa Nayaka seem to have tried to secure Portuguese aid by offering them some more ports in Kanara. Though no fortress was offered, it is interesting to note that this alternative possibility was taken into account in a meeting of the Council of State on December 29. However, the Council felt that it would be undesirable to accept a fortress since the question of succession of the throne of Ikkeri was still unsettled, and such a fortress given to them was bound to be attacked by the rival party, i.e., by Chennammaji, in whose eyes they would be enemies.[38]

Apparently, nothing came of this negotiation and Shivappa was soon suppressed by Chennammaji.

In 1674 the Portuguese captured at the Red Sea Strait, two ships belonging to Chennammaji and sold the cargo, thus inviting trouble upon themselves. As a measure of retaliation, the

Portuguese fleet, which had gone to Kanara to fetch foodgrains, was interned. The Portuguese talked of commencing hostilities, but ultimately agreed to give satisfaction.[39]

Towards the end of 1677 another friction arose between the Portuguese and Chennammaji. The latter allowed the Arabs to take rice supplies and to establish factories at Basrur, Honavar and Mangalore. The Portuguese considered this a violation of the treaty of 1671, as they were deprived of the taxes in the form of anchorage and customs. They sent a fleet to Kanara to suppress the Arab trade and drive them away. However, at Basrur the fleet was held up by the ingenuity of the officials of Bednur, who professed friendship. The delay enabled two Arabs vessels, which had left the Basrur port a day or two earlier with rice supplies, to slip away without being chased. When the Portuguese asked for rice supplies at Basrur, a high rate of 14 *pagodas* a *korji* was quoted, though rice of the same quality had been sold to the Arabs at 8 *pagodas* or even less. The Portuguese realised that the price was raised in order to prevent them from purchasing the commodity which the Kanarese wanted to store up for the Arabs who were expected at the port again. Considering these matters on December 16, the Viceroy-in-Council decided that the Kanarese should be persuaded to give rice at a reasonable price but hostilities should be commenced if they insisted upon supplying the commodity to the Arabs. Ships and houses at the Kanarese ports were to be burned. However, before launching the attack, the factors and their families were to be taken into safety. The Arab ships, which might be at the ports, were not to be allowed to sail out; and those which wished to enter were to be prevented from doing so. If the Bednur ruler desired, after the war to resume commercial relations according to the treaty of 1671, compensation for damage and losses was to be demanded as per the very treaty.[40] Hostilities were actually begun soon after.

In March 1678 the prince of Kanara, Virabhadra Nayaka, probably the son of Basavappa Nayaka, adopted son of Chennammaji, and the prince's captain-general, Timmanna Nayaka of Kasaragod, wrote to the government of Goa, soliciting aid from the Portuguese against Chennammaji. Virabhadra stated that the kingdom of Bednur belonged to him by right and that he intended to take possession of it. He requested the Portuguese to attack by sea, while he marched by land. In return for their help, he assured them their former possessions in Kanara. Virabhadra and Timmanna sent their letters to Goa through two envoys who were commissioned also to secure 400 soldiers from Ankola and Caroalle (?). The envoys were to take these men by sea in seven vessels. The Portuguese were requested to allow these vessels free passage, thus enabling the men to land at a convenient point in Kanara. The Governor-in-Council who met on March 30 to consider these matters, decided to respond favourably.[41] Their main aim was to embarrass Chennammaji as much as possible. Virabhadra must have been a mere child and he might have been a tool in the hands of Timmanna who probably was in revolt against the queen. Virabhadra's claim was rather flimsy and uncommon, as his father, Basavappa was alive and was the rightful heir after his adoptive mother, Chennammaji. It cannot be said that the Portuguese were not aware of all these. Yet any weapon was good enough for them to beat the queen with for having admitted the Arabs into her ports and depriving Goa of rice supplies.

Nothing came of this negotiation. Perhaps, Virabhadra and Timmanna were quickly suppressed. By December Basavappa himself began to negotiate with the Portuguese for peace. Probably acting on behalf of the queen he sent an ambassador, Krishna Nayaka, with a letter and a present to the Governor. Basavappa emphasised the 'ancient' friendship that existed between the Kaladi rulers and the Portuguese and pointed out that though he had been maintaining peace, the Portuguese generally inconvenienced the navigation of his ships and repressed some of them. He demanded their restitution. Krishna Nayaka was empowered to conclude a treaty on the basis of the terms and conditions of which he was given a list.[42] Malliopa, probably Mallappa Malo, who was known well to the Portuguese, also wrote to the Governor on the above lines.[43] After several meetings between Krishna Nayaka and him, and a meeting of the Council of State on December 10 to consider the proposals of Basavappa[44], a treaty of perpetual peace, alliance and commerce as signed in Goa on December 15, 1678.[45]

The first part of the treaty contained conditions on the part of the Portuguese in 19 clauses, and the second part had 10 clauses of conditions on the part of Basavappa. The Portuguese conditions were (1) the king of Kanara should give a compensation of 30,000 *xerafins*. He should not demand satisfaction for his ships which were captured by the Portuguese until then, justly or unjustly. The latter on their part would not demand the arrears of tribute and customs duties and also other losses caused by the king; (2) the king should give tribute as of old in Mangalore and Basrur; (3) the king should give the Portuguese a factory, together with surrounding grounds, at the port of Mangalore. He should supply at the site, stone, lime and wood, free of cost, to construct the factory. The Portuguese, however, would pay the officials employed in the construction of the factory; (4) in addition to the tribute under clause 2, the king should pay another tribute of 1,500 bags of clean and good rice every year at the factory of Mangalore; (5) the factory of the timber yard of the Arabs should be razed to the ground. Henceforth, the king should not allow the Arabs to trade at his ports and lands. If any Arab ship was found at his ports, the Portuguese should be free to attack and capture it. The present treaty should not be considered as violated because of such an attack on the Arabs; (6) ships belonging to the king or to his vassals should not sail into the ports of the enemies of the Portuguese, particularly the Arab ports. A ship violating this provision would be subject to confiscation by the Portuguese; (7) none of the ships of the king or of his vassals should navigate without a Portuguese passport. A fee would be charged while issuing a passport, except for the two passports of the two royal ships of Basavappa. A passport issued by the factor of Mangalore was sufficient for ships navigating between Kanyakumari and Diu; but for ships sailing for Bengal or the east coast of India or the Red-Sea Strait or the Persian Gulf, passports should be obtained from the Secretary of State in Goa. Even those ships which sailed to Goa in the company of Portuguese ships should possess passports issued by the factor of Mangalore. Any ship violating these provisions would be seized by the Portuguese; (8) the factory of Mangalore should have all the privileges as if it were a fortress, and former customs duties, anchorage and other customary taxes should be paid to the factor. Basavappa's officials should assist the Portuguese in this respect; (9) within the factory compound the Portuguese should be allowed to have shops for tobacco, foodgrains, liquors and other customary articles. Five cargoes of provisions a day should be allowed to be taken to these shops free of tolls imposed by Basavappa; (10) the Portuguese should be allowed to erect a church within their factory compound. The priests should be allowed to punish rebels, probably those Christians who did not live according to the dictates of the church. The king's *thanadars* and *manegars* should assist the Portuguese in this connection; (11) disputes among Christians even if the latter were residents in the territories of the king, should be subject to settlement by the factor along with the priests; (12) priests, missionaries and other Portuguese nationals, who travelled through Basavappa's kingdom on the way to others, should be allowed free passage. No tolls should be collected for the baggage and other paraphernalia, save for merchandise; (13) the king should give land and licence to establish churches in his territories, particularly in Mirjan, Chandrapura, Honavar, Bhatkal and Kalyanpur; (14) if any pirates, being subjects of the king, took Portuguese ships, the king should undertake to restore the ships with the cargoes and punish the pirates; (15) the Portuguese should be allowed to have warehouses for foodgrains within the factory compound. They should be allowed to have a fence around the factory and possess guns, *bacamartes*, *arquebuses* and muskets for defence against thieves; (16) slaves, who might run away from their Portuguese masters to the king's territories, should be returned without any payment being charged; (17) the king's officials should treat the factor with respect. If they desired to meet him they should seek his permission first. They should not have any gallows and other means of violent punishment within the factory compound; (18) Portuguese merchants should be free to store their articles of trade within the factory compound. They should be required to pay taxes only on those articles which they sold; (19) the factor should be allowed to bring, free of imports, whatever was necessary, from the king's territories for consumption in the factory.

The following were the conditions on the part of Basavappa: (1) the Portuguese should aid him with their warships against his enemies, provided the latter were not their friends. They should not ally themselves with his enemies; (2) aid should be given against the Arabs, if the latter attacked his lands; (3) the Portuguese should not establish oil mills in the factory; (4) in case of storm, free passage should be given to the king's ships, no taxes being imposed, save on what was sold; (5) Kanarese ships sailing into the ports of Goa should be subjected to nothing more than the customary dues; (6) the priests residing within the king's territories should neither convert any one by force, nor take orphans, nor kill cows; (7) the Portuguese captains and captain-majors of the fleets, carrying the ships of rice, should not compel the proprietors to give them loads of rice or any other bribes; (8) Basavappa should be given license to fetch horses from Congo or Hormuz; (9) those of his ships, which sailed into the ports of Arabia, could be captured by the Portuguese; (10) if a Portuguese subject committed any offence against a subject of Basavappa, the latter's officials would complain to the factor who should do justice, and if he failed, a complaint would be made to the Viceroy or Governor who should order justice done. Similarly, if a Kanarese subject committed offence against a Portuguese subject, the factor should complain to the King's officials who would order justice done.

By February 1679, Chennammaji arranged to pay 30,000 *xerafins* to the Portuguese, as we learn from a letter dated 21st of the month, written by Krishna Nayaka to the Governor.[46] Regarding the yearly tribute of 1,500 bags of rice, she issued an order on August 1, commanding Nallappa, in whose jurisdiction were the revenues of Honavar and Kundapur, to remit the tribute every year through Krishna Nayaka. In June or July 1680 the first tribute of 1,500 bags of rice seems to have been collected through Fr. Manoel Themudo whom the Governor sent to Kanara for the purpose.[47]

Portuguese relations with Chennammaji seem to have been cordial after the conclusion of the treaty of 1678 until 1695. However, in the first half of 1695 an occasion arose for hostility. An Arab fleet attacked a Portuguese fleet off Mangalore and burnt some *sanguichos* and damaged some *parangues*. The Portuguese believed that the queen had betrayed them by informing the Arabs of the weakness of the Portuguese fleet and that the governor of Mangalore, vassal of the queen, had assisted the Arabs. The factor of Mangalore was sent to Bednur to protest and demand satisfaction. He was also to countermine the negotiations of the Arabs with the queen.[48] It is not known whether the pretext was fruitful.

Under the treaty of 1676 the Portuguese were entitled to capture Kanarese ships, if the latter traded with enemy ports, particularly with Arab ports. In November 1695, there was an acute shortage of rice in Muscat. Knowing this, many Kanarese merchants desired to take ship-loads of rice to that region. The Portuguese decided to intercept these ships on the high seas and bring them to Goa where their future was to be determined subsequently. The Kanarese merchants desired to trade with Congo also and sought Portuguese passports. Though under clause no. 9 of the treaty the Portuguese were expected to grant such passports, they decided neither to issue nor to say so, but to delay the issuance until Chennammaji sent her envoys specially for the purpose. It was expected that if no rice supplies were allowed to Muscat for one year, the Arabs would be weakened.[49]

The minutes of the meeting of the Council of State held on March 29, 1697, show that Chennammaji died a little before this date. The Portuguese decided to send a present to Basavappa Nayaka, the new king, and congratulate him on his accession to the throne of Ikkeri.[50]

During the reign of Basavappa and thereafter in the first half of the 18th century, the Portuguese were preoccupied in excluding the Arabs from Kanara. In August, 1698 the factor of Mangalore reported to the Viceroy that what seemed to be Arab ships were anchored at the port of Mangalore and that the Arabs not only purchased rice at the port, but appeared to have the intention of establishing a fortification there. The authorities at Goa decided to write to Basavappa, probably to protest against his encouragement to the Arabs. At the same time they dispatched two frigates to Mangalore with orders to destroy the Arab ships if found at the port. Besides, the frigates were to procure rice from Mangalore for being sent to Mombasa.[51] It is not possible to say what exactly ensued, though it may be inferred from a letter dated May 18, 1699 written by the Viceroy to Basavappa, that some kind of understanding was arrived at between the two, for Basavappa sought Portuguese aid against the Marathas who occupied an island off Honavar. The Viceroy assured assistance, not immediately but in September by which time, however, the Marathas gave up the island and the Portuguese aid, which was sent in November became unnecessary. In the same letter the Viceroy took the opportunity to complain of the non-payment of import and export duties due to the factory of Mangalore, of the detention of a Portuguese, and of the non-cooperative attitude of the administrator of Mangalore.[52] Basavappa readily removed the causes of these complaints of the Viceroy, as we learn from another of the latter's communications on January 29, 1700. The Viceroy assured him all the possible aid against his enemies, provided he and his vassals did not have dealing with the Arabs. In order to show that he had no ill-will towards Basavappa, he blamed the Nayaka's ministers for past violations of the provisions of the treaty of 1678.[53]

In February 1701 Basavappa sent an ambassador with a present to the Viceroy and sought Portuguese passports for his merchant ships. The Viceroy granted the passports, taking the opportunity, however, to complain again of Basavappa's inconstancy and non-conformity to his promises and of his favour to the Arabs. He emphasised that Basavappa should allow free passage to the Portuguese navy and merchant fleet, as also to the factor of Mangalore, missionary priests and vicars of churches; that the king should order punctual payment of customs dues and the yearly tribute of rice as per the treaty of 1678; and that he should not admit Arabs, enemies of the Portuguese, into his ports. He sent a reciprocal present and assured the king all assistance against his enemies, provided he did "what ought to be done", no doubt, referring to the king's obligations under the treaty.[54]

Basavappa did not heed the Viceroy's request not to admit Arabs into his ports. From a letter of January 7, 1702 written by the Governor to the King of Portugal, we learn that their predecessor had warned Basavappa that warships would be sent to the ports of

Kanara if the Arabs were allowed any trading centre there. In spite of this, Basavappa seems to have continued to favour the Arabs, whereupon the Governor decided to order the warship, *Nossa Senhora de Valle*, to sail unto the Kanarese ports and prevent the Arabs from establishing their trading centre.[55] In reply to this letter, the King of Portugal, writing on March 5, approved of the Governor's intention of hindering the Arabs in Kanara, but pointed out that the most effective way of all the possible means to be used against the Arabs would be to procure rice supplies from Kanara, for the Arabs depended upon the rice from that region for their sustenance.[56]

In April or thereabout, 1702, the Portuguese captured a boat belonging to Basavappa though it possessed a Portuguese passport. Their excuse was that the ship carried some Arabs and certain prohibited articles like iron and bamboo intended to be taken to Muscat. The ship was brought to Goa and its cargo of rice, etc, was sold to the credit of the royal treasury. The Arabs, of course, had escaped. Basavappa seized the vicar of Honavar who was suspected to have given the information to the Portuguese authorities that the ship carried Arabs and that it was to sail to Muscat. The factor and the vicar of Mangalore, as also the vicar of Basrur, were interned. On receiving the news of Basavappa's action, the Governor-in-Council meeting on May 22 decided to "chastise" him for his "insolence" but after the rainy season. In the meantime, those merchants of Kanara, who were found in Portuguese territories, were to be interned as an immediate retaliation.[57] Basavappa relented. In July, or perhaps earlier, he released the vicar of Honavar and removed the guard on the factor of Mangalore and others. After this gesture of good will he sent an envoy to Goa to seek the release of the ship. By this time he seems to have engaged in a war against the Nairs of Malabar and therefore, he apparently desired no additional hostility with the Portuguese. He required their assistance, instead. The Portuguese, however, decided to demand satisfaction for his action against the factor and the vicars. If he were to refuse, hostilities were to be commenced against him. Besides, all Kanarese ships which did not have

Portuguese passports or which carried goods prohibited under the passports issued, were to be seized.[58]

Some sort of understanding seems to have followed between the Portuguese and Basavappa, for the Council of Finance passed a resolution on October 10, 1703 authorising the factor of Mangalore to spend a sum of 300 *xerafins* a year as presents to the king of Kanara.[59] Further, from a letter dated December 11, written by the Viceroy to the King of Portugal we learn that the Portuguese aided Basavappa against the Malabaris whose embarkations and pirate ships were expelled by the captain-major of the fleet of the south. Basavappa thanked the Portuguese for the relief given.[60]

However, trouble started again. The merchants of Kanara, who always followed a course which was in their own interests, traded with the Arabs. In fact, the Kanarese ports were closed to the Portuguese and their merchant fleet was refused rice supplies, as we learn from a letter dated May 1, 1704, written by the Viceroy to the nawab of Konkan.[61] By June there was scarcity of foodgrains in Goa. The Portuguese decided to secure supplies from the north and hoped that Basavappa would feel the loss of more than one million in gold, rupees and *patacas*, which they used to invest in his territories for provisions every year.[62] At any rate, Basavappa sent messengers in August, proposing settlement of mutual differences. The Portuguese believed that he relented because of the show of force in the form of four frigates which the Viceroy had sent to hinder his sea trade and to do other acts of hostility. Nevertheless, the Viceroy-in-Council meeting on August 12, decided to negotiate for a peace settlement.[63]

The Dutch, with whom the Portuguese were at peace by then, offered to supply foodgrains from Basrur where they had a factory. The Viceroy thanked them saying that he had procured sufficient rice from the north and therefore, did not need any more. He assured them however, that he would willingly accept their offer in case of need.[64]

From a letter of December 4, 1704 written by the Viceroy to the King of Portugal, we get details concerning the causes that led to the hostilities of the year. The Arabs persuaded Basavappa to deny food supplies to the Portuguese. Fearing the powerful Arab navy, which was believed to be on the way from Arabia, Basavappa obliged. He told the Portuguese that he would not allow them any rice supplies unless the ship captured during the vice-royalty of Almotace-Mor was restored and with this he closed his ports to their ships. The Portuguese retaliated by detaining one of his *pataxos* loaded with areca, whereupon he seized one of their captains, 16 or 18 soldiers and some mariners who were found in his territories. Besides, he withheld payments to their merchants. Some Portuguese *parangues*, which could not slip away in time, were also detained. The Portuguese not only sent four frigates to Kanara in August to hinder the Kanarese sea trade, but defeated the Arab navy off Surat. These developments, and the fear of more warships being sent to Kanara by the Portuguese, compelled Basavappa to release some of the Portuguese prisoners and all their *parangues*, and send an ambassador to Goa. The Viceroy refused to deal with the ambassador until all the prisoners were released and the Portuguese merchants were paid their dues. Basavappa obliged and hostilities were suspended.[65] Soon, the Viceroy's hope of getting rice supplies from Kanara seems to have fulfilled, for in another letter which he wrote on January 15, 1707 to the King of Portugal, he refers to Basavappa's observation of the "many conditions which I imposed upon him anew in the provisions of ratification of the peace which I adjusted with him".[66] This new treaty was concluded in February 1707. The treaty as a whole is not traceable, but a few of its clauses are found mentioned in the *Livro da Correspondencia da Canara*. These clauses are: (1) Basavappa should supply stone, lime, etc. for erecting a factory in Mangalore at a site most convenient to the Portuguese. (2) He should pay an annual tribute of 1,500 bags of "clean and white" rice. (3) Both the Kanarese and Goan merchants should be permitted to take rice from Kanara for sale in Goa. (4) The import and export duties levied at the ports of Mulki and Manjeshwara should belong to the Portuguese. (5) An embarkation belonging to Basavappa, but which had been repressed by the Portuguese, should be returned to its master. It may be noted that the treaty of 1678 was not considered null and void on the conclusion of this treaty of 1705.[67]

Towards the end of 1707 a Portuguese fleet of merchant ships with convoys, went to Kanara to secure food supplies; but the work was found difficult on account of the Arabs who also came there with a strong navy of 14 ships.[68] The Arabs apparently desired to take possession of Honavar, Basrur and Mangalore. At Honavar they landed more than 2,000 men with a view to take the place; but Basavappa's men repulsed the attack, causing them much loss in men and arms. From there the Arabs proceeded to Mangalore where they confronted the Portuguese who, having been re-inforced in the meantime, engaged them in many a battle and drove them away from there too. At Basrur also they were worsted by the Portuguese. These battles between the Portuguese and the Arabs, off the Kanara ports, took place in the first few months of 1708.[69]

In 1712 the Portuguese seized a ship belonging to Basavappa with horses on board, for it did not have a passport and was carrying some articles of trade prohibited under previous treaties. Basavappa was also accused of quoting exorbitant prices for rice and ill-treating Portuguese officials and soldiers who went for securing supplies. An ambassador was sent to Goa to secure the restitution of the ship, but the Viceroy justified its capture. Basavappa insisted upon the restitution and ordered his men, upon pain of death, that no rice should be supplied to the Portuguese. The Viceroy retaliated by sending a fleet of 13 warships with orders to open all possible hostilities against Basavappa; repress his embarkations, take his ports and prevent any rice from being exported.[70]

The fleet carried 350 men-of-war with Joseph Pereira de Brito as captain-major. It departed from Goa on January 15, 1713 and three days later reached Kumta where he confronted eleven of Basavappa's embarkations which were burnt. From Kumta the fleet proceeded to Honavar whose fortress the captain-major intended to capture. However the fortress was well-garrisoned. The defenders, perceiving the impending attack, were ready to withstand. The captain-major thought it inopportune to attack and sailed ahead to Basrur where he reached on the 21st. The fortress of Basrur was attacked so vigorously from the river that a wall came down pretty soon and the Portuguese soldiers landed. Until the midnight they engaged themselves in burning the inhabitants' dwellings and setting fire to ten *parangues*, one galleon and a ship which were anchored in the river. A nearby battery, which was being guarded with men and artillery, was invested on the following morning and taken. A rich habitation near the battery was burnt; so also another set of 10 embarkations, small and big was turned into ashes. The greatest loss was caused there when a store house of foodgrains, sufficient to fill several ships, was burnt down. The captain-major removed to his fleet nothing but the pieces of artillery which he found in the fortress and the battery. The fortress itself was demolished. On the 23rd, the fleet arrived at Kalyanpur where there was a fortress with seven bulwarks. In spite of incessant fire from the fortress, some small ships of the fleet entered the river and burnt the Kanarese ships anchored within. On the following morning the fortress was taken by assault. It was demolished after its artillery was removed to the fleet. On 25th the fleet reached Catapally (Katpadi?) where the soldiers were landed in three divisions. No edifice remained unburnt within the range of more than three leagues from the port. The Kanarese embarkations at the port were also set on fire.

Next, the fleet proceeded to Mulki where it reached on the 27th. The local chief offered to negotiate peace terms with the captain-major. However, the latter thought that it was a cunning device to delay matters until the chief received re-enforcements. Therefore, an attack was commenced forthwith. On the following morning the Portuguese found themselves at the foot of a fortress where 1,500 Kanarese soldiers were ready to defend. There ensued a keen contest, but ultimately the Kanarese were put to fight. After burning and devastating the habitations, the Portuguese sailed down to Mangalore where they arrived on the 30th. The defence force of that place consisted of 4,000 foot soldiers and 1,500 cavalrymen. The entire fleet of the Portuguese entered the river and commenced a battle.

After two days of furious fighting, the governor of Mangalore sought a cease-fire, saying that he would get Basavappa's instructions. The captain-major granted the request, but continued to prevent embarkations from sailing out of the ports of Kanara. However, even by the middle of April Basavappa did not show any sign of coming to terms and the rainy season was about to set in. The Viceroy, therefore, instructed the captain-major to return to Anjediv. On the way he was commanded to destroy Kumta, Gokarna and Mirjan. He faithfully carried out this command. The temple of Gokarna was burnt on this occasion. Thus, a fleet of thirteen ships with a small force of 350 men laid waste the coast of Kanara from Mirjan to Mangalore. Four fortresses were destroyed, 82 ships were burnt, many habitations were set on fire, and 600 or so of the Kanarese soldiers and others were killed. The material loss caused to Basavappa was calculated at five million *pagodas*. Among the Portuguese soldiers, only twelve were killed and thirty wounded. The captain-major too died, but owing to sea-sickness.[71] From another of the Viceroy's letters to the King of Portugal, we learn that the Portuguese enriched themselves during the course of these hostilities by capturing two galleons of Basavappa, one loaded with rice and the other with arecanuts.[72]

At last, Basavappa wrote to the Viceroy on December 28, 1713 and sent Kaddase Damarasa Prabhu with the letter to Goa for peace negotiations, who was empowered to conclude a treaty,[73] which was done on February 19, 1714.[74] The treaty was divided into two parts, the first part containing 25 clauses of Portuguese conditions and the second part comprising Basavappa's conditions in 13 clauses. The Portuguese conditions were: (1) Basavappa and his successors should be loyal friends of the Portuguese, friends of their friends and enemies of their enemies. He should assist them against their enemies; (2) to (7) These clauses related to Christians and missionaries. The factor of Mangalore and its vicar were to be judges in respect of disputes between Christians or between Christians and Hindus. Wherever the factor's jurisdiction did not extend, the priests were to be judges. Provision was made to appeal to the government of Goa, if decisions were unsatisfactory. The Christian women, who led an unchaste life, were to be handed over to the factor. Christian children were neither to be purchased nor to be enslaved. So also, wives and children of Christian soldiers were not to be purchased or enslaved. A Christian of Goa or any other part of the Portuguese possessions, who embraced any of the Hindu castes, should be taken by the church officials and sent to

Goa; in doing this the church officials were not to be obstructed. Clauses 6 and 7 provided for the construction of churches and free movement of missionaries, like clauses 10 and 11 of the first part of the treaty of 1678; (8) Basavappa should give the Portuguese a war compensation of 30,000 *xerafins*; (9) The arrears of the rice tributes amounting to 3,150 bags, or whatever was actually due, and the arrears of customs due, should be cleared; (10) The annual rice tribute should be raised from 1,500 to 1,900 bags; (11) The import and export duties should be paid to the Portuguese at Mangalore as before; (12) This clause, like clause 3 and 15 of the treaty of 1678, provided for the supply of materials on the part of Basavappa to construct a factory, or to repair the existing one, at Mangalore and for the equipment of the factory with arms; (13) This clause was similar to clause 17 of the previous treaty. The factory was to be treated as if it were a fortress; (14) The Portuguese should be allowed to establish warehouses inside the factory compound; (15) Basavappa should not have any dealings with the Arabs. If the latter were found at his ports, the Portuguese were to be free to attack the Arabs. The treaty was not to be considered violated on account of such an attack; (16), (17) and (18) were similar to clauses (6) and (7) of the previous treaty; (19) This provision related to runaway slaves and was similar to clause 16 of the previous treaty; (20) The Portuguese should be given preference vis-a-vis other powers, in giving rice supplies; the Portuguese should never be denied such supplies; Kanarese and Portuguese merchants and their ships carrying rice should be allowed free passage between Kanara and Goa; (21) Each of the rice bags taken by the merchants of Mangalore to Goa should measure two *mãos* of *curós*, each *curó* being eight measures. If the bags measured less, the Portuguese were to be free to confiscate them; (22) Basavappa should pay the value of the vessel (*palla*) taken by the Maratha in 1711 off Honavar, if it was adjudged that the *thanadar* of Honavar had given aid to the Marathas in this respect; (23) He should order Upendra Kamath, former customs officer of Mangalore, to pay the dues of import and export duties to the factor of Mangalore; (24) The latter should be free to purchase wood and send it to Goa unhampered; (25) Prabhu, ambassador of Basavappa, should maintain a *saraf* (*xeraffo*) at Goa to weigh and test the gold to be taken to Kanara.

The second part of the treaty contained the following conditions on the part of Basavappa: (1) the Portuguese should aid him with their fleets against his Asiatic enemies who are not their friends; (2) They should defend his ports, particularly against the Arabs; (3) The Portuguese should issue, free of charge, two passports a year to two ships belonging to him to bring horses from Hormuz or Congo; but such ships were to be subject to confiscation by the Portuguese if they carried on board horses from any of the ports of Imam of Muscat or brought by Arabs. In order to be free from suspicion, the captains of such ships should obtain certificates from the Portuguese factor of Congo showing that the horses were taken from Congo or Hormuz; (4), (5) and (6) were similar to clauses 5, 6, and 7 of the previous treaty; (7) Even those of Basavappa's ships, which possessed passports, were subject to confiscation if they were found at the ports of Arabia; (8) Basavappa's subjects were not to pay tolls at the fortresses and lands of the Portuguese; (9) The Portuguese should return, with the cargo, two ships seized from him in the previous year. If the ships were already sold, the Portuguese should give the cash gained from the sale; (10) Both parties to the treaty should forget the mutual offences that might have been committed and should not demand any compensation; (11) No oil mill should be established in the factory; (12) Kanarese ships, which went to Goa with the cargo of rice, should not be maltreated there. The rice taken from such ships should be paid for promptly; if not, the proprietors of the cargo were to seek justice by complaining to the Portuguese authorities; (13) Whenever there were disputes or differences between the two parties to the treaty, no hostilities should be committed by the one against the other while an ambassador was sent for negotiations.

Sending a copy of the treaty to the King of Portugal, the Viceroy commented that the oriental kings respected the Portuguese as long as the scars of the wounds caused by the Portuguese arms lasted.[75] The King thanked him for his iron policy towards Basavappa and for securing a treaty with such favourable terms.[76] However, in November, 1714 there occurred an incident which was about to cause trouble. A ship belonging to "a man of importance" in the court of Somashekhara Nayaka II (1714-39), who had succeeded Basavappa in the meantime, entered the port of Mormugao to take shelter there against a storm, no doubt with Portuguese concurrence. On examining the passport it was found that the period of its validity had already expired. The ship was interned for the time being. On November 19, the Viceroy-in-Council decided that the ship should be allowed to sail away, for it was not considered worthwhile to incur the hostility of the new ruler of Bednur by confiscating a ship which contained a small cargo and which had entered the port in the good faith.[77] This kind of detention and release of Kanarese ships took place occasionally. Towards the end of 1722 a galley of Mangalore was detained, because it brought horses which were prohibited under the passport given. However, the galley was released, because the Kanarese intended to raise exorbitantly the price of rice, which was necessary for the sustenance of Goa and also because the Portuguese relations with the English were uneasy in those days.[78] The Viceroy wrote to the regent of Keladi, saying that the vessel was released in order to preserve peace with Kanara.[79]

Again in January 1727 a Kanarese ship named Ishwari Mahamai, entered the river Mandovi and was detained, for its passport was found illegal and it carried horses without permission. The Viceroy-in-Council decided on January 20 that the ship should be restored but after ensuring cargoes for the southern fleet. Besides, at the time of returning the ship, a declaration was to be made that the restitution should not be cited as a favourable precedent, implying thereby that detained ships might not be returned in the future. The ship in question belonged to the regent of the kingdom of Keladi,[80] Nirvanayya,[81] who wrote to the Viceroy seeking the restoration of the ship. He responded on January 31 saying that it would be restored without the cargo. At the same time he also wrote to the factor of Mangalore that the latter should promptly inform him if the regent refused to accept the vessel without the cargo and denied rice supplies to the Portuguese so that he could decide on the measures of a suitable reprisal.[82]

The regent was apparently bent on securing horses and delaying the payment of tributes to the Portuguese in order to bring pressure upon them. The Viceroy wrote on January 27 to the factor of Mangalore instructing him to make it clear to the regent that the Portuguese had a just right to suppress ships carrying unlicenced horses and that if the due tributes were refused, they would consider the peace treaty as violated. At the same time he proposed to strengthen the fleet at Mangalore by dispatching a few more frigates in order to prevent the Kanarese ships entering or leaving the port until the question of the payment of the tribute was settled.[83] However, from another letter written by him on March 8 to the captain-major of Kanara, and the southern coast, we learn that the Portuguese were not eager to clash with Somashekhara. The captain-major no doubt was instructed to make persistent efforts to secure the rice tributes, if he found Somashekhara hesitating to give; but at the same time he was authorised to sell explosives and shots to Somashekhara or to the regent, if the war material were sought by either of them for defence against the Marathas[84] who were then invading the territories of Karnataka.

In the meantime, Somashekhara became displeased with the Christians and kept under custody the vicar of the church of Our Lady of Miracles of Mangalore. On May 14, 1727, the Viceroy wrote to Somashekhara a threatening letter demanding the punishment of the governor of Mangalore and the release of the vicar: "I cannot persuade myself that the governor of Mangalore had an order from Your Highness to violate the treaty concluded with this State as I do not suppose that Your Highness has forgotten the price which it cost you, and much less the oath which ought to be observed; and thus I expect that Your Highness should soon order to punish him as he deserves for having insolently violated it without reason when on my part nothing of what was stipulated (in the treaty of 1714) had been unfulfilled."

The Viceroy continued to say that he would declare war if "nothing suffices to persuade Your Highness to moderation which, ought to prevail in these proceedings". Regarding the detained ship, he expressed his disbelief that it was Somashekhara's (assuming that the regent would act in the name of the king), for he could not imagine that "having permission, as you have, to obtain the passport free of charge, (the ship) should have sailed without it, risking detention by virtue of the very conditions of the treaty".[85]

Writing on June 4 to Fr. Agostinho Machado, who was probably endeavouring to reconcile Somashekhara with the Christians of Kanara, the Viceroy assured him that he would not give into hostilities and disgraceful acts on the part of Somashekhara. Fr. Machado was authorised to tell the latter "that should a war break out, I shall not consent another peace treaty to be concluded with him with those advantages: and he can rest assured that he will not have an opportunity to request the restitution of the carcass of a ship on similar occasions." Regarding rice, which Somashekhara could prevent from being supplied to the Portuguese, Fr. Machado was to state "that I am in good peace with Sahu Raja", the Maratha ruler who would provide all his rice supplies to Goa. He was also authorised to assure Somashekhara that the latter's complaint that the Portuguese navy had committed excesses against him would be considered and the guilty officials would be punished.[86] We are not told what these excesses were.

Fr. Machado wrote to the Viceroy on June 6 remitting a statement of offences committed by the Portuguese as listed by the regent. He could not convince Somashekhara that the detention of the ship was justified under the treaty of 1714. Responding to him on June 30, the Viceroy told him to point out that the Portuguese always desired peace with Somashekhara and that is why the latter was aided against the Marathas who in fact could have been invoked to attack his territories instead. Fr. Machado was also to say that the detained ship not only did not possess a legitimate passport, but did not have even a letter from Somashekhara declaring that it was his. Nevertheless, he was instructed to agree to restore the ship, without its cargo, which was of very little value, if Somashekhara was found prepared to stop demonstrations of war.[87]

On the same day, namely June 30, the Viceroy wrote to the factor of Mangalore also appreciating his persistent efforts to secure peace for the Christians and to restore the priests to their offices. He remitted to him the letters from Bednur, together with his own replies, so as to facilitate the factor's further efforts. The latter was to protest against the governor of Mangalore who refused to give sandalwood and customs dues. If these were given, the factor was authorised to give the customary presents to the regent. The detained ship was not to be restored, because restitution would mean indirect approval of the violation of the treaty on the part of Somashekhara and it would damage the reputation of the Portuguese arms.[88]

However, before the Viceroy's letters could reach Fr. Machado and the factor, Somashekhara wrote to him on June 27, informing him that he had ordered cessation of offences against the missionaries and other Christians. Responding to this letter of July 1, the Viceroy hoped that Somashekhara would "desist from the motive which you have given me to complain, and being so, as I hope, Your Highness will observe the effects of the desires which I have of conserving your friendship."[89] Simultaneously, some doubtful points in respect of the treaty of 1714 were clarified. Clause no. 13 had provided that the Portuguese could maintain guns, *bacamartes*, *arquebuses* and muskets and other arms which were necessary. The regent, Nirvanayya, complained that the factor placed pieces of artillery before licences were obtained. The Viceroy urged that this should not become a cause of violation of the treaty since most of the arms were of small capacity. So also, the treaty did not specify the time of the arrival of the Portuguese fleet at Mangalore. However, it always came in November or December and this practice was to be considered regular. Next, it was confirmed that even the royal ships of Bednur would be subject to confiscation, if they did not carry passports issued free by the Secretary of State in Goa. Portuguese obligation to aid Somashekhara against his enemies, if the latter were not their friends, was also confirmed, and the example of the aid offered in the previous year against the Marathas, in case the latter were to descend on the coast of Kanara, was cited. Promise to punish Portuguese officials and soldiers who were legitimately accused of excesses against the Kanarese, was made. However, the ship which was detained legally was not to be restored.[90]

Yet on July 2 the factor of Mangalore complained that Somashekhara continued his prohibitions on arms, customs dues and cargo of sandalwood. Replying on July 24, the Viceroy sent a letter to the regent through the factor. The following complaints were included in the letter to the regent: (1) Arabs were permitted into the Kanarese ports from where they took rice supplies and other necessities, (2) Somashekhara sent his ships with cargoes of food- grains and ammunitions to Arab ports from where he brought horses, (3) he did not restore fugitive slaves and soldiers, (4) Melondin, enemy of the Portuguese, was allowed food supplies and permitted to sail out from the Kanarese ports to rob Portuguese embarkations, (5) missionaries were arrested and Christians were ordered out of Kanara, (6) sandalwood supplies, custom dues and arms were prohibited contrary to the terms of peace.[91]

In the beginning of August, or more probably towards the end of July, some Portuguese soldiers robbed a temple in Kanara and killed a *yogi* therein. It is not clear which was the temple attacked and where exactly it was located. Somashekhara apparently demanded satisfaction. Fr. Machado was instructed by a letter of the Viceroy on September 9 to assure Somashekhara that the culprit would be punished. He was also told to offer Portuguese firemen to assist him against Mysoreans.[92] A soldier, who was guilty of attacking the temple had escaped. The Viceroy instructed the factor of Mangalore to get him arrested either by himself or with the assistance of the governor of Mangalore. The latter, however, was to be required to assure the factor that he would not punish the culprit. The factor was to punish him on receiving further orders from the Viceroy.[93] In the guilty atmosphere in which the Portuguese found themselves, caution was taken by them not to offend Somashekhara anymore. Thus, the Viceroy desired to attack Arab ships if they were found in the Kanarese ports; but before doing so the governor of Mangalore was to be informed by the factor. The attack was to be deferred if the governor hesitated to permit it.[94]

Though Somashekhara had ordered the release of missionaries and the Viceroy had been cautious in his relations with him, there was no sign of the rice tribute. The latter became anxious and wrote to Fr. Machado on March 20, 1728: "I have to await always whether the fleet would return and whether they would pay the tribute; but the news from the factor only confirms the doubt (of securing the tribute) which ought to necessitate much force, it (the payment of tribute) being the principal part of the friendship; and on it depends not only the glory of this tribute, but the conservation of Anjediv". He further said that if the tribute was paid he had "no hesitation to order the (detained) ship to the king, nor to write to Lisbon (to the King of Portugal), concerning the (restoration of the) cargo, nor to show other gallantries to the regent". Fr. Machado was commissioned to agree to negotiate a new treaty, if Somashekhara were to suggest such a course. Supplies of rice at a fixed price were to be ensured for every year in the new treaty. In return, more liberal passports and supplies of salt at a fixed price were to be produced.[95]

On April 5 the Viceroy forwarded three concrete terms to be proposed to Somashekhara, (1) the Portuguese would purchase 70,000 bags of rice every year at the rate of 12 or 14 *pagodas* whether the prevailing market rate was cheap or dear. If more rice was to be purchased, the prevailing market rate would be paid for the additional bags. The Portuguese would supply in return 60,000 bags of salt every year at a fixed price proportionate to the fixed rate of rice, (2) if Somashekhara was prepared to pay more than 5,000 bags of rice every year as tribute, the Portuguese would issue passports free of charge to all ships, royal or others. However, failure to possess a passport would make a ship liable to confiscation. Those ships which brought horses should give two horses to the Portuguese, (3) Somashekhara should not allow Melodin into the Kanarese ports. If the latter's ships were found in any of them, the Portuguese should be free to attack and destroy the ships. In return, the Portuguese would aid Somashekhara against his enemies.[96] Nothing concrete followed until the latter half of October.[97] In fact, the Viceroy seems to have expected hostilities to ensure, for on November 10 he wrote to the general of the North to secure rice from the north, in case war should break out in Kanara.[98]

Open hostilities did not follow, however. At this stage Sundardas Vishnudas, resident at Mangalore, owner of four ships and procurator of the Portuguese in Kanara, took over negotiations for peace side by side with Fr. Machado. The regent, Nirvanayya was apparently a partner of Ramdas in business. Clarifying the policy of issuing passports and detaining ships which navigated without then, the Viceroy wrote to Ramdas on November 22, 1728 that the King of Portugal was the lord of the sea and as such he confiscated these ships which did not gain the liberty of navigation by obtaining passports from his servants. Ramdas himself was assured of Portuguese protection under the system of passports and the Viceroy hoped that he would send ship-loads of rice to Goa. Ramdas, who desired to send his ship to Persia, was offered not only passports, but the protection of the Portuguese navy proceeding to Mombasa and Patte in December. The Viceroy asserted that he always desired peace with Somashekhara. He requested Ramdas to have released the ship of Simão Dias and two Christians[99] who were apparently detained in Kanara in the meantime as an act of reprisal. In return he assured Somashekhara a new ship worth 30,000 *pardaus* for the detained one had become unserviceable by then. Writing of this to Fr. Machado, he said that the sale price of the ship of Simão Dias was also to be negotiated and settled at Goa. If Fr. Machado was authorised by Somashekhara for this purpose, he required that he should come with the king's letter. He was requested also to labour for sending some rice to Goa where the price was as high as 5 *xerafins* (Rs. 6) a bag of two *maõs*.[100]

Somashekhara sent one of his men to examine the new ship offered by the Viceroy. The ship was considered small and the latter offered to give a better one. Somashekhara also desired that passports should be issued to his ships but the Viceroy wanted to know if the former actually possessed the ships for which passports were sought; if no,, he assured her passports at the secretariat in Goa. As for Somashekhara's proposal that he should be free to bring the cargo of horses, the Viceroy expressed his inability to give a general licence but if a new treaty was concluded with the terms proposed by him, such a freedom was assured.[101]

The promised new and better ship was sent in March 1729.[102] No new treaty was concluded but relations between Somashekhara and the Portuguese became cordial. In 1731 no additional factory site was offered to the Portuguese who, however, did not accept it. The reason for the rejection is not indicated.[103]

On January 15, 1732 Fr. Machado informed the Governor of Goa that Somashekhara was hard-pressed by his enemies, probably the Malabaris. In response, he said that he would instruct the captain-major of the southern fleet to extend necessary assistance to Somashekhara.[104] The latter seems to have made his own proposals regarding the exchange of rice and salt at a fixed rate, offering to pay an additional tribute of 600 bags of rice, making the total 2,500 on condition that warships be sent to him in September. The Governor of Goa expressed his inability to take a decision then on these proposals.[105] Count of Sandomil, who succeeded then as Viceroy, wrote to Fr. Machado on November 29 informing him that he had just dispatched a frigate with explosives and shots to assist Somashekhara against his enemies.[106] This was, in fact, the first help sent to Somashekhara, though additional help was sent late with two chiefs of artillery.[107] No assistance could be sent from Goa before November, as the Viceroy explained in his letter of May 12, 1733 to Raghunatha Odeyar, governor of Mangalore, for the fleets of north and south came to Goa very late and it was undesirable to send any ships in the rainy season.[108]

The factor of Mangalore was instructed to place a Portuguese flag at the high plateau at the bar of Mangalore so that it would not be occupied by the forces of Somashekhara.[109] The latter paid the rice tribute of 1,900 bags for the year 1732 and he seems to have been regular for some years past in paying this tribute, for we do not hear of any complaint being made by the Portuguese in this respect. Generally, this rice was assigned to the sustenance of the fortress of Anjediv[110] which was the only fort left to the Portuguese off the Kanara coast.

The Portuguese took advantage of Somashekhara's occupation with the Malabaris to fortify the high plateau at the bar of Mangalore. The Viceroy wrote to the Secretary of State, Portugal, on December 13, 1733: "The king of Kanara requested me to assist with embarkations of war to convey his (embarkations) carrying provisions to the army which he has in the lands that he has just conquered from the Nairs, in which lands he is continuing the war against Cannanore which has vigorously resisted him; I have, on account of the dependence which the State has on the provisions which are customarily taken from his ports, as also to facilitate myself with the work which is actually in progress to fortify the elevated place at the mouth of the river near the factory, which we possess in the port of Mangalore, assisted him with the embarkations sought".[111]

The factor of Mangalore was instructed to do his best to conclude an agreement with Somashekhara, providing for regular rice supplies from Kanara, at the rate of 13 to 14 *pagodas* a *korji* in return for salt supplies at a mutually agreed rate.[112] It seems that a contract was in fact concluded in this respect, for the Viceroy wrote to the captain-major of the fleet of Kanara on March 22, 1734: "I understand that Your Majesty fulfilled with prudence what I expected of you, which has satisfied me greatly; and not less (satisfaction) the form of the agreement of prices for rice and salt (concluded) at the factory (of Mangalore) in your presence". From the same letter we understand that the Portuguese had almost completed the fortification of Mangalore by the time their assistance facilitated Somashekhara's occupation of the fortress of Karlai in the kingdom of Cannanore. The Viceroy authorised the captain-major to hand over to the factor of Mangalore four pieces of artillery to be mounted "on the fortress" of Mangalore.[113]

It seems that the governor of Mangalore, Raghunatha Odeyar, had given clear permission to the Portuguese to construct the 'small fortification'. After his victories in Malabar, Somashekhara changed his mind and ordered that the work should be discontinued. Perhaps, he feared that the Portuguese might use it against himself one day. The factor of Mangalore was induced to go to Raghunatha's house where he was detained for some days and at the same time Kanarese soldiers were placed in the fortification. However, Somashekhara changed his attitude again, apologised for ill-treating the factor, restored the fortification and permitted its completion "in a form that it should not look like a fortress, but a strongly built house".[114] The reason was Somashekhara's intention to continue the war of conquest in Malabar; but the ruler of Cannanore and the English at Tellichery were inviting the Portuguese to ally with them against him.[115] The Portuguese, however, preferred to come to terms with him, because they depended very much upon the rice supplies from his territories.[116] Yet, it may be pointed out that the Viceroy had half a mind to wage war against Somashekhara, for the latter did not satisfy all that was expected of him. However, the Portuguese military position was not strong enough then. He therefore instructed the factor of Mangalore to dissemble with Somashekhara, give the latter customary presents and procure rice supplies of which Goa was in dire need. Simultaneously, he wrote to the English and the king of Cannanore that he would join them against Somashekhara, if he did not give full satisfaction for maltreating the factor.[117]

At last, towards the end of 1736 the differences between the Portuguese and Somashekhara were settled to the entire satisfaction of the former. Somashekhara expected their aid against Cannanore, though they were not in a position to extend it.[118]

In 1737, the Marathas began to invade Portuguese territories. Somashekhara seems to have remained faithful towards the latter. In May, 1738 he informed them that the Marathas planned to invade the island of Goa (Ilhas) by land and sea.[119]

Somashekhara Nayaka II died in 1739 and his nephew, Basavappa Nayaka II (1739-55), succeeded him. The new king's relations with the Portuguese were cordial, on the whole, throughout his reign. However, the Portuguese did not have a high opinion about him. "The king of Kanara is more rich than powerful. The traffic in rice with the whole of Malabar and part of Muscat is the cause of a great influx of money into his kingdom. We have in his dominion a factory at Mangalore. We have been at peace for some time with this Prince, and it is the utmost importance to us that this peace and friendship should be preserved inviolate. It may seem absurd to say that this potentate is much more rich than powerful, but such in the case, for the money, as fast as it comes into his kingdom, is hoarded up in his treasure, and no use is made of it at all. He will not permit any fortification to be erected in his dominions, in case they should at any time be invaded and the enemy establish himself in them".

"Nor has he a large army, so that his expenses are not heavy. During the last two years the Angria has twice invaded Mangalore and Honavar and sacking these ports has carried off some valuable booty. To prevent a third invasion he had informed me that he proposed to build a fleet".[120]

Basavappa sought Portuguese assistance not only against Tulaji Angria but also against the French. In neither case did he receive any effective aid. Tulaji frequently attacked the ports of Kanara, sacking and damaging them. In January, 1747 he carried away from Mangalore a considerable amount of booty which he secured from the Portuguese factory there and from the palace of the local governor of Basavappa. The Portuguese found themselves helpless at Mangalore as most of their forces were engaged against the Bhonsles.[121] Basavappa too had sent a *palla* under the command of Tricamdas, probably Trivikrama Dasa, to aid the Portuguese against the Bhonsles. Trivikrama did well in the battle and Basavappa received written thanks from the Viceroy, Marquis of Castelo Novo.[122]

In order to prevent future assaults on Mangalore by Tulaji, the Viceroy decided to secure Basavappa's permission to fortify the factory. Accordingly, he instructed the factor to study the condition of the factory consequent to Tulaji's attack and to endeavour to convince Basavappa and his governor of the desirability and necessity to strengthen the factory.[123] Basavappa, however, hesitated to allow the fortification. Probably he feared that the fortress might be used by the Portuguese against himself one day, as the Portuguese were not known to be lovers of peace as far as their relations with Ikkeri was concerned.

In the meantime, Tulaji opened peace negotiations with the Portuguese,[124] which, however, were not satisfactory to the Portuguese who continued to consider him an enemy throughout 1747 and the first half of 1748. As a result, the captains of Portuguese fleets had instructions to attack his fleets, if possible, whenever and wherever found.[125]

When time came for the next possible attack on the Kanarese ports by Tulaji Angria in the winter 1747-48, Basavappa sought Portuguese aid against him. The Viceroy responded in his letter of December 26, 1747 that he had already dispatched two ships and an embarkation to the coast of Kanara, not for its defence but to suppress it. For the governor of Honavar had allowed the Bhonsle's ships into the port there and Ismail Khan, captain of a Portuguese fleet, who wanted to take into task the Bhonsle's fleet, had been prevented from doing so. The Viceroy requested Basavappa to punish the governor. He also pointed out that if Tulaji Angria had successfully attacked Mangalore in the previous year the fault lay in Basavappa himself and that Tulaji Angria might not attack again if the factory there be fortified.[126] He instructed the factor of Mangalore also to complain of the governor's proceedings, expressing surprise that Basavappa should seek Portuguese aid against his enemy while assisting theirs. The factor was told also to ascertain the truth of the news that Tulaji Angria was erecting a fortress in Ramataly (?), probably a place on the coast of Kanara.[127] Further, the factor was commanded to continue his efforts to get Basavappa's permission to fortify the factory.[128]

In the summer of 1748 Basavappa came down to Mangalore personally, probably with a view to better defend the place from Tulaji Angria's possible attack. While in Mangalore, Basavappa wished to witness a Portuguese company of grenadiers in exercise. The Viceroy reluctantly agreed that such a company be landed from the southern fleet for one day for the benefit of Basavappa.[129] Ultimately, however, no such exercise was arranged.[130] It might not have been a mere curiosity on the part of Basavappa, as the Portuguese thought. He might have intended to introduce reforms in his own army after witnessing the Portuguese methods of organisation.

There arose certain points of difference between Basavappa and the Portuguese during the latter half of the year 1748. The Nayaka withheld the payment of certain dues to the Portuguese and did not permit the erection of new churches. He also complained that the main factor which enabled Tulaji Angria to enter Mangalore and sack it was the easy access at the Portuguese factory. The Viceroy wrote back on November 4 that if 10 or 12 galliots were sufficient to enter and damage Mangalore, it was Basavappa's fault; and that the Portuguese had pointed out several times the necessity to fortify the factory, but in vain. He concluded by saying that he might be compelled to send a Portuguese fleet to Kanara, not to defend the coast but to attack it in order to make good the injustice of the Nayaka in refusing to pay off the dues and to allow the due privileges to the Christians as per the treaty of peace of 1714.[131]

In the meantime, peace negotiations between Tulaji Angria and the Portuguese were not discontinued.[132] In the latter half of 1748 the negotiations entered a satisfactory stage and the captains of Portuguese fleets were instructed to treat his fleet as of a friend.[133] However, before a definite treaty was concluded Tulaji attacked Mangalore again in November 1749. He sacked not only the port of Mangalore, but robbed there two vessels belonging to the Portuguese. The latter threatened Basavappa that they might abandon the factory in view of Tulaji Angria's continued attacks and Basavappa's refusal to allow the fortification of the factory. However, in reality they did not intend to give up the factory, for they feared that the English or the French might occupy the port. This eventuality was heartily detested by the Portuguese.[134] Writing to Basavappa on November 27, the Viceroy pointed out that Tulaji Angria would continue to attack Mangalore as long as he found it open and unfortified, for he was a "thief by profession". The Viceroy had no objection in fortifying the factory, but at Basavappa's cost.[135] In the letter of protest which he wrote to Tulaji Angria, he required that he should return all that was taken from the two vessels of the Portuguese at Mangalore so that peace negotiations could become fruitful. It is noteworthy that not a word of protest was uttered by the Viceroy on behalf of Basavappa.[136]

Basavappa complained that the factor of Mangalore did not do his best to prevent Tulaji Angria's incursion into the port. In response, the Viceroy alleged that the governor of Mangalore and others did not defend well and that they ran away from the ports instead. He warned Basavappa that the Angria was planning to capture Mangalore, *inter alia*, and therefore he should pay more attention to its defence.[137]

In March, 1750 Tulaji Angria attacked and captured the fortress of Honavar. Though he abandoned it soon, he took away with him not only a large amount of booty but also about 1,500 eminent men from Honavar with a view to extract a huge ransom for their liberty.[138] Gokarna was another place which he attacked and sacked. The Viceroy expressed his surprise that 'a pirate like Angria' should have attacked the territories of Kanara with impunity, whereas he dared not to attack the lands of less powerful kings. Basavappa proposed that the Portuguese and the Kanarese fleets should join hands against Tulaji Angria. The Viceroy thought that this alone would not suffice. He proposed that the Portuguese should be allowed to have factories at the ports of Honavar and Basrur also, with the permission to fortify the factories including that of Basavappa.[139] Basavappa seems to have indicated his intention to have new ships built. The Viceroy instructed the factor of Mangalore to find out if the intention was implemented and let him know before Basavappa's reply to his proposals came.[140]

In the latter half of October, news reached Goa that Tulaji Angria was preparing a strong fleet and was collecting considerable amount of war materials. The Portuguese thought that his intention was to capture some part of the Kanarese coast and to fortify it. Basavappa was informed accordingly.[141]

Towards the end of October or early in November Basavappa wrote to the Viceroy, but did not care to respond to the latter's proposals referring to factory sites at Honavar and Basrur, and the fortification of the factories. However, he repeated his request for Portuguese aid against Tulaji Angria.[142] The Viceroy responded by expressing his willingness to aid, but emphasized that an agreement regarding the Portuguese proposals was important.[143] However, such an agreement never came into existence.

Early in 1751, the Marathas and Basavappa seem to have come to an understanding, for from a letter written by the Viceroy to the factor of Mangalore on January 15, we learn that a Maratha fleet of six galliots sailed to the Kanarese coast with letters and presents to Basavappa.[144] After his attack on Kanara in March 1750, Tulaji did not attack its ports any more. In the meantime peace was established between him and the Portuguese also.

In October 1751 Basavappa opened war against Cochin. He requested the Viceroy not to permit the merchants, subject to Portuguese jurisdiction, to sell the rice which they took from Mangalore at the ports of Malabar.. He readily agreed and issued instructions to the factor of Mangalore to this effect.[145]

Basavappa also sought aid from the Portuguese, probably in the form of ammunitions, which were sent towards the end of December.[146]

By December the French at Mahe joined hands with the Malabaris against Basavappa. They urged the Portuguese to aid them with arms and men, and open hostilities against him at his ports. Though the Portuguese were on friendly terms with the French, the former did not wish to oblige the latter in this respect. The Viceroy instructed the factor of Mangalore that any European nation that tried to attack the port of Mangalore be opposed.[147] In the meantime Basavappa suffered a defeat at the hands of the forces of Cochin.[148] He sought further aid from the Portuguese. In response, the Viceroy informed him that he could not but be neutral, for the French had also sought aid, and on being denied, they had requested the Portuguese to deny it to Basavappa also. The Viceroy pointed out that the treatise of peace between the Nayakas of Ikkeri and the Portuguese expressly declared that the latter should aid the former only against Asiatic enemies who were not allied with the Portuguese. Since the aid sought now was against a European power, an ally of the Portuguese, they were not bound to aid Basavappa. However, the Viceroy decided to be neutral as both the belligerents were his allies.[149]

In January 1752 Basavappa was defeated again, with greater damage than before.[150] In the latter half of February the Viceroy began negotiations with the French in order to bring about peace between them and Basavappa. Writing to the renowned French Governor-General at Pondicherry, Marquis de Dupleix, he offered to mediate between the belligerents and requested Dupleix to let him know his terms of peace.[151] Basavappa was informed of this movement.[152] By September the French and Basavappa were ready to negotiate for peace. The former informed the Viceroy that their main requirement of a proposed treaty of peace was to be allowed to retain the fortresses that they were in possession of, by them, in Malabar. Informing Basavappa of this, the Viceroy requested him to indicate his terms of peace.[153] The Nayaka, however, did not respond to this letter. Instead, he began direct negotiations with the French and sent his ambassadors to Pondicherry in the beginning of 1753.[154]

In the meantime Basavappa was reportedly defeated by the Malabaris who took from him the fort of Chandragiri. He requested the Portuguese to convey his ships, carrying provisions, to the fortress of Decle (?) and that of Hosadurga. The Portuguese excused themselves, though they used to give such convoys to the French and the English. The factor of Mangalore, through whom the request was made, was instructed to say that he had the Viceroy's permission to grant the request, provided there was no delay involved. The factor was to show greatest eagerness to execute this conditional order, but in fact he was not to implement it.[155] However, Basavappa's request for war materials from the Portuguese met with better success. In January 1754 he sought 500 *bambas* and 500 grenades against payment. The Portuguese supplied 500 grenades, but only 300 *bambas*, for the stock of the latter was inadequate.[156] Ultimately, the war of Malabar ended in losses to Basavappa. His territories did not go beyond Chandragiri which he retook from the Malabaris.

Basavappa was succeeded by Chenna Basavappa Nayaka (1755-57) who was followed by the last ruler of the dynasty, Rani Virammaji (1757-63). In both the reigns the Portuguese generally had good relations with Kanara but for the occasional minor complaints that the Portuguese officials were not treated well or that Portuguese ships were detained without cause. On every occasion the complaint was heard and justice done.

In January 1763 Hyder Ali, *de facto* ruler of Mysore, defeated Virammaji and occupied Bednur, thus bringing the rule of the Keladi dynasty to an end. Portuguese records do not show any aid sought by the queen from the Portuguese. Probably, she had no time to seek and obtain it as Hyder Ali's attack was sudden and well-planned. Immediately after his victory, Hyder Ali wrote to the Portuguese and established friendly relations with them. The Portuguese proudly record that he "was the first who wrote to the most illustrious and the most excellent lord, Count of Ega, Viceroy and captain general of India.[157] A new chapter was thus opened in respect of the Portuguese relations with Kanara.

REFERENCES

1. P.S. Pissurlencar, *Agentes de Diplomacia Portuguesa na India*, pp. 57-9.
2. *Assentos*, IV, pp. 32-33.
3. *Ibid.*, p. 33.
4. K.D. Swaminathan, *The Nayakas of Ikkeri*, pp. 102-3.
5. English records refer to this invasion of the Bednur kingdom by the Adil Shah, saying that Bhadrappa fled to the woods for protection. Later on, the Adil Shah extracted seven lakhs of *pagodas* from him (*EF*, 1661-1664), pp. 260-1, 237, 239).
6. *Assentos*, IV, p. 527.
7. *Ibid.*, pp. 530-1.
8. *EF*, 1661-1664, p. 342.
9. *Ibid.*, p. 343.
10. *Ibid.*, p. 349.
11. *Assentos*, IV, p. 553.
12. *Ibid.*, p. 534-5.
13. *Ibid.*, pp. 535-6.
14. *Ibid.*, p. 537.
15. *Ibid.*, pp. 537-8.
16. *Ibid.*, pp. 552-3.
17. *Ibid.*, pp. 540-1.
18. *EF*, p. 349.
19. *Assentos*, IV, p. 542.
20. They seem to have tried to possess it themselves by placing their flag on its walls. But this act was so much resented by the Kanarese that they took down the flag and tore it asunder. The Portuguese, coming to know of this incident, laughed in their sleeves (*EF*, p. 350).
21. *Assentos*, IV, p. 543.
22. *Ibid.*, pp. 545-7. Letters of November 25 and 26, 1664.
23. *Ibid.*, p. 546. Letter of November 25, 1664.
24. *Ibid.*, p. 548. Letter of December 11, 1664.
25. *Ibid.*, pp. 549-52.
26. *Assentos, IV,* p. 555.
27. *Ibid.*, p. 171.
28. *Ibid.*, p. 175.
29. *Ibid.*, p. 176.
30. *Ibid.*, p. 169.
31. *Ibid.*, pp. 564-5.
32. *EF*, 1668-1669, p. 111.
33. J.F.J. Biker, *Colecção de Tratados e Concertos de Pazes*, IV, pp. 192-4.
34. *Assentos*, IV, pp. 216-7.
35. Biker, *op. cit.*, pp. 189-92.

36. Abbé Carré, *Travels of ...*, tr. Fawcett and Fawcett, III, p. 699; *EF*, 1670-1677, p. 308.
37. *KNV*, pp. 128-9; *EF*, 1670-77, pp. 308-9.
38. *Assentos*, IV, pp. 226-7.
39. *Ibid.*, pp. 233-4, 236, 240.
40. *Ibid.*, pp. 274-5, 278-80.
41. *Ibid.*, pp. 314-5. Neither N.L. Rao nor K.D. Swaminathan refer to this revolt of the young prince in 1678. *KNV* also does not throw any light on this event. The revolt was probably nipped in the bud and therefore it did not attract anybody's attention.
42. Biker, *op. cit.*, IV, pp. 212-3.
43. *Ibid.*, pp. 213-4.
44. *Ibid.*, pp. 205-6; *Assentos*, IV, pp. 338-9.
45. Biker, *op. cit.*, pp. 207-12.
46. *Ibid.*, p. 214.
47. *Ibid.*, p. 215.
48. *Assentos*, IV, pp. 487-8.
49. *Ibid.*, p. 499.
50. *Ibid.*, V, p. 42. Swaminathan, *op. cit.*, p. 125 mentions that the queen "seems to have died in 1698". This is obviously incorrect in view of the clear indication given by this document, which says: "the queen being dead", Basavappa Nayaka should, on his accession, be complimented in the manner indicated.
51. *Assentos*, V, pp. 57-8.
52. Appendix no. I. See also *LCC*, I, 1698-1720, fl. 5. Viceroy's letter to Basavappa, October 31, 1699.
53. Appendix no. II.
54. *LRV*, no. 5, fl. 44; *APO-BP*, tomo I, vol. III, pt. 1, pp. 94-5. K.D. Swaminathan, *op. cit.*, p. 275 includes a translation of this letter at Appendix no. 13 of his book. The translation is full of errors. The Viceroy did not order "that the price of rice should be promptly paid" to Basavappa but told the latter to pay "all the quantity of rice of tribute in accordance with the provision" of the treaty. The "previous dues" or arrears were not on the part of the Portuguese as the translation indicates, but on the part of Basavappa, who was requested to clear them up with the Portuguese. There is no reference in the original to "our not receiving remittance". So also the original does not refer to the "traditions" of the Arabs, but to their treacheries. The Viceroy did not remit "letters", but *cartazes* or passports.
55. *Monções*, no. 65, fl. 253; *APO-BP*, pp. 136-7.
56. *Monções*, no. 67, fl. 71; *APO-BP*, pp. 143-4. K.D. Swaminathan, *op. cit.*, p. 127 (footnote no. 9) refers to this letter but wrongly says that it was written by the Portuguese to Basavappa.
57. *Assentos*, V, pp. 134-6.
58. *Ibid.*, pp. 136-9.

59. *APO-BP*, p. 204.
60. *Monções*, no. 67, fl. 12; *APO-BP*, p. 223.
61. *LRV*, no. 5, fl. 83; *APO-BP*, pp. 238-9.
62. *Assentos*, V, pp. 163-4.
63. *Ibid.*, pp. 166-7.
64. *LRV*, no. 5, fl. 87; *APO-BP*, pp. 260. Viceroy's letter to the Dutch factor of Basrur, October 13, 1704.
65. *Monções*, no. 68, fl. 195; *APO-BP*, pp. 266-8. K.D. Swaminathan, *op. cit*, p. 128 refers to this letter, but inaccurately says that there was a skirmish in December, 1704. The letter actually recounts the past skirmish and the events that led to a settlement of the differences before the date of the letter.
66. *Monções*, no. 69, fl. 108; *APO-BP*, pp. 393-4.
67. *LCC*, I, fls. 42, 96-97.
68. *LRV*, no. 7, fl. 12; *APO-BP*, p. 435.
69. *Monções*, no. 73, fl. 1; *APO-BP*, pp. 453-6. K. D. Swaminathan, *op. cit*, p. 128 says that "In 1707 the Portuguese invaded the territories of Basavappa Nayaka and attacked the port of Mangalore. But the forces of Basavappa were able to put up a stiff resistance and the Portuguese were compelled to suspend hostilities. Basavappa Nayaka deputed Damarasa Prabhu as his ambassador to Goa with a letter to conclude peace with them". These are baseless statements. It was the Arabs and not the Portuguese, who invaded the territories of Basavappa. The latter resisted the Arabs stiffly and the Portuguese were glad to fight the Arabs on the occasion, though more for their own sake than for Basavappa. As has been shown elsewhere, Damarasa Prabhu was sent to Goa towards the end of December 1713, and his embassy had nothing to do with the event of 1707-8.
70. *Monções*, no. 78, fl. 124; *APO-BP*, tomo I, vol. III, pt. II, pp. 79-80. Viceroy's letter to the King of Portugal, January 1713.
71. *Monções*, no. 79, fl. 254; *APO-BP*, pp. 90-4. Viceroy's letter to the King of Portugal, January 17, 1714. Swaminathan, *op. cit.*, pp. 278-80 includes a translation of this letter. However, to say the least, the translation is concocted and, at many places makes no sense at all.
72. *Monções*, no.79, fl. 248; *APO-BP*, pp. 88-9. Letter of January 15, 1714.
73. *APO-BP*, p. 83.
74. *Ibid.*, pp. 97-106; Biker, *op. cit.*, vol. V, pp. 280-8.
75. *Monções*, no. 80, fl. 160; *APO-BP*, p. 151. Viceroy's letter of January 5, 1715.
76. *Monções*, no. 80, fl. 160; *APO-BP* pp. 187-8. King's letter of October 17, 1715. K. D. Swaminathan, *op. cit.*, p. 139, footnote 20, makes baseless statements referring to this letter and that of January 5, 1715.
77. *Assentos*, V. pp. 289-92. There was no plan to send an expedition against Somashekhara as K.D. Swaminathan, *op. cit.*, p. 139, footnote 21, would like us to believe. The document which he refers to in this respect is simply an order of the Viceroy to the general of Bardez to recruit 60 mariners to serve in the fleet of Kanara.

78. *Assentos*, V, pp. 369-92.
79. *LRV*, no. 7, fl. 26. Letter dated December 9, 1722.
80. *Assentos*, V, pp. 372-3. The Regent is referred to as minister also.
81. *Ibid.*, p. 370.
82. Appendix no. III and also no. IV.
83. *LRV*, no. 7, fl.41; *APO-BP*, tomo I, vol. III, pt. IV, pp. 39-40.
84. *LRV*, no. 7, fl. 43; *APO-BP*, tomo I, vol. III, pt. IV, pp. 41-2.
85. *LRV*, no. 7, fl. 45; *APO-BP*, tomo I, vol. III, pt. IV, pp. 48-9.
86. *LRV*, no. 7, fl. 46; *APO-BP*, tomo I, vol. III, pt. IV, pp. 49-51.
87. *LRV*, no. 7, fl. 47; *APO-BP*, tomo I, vol. III, pt. IV, pp. 58-60.
88. *LRV*, no. 7, fl. 46; *APO-BP*, tomo I, vol. III, pt. IV, pp. 60-2.
89. *LRV*, no. 7, fl. 47; *APO-BP*, tomo I, vol. III, pt. IV, pp. 62-3.
90. *LRV*, no. 7, fl. 48; *APO-BP*, tomo I, vol. III, pt. IV, pp. 63-4.
91. *LRV*, no. 7, fl. 49; *APO-BP*, tomo I, vol. III, pt. IV, pp. 65-6.
92. *LRV*, no. 7, fl. 53; *APO-BP*, tomo I, vol. III, pt. IV, pp. 69, 71.
93. *LRV*, no. 7, fl. 51; *APO-BP*, tomo I, vol. III, pt. IV, p. 70.
94. *LRV*, no. 7, fl. 55; *APO-BP*, tomo I, vol. III, pt. IV, pp. 71-2. Viceroy's letter to the factor of Mangalore of October 2, 1727.
95. *LRV*, no. 7, fl. 60; *APO-BP*, tomo I, vol. III, pt. IV, pp. 91-2.
96. *LRV*, no. 7, fl. 64; *APO-BP*, tomo I, vol. III, pt. IV, pp. 94-5. Swaminathan, *op. cit.*, pp. 139-40, includes a translation of the first proposal. The translation is singularly inaccurate.
97. *LRV*, no. 7, fl. 70; *APO-BP*, tomo I, vol. III, pt. IV, p. 124.
98. *APO-BP*, p. 125.
99. *LRV*, no. 7, fl. 73; *APO-BP*, tomo I, vol. III, pt. IV, pp. 126-7.
100. *LRV*, no. 7, fl. 74; *APO-BP*, tomo I, vol. III, pt. IV, pp. 129-30. Viceroy's letter to Agostinho Machado of November 29, 1728.
101. *LRV*, no. 7, fl. 75; *APO-BP*, tomo I, vol. III, pt. IV, pp. 130-1. Viceroy's letter to Sundardas of December 17, 1728.
102. *LRV*, no. 7, fl. 77; Viceroy's letter to Sundardas of March 16, 1729.
103. *Ibid.*, fl. 94. Viceroy's letter to factor of Mangalore of April 3, 1731; fls. 95-6, Viceroy's letter to Agostinho Machado of May 2, 1729.
104. *Ibid.*, fl. 101; *APO-BP*, tomo I, vol. III, pt. IV, p. 287. Viceroy's letter to Agostinho Machado of January 1, 1732.
105. *LRV*, no. 7, fl. 102; *APO-BP*, tomo I, vol. III, pt. IV, p. 288. Governor's letter to Agostinho of March 1, 1732.
106. *LRV*, no. 7, fl. 105; *APO-BP*, tomo I, vol. III, pt. IV, pp. 289-90.
107. *LRV*, no. 7, fl. 132; *APO-BP*, tomo I, vol. III, pt. IV, p. 321. Viceroy's letter to Somashekhara of March 23, 1734.
108. *LRV*, no. 7, fl. 121; *APO-BP*, tomo I, vol. III, pt. IV, pp. 303, 304.
109. *LRV*, no. 7, fl. 105; *APO-BP*, tomo I, vol. III, pt. IV, pp. 289-90.
110. *APO-BP*, tomo I, vol. III, pt. IV, pp. 292, 297, 351. Of course 1,900 bags of rice alone were insufficient. 1,100 bags more were provided.
111. *Monções*, no. 102-B, fl. 780; *APO-BP*, tomo I, vol. III, pt. IV, pp. 307-8. Also see Viceroy's letter to the factor of Mangalore of February 27, 1733, in

which the factor was ordered to carry out the work of fortification (*LRV*, no. 7, fl. 108; *APO-BP*, tomo I, vol. III, pt. IV, p. 299).

112. *LRV*, no. 7, fl. 108; *APO-BP*, tomo I, vol. III, pt. IV, p. 299.
113. *LRV*, no. 7, fl. 130; *APO-BP*, tomo I, vol. III, pt. IV, p. 320.
114. *Monções* no. 103, fl. 911; *APO-BP*, tomo I, vol. III, pt. IV, pp. 343, 345-6. Viceroy's letter to the King of Portugal of January 25, 1735.
115. *LVR*, no. 7, fl. 132; *APO-BP*, tomo I, vol. III, pt. IV, p. 326, 328. Viceroy's letter to factor of Mangalore of October 26, 1734.
116. *Monções* no. 103, fl. 911; *APO-BP*, tomo I, vol. III, pt. IV, pp. 345-6.
117. *LRV*, no. 7, fl. 147; *APO-BP*, tomo I, vol. III, pt. IV, pp. 350-1. Viceroy's letter to the factor of Mangalore dated February 9, 1735.
118. *Monções* no. 106, fl. 9; *APO-BP*, tomo I, vol. III, pt. IV, pp. 428-9. Viceroy's letter to the King of Portugal of December 22, 1736.
119. *Assentos*, V, p. 471.
120. F. C. Danvers, *The Portuguese in India*, II, p. 423.
121. *LCC*, II, 1747-1769, fl. 1. Viceroy's letter to Basavappa of January 31, 1747.
122. *Ibid.*, fl. 2. Viceroy's letter to Basavappa of February 2, 1747.
123. *LRI*, no. 14, fls. 6-7. Viceroy's instructions to José Antunes Branco, factor of Mangalore; *LCC*, II, fl. 8. Viceroy's letter to the same factor dated October 2, 1747.
124. *LRV*, no. 12, fl. 65. Viceroy's letter to José de Souza Fernandez of February 13, 1747 and fl. 89. Viceroy's letter to Tulaji of August 22, 1747; *LCC*, II, fl. 9, Viceroy's letter to the factor of Mangalore dated October 14, 1747.
125. *LRI*, no. 14, fls. 12, 15, 50. Viceroy's instructions of February 2, 1747; March 27, 1747 and March 20, 1748, respectively.
126. Appendices V and VI.
127. Appendix VI.
128. *LCC*, II, fl. 13. Viceroy's letter to the factor dated February 16, 1748.
129. *Ibid.*, fl. 15. Viceroy's letters to the Commandant of the southern fleet dated March 14, 1748 and to the factor, dated March 26, 1748, respectively; and fl. 18, Viceroy's letter to the factor dated April 8, 1748.
130. *Ibid.*, fl. 18. Viceroy's letter to the factor dated April 24, 1748.
131. Appendix, VII; and also *LCC*, II, fls. 23-4. Viceroy's letter to the factor dated November 3, 1748.
132. *LRV*, no. 12, fls. 136-7, 147, 163-4, Viceroy's letters to Tulaji dated March 30, 1748, May 6, 1748 and July 19, 1748, respectively.
133. *LRI*, no. 14, fls. 66, 116, Viceroy's instructions dated October 24, 1748 and March 9, 1749 respectively; also *LCC*, II, fl. 28, Viceroy's letter to commandant of the southern fleet, Francisco da Cunha de Araujo dated March 9, 1749.
134. *LCC*, II, fl. 38. Viceroy's letter to the factor dated November 21, 1749.
135. Appendix VIII.
136. Appendix IX.
137. Appendix X.

138. Appendix XI.
139. Appendix XII.
140. *LCC*, II fl. 52. Viceroy's letter to the factor dated August 20, 1750.
141. *Ibid.*, fl. 53. Letter of Luis A. Dantas, Secretary of State dated October 24, 1750.
142. *Assentos*, V, pp. 688-9.
143. *LCC*, II, fl. 55. Viceroy's letter to Basavappa dated November 9 (?), 1750.
144. *Ibid.*, fl. 59. Viceroy's letter to the factor dated January 15, 1751.
145. *Ibid.*, fls. 72-4. Viceroy's letter to Ayyappayya, governor of Mangalore and to José Antunes Branco, factor of the same place dated November 15, 1751 and November 15/16, 1751 respectively.
146. *Ibid.*, fls. 75-6. Viceroy's letter to the ministers of Basavappa dated December 28, 1751.
147. *Ibid.*, fls. 76-7. Viceroy's letter to the factor dated December 12, 1751.
148. *Ibid.*
149. Appendix XIII.
150. *LCC*, II, fl. 78. Viceroy's letter to the factor dated January 18, 1752.
151. *Ibid.*, fl. 80. Viceroy's letter to the factor dated February 9, 1752.
152. *Ibid.*, fl. 82. Viceroy's letter to Basavappa dated March 13, 1752.
153. Appendix XIV. Also *LCC*, II, fls. 91-2. Viceroy's letter to the factor dated September 28, 1752.
154. *LCC*, II, fls. 93, 96. Viceroy's letters to the factor dated November 23, 1752 and February 25, 1753, respectively.
155. *Ibid.*, fls. 98-9. Viceroy's letter to the factor, March 23, 1753.
156. *Ibid.*, fl. 107.
157. *Ibid.*, fl. 155.

10

THE PORTUGUESE AND CHRISTIANITY IN KANARA

Christianity was not unknown in Kanara before the Portuguese arrived. About 1493 a cross was caught in the net by some fishermen, off Mangalore. It was of olive wood, well-finished and one span and a half in length. The fishermen thought that the cross was a venerable object, for they caught abundant fish of various sorts at the same spot, thus enriching themselves. They handed over the cross to the Bangar chief from whom it was obtained by Miguel de Almeida in 1611 and taken to Goa.[1] In fact, it is said that there might have been a Christian community in Mangalore. For on November 19, 1502 some Christians of Mangalore "and other interior places" went with presents to Vasco da Gama who was in Cochin. They also presented a letter from the "lord of all those territories, who has abcut 30,000 people within his jurisdiction" and who offered to become a vassal of the King of Portugal. These Christian ambassadors told da Gama that "they had their bishops and all of them said the mass. They also told him, among other things, that they "undertook grand pilgrimages to the sepulchre of the blessed St. Thomas."[2] One may not find it easy to believe that the chief of Mangalore should have offered vassalage to Portugal on his own and should have sent his "Christian" ambassadors to Cochin to meet the Portuguese admiral for the purpose. It may be noted here that the first of the Portuguese who arrived in India mistook non-Muslims for Christians. They were virtually ignorant of the existence of the Hindu community, though within a few years they became aware of their mistake.

Further, some crosses, painted black and red, were discovered by the Portuguese while digging up for laying down the foundation of the fortress built in Anjediv in 1505. Commenting upon these findings, Paulo da Trindade says that they appeared to have belonged formerly to a "chapel or church of Christians". He continues to say: "This is not difficult to believe, because the glorious St. Thomas travelled all these parts of the Orient, propagating the Christian faith and converting many unbelievers."[3] However, it is difficult to say whether the findings were in fact Christian crosses or some other objects which looked like crosses and were actually some instruments prepared by Hindus for astronomical observations.[4] Even if it is granted that there were Christians in Kanara before the Portuguese arrived, the community of the former must have disappeared by 1498. It did not matter, however, for they never hesitated to establish a new community of Christians by converting the people of Kanara whenever an opportunity offered itself.

The first Portuguese missionaries, who began their propagation activities in Kanara were Franciscans. In 1500, eight friars under the leadership of Henrique of Coimbra landed in Anjediv, in the company of Pedro Alvares Cabral.[5] The friars endeavoured to convert the natives of Anjediv. Trindade says that the natives went to the friars without any fear and "participated in the mass which they said and in the propagation which they preached, demonstrating happiness in seeing their ceremonies. And, though they (the friars) did not know their language and thus could not declare to them the mysteries of our holy faith, they did it in the manner which was possible for them, telling them by signs that they should give up the idols which they had in their homes, and showed to them the sacred sign of the cross and other images which they (the natives) gladly kissed and reverenced." The friars had great desire to continue to be at Anjediv in order to convert all the people there. However, Cabral had to proceed to Calicut and they too had to go along with him. Though they desired to return to the place later on, God willed otherwise.[6] None of them ever landed in any of the territories of Kanara, though Luis de Salvador played an important role as Afonso de Albuquerque's envoy to Vijayanagara. It is claimed that the Vijayanagara emperor, Vira Narasimha, not only listened to the preachings of Salvador, but allowed the latter to propagate the "holy faith" in his territories and construct churches.[7] In spite of this permission, Salvador does not seem to have indulged in propagation in Kanara.

In 1505 Francisco da Almeida destroyed a temple that he came across on the island of Anjediv and used the stone of the edifice for the construction of the fortress. Some Franciscans had accompanied him. A chapel might have been built for the benefit of the garrison, though no specific reference is made to such a building. However, the chapel might have disappeared along with the fortress, when the latter was destroyed in 1506.[8]

In 1683 a church dedicated to Our Lady of the Blossoms (*Nossa Senhora das Brotas*) was established on the island.[9] The church was meant for the garrison of the fortress, which was built on the island in the previous year, and "to administer the sacraments to other Catholics who might take up residence there or on the mainland".[10] In 1733 there were 505 Catholics on the island.[11] Most of them were "old Catholics belonging to the garrison or its followers and dependents, but it might be that the friars made some conversions either on the island or on the mainland."[12]

Mangalore and its neighbourhood became another centre of early missionary activities. In 1526 the Franciscans established a regular mission in Mangalore.[13] In due course they built three churches– one in Mangalore dedicated to Our Lady of the Rosary, another in Ullala for Our Lady of Mercy and the third in Farangipet dedicated to St. Francis of Assisi.[14]

In 1533 the diocese of Goa was created by a bull of Pope Clement VII and confirmed in 1534 by Pope Paul III. The diocese included all the lands from Cape of Good Hope to China, including no doubt, India. Kanara, thus came under the charge of the bishop of Goa. However, nothing worth noting was done by the bishop to propagate Christianity in Kanara. Even the great missionary, St. Francis Xavier, who worked zealously in India and other parts of the Orient, from 1542 to 1552 did not visit Kanara, though he did not fail to see the possibilities of conversion in this coastal region. For he wrote on September 18, 1542, "We have great hope that many Christians will be made here" in Kanara.[15] It is possible that he sent his assistants to Kanara for propaganda there and the rectory of Basrur, which Nazareth refers to,[16] might have been established some time during this period.

The Catholics of Kanara take pride in the fact that the ship, carrying the body of St. Francis Xavier, touched the port of Bhatkal in 1554 while it was being taken to Goa. A miracle occurred there. The wife of António Rodrigues, factor of Bhatkal, was seriously ill. She was taken to the ship to see the body. She recovered health the moment she saw it.[17] Already in 1552, an attempt was made to convert some people in Bhatkal, but no concrete success attended the effort.[18]

In the latter half of the 16th century, the Portuguese entrenched themselves in Kanara by building fortresses in Mangalore, Basrur and Honavar. In each of these a church was built. A vicar, with several assistants, was put in charge of each. The primary purpose of these was to serve the spiritual needs of the Portuguese soldiers. It is probable that whenever there was a zealous vicar in charge of a church he might have endeavoured to convert the local people. The number of conversions, however, must have been very small.

A few Catholic families of converts of Goa might have migrated to Kanara as a result of the activities of the Inquisition which was established in Goa in 1560. The converts could not give up completely their pre-conversion customs and habits, which the Inquisition would not tolerate. In the process of enforcing conformity it created a sense of insecurity among the converts who found scarce protection for their life and property. Some of them, therefore, left Goa and settled down in Kanara.[19]

G. M. Moraes, says that the majority of the Kanara Christians came from Goa owing to the troubles and scarcity conditions in the latter place caused by enemy attacks and natural calamities like famines and epidemics. 1553 was a year of famine. In 1570 and 1683 respectively, Goa was subjected to enemy attacks. In 1570 and 1635 there were epidemics. Besides, in general, the agricultural products of Goa were not adequate enough to sustain the Goans. All these were said to have forced many Goans, Christians and Hindus, to leave their homelands for Kanara.[20]

It is true that the majority of the Kanara Christians were immigrants from Goa. However, migration until the middle of the 17th century seems to have been negligible. Or, even if many might have migrated, most of them might have returned to Goa when conditions became normal in the latter region. For Pietro Della Valle, who visited Kanara in 1623, found churches and priests in Kanara but he makes no reference to any Christian settlement or community as such in any of the towns and ports that he visited. In Mangalore he came across three churches, namely, the Sé, or Cathedral of Our Lady of Rosary, within the fort, La Misericordia and St. Francis without". He added: "Yet in Mangalore there are but three ecclesiastical persons in all; two Franciscans in São Francisco and one vicar to whose charge with small revenues belong all the other churches."[21] Della Valle roamed about in Mangalore, but apparently did not find any Christian settlement. Writing about Honavar, again, he mentions two churches, but no Christian community.[22] António Bocarro, writing in 1635, says positively that there was no Christianity in the kingdom of Ikkeri, including, no doubt, Kanara. He wrote: "We do not have any Christianity in the lands of this king of Kanara and as all are Hindus, the aversion they have for receiving our sacred faith is so great that it is rare that any one had been converted so far." He thought that it was owing to the lack of knowledge of Kannada on the part of the missionaries who could otherwise have written in Kannada the commandments and principles of Christianity for the benefit of the Kanarese. He also points out that no missionary moved about in the kingdom of Ikkeri. However, he mentions that there were churches in the various Portuguese fortresses. Thus, in Basrur there were two churches, one named the Sé, inside the fortress, and the other named Mia (mother?) just outside. The former was meant for captains, soldiers and others within, and the latter for the *cazados*. So also, in Mangalore, Honavar and Gangolly there were churches attached to the fortresses.[23] It may also be added here that there is no clause providing for the protection and privileges of Christians in Kanara in the treaties of 1631 and 1633 entered into between the Portuguese and the rulers of Ikkeri. On the other hand, there are several such provisions in the treaties of 1678 and 1714. This indicates that a large number of Christians came to settle down in Kanara during the latter half of the 17th century. Thus, Fr. Giuseppe de Santa Maria, a Carmelite friar, who passed through Kanara in 1656-7, could say that there were 6,000 Christians in the kingdom of Ikkeri, though only one Jesuit priest, namely, Spinola, was available for their religious requirements.[24] This number went on increasing. From a letter of the Viceroy to the King of Portugal, dated August 13, 1747, we learn that about 5,000 Christians fled from Goa to Kanara during the course of the Maratha invasion of Goa beginning in 1738.[25] There were about 30,000 Christians in the kingdom of Ikkeri when it fell into the hands of Hyder Ali in 1763.[26]

A reference may be made to some missionaries and their activities in Kanara. In 1580 the Franciscans built a church dedicated to St. Anthony in Mangalore, Fr. Fernando da Paz being its custodian. He and his successors accomplished a free conversions there. An interesting account is given of a Hindu convert. He had a vision where after he longed to be a Christian. Said he soon after his conversion: "I, gentlemen, had in my heart since long (a desire) to make myself a Christian and to receive the faith of Christ, believing to be the true faith after I had a vision which I shall presently narrate. But until now I am not disposed for this ... on account of my wife, who always contradicted me regarding my sacred proposal. But, as God is merciful, (He) had the kindness to remember me, giving powers to me to overcome all the difficulties which my wife, as a Hindu and captive of idolatry, put before us." The vision that he saw was a procession of priests of the Order of St. Dominic which came from the side of the territories of the Bangar chief on the occasion of the death of a Dominican priest, who resided in the church of the Misericordia in Mangalore. The processionists, carrying candles in their hands, went back to the same direction. The element of surprise in the vision was the fact that so many Dominican priests were not to be found in Mangalore or its neighbourhood, though some were there in Cochin, Goa and Chaul. The convert was recruited a soldier in the Portuguese army.[27] This might, in fact, have been the incentive for his conversion.

A church dedicated to Our Lady of Conception, was built in Gangolly which was occupied by the Portuguese in 1630. It was the work of two Franciscans, Fr. Francisco Cordeiro and his companion, Fr. Jorge da Conceição, who, "as a signal of the war which they had to wage against the Hindu population there, destroyed and razed to the ground a great temple which existed near the site where the fortress (St. Miguel of the Portuguese) was established." It was a temple dedicated to Lord Shiva and was richly endowed with a revenue of 1,000 *pagodas* or 3,000 *xerafins*. There was in the temple "as an idol, a *linga,* which is a certain thing which they (the Hindus) consider divine, which, being ignoble and sordid, is not mentioned (by me) what it is." The church was built in the very place of the destroyed temple. At the same time, it is claimed that Gangolly was given to the Portuguese by the merchants of Basrur on the condition that only Franciscans should be allowed there.[28] However, in the official documents of the Portuguese there is no reference to such a condition.

By far, the greatest of the missionaries of Kanara was Fr. Joseph Vaz who was in Kanara from 1681 to 1684 and again in 1686. However, he had to work under difficult circumstances, for the conflict of jurisdiction between the *Padroado*[29] of the Portuguese King and the Sacred Congregation of the *Propaganda Fide*[30] entered Kanara in the latter half of the 17th century. The Pope appointed Thomas de Castro, a brahmin Christian of Goa as bishop of Fulsivelum and vicar apostolic of Kanara and other places. He, who as in Rome, reached India in 1674 by land via Syria and Babylon. He adopted this route in order to avoid the Portuguese who did not approve of his appointment. Besides, it was repugnant to them that an Indian should have been appointed to such a high position in the church.[31]

Bishop Castro began his missionary work with zeal. Though he made Mangalore his headquarters, he paid attention to Basrur, Barkur, Mulki, Kalyanpur and other places of Kanara. From the very outset the *Padroado* tried to hinder his activities by forbidding the Christians of Kanara from receiving sacraments at his hands, or at those of his prelates, unless he produced the bills conferring the jurisdiction over Kanara to him. He responded by excommunicating those who received sacraments at the hands of the missionaries of the *Padroado*.[32]

In 1681 the Church chapter of Goa appointed Fr. Vaz as the vicar forane of Kanara. He actually desired to go to Ceylon but realising the need of a good missionary in Kanara, particularly to counteract Castro, the Chapter sent him to Kanara. He acted very tactfully. His humility and honesty of purpose won him laurels. He did not declare open hostility against Castro. Instead, he approached him and requested him to show the papal documents of appointment, which the chapter of Goa had declared fraudulent. On finding the documents legitimate, he proposed to the bishop that he should not excommunicate any more Kanarese Christians until the question of jurisdiction over Kanara was settled by the chapter to whom he proposed to write on the matter. He agreed. However, neither the chapter nor the archbishop was prepared to recognise the jurisdiction of Castro. The matter was referred to Rome. Fr. Vaz, being told of this, prostrated himself at the feet of Castro, requesting him not to excommunicate Kanarese Christians who received sacraments from the missionaries of the *Padroado* until the Pope settled the matter. The sincere humility of Fr. Vaz won the heart of the bishop. Both continued their respective missionary activities until Castro died in 1684.[33]

Bishop Castro secured a plot of land at Mangalore from queen Chennammaji. He built the first church of Our Lady of Miracles on this site. At his death, his body was buried in the church, which, however does not exist today. On its site we find only a cemetery and the grave of the bishop cannot be identified.[34]

Fr. Vaz worked in Kanara for about three years. During this short period he became very popular among the Christians there. He improved the church of Our Lady of the Rosary at Mangalore and built two new churches in Basrur and Gangolly, dedicated to Our Lady of the Rosary and Immaculate Conception, respectively. Where there were Christian communities, but no churches, he erected small huts and asked the Christians to gather in these huts and offer prayers even though there were no priests. He called such gatherings *irmandades* (brotherhoods) and visited them as often as possible.[35]

From a letter of his we learn that there were Christians in Bantwal and Arkol who went to the church in Mangalore on important festive occasions and for sacraments. So also there were Christian communities at Bhatkal, Kalyanpur, Sirul and Gandalim (?) who depended upon the vicar of Basrur. The Christians of Kumta and Chandavar went to him at Honavar. Fr. Vaz urged his superiors in Goa to send more priests to Kanara so that those Christians, living so far away from the centres where there were churches could avail the services of the additional priests.[36]

Returning to Goa in 1684, Fr. Vaz organised the Congregation of the Oratory of Goa. He came back to Kanara in March, 1686 and worked there again for nine months after which he left for Ceylon. This time he was not called upon to waste his energy on the conflict of jurisdiction, for the Pope had not appointed any regular successor to Bishop Castro. The latter had nominated, before his death, Joseph de Castro, his relative, as vicar general but the successor had to promise not to exercise his powers until further orders from the Pope, who did not send any. Joseph de Castro died in 1700 and the conflict of jurisdiction disappeared completely.[37]

A few words may now be said regarding the non-religious activities of the missionaries in Kanara. They generally participated in the wars that were waged in that region, for the success of their mission depended largely upon the political successes of the Portuguese in the region. Sometimes it was a priest, with a cross aloft in his hand, who led the vanguard. Thus, three Jesuit chaplains accompanied the Portuguese expedition against Ullala in 1568. One of them, Fr. João Francisco Estefonio "always marched in the front with a holy cross aloft, animating the soldiers to fight".[38] Similarly, five priests participated actively in the battle of Mangalore in 1619 against Venkatappa Nayaka. Three of them were Augustinians and two Franciscans. Fr. Diogo Homem, one of the two Franciscans marched by the side of Gomes da Silva, captain of the vanguard. He carried "a lance in his right hand and a cross on his breast". He was, however, killed along with two Augustinians. The remaining two escaped death and retreated to the fortress along with the remnant of the vanquished Portuguese soldiers. After this crushing defeat, the Hindu temple which was within the Portuguese fortress, was destroyed on the Viceroy's orders.[39] This was probably at the instance of the missionaries who might have desired to avenge the death of the fathers just mentioned.

It was common to employ missionaries as ambassadors. We have seen while discussing the Portuguese relations with the Nayakas of Ikkeri, that many of the Portuguese ambassadors to the Nayakas were priests. Besides this, in political counsels the clergy was given an important place. The factors in Kanara could deliver judgements in respect of cases involving Christians only in the company of the vicar attached to the church of the factory. Where there was no factory, the priest of the church of the locality was empowered to settle disputes between Christians on the one hand, and between Christians and Hindus on the other.[40]

Sometimes the priests acted as informers. As we have seen in 1702 Basavappa Nayaka imprisoned the vicar of Honavar, who was suspected of having informed the Portuguese authorities that a ship, carrying some Arabs and certain prohibited articles, was about to sail for Muscat. The ship was captured by the Portuguese.[41] Many a time the Nayakas of Ikkeri arrested or otherwise harassed the Christians in Kanara whenever there were hostilities between the Nayakas and the Portuguese. This was done in 1668.[42] In 1702 the vicar of Basrur was interned while that of Honavar was imprisoned.[43] Again, in 1727 the vicar of Mangalore was kept under custody by Somashekhara.[44] Some priests were arrested by Basavappa Nayaka II in 1746 for having built a new church at Bantwal without his permission, though the Portuguese contended that no such permission was necessary under the treaty of 1714.[45]

The Portuguese government in Goa did whatever was possible to safeguard the interests of the missionaries and Christians in Kanara. This is particularly evident during the last hundred years of the Ikkeri rulers. In the various treaties that were entered into between the Portuguese and the Nayakas, provisions were included to protect the interests of the church and its flock. We have seen what these provisions were in the treaties of 1678 and 1714.[46] The missionaries received all the encouragement from the government in their conversion activities. In January 1751 Basavappa's ministers complained to the Viceroy that a missionary, working in the region of Kalyanpur and Bàrkur, was trying to convert a brahmin, Manhant Shankarayya, resident of Kalyanpur, and his wife to Christianity by force. In reply the Viceroy denied to have received any information in this respect, but promised to command the missionary to "proceed as per justice", for his intention was not to "consent to violences".[47] By July, however, the couple was sent to Goa where they were converted and baptised. Shankarayya became Francisco and the Viceroy, Marquis of Tavora, his godfather. The relatives of Shankarayya seem to have tried to deprive him of his property. The Viceroy commanded the factor at Mangalore to do his best to get Shankarayya his property.[48] The factor might have carried out the instruction, though we do not find any documentary evidence to this effect.

Before concluding this chapter, I may allude to the claim of some pious Christians that sometimes even Hindus venerate crosses and churches. The Count of Linhares (1629-35) records in his diary an interesting episode in this regard. A cross was erected at the distance of a gunshot from the Portuguese fortress of Gangolly. One night, however, it was removed by the local *thanadar*, assisted by a few men, and was taken to Virabhadra Nayaka. Misfortune befell all the twenty men who thus stole it away; they died all of a sudden. What is more all others who scornfully placed their hands upon it, also fell dead. Presently, Virabhadra, seeing the fate of his men, ordered that the cross be restored to the Christians. In the meantime, it was very much venerated and worshipped by the Hindus with flowers.[49]

REFERENCES

1. Francisco, de Sousa, *Oriente Conquistado*, pt. I, conquista I, div. I, pp. 24-6.
2. *APO-BP*, tomo I, vol. I, pt. I, pp. 266-7.
3. *CEO*, I, p. 91.
4. Gerson da Cunha, "An Historical and Archaeological Sketch of the island of Angediva", *JBBRAS*, no. xxxi, vol. xi, 1875, p. 303.
5. A. da Silva Rego, *História das Missões do Padroado Português do Oriente*, vol. I, pp. 153-4. The friars were Henrique de Coimbra (superior), Gaspar, Francisco da Cruz, Simão de Guimarães, Luis de Salvador, Messeu, Pedro Neto, and João de Vitória.
6. *CEO*, II, pp. 226-7. António José de Heredia in "O Christianismo na India antes da erecção da diocese de Goa", *Memória Histórico-eclesiástico de Arquidiocese de Goa, 1533-1933*, p. 20 mentions that 22 or 23 were baptised by these friars in Anjediv.

7. *CEO*, III, p. 284. See also *Documentação*, I, p. 34. footnote 1.
8. *Lendas*, tomo I, pt. II, p. 562.
9. M. F. Gabriel de Saldanha, *História da Goa*, II, p. 284.
10. Achilles Meersman, "The Chapter list of the Madre de Deus Province in India, 1569-1790", *Studia*, July 1960, p. 183.
11. Viriato de Albuquerque, *Senado da Goa*, p. 447.
12. Meersman, *art. cit.*, p. 184.
13. António José de Heredia, *art. cit.*, p. 28; J. Sturrock, *The South Kanara District Manual*, p. 68.
14. I. Carmo, "O Cristianismo no Canara", *Boletim Eclesiástico da arquidiocese de Goa*, November 1951, p. 174. Also, Severine Silva, *History of Christianity in Canara*, I, p. 37.
15. J. Gerson da Cunha, "The Portuguese in Kanara", *JBBRAS*, vol. xix, 1895-97, p. 251.
16. C.C. de Nazareth, *Mitras Lusitanas no Oriente*, I, p. 171.
17. Felippe Neri Xavier, *Resumo Histórico da Maravilhosa Vida, Conversões e Milagres de S. Francisco Xavier*, p. 221.
18. *Documentação*, V, p. 254.
19. S. Silva, *op. cit.*, pp. 43-4.
20. George M. Moraes, *Mangalore*, pp. 58-60.
21. Pietro Della Valle, *Travels of...*, ed. Edward Grey, II, p. 301.
22. *Ibid.*, p. 203.
23. *APO-BP*, tomo IV, vol.II, pt. I, pp. 309, 311, 317, 320.
24. G. di Santa Maria, "Prima speditione", quoted by G. Moraes, in *Mangalore*, p. 60.
25. *Monções*, no. 120-B, fl. 523.
26. MMDLT, "History of Hyder Shah", quoted by G. Moraes, *op. cit.*, p. 61.
27. *CEO*, II, pp. 237-8.
28. *Ibid.*, pp. 236, 242.
29. *Padroado* implies the privilege of patronage conferred on the Kings of Portugal by the Popes. The former were authorised to recommend candidates for bishoprics or other ecclesiastical benefices in the territories discovered by the Portuguese. This privilege was given right from 1481. In return, the Portuguese were to protect Christians in the territories which came under their control or influence. The names recommended were generally accepted by the Popes.
30. The department of the Sacred Congregation or Propaganda Fide was instituted in 1622 by Pope Gregory XV. The purpose of this organ was to convert the Orient to Christianity directly through missionaries appointed by the Pope. In the 17th century the Portuguese were not always in a position to discharge their responsibility of the Padroado on account of the series of defeats suffered by them at the hands of the Dutch.
31. S. Silva, *op. cit.*, I, p. 61.
32. C.C. de Nazareth, *op. cit*, I, p. 185; Arsenio Tomaz Dias, "Acção e Traços Biográficos dos Prelados", *Memória histórico-eclesiástica de Goa, 1533-1933*, p. 118; S. Silva, *op. cit.*, I, p. 62.

33. For a full account of Fr. Joseph Vaz's proceedings in Kanara one may read: Sebastião Rego, *Vida do Venerável Padre José Vaz*, 3rd ed., pp. 31-53; S. G. Perera, *Life of the Venerable Fr. Joseph Vaz*, pp. 19-35; S. Silva, *History of the Christianity in Canara*, I, pp. 64-72.
34. S. Silva, *op. cit.*, I, pp. 68-9.
35. S. do Rego, *op. cit.*, p. 33. Also S. Silva, *op. cit.*, I, p. 71 and Euchides Rogaciano Dias, *Rèsumo da vida do Venerável Padre José Vaz*, pp. 11-12.
36. Sebastião Rego, *op. cit.*, pp. 51-2, footnote 10. This letter is dated September 14, 1681 and is addressed to the Chapter of Goa. For its English translation see S. G. Perera, *op. cit.*, pp. 28-30. Also S. Silva, *op. cit.*, pp. 65-6.
37. S. G. Perera *op. cit.*, pp. 44-5; S. Silva *op. cit.*, pp. 68, 71-2.
38. Francisco de Sousa, *op. cit.*, pt. II, con. I, div. I, p. 30.
39. *CEO,* II, pp. 239-42.
40. *Supra*, p. 251.
41. *Supra*, p. 245.
42. *Supra*, p. 235.
43. *Supra*, pp. 245-6.
44. *Supra*, p. 255.
45. *LRI*, no. 14, fls. 6-9, Viceroy's instructions to the factor of Mangalore, 31.1.1747.
46. *Supra,* pp. 241, 251.
47. *LCC*, II, fl. 59.
48. Appendix, XV.
49. Conde de Linhares, *Diário de*, tomo II, pp. 148, 201.

11

THE PORTUGUESE TRADE AND COMMERCE IN KANARA

The primary object for which the Portuguese came to India was trade. To be sure, their commercial activities in Kanara throughout the period of our study form an interesting chapter. Pepper and rice are the two important articles of trade which attracted them to the region.

The first century of the Portuguese history after the discovery of the searoute to India was marked by their monopoly of spice trade between the East and the West. It is needless to say that Kanara too was subjected to this monopoly. They attempted to secure all the exportable pepper from this region. Thus, in 1502 the Bhatkal chief was compelled to agree not to trade in pepper, except with the Portuguese, lest his ships be burnt.[1] In the treaty of November 2, 1540, between them and the chief of Gersoppa, we find a clause that no pepper should be exported by the latter.[2] It implied that this article should be sold only to the Portuguese and not to the Arabs. From another document of 1574,[3] we learn that the queen of Gersoppa was obliged to sell the Portuguese 500 *khandis* of pepper at 25 gold *pagodas* a *khandi*. However, there was hostility between the two parties in 1570s and therefore she did not fulfil her obligation.

In the 17th and 18th centuries, the situation was different. By then the Portuguese had lost their trade monopoly in the East to the Dutch and the English, and had become weak politically and militarily. They were, therefore, unable to impose their monopolistic conditions on the Nayakas of Ikkeri, who were now masters of Kanara. On the other hand, the latter wanted to impose a condition that the Portuguese should compulsorily purchase from them every year a definite quantity of pepper at a fixed price. The Portuguese did their best to free themselves from this condition. By the treaty of 1631 with Virappa Nayaka they endeavoured to keep the pepper market open and free. They, no doubt, desired to have substantial quantity of pepper from Kanara, but they wanted no obligation either on their part to purchase or on the part of Virappa to sell, compulsorily.[4] However, Virappa was a usurper and Virabhadra, who got rid of him, was not prepared to accept this term. By the treaty of 1633, which he concluded with the Portuguese, the latter were obliged to purchase 350 *khandis* of pepper from him every year at the rate of 22 *pagodas* a *khandi*.[5] Subsequently, as we have seen, Virabhadra demanded more than the agreed price and disputes arose. During the reign of Shivappa (1645-60) the reluctance or inability of the Portuguese to purchase substantial quantities of pepper from him became one of the primary causes of the war which led to the loss of their fortresses in Kanara. In the treaties of 1671, 1678 and 1714, however, there was no clause for compulsory purchase or sale of the commodity between them and the Nayakas of Ikkeri.

The Portuguese depended heavily upon the rice supplies from Kanara. They secured much of the commodity by way of tributes exacted from local chiefs. They bought the rest. In 1502 they imposed on Bhatkal an annual rice tribute of 1,500 bags,[6] which was increased to 2,000 bags in 1509.[7] In 1540, Gersoppa agreed to pay them an annual tribute of 2,000 bags of rice. In addition, the chief of Gersoppa consented to sell 8,000 bags or more at a rate which was being paid formerly,[8] implying thereby that the Portuguese used to purchase rice from Gersoppa at an agreed price prior to 1540. In 1548 Bhatkal revived the annual tribute of 2,000 bags of rice,[9] which seems to have been stopped for some years. By 1554 the chiefs of Honavar and Basrur bound themselves to pay annual rice tributes of 2,000 and 500 bags, respectively.[10] This practice of securing rice by means of treaties was continued in the 17th and the 18th centuries. By the treaty of 1631 they obtained an annual tribute of 500 bags from Virappa Nayaka; by that of 1678,

1,500 bags from Chennammaji; and by that of 1714, 1,900 bags from Basavappa Nạyaka. Not that they always got the tributes. Whenever there was hostility between them and Ikkeri rulers or when the latter were strong enough to refuse, no such tribute was given. Thus, in the treaty of 1633 there was no provision for a tribute. So also, they did not receive any rice tribute during the reign of Shivappa Nayaka.

Ample references can be found in Portuguese chronicles and documents to the Portuguese purchases of rice supplies from Kanara. Francisco de Almeida and Afonso de Albuquerque secured rice from Honavar through Timmayya, who gained much profit, for he could secure foodgrains from Kanara almost for nothing as they were available there in abundance.[11] A large ship was loaded at Bhatkal with rice and other articles in 1516.[12] In 1525 Simão de Menezes was sent to Basrur and Bhatkal for provisions and he actually secured rice.[13] The treaty of 1540 with Gersoppa shows that the Portuguese purchased every year a considerable quantity of rice, probably about 8,000 bags, from that region.[14] In the chapters concerning the Portuguese relations with the Nayakas of Ikkeri, many references have been made to the importance that the former attached to the rice supplies from Kanara.

Other articles of trade which the Portuguese secured from the region were sugar, iron, ginger, choir, saltpetre, wood and timber. In 1498 Vasco da Gama had taken the sample of cinnamon from Anjediv,[15] but it is not known if this article was purchased by the Portuguese from Kanara in due course. In 1508 Timmayya offered to sell to the Portuguese cloves, camphor and black-wood.[16]

In exchange for the articles of trade which they purchased in Kanara the Portuguese sold there several articles which they brought with them from Portugal and other countries. Horses, copper, quicksilver, vermilion, coral, lead and salt were the important articles they sold in Kanara. It was calculated that the copper, quicksilver, vermilion and coral, which the fleet of João da Nova had in 1501, were worth 15,000 *pardaus* at the rates prevailing in Bhatkal. The Portuguese considered the rates very high and, therefore, sold much of these articles there and then whereby they gained considerable profit.[17] A reference is found to the Portuguese slave trade in

Bhatkal in 1540's. The orphans, who fell into their hands, were sold into slavery to the Muslim merchants at Bhatkal for a price of four *pardaus*.[18]

The price of the various articles exchanged between the Portuguese and the Kanarese is scarcely indicated in Portuguese sources as far as the 16th century is concerned. Nevertheless, Duarte Barbosa mentions that a bag of sugar cost only three and one thirds rupees in Bhatkal. From the financial statement of 1574[19] we learn that the queen of Honavar (Gersoppa) had agreed to sell pepper to the Portuguese at the rate of 25 *pagodas* a *khandi*. More information regarding prices can be obtained in respect of the 17th and the 18th centuries. In a royal ordinance dated March 19, 1612, the King of Portugal specified that a price of twenty eight and a half to twenty nine *pagodas* to be paid for a *khandi* of pepper of Kanara, which was considered superior to that of Cannanore.[20] By the treaty of 1633 the Portuguese agreed to purchase annually 350 *khandis* of pepper from Virabhadra Nayaka at the rate of 22 *pagodas* a *khandi*. Earlier, in 1630, they endeavoured to secure pepper from Basrur at the rate of 56 *xerafins* a *khandi*.[21] This is a very low quotation. The Portuguese themselves were not sure of getting it at this price and it is not indicated whether they really secured the commodity so cheap. Soon after the treaty of 1633 Virabhadra demanded 28 *pagodas* for a *khandi*. This was the price which Shivappa Nayaka also insisted upon subsequently and which the Portuguese were reluctant to pay. The Portuguese were prepared to pay a price of 12 to 14 *pagodas* a *korji* of rice in the beginning of the 18th century.[22]

The price of the different articles, of course, did not remain steady. Many a time it was rigged up owing to war condition or competition. The Portuguese raised the price of their articles if they found the local merchants quoting a high price for theirs. This was a common practice, for the English also did so. In 1637 the latter offered to purchase pepper from Virabhadra Nayaka at the rate of 30 *pagodas* a *khandi* in exchange for lead at the rate of twenty two and a half *pagodas* a *khandi*. The Portuguese pointed out that the English sold the same lead to them at the rate of 20 *patacas* or about 12 *pagodas* a *khandi*, and that they also were willing to pay Virabhadra 30 *pagodas* a *khandi* of pepper, instead of the contracted 22 *pagodas*, if he was prepared to purchase lead from them at the rate quoted by the English.[23] In 1677 the Kanarese quoted 14 *pagodas* a *korji* of rice; but the Portuguese complained that the Arabs got the same rice from Kanara for 8 *pagodas* or even less.[24] In the time of war, the Portuguese found it difficult to procure any supplies from Kanara and even if anything was secured it was at an exorbitant rate. We have seen how the Nayakas of Ikkeri blocked the supply of provisions to the Portuguese whenever there was hostility between the two parties.[25] In 1619 the Portuguese had to pay more than double the normal price for anything they purchased in Mangalore, because of their hostility with Venkatappa Nayaka and the resultant scarcity condition created by the Nayaka.

The Portuguese used local weights and measures in their commercial dealings with the Kanarese. In 1501 they sold copper, quicksilver, vermilion and coral at Bhatkal by the local bar, meaning *bhara* or burden, which was then equivalent to three and a half quintals (205.632 kgs.).[26] However, there were different bars in Bhatkal for different commodities in 1554. Thus, to weigh copper iron, cinnamon and choir the bar of 212.058 kgs. was used. The bar for sugar weighed 192.780 kgs. Legume and coral were weighed by a bar of 11.016 kgs only. Sometimes sugar was weighed in bags also, each bag being 77.112 kgs.[27] The bars differed from place to place too. For instance, the bar of Honavar, which was equivalent to 201.960 kgs. differed from the various bars of Bhatkal.[28] In 1574, a *khandi* of pepper in Honavar weighed 220.320 kgs.[29] In the 17th and 18th centuries the Kanarese pepper seems to have been purchased by the Portuguese in terms of this *khandi* of 220.320 kgs. In the treaty of 1671 there was a clause that the Portuguese should use local weights and measures.[30]

The Kanarese *korji*, a measure meant for rice, was used by the Portuguese for dealing in this commodity in Kanara in the 17th and 18th centuries. It seems to have weighed 1,640.52 kgs. as at present.

It is difficult to have a clear picture of statistics regarding the quantity of goods exchanged between the Portuguese and the Kanarese year by year. By 1554 the former obtained 6,500 bags of rice annually from Honavar, Bhatkal, Gersoppa and Basrur. At the same time, 8,600 bags of rice were expected from other parts of Kanara by future treaties or other arrangements.[31] In addition to this they might have secured further rice supplies by means of purchases as the treaty of 1540 with Gersoppa would suggest.[32] When Gangolly was occupied in 1630, they expected to benefit by the 20,000 bags of exportable rice from there.[33] It seems that the annual rice supplies required by the Portuguese in the 18th century were 70,000 bags which they endeavoured to secure from Kanara by means of an agreement with Somashekhara Nayaka of Ikkeri. In return for this, 60,000 bags of salt were to be supplied to the Nayaka.[34]

As we have seen, the Portuguese secured by means of treaties the monopoly of pepper supplies from Gersoppa[35] and Basrur.[36] However, it is not known how much of pepper was secured from Kanara this way. From the financial statement of 1574,[37] we learn that the queen of Honavar was obliged to sell 500 *khandis* but she did not do so in the 1570s owing to hostility between her and the Portuguese. Towards the end of the 16th century, the latter seem to have purchased 3,000 *khandis* of the commodity every year from Kanara as a whole.[38] In the beginning of the 17th century, however, they purchased only 1,000 quintals a year.[39] In 1620s, the Gangolly-Basrur region alone exported annually 1,500 *khandis*.[40] In the middle of the 17th century Shivappa Nayaka insisted that the Portuguese should purchase from him 1,000 *khandis* of pepper in the year of a proposed agreement and 500 *khandis* subsequently every year.

In order to secure the various supplies from Kanara the Portuguese seem to have invested 500,000 *pagodas* every year in the region in the middle of the 17th century[41] and "more than one million in gold, rupees and *patacas*" in the beginning of the 18th century.[42]

On occupying Goa in 1510, Albuquerque found that Muslim and Hindu coins were in circulation there. He, however, issued his own coins equivalent to the local ones. The man who was authorised to mint coins was a Shetty of Bhatkal.[43] The coins of Goa and Kanara were equal in exchange rate. That is why António Nunes, writing in 1554 could indicate that the currency of Bhatkal (or other places of Kanara) was similar to that of Goa.[44] However, in due course some variations cropped up, as the Portuguese varied the value of their coins now and then. Then, in the treaty of 1633, we find a clause wherein 100 *pagodas* of Ikkeri were considered equal to 102 São Tomes which were gold coins of Goa.[45] The exchange rate thus being 1 to 1.02 between the Ikkeri pagoda and the São Tome of Goa. In the 1630s another coin, the *xerafim*, which was current in Goa, was exchanged with the Ikkeri *pagoda* at the rate of 3.5 to 1.[46]

There were roads, some which might have been fit for carts, and medieval means of transport to facilitate trade. There was a road from Bhatkal to Bankapur via Honavar.[47] Goa was linked on with Vijayanagara via Bankapur.[48] Porters, and pack animals like horses, bullocks and asses were the usual means of transport.

Boats and ships were, no doubt, the most important means of transport. The Portuguese sources refer to different types of local vessels. It is very difficult, however, to determine, their size, capacity and mast. The different rates of anchorage levied on different vessels[49] show their greater or smaller capacity and size. Thus, *empaleqa*, *catacoulão* and *calamute* were the smallest of these local vessels; larger than these were *parao*, *manchua* and *sanguicel*; then came pinnace, *cathia* and *gundra*, followed by *taurim*, *paquel* and *zambuco*; there were also big *taurim* and big *paquel* and *nau*, which were the largest of the local ships. These were vessels which were common on the coast of Kanara and Malabar in the 16th century. *Pataxo*, *periche* and *palla* were added in the following centuries. The Portuguese had their galleys, galleons and galliots in the 16th and 17th centuries, and these were reinforced by frigates in the 17th and 18th centuries. They used the word *nau* to indicate these ships.[50] *Navios* stood for vessels in general. It is difficult to say what the freight charges were for carrying goods from one place to another by these vessels.

A few words may now be said regarding the Portuguese control over Kanarese trade and the organisation and the nature of their commercial dealings in the region. They declared themselves lords of the sea and as such they imposed conditions on the local chiefs with regard to the latter's coastal and overseas trade. As early as 1502, da Gama, after burning the port of Bhatkal, told its chief that the King of Portugal was the "lord of the sea and of the whole world, as also of all this coast; by reason of which all the rivers and ports, which had navigation, ought to obey him, and pay tributes to his men who moved about in his fleets." He also declared that the ships of Bhatkal would be burnt if the chief traded in pepper or dealt with the Arabs or sent his ships to Calicut.[51] The chief agreed to pay an annual tribute of 1,000 bags of fine rice, and 500 bags of coarse rice, and to refrain from doing the forbidden.[52] Albuquerque attempted to secure Krishna Deva Raya's permission to erect a fortress, or at least a factory, at Bhatkal in order to control its trade. He did not succeed in obtaining the permission but after occupying Goa in 1510 he employed some captains to compel merchant ships to sail into the port of Goa, thus damaging the sea trade of Bhatkal.[53]

The Portuguese always endeavoured, either by force or by agreements with local chiefs, to exclude from Kanarese trade their enemies and rivals, particularly the merchants of Calicut, the Arabs, the Dutch and the English. Many a time the local chiefs themselves were punished for allowing the rivals to trade with the Kanarese ports. In 1513 Albuquerque sent some of his captains to Bhatkal and Mangalore to take possession of some of the Calicut ships which were on their way to the Red Sea Strait. If the local chiefs were not to cooperate with the captains by allowing them to take the ships, the trade of the ports was to be hindered until the ships were secured. The chiefs, however, did not resist and the captains took the ships with goods.[54] In 1525 the Portuguese destroyed a few of the Calicut ships which were trading at Mangalore.[55] We have seen how a Hindu merchant of Mangalore, the Shetty of Mangalore, was punished and the city was burnt in 1530, because he had commercial dealings with the merchants of Calicut.[56] So also, in 1558 Mangalore experienced the Portuguese brutality for the dealing with their enemy ships from Malabar.[57] In the 17th century the Portuguese could not exclude the Dutch and the English from Kanara by force. However, they did their best to prevent these rivals from gaining a foothold in Kanara by urging the Nayakas of Ikkeri not to admit the rivals. Sometimes their efforts were crowned with success. Thus, we find the English factory of Bhatkal being destroyed in 1639 at their insistence; but in 1642 the former was reinstated there.[58] In their treaties with the Nayakas of Ikkeri in 1678 and 1714, the Arabs were excluded from Kanara. However, many times these provisions were not observed and the Arabs were allowed to trade at the Kanarese ports by the Nayakas. On such occasions the Portuguese attempted to expel the Arabs by force and punish the Nayakas simultaneously.[59]

Occasionally the Portuguese attempted to encourage the Kanarese to trade with them, while endeavouring to exclude other traders from elsewhere. Thus, by a Charter of October 21, 1522, the King of Portugal freed the merchants of Bhatkal, Honavar, Mangalore, Mirjan, and Basrur from the entrance duty of four and a half percent, which was continued to be collected in respect of the articles coming into Goa from other than Kanarese territories.[60] This was an encouragement to the Kanarese merchants to trade with Goa.

The Portuguese organised their commercial affairs with the East through what may be termed as the 'fortress-factory' system.[61] In Kanara they had fortresses between 1568 and 1654, and more often than not, the captain of a fortress was also its factor. Before the establishment of these fortresses and after their loss, trade dealings were organised through a factory. However, it does not mean that the Portuguese always had a factory in Kanara. Their first factory in the region seems to have been established at Bhatkal in 1540 or thereabouts though they had commercial contacts with Kanara right from 1498. Castanheda tells us that the Governor sent in 1517 João Gonçalves de Castelo Branco to take possession of Bhatkal and leave a man with a factor to purchase all the available saltpetre there.[62] However, he does not indicate whether the place was actually taken and whether the factor was successful in securing the article mentioned. He does not clarify also whether the Governor intended to have a factor at Bhatkal on a permanent basis, if the place was to be taken. Gaspar Correa, referring to the incident of 1542, already described,[63] definitely mentions an established Portuguese factory at Bhatkal.[64] However, this factory seems to have been discontinued after the establishment of the fortresses in

1568-69, for no reference thereafter is found to any factory at Bhatkal. In 1660s it appeared that the Portuguese would get back their lost fortresses of Kanara; but the Dutch came in their way. By virtue of the treaty of 1671, however, they established a factory at Mangalore, which was perpetuated by the subsequent treaties of 1678 and 1714.

The 'fortress-factory' system was headed by a captain-cum-factor, though for some years in the beginning (1568-70) these offices were entrusted to the care of two different persons. A reference had already been made to the administrative and financial arrangements of the system.[65] It may only be mentioned here that the system was not only the centre of the Portuguese commercial activities but also of their political and religious affairs in Kanara.

The Portuguese could control the commerce of Kanara more or less effectively to their own advantage through the system as long as they were unchallenged either by local chiefs or by European rivals. However, in the 17th century, the Nayakas of Ikkeri, the Dutch and the English became a formidable challenge to their monopoly and they had to give in. While losing, however, they endeavoured to retain whatever commercial advantages were possible by means of treaties with the Nayakas of Ikkeri. Thus, under the treaty of 1633 Virabhadra was to allow supplies of rice and other foodgrains to the Portuguese; to permit them to take necessary wood from his territories for their shipyard; not to impose upon them more taxes than was customary; to provide them with 24 masts for their vessels; and to allow them to purchase pepper freely, other than the quantity of 350 *khandis* which they had to purchase from him compulsorily every year.[66] It is not necessary to repeat here what commercial advantages they secured under the treaties of 1671, 1678 and 1714, as they have been indicated earlier.

Even as they were weak and impotent in the 17th and the 18th centuries, the Portuguese continued their attempt to control the overseas and coastal trade of Kanara in keeping with their notion that they were the lords of sea and therefore one could carry on sea trade only with their permission. To be sure, they did not bother their European rivals with their notion; but they did try to impose it particularly upon the Arabs and other non-European traders. The means by which they attempted to lord over the sea trade was the system of *cartazes*, meaning permits or passports.

The system seems to have been introduced in the first half of the 16th century itself. The first reference to it with regard to Kanara is in 1548. Simão Botelho, speaking of the treaty of that year between the Portuguese and the Bhatkal chief, says that the latter had agreed to the condition that the former could have a factor at Bhatkal "in order to issue passports to the ships which sailed out from the said port", and to carry on Portuguese commerce there.[67] In the treaties of 1633, 1671, 1678 and 1714 between the Portuguese and the Nayakas of Ikkeri there were provisions imposing upon the latter the obligations to secure *cartazes* for their merchant ships. Even the royal ships were subject to this obligation.[68] Ships, sailing without *cartazes* were subject to confiscation by the Portuguese. We had occasion to refer to such incidents of confiscation during the course of our discussion concerning Portuguese-Ikkeri relations.

A fee was generally charged while issuing *cartazes*, though some specified number of royal ships of Ikkeri were given *cartazes* free of any charge.[69] For instance, under the treaty of 1678 two free *cartazes* were to be issued to Basavappa Nayaka. A *cartaz* generally specified the ports to which the ship was prohibited to go for trade and also the articles of trade which could not be carried on board. Arab ports were forbidden and ships sailing into them, or violating other conditions, were subject to confiscation.[70] So also, horses were a Portuguese controlled article of trade. No Kanarese ship was allowed to carry or deal in horses without specific *cartaz*. In 1728 the Portuguese told Somashekhara Nayaka that they would issue *cartazes* free of any charge to all Kanarese ships, royal and others, and allow them to deal in horses, provided that he agreed to pay an annual rice tribute of more than 5,000 bags and two horses for each ship which brought the animals.[71] Nothing came of this proposal.

The Portuguese entered into commercial dealings with the Kanarese merchants in different ways. The 'factory' or 'fortress-factory' system was the centre of trade transactions. However, before its establishment the Portuguese sailed into the Kanarese ports from time to time, sold their goods there or purchased whatever they needed. Normally, an interpreter assisted them in communicating with the local merchants. In course of time they found it inconvenient to go themselves to the interior and negotiate business transactions with local dealers. They therefore evolved the practice of appointing Goan or Kanarese merchants as their procurators in Kanara. Thus, by a vice-regal order of November 15, 1595 Santopá and Mango Sinai, two merchants of Goa, were appointed to procure and supply 3,000 *khandis* of pepper from Kanara. The commodity was to be delivered to the Portuguese at their Kanarese fortresses.[72] Sundardas Vishnudas, resident of Mangalore and owner of four ships, was the Portuguese procurator in Kanara in 1720's and 1730's.[73]

The Portuguese were notorious for their malpractices and ill-treatments of the Kanarese merchants and ships. As Gaspar Correa remarks, it was common for them to indulge in malpractices such as forcibly taking articles of trade from local merchants, as they did at Bhatkal in 1542.[74] Francisco de Mello e Sampaio, who became captain of Basrur in 1583, damaged the trade of that port so much by forcibly taking goods at a low price that the local merchants attempted to drive the Portuguese away from there, though unsuccessfully.[75] There were also instances of captains who levied and collected illegal imposts from merchants at Basrur, contrary to vice-regal orders, as a document dated October 13, 1591 informs us that five *larins* were collected illegally from Muslim merchants for every *korji* of rice purchased by them at Basrur.[76] Sometimes the Portuguese confiscated Kanarese ships and sold their goods for sheer profit. They gave as low a compensation as possible if the Nayakas of Ikkeri threatened and demanded satisfaction.[77]

REFERENCES

1. *Lendas*, tomo I, pt. I, p. 291.
2. Simão Botelho, "O Tombo de Estado da India", *Subsidios*, pp. 257-8.
3. *Orçamento*, p. 95.
4. *Supra*, pp. 175-6.

5. *Supra*, p. 183.
6. *Lendas*, tomo I, pt. I, p. 291.
7. *História*, II p. 441.
8. Botelho, *op. cit.*, pp. 257-8. *The Gazetteer of the Bombay Presidency* (vol. XV, pt. II, *Kanara*, p. 114) wrongly says that 8,000 bags of rice were the past tributes.
9. Botelho, *op. cit.*, p. 243.
10. *Ibid.*, pp. 246-8. *The Gazetteer of the Bombay Presidency* (*op. cit.*), p. 114 proceeds to say that Agrakona, Ankola, Kumta and Mirjan also paid certain rice tributes to the Portuguese by 1554. This, however is not true. Simão Botelho, whom the *Gazetteer* also quotes, mentions these places under the title: "The rivers which can pay tributes" *(Os rios que podem paguar pareas)*, implying clearly that they were not paying the tribute already. The author estimated the figures of possible tributes that could be collected in the future from these places. This is all the more clear from the main heading of the whole list: "These are the tributes of rice which the king, our lord, has in this coast of Goa as far as Cannanore, *and also some rivers which can pay, if they are bound for this purpose*" (emphasis mine). Honavar, Bhatkal, Basrur are included in the first category of places which were actually paying the tribute by 1554. Agrakona, etc. are included in the second category of places from where certain tributes were expected in the future, if the Portuguese were to bind these places to pay by entering into treaties with them.
11. *Lendas*, tomo I, pt. I, p. 579.
12. *Ibid.*, p. 469.
13. *História*, VI, pp. 291-92.
14. Botelho, *op. cit.*, p. 257.
15. A. Velho, *Roteiro da primeira viagem de Vasco da Gama*, p. 71.
16. *Cartas*, III, p. 303.
17. *Lendas*, tomo I, pt. I, pp. 239-40.
18. *Documentação*, III, p. 211.
19. *Orçamento*, p. 95.
20. *DRI*, II, p. 228.
21. *Assentos*, I, p. 257.
22. *Supra*, p. 259.
23. *Assentos*, II, p. 168.
24. *Ibid.*, IV, p. 279.
25. *Supra*, pp. 171, 184-85, 249.
26. *Lendas*, tomo I, pt. I, p. 239.
27. António Nunes, "Livro dos pesos, medidas e moedas", *Subsidios*, pp. 32, 45.
28. *Ibid.*, pp. 33, 50.
29. *Orçamento*, p. 95.
30. *Supra*, p. 236.
31. Botelho, *op. cit.*, pp. 246-8, 257-8.
32. *Ibid*, p. 257.

33. *Assentos*, I, p. 555.
34. *APO-BP*, tomo I, vol. III, pt. IV, p. 94.
35. Botelho, *op. cit.*, p. 258.
36. *LCF*, fl. 42.
37. *Orçamento*, p. 95.
38. *APO-CR*, III, p. 567.
39. *Assentos*, I, p. 115.
40. Henry Heras, "Expansion Wars of Venkatappa Nayaka", p. 7.
41. *Assentos*, II, p. 13.
42. *Assentos*, V, p. 163.
43. J. Gerson da Cunha, *Contribuções para a estudo da numismática Indo-Portuguesa* p. 21.
44. António Nunes, *op. cit.*, pp. 61-2.
45. *Assentos*, I, p. 570.
46. *Ibid.*, p. 539.
47. Robert Sewell, *A Forgotten Empire*, p. 119.
48. *Ibid.*
49. *APO-CR*, V, pt. III, p. 1518.
50. Charles R. Boxer, *The Carreira da India*, p. 2.
51. *Lendas*, tomo I, pt. I, p. 290.
52. *Ibid.*, p. 291.
53. *Commentários*, III, pp. 50-1.
54. *Commentários*, IV, p. 79.
55. *História*, VI, p. 291.
56. *Supra*, pp. 88-91.
57. *Supra*, pp. 91-2.
58. *Assentos*, III, p. 654; *EF*, 1642-1645, p. 109.
59. *supra*, pp. 238-9, 244, 246-8.
60. *APO-CR*, V, pt. III, pp. 1553-4.
61. *Orçamento*, p. 443.
62. *História*, IV, p. 433.
63. *Supra*, pp. 78-81.
64. Botelho, *op. cit.*, p. 243.
65. *Supra*, pp. 110-19.
66. *Assentos*, I, pp. 569-70.
67. Botelho, *op. cit.*, p. 243.
68. For details see the relevant provisions of the said treaties in chs. 7 and 9.
69. A fee of Rs. 10 for every 100 *khandis* was charged at Mangalore in the 18th century. In addition, the charges of writers and other officials were also collected along with the fee (*LRI*, XVI, fls. 65-6, 174-5). A fee of Rs. 10 only was charged in Goa (*Livro das cartazes*, no. I, 1704-1766, fls. 54-56, etc.).
70. Appendix XVI.
71. *APO-BP*, tomo I, vol. III, pt. IV, p. 94.
72. *APO-CR*, III, pp. 567-8.

73. *Assentos*, V, p. 378.
74. *Lendas*, tomo IV, pt. I, pp. 257-8.
75. *D-DC*, X, pt. I, pp. 381-2.
76. *APO-CR*, III, pp. 335-6.
77. *Assentos*, II, pp. 543-5; IV, pp. 239-40.

CONCLUSION

We have completed our narrative of the political, religious and commercial activities of the Portuguese in Kanara up to a definite stage of the history of the region, namely, the downfall of the Keladi dynasty and the establishment of Hyder Ali's rule in 1763. It is rather regrettable that extant Kannada sources throw very little light on the Portuguese-Kanarese relations. Even the *Keladinripa Vijaya* of Linganna Kavi says precious little on this subject. Most of the information we have is to be found only in Portuguese sources or other records of the Western powers who came to India. The lack of contemporary Kannada chronicles and records on the Portuguese-Kanarese relations may be attributed to the general lack of a sense of history among our countrymen, not only in the past but even today to a great extent.

The Portuguese relations with Kanara were marked by a belligerent attitude. They shaped their policy generally from a position of strength whenever it was possible. This was particularly true of the 16th century when no Indian ruler possessed a navy strong enough to curb their belligerence and when their power in the East was unchallenged by any other European country. They extracted tributes from the Kanarese chiefs and imposed trade conditions upon them. If any chief failed to abide by these arrangements, his ports and boats were attacked and damaged. Even on the loss of their fortresses of Kanara in the middle of the 17th century and thereafter when their power was not worth the name, they followed a policy based upon force. They would only wait until the annual fleet arrived from Portugal and, on its arrival, use it to hinder the trade and commerce of Kanara, or to damage the latter's ports and vessels. This was the method by which they endeavoured to get what they wanted from the Nayakas of Ikkeri.

We find frequent references to such incidents in Portuguese sources, as we have seen. The Nayakas, after Shivappa, were not strong enough to punish the Portuguese for these acts of violence.

Of course, there were exceptions to this general policy of force. For instance, Albuquerque, the greatest of the Portuguese conquerors and statesmen, was careful not to indulge in belligerence in Kanara. He tried to get concessions by negotiations and did not use force when negotiations failed. He was, no doubt, influenced by the aid given to him by the king of Gersoppa and the latter's officials in occupying Goa; and also by a desire to be on friendly terms with Vijayanagara in which empire Kanara was included. However, he endeavoured to damage Kanarese commerce by compelling the ships from Arabia and Persia to sail to Goa and by excluding the ships of Calicut from the Kanarese ports.

The political, commercial and religious activities of the Portuguese in Kanara were intermingled. However, commerce may be considered as the most decisive factor which influenced their policy towards the region. If they wished to possess fortresses in Kanara, it was mainly in order to control the commerce of the region. Not that they never had the ambition of establishing a territorial empire in India; but they did not succeed in doing so. No empire worth the name was ever established by them, though Albuquerque and some others did their best towards the fulfillment of the ambition. The declared purpose of the Portuguese in establishing fortresses in Kanara was generally commercial. Albuquerque desired a fortress in Bhatkal for that purpose. Luis de Ataide established fortresses in Honavar and Basrur in order to exclude the Malabaris from the trade and commerce of the Kanarese ports. The fortresses of Mangalore and Gangolly also served the same end. If the Portuguese participated actively in the local political struggles, aiding one chief against another, the main purpose was to safeguard their own commercial interests in the region. Their endeavour was to see that no single chief became strong enough to deprive them of their privileged position there. To aid one local chief against another was a common practice of the European powers in the process of colonization and empire building. The

Portuguese did not acquire an empire worth the name; but they did safeguard their commercial interests in Kanara, as long as they could, by this usual means.

Some of the Nayakas of Ikkeri like Venkatappa I and Virabhadra were too strong and powerful for the Portuguese to cope with. Therefore, the latter generally felt happy whenever the former were in trouble, either because the Nayakas were attacked by their neighbourhood, that is, by their neighbouring potentates or because their own feudatories were in revolt. The reason was that the Portuguese found their own strength in the weakness of the Nayakas. The Adil Shahi rulers of Bijapur proved to be stronger than the Nayakas. The Portuguese, therefore, rarely helped Bijapur against the latter; but sometimes they aided the Nayakas whom they did not want to see thoroughly beaten by the Adil Shahis, for the latter were considered more dangerous as neighbours. The Portuguese became uneasy if the Nayakas settled their differences with Bijapur and began to gain greater strength in other quarters. They also did not hesitate to aid the revolting feudatories of the Nayakas with a view to keep the latter engaged and weak. Under the rule of a strong Nayaka the Portuguese had no opportunity to carry on as they pleased in Kanara, particularly in commercial matters. Such a strong Nayaka certainly desired to share commercial benefits with the Portuguese by raising the price of articles of trade of Kanara or by levying additional imposts on sales and purchases and on imports and exports.

The Portuguese built their fortresses in Kanara in 1568-69. The time chosen for the purpose is noteworthy. It was about 3 years after the battle of Talikote where the glory and the might of the Vijayanagara Empire had departed. The successors of Rama Raja who was defeated and killed in the battle field, became fugitives and many of their vassals declared themselves independent. It was a period of confusion within the Empire and the Portuguese successfully fished in the troubled waters. To be sure, they desired to have at least one fortress in Kanara right from 1505. One was actually built in Anjediv that year; but Anjediv was virtually nobody's land then and, besides, in the following year the fortress was destroyed. The Portuguese then tried to get a site in Bhatkal by negotiations; but failed. Probably they did not dare to capture or establish by force any fortress in Kanara as long as the Vijayanagara Empire was united and powerful.

In fact the Portuguese followed an opportunistic policy in Kanara. They were always ready to exploit the weakness of the Kanarese chiefs and to benefit from the internal revolts and confusions. If the people of Basrur needed their aid, they would endeavour to get pepper from the former at nearly half the market rate and to ensure many other privileges. If there were revolts within the kingdom of Ikkeri or if the latter were attacked from outside, the Portuguese would encourage the rebels and try at the same time to acquire additional lands or fortresses or privileges for themselves.

One of the redeeming features of the Portuguese policy in Kanara was their staunch loyalty to one of their allies, namely the Bangar chief. No doubt, they were motivated by their own interests; nevertheless, many a time they aided him with great risk to themselves. The chief had given them on his own accord a site in Mangalore to build their fortress in 1568, besides, giving them many other concessions. Ever since then he was considered a friend and brother-in-arms to the King of Portugal. In due course he was aided against the chiefs of Ullala, and the Nayakas of Ikkeri. In their battle with Venkatappa, waged on behalf of the Bangar chief, they suffered a good deal of loss in men and materials. Later on, when the chief lost everything in spite of their help they did their best for him to secure the most favourable terms possible by means of a treaty with the Nayaka. The King of Portugal did not fail to instruct his viceroys and governors to restore the kingdom of Bangher to its chief, whenever an opportunity arose, by waging a war against the Nayakas.

Another feature of the Portuguese policy in Kanara was their application of whatever political hold they had in Kanara to the service of Christianity by protecting Christians and missionaries in the region. This was particularly true of the 17th and 18th centuries when there was a considerable number of Christians and churches in Kanara. The treaties between the Portuguese and the Nayakas of Ikkeri included provisions, as we have seen, to secure the freedom of movement for missionaries, the right to build churches at different places, the privilege for Christians not to be under the legal system of the Nayakas but of the Portuguese and so on. If the Nayakas imprisoned priests or imposed restrictions on the Christians, the Portuguese did not hesitate to threaten hostilities against the Nayakas. Whenever any Kanarese was converted to Christianity full Portuguese support was given to the convert to secure for him his property which, sometimes, the relatives of the convert endeavoured to deprive him of.

Kanara became a granary for the Portuguese. Most of the rice required for them for sustaining Goa and other possessions like Hormuz, came from the lands of Kanara. Sometimes they secured it from the North, that is, from the Konkan and Gujarat; but it was difficult to do so particularly in the 17th and 18th centuries on account of one or another hostile power there like the Dutch or the Adil Shahis of Bijapur or the Marathas. Their dependence on the Kanarese rice shaped their relations with the rulers of the region. Many a time they had an ardent desire to commence hostilities against the Nayakas of Ikkeri or to give open assistance against the latter; but the fear that the rice supplies would be stopped from the lands of Kanara restrained them. Sometimes they opened hostilities and made brave efforts to secure rice from the north; but generally it ended in scarcity in Goa and other places under their control.

Appendices

Appendix I

To the king of Kanara

I have written to Your Highness that by September I would send the navy against the Marathas who have taken the Island of Honavar, it being impossible (for the navy) to go at the time when Your Highness sought for it, as it was impossible to return on account of the monsoon; and that in the (monsoon) the Marathas would not be able to cause any damage, as the experience showed in the ease with which they left it (the island). The governor of Kanara (Mangalore) maltreated my good will so much that he says that the churches of the Christians should be destroyed; and (regarding) the payment of the tributes which you entrusted for this State, (he says) that the due, being so small, comes to nothing; so also he commanded the revenue-farmer that he should not collect the import and export duties which belonged to the factory of (His) Majesty (King of Portugal); and (he says) that this State is so powerful and the tribute and the import and export duties are such a small thing that it serves (the State) little. And Your Highness has much profit from the gold which goes from her for the purchase of rice, as the experience demonstrates; and thus it is more advantageous (for you) to have friendship (with) the State than for it with Kanara (you); and if Your Highness does not desist from the maltreatment which you have meted out to the Portuguese, the vassals of the king, my lord, and (from the maltreatment regarding) the import and export duties and the tributes, this State would know what it should do; and at the same time, Your Highness send an envoy to the Maratha king, enemy of the State, without informing me; the envoy came to my presence and I did not arrest (him) owing to my greatness. I expect a reply to this letter with all brevity to enable me to decide what would suit more to the service of the King, my lord. Your Highness may consider this point and afterwards your vassals may not complain of the loss that may ensue. Your Highness may do me the service of handing over one Vicente Rodrigues, who was the interpreter of the factory of Mangalore, who it is who goes on communicating those frauds and correspondence which Your Highness has with the Arabs, enemies of this State, dealing with them secretly. These and other things serve to demonstrate the little friendship and fidelity which you have towards this State; especially (the little friendship and fidelity of) the minister who commands. I hope that Your Highness will give me all satisfaction and also (satisfaction) of the delay which the navy experienced at the port without being loaded in time which was the cause of all this damage.

May God enlighten Your Highness with his divine grace.

Goa, May 18, 1699.

António Luis Gonçalves de Camara Coutinho.

Appendix II

To the king of Kanara

I received the letter which Your Highness sent to me in reply to that which I wrote to you when I sent the navy of this State to those ports of Kanara. In which (your letter) I see Your Highness to have satisfied the instances of my cause by commanding to raise the tolls and the tributes of foodgrains and salt, and simultaneously to have satisfied the rice (tribute) which was due and (to have rendered) the port of Honavar unimpeded to bring from there the masts which, by the order of the royal treasury, had been purchased for the shipyard of this city (of Goa). I never doubted that Your Highness would thus implement your term(s) and resolution, because the affection of our friendship and the provisions of the peace (treaty) concluded between Your Highness and this State do not permit the want of observation of this accord. However, side by side I find many causes of the scandal of unfulfilling ... some conditions of the said treaty of peace, the most essential being Your Highness admitting in your ports the greatest enemies of this State, as the Arabs are, giving them open commerce and simultaneously (giving them) consent to commit a crime so scandalous as it was to rob and damage a church. And in view of an excess so stupendous as this I am obliged to tell Your Highness that you are responsible to give me satisfaction for it by commanding to hand over the said Arabs and not to admit any one any more into those ports because if I find the savage(s), Your Highness may receive great damage with the cause it may give me to alter the provision of the peace (treaty) in view of the correlation and communication which you have with the enemies of this State without warning, whereas you ought to treat the friends (of the State) as friends and (its) enemies (as) enemies; and if Your Highness carries on in this way (as per the treaty), as I hope that you will do, it is certain that you would find my enthusiasm very prompt to succour and defend from all the enemies who might intend to cause you in those ports the slightest damage, because at all times I would ensure the suppression (of enemies) with the fleets of this State just as I did this year, and with still more advantage (when you would be) requesting it on the necessity of the occasion. The complaint which Your Highness makes to me of the captain-major of the navy is very strange to all reason, because in the hands of Your Highness lies the remedy (of the complaint); and it boils down to Your Highness not permitting the Arab vessels to load rice at your ports; nor so little ... those of the vassals of Your Highness in order to take in them the said rice to Muscat ... that Your Highness, with lame excuses favoured more the cause of the Arabs than that of this State and did not keep the royal promise and just correspondence which (you) ought to have with the Majesty, the King, my lord, and consequently with all his vassals; however, I do not give full credit to any of this, because I suppose that all these disorders resulted from the ambition of some ministers of Your Highness. And I expect that Your Highness will give such a just satisfaction to all these particulars that with it improves (all the) more our friendship; to be so alone suits Your Highness.

May God guide and enlighten Your Highness with his divine grace.

Goa, January 29, 1700.

Appendix III

To the regent of the kingdom of Kanara, Nirvanayyanavaru

I am in receipt of the letter of your majesty, esteeming the news of your health.

My intention too is to preserve the friendship of this State with that kingdom, and also not to consent the violation of the peace (treaty) lately concluded, as it is signed by the ambassador (of) the king of Kanara; and the conditions are that the vessels of the said king, which wanted passports in order to fetch horses shall be given only for two at this secretariat, free of fees, and that the others which came with them (vessels) shall be considered captives even though they may bring passports; in contradiction to which terms proceeded the vessel *Ishwari* in the same way as she has done at other times; though it was the same vessel and through which I took the decision of desiring to restitute to Your Majesty without the cargö, I ought not to take (the decision) of handing over what is brought; and this decision is what I informed Your Majesty, which I ought not to change.

The vessel goes along with the navy; and as long as Your Majesty does not take proper decisions, it (the vessel) will serve to accompany (the navy) when the latter has to return (to Goa). You offer me nothing more (than taking proper decisions). Our Lord etc.

Goa, January 31, 1727.

João de Saldanha da Gama.

Appendix IV

To the factor of Mangalore, Mathias Rodrigues Chaves

I am in receipt of your letter with that of the regent of Kanara; and granted that he tells me that he does not want the vessel without the horses and the cargo, I think to send it in this way (without the horses and the cargo); in case he does not accept, you shall let me know with promptitude, so that I can think of the punishment which he deserves; and when he does not consent that rice be taken, (I can think) of a remedy with which I have to make the shortage.

Goa, January 31, 1727.

João de Saldanha da Gama.

Appendix V

To the king (of) Kanara

I received the letter of Your Highness at the time when I have already sent twice one ship with a *palla* to that coast, and now have sent lately another ship and various galliots of war in order to free the commerce and to suppress the ports of Your Highness; but allow me to tell you that the retaliation is not equal to what this State experiences with some of the governors of the ports of Your Highness and it means that I send embarkations to that coast if the governors of the ports of Your Highness give in them entrance to the enemies of this State, as it lately happened in Honavar where two galliots of the Bhonsle gathered in order to perturb the merchants who might come to Goa with their goods, the said governor defending them in such a way that they took masts and artillery. He sent words to Ismail Khan, who went there with five galliots of the State, that those which were found in that port were of Melondin, and not of the Bhonsle, the contrary being the case. So, I expect that Your Highness shall punish the said governor so that the same thing will not occur in case of other governors.

If in the last year the port of Mangalore experienced the invasion of the Angria, it was because I was found occupied in Rery (Raigad). I hope that this year he may not have the same impudence. If our factory were not open, and if the men who defended the port could take position in it, perhaps the Angria would not dare to enter it; but in the state in which it is found, necessarily it has to give in when any enemy comes, by not having (by means) with which to defend.

May God enlighten Your Highness with his divine grace.

Goa, December 26, 1747.
Marquis of Castelo Novo.

Appendix VI

To the factor and governor of Mangalore, José Antunes Branco

I received the letter of the factor and governor of Mangalore, José Antunes Branco, of December 19 and I appreciate much that those people should be satisfied with the delivery of the boat. I am the one who has the occasion to contend with the lord of that coast of Kanara, because the governor of Honavar is giving shelter to the Bhonsle in order to gather in his ports to attack our embarkations, so much so that one Ismail Khan repressing the two galliots that moved about there, the governor wanted to defend them, saying that they were the Malvan, and as he (Ismail Khan) could not prevail upon (the governor) they took from (the port) masts and artillery and the men gathered on the land, who, through the news I have from those who move about and give me information, continue the piracy.

The king of Kanara wrote to me here through a messenger, asking me embarkations against the Angria who, he feared, might make an incursion as in the last year. I responded to him that in no year did our embarkations anticipate so much as in this, because I had already dispatched there a frigate and a *palla* and various *manchuas*. Actually there moves about one frigate. However, there was no stranger a thing than he asking me aid against his enemies (when) he is giving good shelter to mine, who are also his at the same time. I complained bitterly of the governor of Honavar, requesting him that he should punish him.

If the king is there, the factor shall make to him a strong complaint about this and shall tell him that unless everything is set right, I am determined to attack the Bhonsle in whichever port he might be; and if he (the king) is not there, the factor and governor shall write in the same form to the said king.

Also, I availed of the occasion when he lamented the incursion which the Angria effected in the last year into Mangalore, to tell him that the fault was his, because our factory, from where the men could be effective to embarrass the entry of the enemy, was open on his own accord and without defence; and that in respect of this he should consider what suited him.

Also, they inform me from those parts that the Angria is erecting a factory in Ramataly (?). The factor and governor shall immediately investigate this matter with every care and, finding it true, shall complain of this also to the king so that it does not embarrass. You shall inform me promptly so that I may take a decision that I may think of and you shall immediately remit the reply of the letter which Domingos Rodrigues remitted to me. Our Lord etc.

Goa, January 4, 1748.
Marquis of Castelo Novo.

Appendix VII

To the king (of) Kanara

I am in receipt of the letter of Your Highness in which you recommend to me the friendship which this State always preserved with the kings of Kanara from olden days. This observation was not necessary, for I have it much in my memory. I should tell you, however, that the friendship between two friends, in order to be perpetual, should be equally reciprocal on each other's part. Of mine, Your Highness cannot have any cause to complain. Nor does the complaint, which Your Highness make regarding my embarkations not going out sooner (than they did) to your ports about two years ago, have any foundation, for it should be well known to Your Highness that I was found occupied then in chastising the Bhonsle, who was the enemy of Your Highness too, defeating his fleet in Aromdem (?) and taking from him Tiracol and Raigad. The Angria took advantage of the time to invade Mangalore. I ought to tell you that every one is obliged, first of all, to defend one's own house and (then) give time to one's friends whom he can help. Then, by the provisions of the peace (treaty), I am not obliged to have a fleet at the ports of Your Highness throughout the year; I ought to have only at the due moment, when the enemies do not embarrass me on another side. If Your Highness has your ports in such a manner that ten or twelve galliots suffice to damage them, it is not my fault. Your Highness says that the principal cause of the Angria's invasion was not to have had fortification at the Portuguese factory and that this situation facilitated the Angria's incursion into Mangalore. On the part of the State, this very consideration was held for several years and by virtue of it the danger to which the port of Mangalore was exposed was represented; but the court of Bednur never attended to this danger. On the contrary, dissensions followed, as Your Highness might remember, in the days of the factor, António Aique Pedro, when he wished to put the factory with some defence. Last year, when Your Highness visited your sea ports, this very thing was represented to you by the factor, José Antunes Branco, thinking that Your Highness would listen to reason; but you did not take any measures in this respect; not regarding the three other propositions which the very factor made to you: the first, concerning the import and export duties which were due as per the treaty; the second, concerning the erection of churches of our holy religion in conformity with the established provision of the peace (treaty); the third, the timber yards should pay the duties which they always paid; even though Your Highness says, in respect of this (last) provision, that the duties of the said timber yards come virtually to nothing, you should not change the custom for this reason. Seeing that I ask from you nothing more than what has been agreed upon, I do not know to what can be attributed Your Highness sending a command to the governor of Mangalore that he should pay these duties and soon after send him the order not to pay them. Such things are not taken recourse to while desiring to conserve friendship. Thus, I hope that Your Highness will reply to me soon concerning the four points declared above and that you will recall what has been agreed upon them in the provisions of the peace (treaty), which alone is what I intend (to be observed). I shall be sorry to be compelled to send my fleet to that coast in order to employ it to have justice done, without giving reasons that I may have.

May God enlighten Your Highness with his divine grace.

Goa, November 4, 1748
Marquis of Alorna.

Appendix VIII

To the king of Kanara

I felt very sorry at the news which the Factor, José Antunes Branco, sent me that the Angria committed a fresh aggression on Mangalore. I was not astonished at his boldness, because whenever he finds the door open, he has to enter through it, as he is a thief by profession, and this very factory (of the door being open) invites him to return to it many times, with damage to Your Highness as well as to your subjects, and to the merchants who gather at that port. As his intention may be to have a port in the south from where he can commit piracy with more convenience, who knows if he wills to establish himself more firmly in Mangalore one day, which will be of worse consequences.

About two years ago, when the Angria did similar damage to Mangalore, Your Highness wrote to me, complaining that I did not have my fleet to defend that port. And I replied to you that I was engaged in a war opened against the Bhonsle as well as against the very Angria. It was necessary to defend my house first and help the friends afterwards as I could; this was the cause that Your Highness, who had the obligation to defend your own land, abandoned it. I did not have the force to defend it and to wish that upon this State ... its defence, without wishing even a little to aid the very State with the very defence. On the first occasion also, when the Angria attacked Mangalore, I wrote to Your Highness that it did not matter that the factory had artillery, if it was open on all sides, and it could not be defended. Now, on this second occasion, he came obviously because the artillery which fired towards the sea embarrassed for a while (only) as the galliots entered inside;

but as the Angria came by land and the subjects of Your Highness did not wish to assist the factory to defend, which is what could be done without abandoning it. On these considerations, it may be that I may decide to command to remove all the artillery in order not to be suffering every day this attack of the Angria and the complaints of Your Highness and of those people. And if I suppress this course of action for the time being, it is to expect the reply to Your Highness and see your decision, because I shall, as your good friend, wish to contribute whatever is possible to the defence of your country and of your subjects; but this does not free Your Highness from what you should do on your part also to defend him, because this obligation is incumbent more on you than on me.

I have no desire at all to fortify the factory, because what it should serve me is to augment the expense ... Your Highness may take, in this matter, whatever decision you may think of, which all, whatever it is, be of indifference to me. I shall only desire to have many occasions in which to show you the great willingness which I have to serve you and to defend your subjects, and to preserve for ever a loyal friendship.

May God enlighten Your Highness with his divine grace.

Goa, November 27, 1749.
Marquis of Alorna.

Appendix IX

To Tulaji Angria Sarquel

Through the esteemed hand of Ismailji Nacoa, I received the letter of Your Majesty, when I least expected him, because while we were negotiating for a good and loyal friendship and Your Majesty were intending to press upon this State in order to better succeed in the object which you have against the common enemy, the Bhonsle, how could I believe that Your Majesty would attack the port of Mangalore, where one comes across a Portuguese fortress, obliged to be defended on account of a treaty of peace with the king of Kanara, and (you would) rob at the port whatever was found in the (*pataxo* of Philipe de) Valadares and an embarkation of war which was anchored there this winter? This convinced me that Your Majesty did not desire peace but treated us as enemies. If it is not so, Your Majesty may please tell me the effect which I can expect from this peace, which Your Majesty intend, at such a happening. If it is supposed that it was done contrary to the order of Your Majesty, it is necessary in order to convince me, that Your Majesty order to restore what was taken at that port from the said *pataxo* of Philip de Valadares, as contained in the enclosed list; and an anchor and a small anchor, along with the other things which were robbed from the embarkation of war.

Goa, December 14, 1749
Marquis of Alorna

Appendix X

To the king of Kanara

I received two letters of Your Highness. In one of them you tell me that you are surprised at the incursion of the Angria into the port of Mangalore. I am surprised all the more at the intention of the vassals of Your Highness to deceive you, relating to you the event very differently from what happened, because my factor is not obliged to guard the port as they tell Your Highness, except in the manner which is possible for him; nor could he do anything more than what he did in an open place, without any defence, because Your Highness never consented that the fort, where the pieces of artillery are, be enclosed. A house, without doors and open on all sides, can neither be guarded nor defended. If the shots which the factor discharged, did not produce effect, it is not much of a wonder, because the shots, which are discharged from above, below and from land to sea, are always uncertain, as the embarkations are found in continuous movement where the shots cannot be well employed. However, if Your Highness had troops on the land which could embarrass the entry of the embarkations of the Angria, and with other (troops) could embarrass the path of Bolar, you could very well succeed, which would have cost the entry of the Angria very dear. One may calculate that Your Highness might tell me that the factor had troops in order to defend the fort as well as to defend the path of Bolar. As the vassals of Your Highness did not wish to defend their houses and fled to the woods with your very governor, the (Portuguese) forces remained (with) the factor in order to defend the land as well as the river mouth. Already, in another context, I told Your Highness that everyone was obliged to defend one's own house and then expect aid from friends.

It appears that all these past events oblige Your Highness to care much concerning the port of Mangalore, with more care than hitherto. I have reliable information that the Maratha (the Angria) intends to capture the fortress of Malvan and that of Mangalore in order to freely commit piracy on the sea from the North to the Cape of Kanyakumari, and that Hiraji Nayaka is negotiating some treachery against Your Highness, regarding which you ought to have the greatest caution and should provide in time for every eventuality. As a good friend, I shall not omit to help with all that which should be possible for me to aid Your Highness, provided always that I do not become obliged to defend my own house, for Your Highness knows well that every one is obliged first to his own defence and then to another. If the Maratha captures Mangalore, a great danger may befall the whole of the State of Your Highness, apart from the great decrease which your income should have. I hope Your Highness does not scorn this news, because I have it from a very reliable source. Your Highness should fortify the port of Mangalore as much as possible so that this enemy does not execute his intention.

May God enlighten Your Highness with his divine grace.

Goa, January 28, 1750.

I present to Your Highness this piece of damask which the messengers carry.

Marquis of Alorna.

Appendix XI

To the factor of Mangalore, José Antunes Branco

... I suppose that the factor may have there already the news of the attack which the Angria made on the lands of Kanara. He captured the fortress of Honavar. Though he gave it up and went back with his fleet to Griem (?), he carried away, apart from a great booty, nearly one thousand and five hundred important men of Honavar in order to make them pay a high ransom ...

Goa, March 16, 1750.
Marquis of Alorna.

Appendix XII

To the king (of) Kanara

I received the letter of Your Highness through the honourable Trivikrama Dasa and I valued much to know from him that Your Highness was free from the just anxiety in which the illness of the king and that of your minister placed you, because I am feelingly interested, as your true friend, in all your happiness and in everything that grieves you. On account of this reason Your Highness cannot doubt that I aided (you) with the greatest willingness to protect your sea coast and to prevent the invasions of any enemy who wanted to attack it. Just for this Your Highness may not ignore that it is necessary to incur more expenses and that when between (two) friends any business, which may be of particular interest to one of them, is proposed, it is necessary that the other has equal interest in the same business, for the laws of friendship cannot oblige to incur excessive expenses with embarkations, and ammunitions of war, and to expose to the mouth of danger the embarkations and the lives of men only for the benefit of the other friends, particularly when he who incurs these expenses has to incur many other expenses in order to defend himself from enemies who are at the door of the house.

Your Highness might have already been informed that it is more than 150 years that the king of Kanara experienced of this State a loyal friendship and a good reciprocity and that on the part of this State none of the provisions of the peace (treaty), which was concluded in 1671 between the Governors António de Mello de Castro and Manuel Corte Real de Sampaio, and the honourable Vittala Malo, ambassador of the illustrious king of Kanara

Somashekhara Nayaka, has been violated; nor the peace (treaty) which was concluded in 1678 between Governor António Paes de Sande, and Krishna Naik, ambassador of the illustrious king of Kanara, Keladi Basavappa Nayaka; nor the peace (treaty) which was solemnised in 1714 between His Excellency Vasco Fernandes Cazar, Viceroy and Kaddase Damarasa Prabhu, ambassador of the illustrious king, Keladi Basavappa Nayaka. And the State having been so faithful in the observance of the said peace (treaties), on the part of the kings of Kanara it had not been so. Though the observance of the said peace (treaties) was promised, they never implemented the first provision of them, in which the king of Kanara is obliged to give the State factories in Honavar, Basrur and Mangalore with their timber yards and enclosures of stone and lime given by the king of Kanara, the State paying to the officials only the cost of labour, and not digging ditches around them, nor (constructing) double walls, but (only) single ones.

During the course of three years, Your Highness has experienced two invasions of the Angria in Mangalore and one in Honavar and Gokarna. Concerning those of Mangalore, Your Highness has always complained that the factors did not defend the port well, without realising the cause that the Factory, open on every side, is not able to resist any enemy even for an instant, nor is it possible to expect the aid of Your Highness when it is attacked. Under these circumstances it is necessary that the Factor abandons it.

Thrice I have represented it this way to Your Highness and you never responded to this point. It is certain that if the Factory is enclosed, it is possible that the enemies may not venture to cause so much damage as they did on the two occasions when they sacked it. However, as this results in the service of Your Highness and that of your people, I did not continue my earnest appeals, because it concerns Your Highness to take measures which you think fit for the better defence of Your Dominions. It is almost an impossible matter that Your Highness intend Mangalore or any other port should resist the intrusions of the enemy without applying to it the means which are necessary to repel their impulse.

I do not know how Your Highness, being a Prince of so much spirit, are not ashamed that a pirate like the Angria, who attacked the coast two days ago, be invading your lands every year, whereas he did not intend this very thing regarding those (lands) of other less powerful Princes, and that he has now the boldness to propose to Your Highness to make yourself his tributary. Your Highness are justly anxious to defeat these aims of his.

The means, which Your Highness pointed out through honourable Trivikrama Dasa, of assembling your embarkations with those of this State, appears very good to me. However, as the success of arms depends upon divine providence, prudence is required that apart from this means, the Ports and the Factories should be in the State that in whatever eventuality that may take place they should be prepared to beat off the enemy. This is to tell Your Highness the pure truth as your friend. Fulfilling on the part of Your Highness what was sworn through the peace (treaties) would not allow me any doubt that the embarkations of this State combined with those of Your Highness would defend that coast. For this it would be necessary that Your Highness send here an intelligent man of yours with whom I should be able to conclude this negotiation, (he) bringing all those powers necessary to solemnise this agreement. May God enlighten Your Highness with his divine grace.

Goa, August 6, 1750.
Marquis of Alorna.

Appendix XIII

To the king (of) Kanara, Keladi Basavappa Nayaka

I am in receipt of the letter of Your Highness, with the regard which I render to your correspondence and to the good news of your health which I always wish you with much happiness.

When Your Highness asked my aid against the Nairs at the beginning of the war which you have against him, I was soon inclined to aid you with efficacy and I was disposed to expedite the aid as soon as my embarkations were disengaged, as I told several times to the Envoy of Your Highness who is found here. In the meantime, the French, who have alliance with me, also requested my aid with arms and men; and telling me (the aid) to be against Your Highness, as they had declared war on you, I undeceived them with the reason of Your Highness being my ally; and thus undeceived, they requested me that since I denied them the aid which they expected, I should not concede it to Your Highness too, and (that) I should be neutral, without declaring myself neither for the one nor (for) the other side.

In order to decide upon this proposal of the French, I examined the treaties of peace and alliance solemnised between Your Highness and my predecessors. Finding that the aid which this State was obliged by means of the very treaties was, with the express declaration, to be only against the Asiatic enemies with whom Your Highness should have war, and (who) might not be allied with the State, I recognised that it (the war) being now with the Europeans, very much allied to me, I had place only for neutrality, and that I ought to adhere to it at the request of the very allies, especially when I denied to them also the aid which they asked me. As I constantly denied (the aid) to them, I ought to proceed this way so that peace is re-established between both the parties.

Appendix IV

To Basavappa Nayaka, king (of) Kanara

I received through this same courier the letter of Your Highness. I was happy with the good news of your health which I hope will always be perfect with much happiness.

At the same time when I received this letter of Your Highness, the reply to what I had written to the French, that you would negotiate for peace through my mediation, also reached me, and persuaded by my letter, they assure me to have the same wish. Your Highness may communicate to me the conditions which you wish to propose on your part, so that compared with those which the French might propose, this negotiation can be conducted with efficacy and be concluded shortly. I already know from their side that their principal article is to retain the fortresses which they are actually in possession of. Your Highness may see what articles may suit you to propose on your part and I shall not omit to interpose with all consideration my good offices so that the peace shall be mutually useful.

Goa, September 28, 1752.
Marquis of Tavora.

Appendix XV

To the new factor José Antunes Branco

Francisco, bearer of this note, who is called Mahant, Shankarayya among the Hindus, resident of the village of Kalyanpur, and his wife, embraced our holy Catholic faith and were baptised in this city of (Goa), and I became their godfather. As they suffered much in order to carry out their vocation and even their property was confiscated for this and (as) they request me that I recommend to the captain, factor and governor of Mangalore, Joseph Antunes Branco, that he (you) may do all the possible diligences for them to be restored of the said property of theirs. I recommend it so to the captain and factor, assuring him (you) that I will have the greatest pleasure if they, by means of the diligences of their captain and factor, Joseph Antunes Branco, secure what belongs (to them). And also to the two servants of the said Francisco and his wife you may do all the favour of which they may need.

Our Lord, etc.

Goa, July 19, 1751.
Marquis of Tavora

Appendix XVI

Passport to the king of Kanara

I, Vasco Fernandes Cezar de Menezes of the Council of State of His Majesty, Viceroy and Captain General of India, etc. make it known to those who see this that, having regard to the king of Kanara (who is pleased) to have requested for a passport for a boat of his to be able to navigate, and in order to favour him this time alone, I am pleased to grant him licence and security for his said boat, by name, Parameshwary, of the declared capacity of 600 *khandis* of Goa in which goes as captain Hanssanabappa (and also) Carrane (?) Pundalika, pilot Mahammadaji, artillery chief Salu, Sarangue Ismael, Tandel (?) Abdul and other men of her navigation and carries for defence 25 men of artillery, 30 guns, 30 swords, 50 spears, 5 anchors, necessary gunpowder, and shot(s) and other war materials, so that in the monsoon, in the month of April and May of the current year of 1714 she can perform her voyage from the port of Mangalore to that of Congo and Hormuz; and she shall not carry male or female slaves (who are) Christians or children of Christians; and having suspicion and information that she carried them, examination will be made of them; making them known to the Provincial Council, even though such children may not be baptised, nor can she carry or bring Abyssinians, Rumes, or Arabs of the lands subject to the Imam of Muscat; nor will she load iron, albino, sulphur, timber, bamboo, (and) mules as merchandise, nor (shall she carry) goods belonging to the Arabs even though they (such goods) may not be among the prohibited; nor shall she carry the Portuguese nor go to any port of those who obey the Imam of Muscat, nor to those of Angria nor of any other prince, or rebel with whom the

State may be at war; and even though all may be prohibited to bring horses I grant, as a special favour to the said king, that this, his said boat, can bring them from the port of Congo or from Hormuz; and (on) reaching that port she shall unload the goods which (one may) take in that factory and customs house, and shall pay therein the duties that are due, for which she shall bring the certificate of our factor on the margin of this passport with the declaration that she took on board the horses in those ports, in order not to have doubt whether she took them on board or not in other ports and (in others) pertaining to the Imam of Muscat; and doing the contrary or going to the prohibited ports, and carrying or bringing forbidden goods, this passport shall not be valid for her and that boat shall be captured and confiscated for the royal treasury. I notify thus to the generals and captain-majors, of the fleets of this State, other captains, officials and persons to whomsoever it concerns, so that they may fulfil and guard it (passport) in this way and may allow this boat to perform her to and fro voyage, without any impediment; and on the expiry of one year, this passport shall not be valid for her; which (passport) shall be sealed with the seal of the royal Arms of the crown of Portugal, and shall declare that this is the seventh passport which was issued this summer, for which he will not pay the duties in this City as being granted to him free of the said duties by one of the articles of the peace (treaty) concluded with the king of Kanara.

Gregory Mathias prepared this in Goa on March 1, 1714, the secretary João Rodrigues Machado, wrote it.

Vasco Fernandes Cezar de Menezes.

As a dispatch from the Most Excellent Lord, Viceroy and Captain General of India, February 27, 1714.

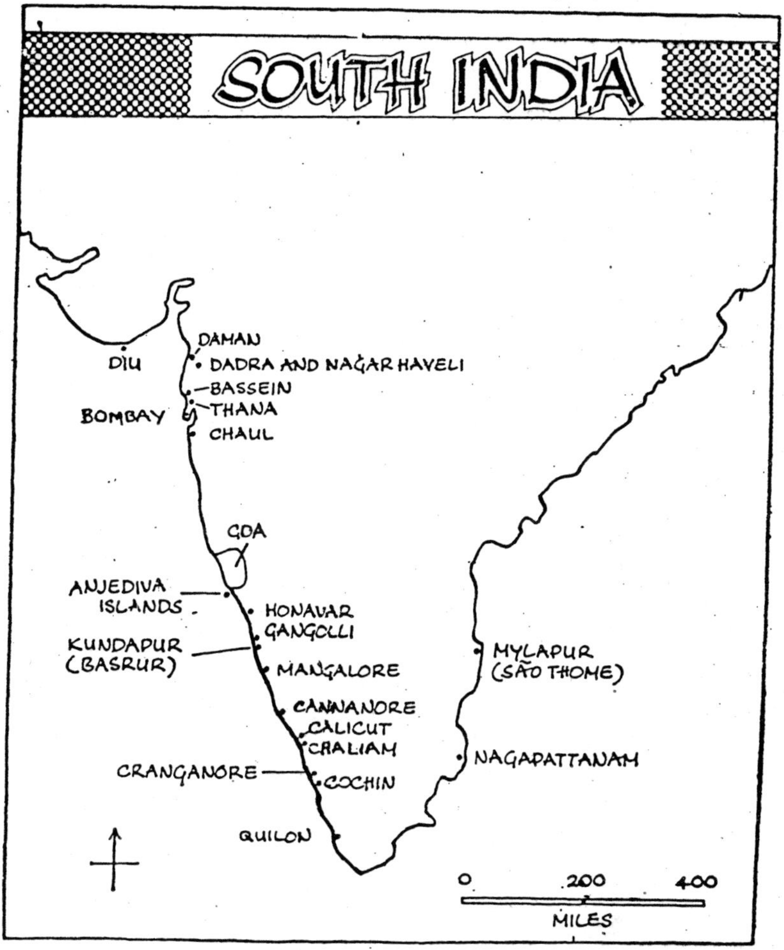
SOUTH INDIA
DAMAN
DIU
DADRA AND NAGAR HAVELI
BASSEIN
BOMBAY
THANA
CHAUL
GOA
ANJEDIVA ISLANDS
HONAVAR
GANGOLLI
KUNDAPUR (BASRUR)
MANGALORE
CANNANORE
CALICUT
CHALIAM
CRANGANORE
COCHIN
QUILON
MYLAPUR (SÃO THOME)
NAGAPATTANAM
0
200
400
MILES

BIBLIOGRAPHY

Unpublished documents

Livro das Monções do Reino (the book of the Monsoons of the kingdom): nos. 65, 67, 68, 69, 73, 78, 79, 80, 82, 102-B, 103, 106, 120-B. Here the word monsoons implies the seasonal correspondence. The volumes contain the annual letters exchanged between the authorities in Goa and Portugal. In addition, reports and other documents are also included. The condition of some volumes is bad.

Livro de Cartazes (The Book of Passports): no. 1, 1704-66 contains the passports issued to merchants and native kings. Useful for understanding the Portuguese control over sea trade. Well preserved.

Livro da Correspondencia do Canara (The Book of Correspondence on Kanara), I (1698-1720) and II (1747-69), contain letters written by the viceroys or governors of Goa to the Nayakas of Ikkeri, Portuguese factors of Mangalore, vicars of churches in Kanara and local governors of Mangalore. Extremely useful for the study of Portuguese relations with Kanara. The first volume is moth-eaten and faded at places. The second volume is in excellent condition of preservation.

Livro de Regimentos e Instruções (The Book of Ordinances and Instructions), no. 14, 1747-52, includes the viceroys' instructions to factors of Mangalore and to captains and captain-majors of Portuguese fleets. Throws light on political, religious and commercial relations between the Portuguese and Kanara. The condition of the volume is fairly good.

Livro de Reis Vizinhos (The Book on the Neighbouring Kings), nos. 1-12, cover the 17th and the 18th centuries and include letters written by viceroys to neighbouring kings and other related documents. The condition of some volumes is extremely bad.

Published documents

Albuquerque, Afonso de, *Cartas de*, vols. I-VII, Lisbon, 1884-1935. Albuquerque's letters to the King of Portugal, his instructions to his subordinate officials, and other documents of his times contained in these volumes are very helpful primary sources for a study of Portuguese relations with Kanara during his period of office, 1509-15.

Biker, J.F.L., *Collecção de tratados e concertos de pazes*, vols. I-VI, Lisbon, 1881-1885. This work includes treaties and concerts of peace between the Portuguese and the chiefs of Kanara, as well as relevant correspondence and other documents.

Documentos Remettidos da India ou Livros das Monções, published by the Royal Academy of Sciences, Lisbon, 5 vols. 1880-1935, include official letters exchanged between Goa and Portugal. The documents relate to the first two decades of 17th century and supply good deal of information regarding Portuguese relations with Venkatappa Nayaka I of Ikkeri and other chiefs of Kanara.

Felner, R. J. de Lima, *Subsidios para a história da India Portuguesa*, Lisbon, 1868, contains the following three works: (a) *Livro dos pesos, medidas e moedas* by António Nunes, written in 1554; (b) *O Tombo de Estado da India* by Simão Botelho, also written in 1554; and (c) *Lembranças das cousas da India*, by an unknown author in 1525. The work of Nunes is useful for a study of commercial activities of the Portuguese in Kanara, whereas the work of Simão Botelho, an honest Portuguese official in the East, is important for studying their political and commercial activities.

Fawcett, Charles, *The English Factories in India, 1670-1677*, Oxford, 1936.

Foster, William, *The English Factories in India*, 13 vols, Oxford, 1906-27. These two works of Fawcett and Foster refer to the Portuguese activities in Kanara and therefore they are good supplementary and corroborative sources to Portuguese documents on their activities in Kanara in the 17th century.

Pereira, A. B. de Bragança, *Arquivo Português Oriental*, 10 vols, Bastora (Goa), 1936-40. These contain extracts from the Portuguese documents preserved in the Historical Archives of Goa. Most of the extracts are from the *Livro das Monções*, *Livro de Reis Vizinhos*, and *Livro de Regimentos e Instruções*. *Roteiro da primeira viagem de Vasco da Gama* and António Bocarro's *Livro das plantas de todas as fortalezas, cidades e povoações do Estado da India Oriental* are also included in the series. Unfortunately the volumes suffer from certain omissions and commissions on account of careless editing and bad printing. This necessitates a research student to go to the originals.

Pissurlencar, P.S.S., *Agentes da Diplomacia Portuguesa na India*, Bastora (Goa), 1952.

Pissurlencar, P.S.S., *Assentos do Conselho do Estado*, 5 vols., Bastora, 1953-57. Extremely useful. The volumes contain the minutes of the Council of State. In addition, other related documents, from the Goa Archives as well as from Portugal, are included, thus making the volumes comprehensive. The footnotes of the editor enhance the value of the collection further. The documents have been edited carefully and accurately. Most of the documents belong to the 17th century, though some are of the 18th century.

Pissurlencar, P.S.S., *Regimentos das Fortalezas da India*, Bastora, 1951, contains ordinances providing for the appointment of officials, military as well as civil, their functions and salaries, the conduct of business and financial arrangements, for the fortresses of the Portuguese in Kanara. In other words, it is particularly useful for a study of administrative arrangements of their fortresses in the 16th century. It throws light also on religious and commercial activities of the Portuguese in Kanara.

Rego, António da Silva, *Documentação para a História das Missões do Padroado Português do Oriente*: India, 12 vols., Lisbon, 1946-58, contain mostly 16th century letters and reports sent from India by Christian missionaries and priests to their superiors in Portugal. Though the documents are mainly of religious interest, they throw light on political and commercial aspects as well. The documents have been edited with care.

Rivara, J. H. da Cunha, *Archivo Portuguez Oriental*, 11 vols, Nova Goa, 1857-1876, contain state papers from the Goa Archives. The documents pertain to the 16th and the 17th centuries. Most of the documents are reproduced in full; but some are summarised by the editor. The editing has been done with care. For my purpose, fascicle no. 3 (vol. 2) and fascicle no. 5 (vol. 3) have been of use.

Sastri, K.A.N. and Venkataramanayya, N., *Further Sources of Vijayanagara History*, Madras, 1946.

Velho, Diogo, *Orçamento do Estado da India (1574)*, Lisbon, 1960. This financial statement of the year 1574 is very useful for a study of the commercial activities of the Portuguese. It shows, *inter alia*, the sources and extent of both income and expenses of the various Portuguese fortresses in Kanara.

Commentaries, Travelogues, Diaries and Biographies

Albuquerque, Afonso de, *Commentários do grande Afonso Dalbuquerque*, 4 vols., Lisbon, 1912-26. This work of the natural son of the great conqueror-statesman, Afonso de Albuquerque, is based on original documents relating to the latter and his times. Though laudatory in tone, the work is fairly reliable and supplies good information on Albuquerque's relations with the Kanarese region.

Barbosa, Duarte, *Livro em que dá relação do que viu e ouviu no Oriente*, tr. Augusto Reis Machado, Lisbon, 1946. Barbosa was a Portuguese official in India from about 1500 to 1561. The book was completed by him in 1516. It is useful particularly for a study of trade and commerce along the Kanara coast, among other regions.

Barbosa, Duarte, *The Book of*, tr. Longworth Dames, I, London, 1918.

Carre, Abbé, *The Travells of*, tr. Fawcett and Fawcett, III, London, 1948.

Dias, Euclides Rogaciano, *Resumo da vida do Venerável Padre José Vaz*, Nova Goa, 1932.

Linhares, Conde de, *Diário do Terceiro Conde de*, 2 vols., Lisbon, 1937, 1943. The Count of Linhares or Dom Miguel de Noronha was the twenty third viceroy of India from 1629 to 1635. The Diary covers only a short period of his office, namely 6.02.1634 to 21.01.1635. Some useful references to Kanara are found in it.

Perera, S.G., *Life of the Venerable Father Joseph Vaz*, Ranchi, 1943. This is the best English biography of Father Vaz, the greatest of the Catholic missionaries to Kanara. It is based on Sebastião do Rego's *Vida do Venerável Padre José Vaz*.

Pires, Tomé, *The Suma Oriental of*, tr. Armando Cortesão, 2 vols. London, 1944. Tomé Pires came from Portugal to India as factor of drugs. He was here for about 9 months in 1511-12 and again for about one year in 1515-16. He wrote his account in 1512-15. He is not as reliable as Duarte Barbosa.

Rego, Sebastião do, *Vida do Venerável Padre José Vaz*, Goa, 1962. This is the best biography of Father Joseph Vaz.

Sanceau, Elaine, *O Sonho da India: Afonso de Albuquerque*, Porto, 1943.

Stephens, H. Mores, *Albuquerque*, Lisbon, 1948.

Valle, Pietro Della, *The Travells of*, 2 vols., tr. Edward Grey, London, 1892. A reliable travelogue by the famous Italian traveller who was in Kanara in October-December, 1623. He comments copiously on the political activities of the Portuguese in Kanara.

Varthema, L. de, *Itinerário*, tr. Vicenzo Spinelli, Lisbon, 1949. Varthema was in India for about four years from 1504 to 1508. He was the first European traveller after Marco Polo. His work is useful particularly for knowing the trade and commerce of Kanara. His account is fairly reliable.

Velho, Alvaro, *Roteiro da primeira viagem de Vasco da Gama*, Lisbon, 1940. This log-book or itinerary of the first voyage of Vasco da Gama (1497-1499), was written by an unknown sailor in da Gama's fleet.

Xavier, Felippe Neri, *Resumo historico da maravilhosa vida, conversões, e milagres de S. Francisco Xavier*, Nova Goa, 1861. This is considered a good biography of the great missionary.

Gazetteers and Manuals

Gazetteer of the Bombay Presidency, vol. XV, pt. II, *Kanara*, Bombay, 1883.

Rao, Hayavadana C., *Mysore Gazetteer*, vol. II, pt. III, Bangalore, 1930.

Sturrock, J., *The South Canara District Manual*, vol. I, Madras, 1894.

Chronicles

Albuquerque, Viriato A.C. de, *O Senado de Goa*, Nova Goa, 1909.

Aragão, A. C. Teixeira de, *Descripção geral e histórica das moedas em nome dos Reis, Regentes e Governadores de Portugal*, III, Lisbon, 1880.

Azevedo, J. Lucio de, *Epocas de Portugal Economico*, Lisbon, 1929.

Barros, João de, *Asia de*, 4 *Décadas*, Lisbon, 1945-1948. Barros was a factor of the 'House of India, Mina and Ceuta', where he had easy access to documents relating to India and therefore could write an authentic account of the Portuguese in India. However, he never visited this country and, besides, as an official historiographer he was subject to government censorship. His work, which covers the period up to 1538, is a little less valuable than those of Gaspar Correa and Fernão Lopes de Castanheda, who express their views freely.

Bocarro, António, *Década 13 da História da India*, 2 vols., Lisbon, 1876. Bocarro came to India in 1615 and served as a soldier for 13 years. In 1631 he was appointed chronicler, and chief keeper of the Goa Archives. He held the office until 1643. His *Década* covers a small period from 1612 to 1617, i.e., the vice royalty of Dom Jeronimo de Azevedo. The work is useful for a study of the Portuguese relations with Venkatappa Nayaka I of Ikkeri and other Kanarese chiefs.

Boléo, Oliveiro, *Descrobrimentos marítimos e explorações terrestres*, Lisbon, 1955.

Boxer, C.R., *The Carreira da India*, Lisbon, 1961.

Boxer, C.R., *Four Centuries of Portuguese Colonisation*, Johannesburg, 1961.

Cambridge History of India, vol. V, Delhi, 1963.

Castanheda, Fernão Lopes de, *História do descobrimento e conquista da India pelos Portugueses*, 9 books, Coimbra, 1924-1933. Castanheda came to India in 1528 and remained here for about ten years. He collected documents for his work diligently and used them with good judgement. His narrative is so very frank and honest that the last two volumes were not allowed to be published because some nobles did not like the way in which their own role was described, as Diogo de Couto tells us. Castanheda's work is indeed reliable and authentic. It stands the test of accuracy wherever it is possible to compare the narrative with original documents. For instance, the account of Vasco da Gama's first voyage is faithful to the unknown sailor's *Roteiro de primeira viagem de Vasco da Gama*. Castanheda brings his work upto 1541.

Correa, Gaspar, *Lendas da India*, 4 tomos, Coimbra (tomos 1-3, 1921-1931) and Lisbon (tomo 4, 1964, 1966). Correa came to India in 1512 and served as a secretary to Afonso de Albuquerque. He might have been in India until 1527. His work covers the period from 1497 to 1550. His narrative concerning Albuquerque's governorship may be considered as reliable. Correa could write frankly and without fear as his work was not published in his lifetime. In fact, his work is rich with honest criticism of the Portuguese authorities.

Couto, Diogo de, *Da Asia, Décadas* IV-XII, Lisbon, 1778-1788. He came to India in 1556 and spent most of his life here until his death in 1616. In 1595 he was appointed chief keeper of the Goa Archives, which was just established. He held the office until 1616. He took up the work where Barros had left, though the former's Década IV includes the last few years covered by Barros. Couto brought the narrative up to 1600. He is more honest and reliable than Barros.

Couto, Diogo de, *Década Quinta da Asia*, Coimbra, 1937.

Danvers, F.C., *Report to the Secretary of State for India in Council on the Portuguese Records relating to the East Indies*, Lisbon, 1892.

Fitzler, M.A.M., *O cêrco de Columbo (1652-1656)*, Coimbra, 1928.

Heras, Henry, *The Aravidu Dynasty of Vijayanagara*, vol. I, Madras, 1927.

Heras, Henry, *The Expansion Wars of Venkatappa Nayaka of Ikkeri*, Calcutta, 1929.

Linganna, *Keladinripa Vijaya* (in Kannada), ed. R. Shama Shastry, Mysore, 1921. Linganna was a Kannada poet who enjoyed the patronage of Basavappa Nayaka II (1739-55). *Keladinripa Vijaya* is eulogical in character and the poet's account up to the beginning of the 17th century is not reliable. Though the narrative of the 17th and the 18th centuries is fairly acceptable, the work throws very little light on Portuguese-Keladi relations.

Lobo, Amaro Pinto (ed.), *Memória Histórico-Eclesiástica da Arquidiocese de Goa: 1533-1933*, Nova Goa, 1933.

Lopes, David, *Chronica dos Reis de Bisnaga*, Lisbon, 1897.

Moraes, G.M., *Mangalore*, Mangalore, 1927.

Nazareth, C.C. de, *Mitras Lusitanas no Oriente*, Lisbon, 1913.

Oruganti, R., *Studies on Krisnadevaraya of Vijayanagara*, Waltair, 1953.

Panikkar, K. M., *Asia and Western Dominance*, Lisbon, 1961.

Pereyra, António Pinto, *História da India no tempo em que a governou o viso-rey D. Luis de Ataide*, Coimbra, 1616.

Rego, António da Silva, *História das Missões do Padroado Português no Oriente: India*, vol. I, Lisbon, 1949.

Rego, António da Silva, *Portuguese Colonisation in the Sixteenth Century: A Study of the Royal Ordinances (Regimentos)*, Johannesburg, 1959.

Saletore, B.A., *Social and Political Life in the Vijayanagara Empire*, 2 vols. Madras, 1934.

Sastri, K.A.N., *A History of South India*, Oxford, 1955.

Sewell, Robert, *A Forgotten Empire*, New Delhi, 1962.

Silva, Severine, *History of Christianity in Canara*, 2 vols. Bombay, 1957.

Sousa, Francisco de, *Oriente Conquistado ...*, 2 vols., Bombay 1957.

Sousa, Manuel de Faria e, *Asia Portuguesa*, 6 vols, Porto, 1945-47. The work was first written in Spanish. The author relied heavily on Portuguese chroniclers like João de Barros, Antonio Pinto Pereyra and others. His work is considered uncritical compilation in which he included imaginary details. The work covers the Portuguese activities in the East up to 1640.

Swaminathan, K.D., *The Nayakas of Ikkeri*, Madras, 1957. An utterly unreliable and misleading work as far as Portuguese-Kanarese relations are concerned. The author is guilty of borrowing detailed information from other works without acknowledging it. I have taken opportunity, *vide* my footnotes, to point out the defective and unreliable character of his translation and use of Portuguese documents.

Venkataramanayya, N., *Studies in the History of the Third Dynasty of Vijayanagara*, Madras, 1935.

Trindade, Paulo de, *Conquista Espiritual do Oriente*, 3 vols., Lisbon, 1961-67.

Vijayanagara Seicentenary Commemoration Volume, Dharwar, 1936.

Whiteway, R.S., *The Rise of the Portuguese Power in India: 1497-1550*, Westminster, 1899.

Journals and Bulletins

Anuário do Seminário Patriarcal de Rachol, Goa.
Boletim Eclesiástico da Arquidiocese de Goa.
Boletim do Instituto Vasco da Gama, Goa (1926-1962).
Boletim do Instituto Menezes Bragança, Goa (1963 onwards).
Journal of the Bombay Branch of the Royal Asiatic Society, Bombay.
O Oriente Português, Goa.
Quarterly Journal of the Mythic Society, Bangalore.
Studia, Lisbon.

INDEX